THE LEADER LOCOMOTIVE

THE LEADER LOCOMOTIVE

Bulleid's Great Experiment

Kevin Robertson

crecy.co.uk

First published 2021 by Crécy Publishing Ltd

All rights reserved. No part of this book may be reproduced or transmitted in any form or by any means, electronic or mechanical, including photocopying, recording, scanning or by any information storage without permission from the Publisher in writing. All enquiries should be directed to the Publisher.

© Kevin Robertson 2021

A CIP record for this book is available from the British Library

Publisher's Note: Every effort has been made to identify and correctly attribute photographic credits. Any error that may have occurred is entirely unintentional.

Printed in Turkey by Pelikan Print

ISBN 978 191080 9853

Crécy Publishing Limited
1a Ringway Trading Estate,
Shadowmoss Road,
Manchester M22 5LH
www.crecy.co.uk

FRONT COVER No. 36001 'resting' at Dormans. Due to the continuing paucity of original colour views of Leader we have made recourse to modern technology and commissioned a limited number of colourisations. Where these appear, they are reported as such. No attempt has been to otherwise interfere with any other images through digital manipulation, apart that is, from the removal of blemishes on the original print/negative. *From a photograph by Harry Attwell. (For further detail see page 136.) Colour by David Williams*

HALF-TITLE PAGE The dream that became a nightmare. No. 36001 during the time of its first visit – and inspection – at Eastleigh 26-29 June 1949. This is No. 1 (smokebox) end and it is interesting to note that the steam-heat pipe is missing. It had certainly been in place at Brighton a few days earlier, which tends to imply it had been removed to examine the oscillating gear (the latter hidden under the longitudinal dustcover above the buffer beam).

TITLE PAGE The steam engine of the future, or just one man's vision? This is the question the following pages attempt to resolve. No. 36001, at Eastleigh shed, 19 August 1950. *Pursey C. Short*

FRONTISPIECE No. 36001 steaming well on its final trial north, passing through Winchester on Thursday 2 November 1950. By this time the dynamometer car had returned to the Eastern Region whilst the load was the heaviest ever hauled at 480t. The engine had left Eastleigh 'cold' and yet despite this and the colossal load at the drawbar on a 1 in 252 rising gradient – the train also heavier than the pullman cars on the 'Bournemouth Belle' – she was travelling at 50mph by the time Litchfield summit was reached, and perhaps even had been for some miles before. All this from a grate area of just 26.52ft. The dream might well be said to have become reality. *From a painting by Malcolm Root. (Copies of this image may be available. Please contact the artist directly at artist@malcolmroot.co.uk)*

REAR COVER MAIN On the way home to Brighton at Falmer with the usual mixed bag of rolling stock in tow. (For further details, see page 141.)

INSET TOP Oxted, a favoured destination for trials and it seemed failures as well. (For further details, see page 147.)

INSET MIDDLE British Railways image taken at Oxted in late 1949 and presenting a dowdy appearance. (For further details, see page 143.)

INSET BOTTOM Seemingly running well on the descent of Falmer bank. (For further details, see page 148.)

Contents

Introduction 6
Glossary 8
Bibliography and Acknowledgements 9

1   The Reluctant Offspring: Brighton, June 1949 11
2   Leader in Concept, from 1882 to 1949 14
3   History and Rationale 17
4   The Last Vestiges of Convention 36
5   The (Iron) Horse Designed by a Committee 46
6   The Sacrificial Lamb: No. 2039 (and No. 1896) 59
7   The Race Against Time 84
8   From Brighton to Eastleigh (More Than Once) and Back to Brighton Again 116
9   'The Great Grey Galloping Sausage' (vis-à vis the Trials from Eastleigh) 158
10 The Final Reckoning 193
11 Conclusions 209
12 'Leader Mk2' 237

Appendix 1: G. Freeman Allen: *The Southern Since 1948* 258
Appendix 2: Les Warnett: *Leader – The Mechanics* 262
Appendix 3: The Views of the Professionals, ... 282
    Including Copies of Correspondence and Biographical Details
Appendix 4: Details of Test Runs: 2039, 36001, etc. 287
Appendix 5: The Colour and Appearance of Leader 294

Index 298

Introduction

At the time of writing in 2020, it was 32 years since my first book on the subject of Leader appeared. That was followed in 1990 by a few more lines on the subject and then a combined edition in 1995; these all by Messrs Alan Sutton. I can honestly say I was certainly not expecting interest to have been as it was at the time. The first printing in 1988 sold out within weeks and was reissued, I think twice. This was all the more surprising as the publisher had clearly got 'cold feet' in the early stages and I suspect would have preferred if I had agreed to cancel our agreement. I refused, with the results just stated.

Time moved on and in 2005/6 Messrs Ian Allan, then the owners of the Oxford Publishing Company imprint, approached me on the subject of a revised edition. This appeared as a hardback in 2007, again sold out, and was reissued as a paperback two years later in 2009.

Why the history lesson in publishing? Well, be assured it has nothing whatsoever to do with seeking kudos, anything like that disappeared many years ago. Instead, in presenting a new appraisal, I have to ensure all is explained so the reader is aware he is not simply getting the same text, all the same images, simply repackaged with a new cover.

So what is different in this new edition? Back in 1988, and again in 2007, my aim had been to present the story of Leader primarily as a factual analysis. From reviews and correspondence, I knew each book was generally well received but I had always felt there was something missing and knew what that was – more detail of the behind-the-scenes goings-on, the trials, and ideally contemporary thoughts from someone who was there, plus, if it were possible to find, confirmation from a contemporary source that I was 'on the right track' with my various conclusions.

Why this last point was important is just that the whole Leader subject remains an emotive topic – still so decades later. If I was to impart my own opinions – opinions I believe based on reasoned judgement – I needed to know I was not simply going off at a tangent. After all I was not there, I never saw the engine and the closest I could hope to get, aside from formal documentary research, was by speaking to those who did indeed have first-hand knowledge.

Back in 1988 – to be more accurate during the research period prior to that time – I had genuinely attempted to speak to as many who had been involved as I could. Mr Bulleid was no more of course – whether he would have discussed matters with me is another point entirely – but I did speak to his son H.A.V. Bulleid, plus people who had worked on the project such as Stephen Townroe, Harry Attwell, John Click, Harry Frith, various erecting shop and maintenance fitters plus footplate staff both at Brighton and Eastleigh. Most were kindness personified; there was one exception, but that is no matter; I had tried and I did my best at the time. The point is that thirty-plus years ago these men were still around, but all are sadly now gone. To put this in context, even an apprentice working on Leader in 1949 would have been at least sixteen years old then and consequently an octogenarian now. Those in more senior positions would have been older, hence whilst incredibly grateful to those who did kindly give of their time and memories, there were others I naturally missed. First-hand knowledge is certainly preferred to second-hand recollections, although all have their place.

Then there was the trawl for images, and certainly more appeared than I ever thought possible, whilst they have also continued to come out of the woodwork – should that really be the metalwork? – since. Again most people I approached were similarly helpful.

However, I will certainly not be so naïve as to suggest this really is the close of the topic; instead it is everything I can realistically bring together at the time of writing, (and the publisher will allow me to include). More may yet emerge, on that I can only say – we will see. I do know of one, possibly two, collections that might yield more but the owner/custodians are for the present unwilling to allow access; it is their prerogative of course.

So getting back to why this version is different. For the first time we have had access to parts of an unpublished manuscript by the late John Click (JGC). Click was a pupil of

Bulleid and was at Brighton both for the first steaming and also some of the early trials of the engine. His recollections of that first steaming – see p.11 et seq – are both fascinating, indeed, it might be said, comic, and also revealing, whilst at the same time sadly too (for the sake of the reputation of No. 36001 and those actually involved) at times verging on the ridiculous. Professional it most certainly was not. This was followed by further experiences on the later trials from Eastleigh, often reported in similar vein.

At the same time some notes appeared from a *Southern Way* contributor related to the late Harold Ware Attwell, who was in charge of the test section at Brighton during the trials of Nos 2039 and 36001. The Attwell recollections were first seen in *Southern Way* No. 41 and at that time, I had no thought about this revised edition. However, their importance warrants their inclusion here, if for nothing else, for the sake of completeness. It is the inclusion of this type of material and similar other new items, assessments and correspondence that make for the practical reissue of a book on this subject. (Some extracts from John Click and Harry Attwell have already appeared in the regular *Southern Way* periodical, but on the basis that books have a different readership than *SW* and it was also much a précised version, they are reproduced in greater detail herein.)

Regular 'followers' of Leader will find some phrases are the same as appeared in the 2007 edition, whilst the actual physical history is similarly matching although I have rearranged and retitled the chapters/sections. I am going to disappoint if you might have thought you were going to find information on a Mk2 Leader, in the UK that is. But there was indeed a Mk2 and that was the Irish version, consequently the JGC papers plus a new batch of photographs from the late Ron Pocklington, who was in Ireland with JGC at the time, mean we can add more detail to that story as well.

As stated, a new edition deserves a new approach, hence the chapter headings are different, some more questions are asked (some answers given to those of last time) and I hope overall a more balanced and mature approach is the result.

But do not expect new conclusions. This remains a 'warts and all' story so some of those involved may not always appear in the best light. If that is the case, then remember this relates just to an individual's involvement with No. 36001 and should not in any way be taken as a reflection upon a whole career. What has been the most difficult is trying to present the case in the light of the circumstances prevailing at the time. Writing this seventy plus years after the actual events, we have the benefit (or otherwise) of hindsight; back in 1949 when No. 36001 first turned a wheel under its own steam Bulleid and his senior staff could rightly be said to have been true pioneers. Whether they were right or they were wrong is still the story I am attempting to unravel in what follows.

This year, 2021, also marks the 70th anniversary of the ending of the Leader engines, the last vestiges of the physical design were scrapped in 1951. I doubt very much I will be around to witness the centennial anniversary so in consequence it is only right I attempt to give the whole concept one last 'Hurrah'.

Kevin Robertson
WEST BERKSHIRE
2019 to 2021

'One' of Leader's predecessors: there were several, the Paget engine, No. 1896; we might even include the Bulleid Pacific design. No 2039, *Hartland Point* is perhaps the best known, seen here probably early in 1948 fitted with sleeve valves and oscillating gear, plus external fabricated exhaust pipes and a less-than-becoming chimney. No. 2039 was meant to prove the inclusion of sleeve valves was viable. It hardly achieved this and the problems experienced with No. 2039 would go on to be replicated in No. 36001.

Glossary

ASLEF	Associated Society of Locomotive Engineers and Firemen. (The main trade union representing drivers and firemen, dating back to 1880.)
BR	British Railways
CIE	Córas Iompair Éirann (Irish [Republic] Transport System)
CME	Chief Mechanical Engineer
CSC	Clifford S. Cocks, Chief Draughtsman, Brighton.
DO	Drawing Office (Brighton)
ECS	Empty coaching stock
GNR(I)	Great Northern Railway (Ireland)
HAV	Henry Arthur Vaughan Bulleid (sometimes known as Anthony) eldest son of O.V.S. Bulleid.
HWA	Harold Ware Attwell, in charge of the testing section at Brighton and deputy to C.S. Cocks.
JGC	John Gaywood Click
KJR	K.J. Robertson (the author)
LNER	London & North Eastern Railway
OVB/OVS	Oliver Vaughan (Snell) Bulleid
MR	Midland Railway
MT	*Modern Transport* journal
RO	*Railway Observer* periodical
SR	Southern Railway (post 1948: Southern Region)

'Leader in service?' Hardly. Instead No. 36001 departs from Brighton on trial – she never went north on the Brighton main line – but No. 36002 did come south! The same image was used by Bulleid in an article for an American journal describing steam locomotive development and using the caption 'Leader in service'. (See page 197.) In reality the engine never took a revenue-earning train of any description.
British Railways

Bibliography and Acknowledgements

'Arthurs' 'Nelsons' and 'Schools' at work. S.C. Townroe. Pub. Ian Allan, 1973 revised 1983.
Article in *Southern Way* by J.M. Dunn and 'A.F.C.'. (J.M. Dunn refers briefly again to the design in his autobiography *Reflections on a Railway Career LNWR to BR* published by Ian Allan in 1966.)
Backtrack – various issues, including November 2005
Bulleid and the Turf Burner. Ernie Shepherd. Kestrel Railway Books, 2004.
Bulleid Last Giant of Steam. Sean Day-Lewis. George Allen & Unwin, 1964.
Bulleid of the Southern, H.A.V Bulleid. Pub Ian Allan, 1977.
Chapelon: Genius of French Steam. Col H.C.B. Rogers. Ian Allan, 1972.
Engine Sheds in Camera. D.J. Hucknall. The History Press, 2005.
Experiments with Steam. Charles Fryer. Patrick Stephens Ltd, 1990.
Journal of the Stephenson Locomotive Society in particular No. 483 of October 1965.
La Locomotive a Vapeur. André Chapelon. English Translation of the original 1950 edition, updated and revised in 2000. UK Publisher Camden Miniature Steam Services.
*Locomotives of the GSR (*Great Southern Railways Ireland). Jeremy Clements and Michael McMahon. Colourpoint, 2008.
Locomotives of the Southern Railway Part . D.L. Bradley. Pub. The Railway Correspondence and Travel Society, 1975.
Locomotives of the LBSCR Parts 2 and 3. D.L. Bradley. Pub. The Railway Correspondence and Travel Society, 1972 and 1974 respectively.
Locomotive Panorama Vol 1. E.S. Cox. Ian Allan, 1965.
Locomotive Panorama Vol 2. E.S. Cox. Ian Allan, 1966.
Modern Transport. Various issues.
Oliver Bulleid's Locomotives. Colin Boocock. Pen & Sword, 2020.
Proceedings of the Institute of Mechanical Engineers, Vol 156, 1947, Presidential Address.
Prototype Locomotives. Robert Tufnell. David & Charles, 1985.
The Railway Gazette. Various issues, but in particular that of 19 November 1948.
Reflections on a railway career LNWR to BR. J.M. Dunn. Ian Allan, 1966.
Ron Jarvis From Midland Compound to HST. J.E. Chacksfield. Oakwood Press, 2004.
Southern Steam. O.S. Nock. David & Charles, 1966 and 1972.
Steam Locomotive Development. Kevin P. Jones. Published by the Library Association in 1969.
The Book of the West Country and Battle of Britain Pacifics. Richard Derry. Pub. Irwell Press, 2008 edition.
The GWR Exposed, Swindon in the days of Collett and Hawksworth. Jeremy Clements. Oxford Publishing Co., 2015.
The Railway Gazette. Various issues, but in particular that of 19 November 1948.
The Railway Magazine. Various issues.
The Railway Observer. Pub. The Railway Correspondence & Travel Society. Various issues from 1948 to 1951.
Ron Jarvis From Midland Compound to the HST. John Chacksfield. Oakwood Press, 2004
The Southern Since 1948, G. Freeman Allen. Pub. Ian Allan Ltd, 1987.
The Southern Way. Various issues. Crécy Publishing.
Southern Way Special No. 17: The Southern Railway Oil-Burning Engines 1946–1951, Kevin Robertson. Crécy Publishing, 2020.
Speaking of Steam. E.S. Cox. Ian Allan Ltd, 1971.
Testing Times at Derby, Alan Rimmer. Oakwood Press, 2004.
Trains Annual 1952. A.F. Cook. Ian Allan.
Unusual Locomotives. Ernest F. Carter. Frederick Muller Ltd, 1960.

Certain other publications referenced are specifically mentioned within the text.

The reader may also find it useful to refer to https://www.steamindex.com/people/engrs.htm#surnt which provides an excellent potted biography of certain of the engineers mentioned in the text.

As before, this book could not have been compiled without the help of many people. The names below are consequently carried over from both the 1988 and 2007 editions but also added to, in consequence of the information contained within. Sadly too many of those named are now no longer with us.

Hugh Abbinnett, Mike Arlott, Mike Arscott at Markits (UK) Ltd, Charles Attwell, H.W. Attwell, C. Banks, John Bell, Eric Best, W. Bishop, Sean Bolan, C.P. Boocock, D.L. Bradley, E. Bramble, E. Branch, Don Broughton, H.A.P. Browne, H.A.V. Bulleid, D. Callender, H.C. Casserley, Derek Clayton, Jeremy Clements, John Click, Terry Cole, Barry and Joe Curl, Brian Davis, Ken Dobson, Peter Dunk, W. Durban, R. Eagle, Les Elsey, John Fairman, Robin Fell, Tony Francis, John Fry, Ted Forder, Harry Frith, Geoff Gardiner, Jack Gardner, W. Gilburt, David Fereday Glenn, Roger Hardingham, Graham Hawkins, C.C.B. Herbert, Dave Heulin, P. Ineson, Bill Jackson, Phil Kelley, Mike King, Graham Long, The Institute of Mechanical Engineers and especially S.G. Morrison, Ron Manley, Henry Meyer, Max Millard, Michael McMahon, Tony Molyneaux, B. Musgrave, S.C. Nash, The National Newspaper Library, The National Railway Museum and especially Phil Atkins and John Edgington, Gerry Nichols and the archives of the Stephenson Locomotive Society, G.L. Nicholson, The Patents Office, Reg Randell, R.C. Riley, John Rooney, Reg Roude, Andrew Royle, The Science Museum, John Scrace, Ian Shawyer, John Scott-Morgan, Tony Sedgwick, Ernie Shepherd, Pursey Short, Roger Silsbury, R.C. Simmonds, Roger Simmonds, Alf Smith, The Stephenson Locomotive Society, A.C. Sterndale, Richard Stumpf, Mrs (Sam) Talbot, Arthur Tayler, Mike Thorp, Dennis Tillman, *The Times* Photographic Library, S.C. Townroe, Mike Turner, J.T. Howard-Turner, Fred Waller, Les Warnett, George Wheeler, D.W. Winkworth, Les Wright, Doug Yarney and Chris Youett.

Two names have been deliberately omitted until now. Malcolm Root, for agreeing at short notice to produce the wonderful painting of the engine on her last run, and David Williams, who also came to the rescue with his superb colourisations. Colour photography was the province of very few back in the time Leader was running and consequently the chances of finding further originals must be stark. However, and as before, if anyone reading this does have more information or images, I suspect my interest in the subject will never totally wane.

The dream that died. The second of the class, No. 36002, outside Brighton works. Visible windows, external pipework from the body to the buffer beam, plus dustcovers over the springs appear to be all that are missing. There was even the suggestion that with less of a rush to complete the engine, she might have been a better prospect and should even have been substituted for No. 36001 on the official trials. In the event, the extra time taken would work against her as she was just two days away from completion when the dictate came to cease work on the class. It would never resume. *John Click/National Railway Museum*

1

The Reluctant Offspring: Brighton, June 1949

Had it not been meant to be deadly serious, the first steaming and then attempted movement of No. 36001 from inside Brighton works to the outside world on 20/21 June 1949 might be said to be no better than a slapstick comedy. Professional men who really should have known better played the part of actors in what in reality was little more than a seaside farce as Leader emerged. John Click takes up the story:

There were irritating last-minute problems, but the works 'Terrier' 377S, came in and stood, panting patiently most of the morning, waiting to pull No. 36001 out. At last No. 377S was needed and snatching on a loose coupling (an old trick), succeeded in moving its heavy load half-way out where it promptly stuck fast. Whether it was lack of power, the tight curve, bad rail joints or (perish the thought) a design problem – or ALL *(the emphasis is JGC's)* those things – wasn't clear; but there was only one way to go – back inside.

Next morning it was decreed by the Chief (this was Laurie Granshaw the Works Manager) that lighting up would be done in the Erecting Shop, a very unpopular move not made since No. 2039's first tests. With the help of a compressed air line feeding the blower ring, steam was made surprisingly quickly and, without completely filling the place with smoke, although it was said that the overhead crane men did ask for fog men to be posted on the crane rails!

Nobody, and it was very wise, really liked the idea of driving No. 36001 out under its own power; so, after the track outside the door had had a facelift, something larger than the works 'Terrier', an E4 tank, had been specially laid on, and tried its luck.

One slip, and ... success? After about an engine length there was a loud bang, a general shout of

Complete – well 99.9% (the numberplates had still to be added) – and into the daylight for the very first time, at Brighton on 21 June 1949, the E4 pulling the engine into daylight. *John Click/National Railway Museum*

With steam issuing, some onlookers watch as the engine is prepared for its first move. *Don Broughton Collection*

'WHOA', and the strongest suggestion that some foul inside or underneath had cleared itself. Something must have broken, but what? Short of taking many covers off, the cause would remain a mystery, for the present at least. The No. 1 bogie frame appeared to be hard against the mainframe to me, and the foul could have been there; but at the next attempt out came the 'Leader', reluctant no longer. There was some protest from the flanges and an impression that the track might burst, but she was safely deposited on the Works siding adjacent to the line from Lewes.

I wanted to be there for the first move; but, calculating that I'd be missed went back to the Drawing Office for a bit. After nearly an hour I slipped out again and they had the boiler blowing off. Granshaw was in No. 1 cab (the chimney end) preparing to move, watched by a large number of erecting shop staff anxious not to miss the fun. Others, like me, who had no business to be there, stood back trying to look at ease and hoping nobody would notice them.

Very significantly, not a soul from the design staff was there or indeed had been invited. Had I been known to the Works Manager as one of Cocks's outfit he would have gone out of his way to have ordered me off 'a bit sharpish'. Granshaw had a lot of testing experience behind him but it was absurd that at least Cocks wasn't there too, after all it was he who knew what everything was supposed to do. Perhaps they knew each other's limitations so well that they dared not meet and risk a very public scene. I hoped OVB would appear and decided to stand my ground if he did (it appears he did not).

At about half past two Granshaw tried the whistle; from which issued water, then steam, but only a wet squeak. He shouted a warning instead; then tugging at the regulator, watched the steam chest pressure gauge and then the ground, anticipating movement. Nothing at all happened.

The Foreman helpfully hinted that the cylinder cocks ought to be opened. This lever wanted a lot of pulling; but water, stutteringly at first, became a series of ever more powerful jets shooting out from both ends, horizontally now and flashing into steam. The unwary, who had not realised that what came out at one end would also come out of the other, moved smartly to safer ground. Hot live steam was at last issuing forth.

Chapelon's principles of having large steam-pipes and big steam-chest volume in relation to cylinder size were all very well in theory, but what an awful lot of water to be evacuated, how great a risk of hydraulic damage, and what would happen in freezing conditions? At least the Drawing Office had had the foresight to put a drain cock at the lowest point in each main steampipe, though it was not an automatic one.

More steam, safety valves lifting and some puzzled individuals. It may be that L.J. Granshaw is in the centre of the group. There has Just been a loud 'bang' and a general shout of 'WHOA'. This is No. 1 end. *John Click/National Railway Museum*

A new diesel locomotive? An electric locomotive perhaps? Speculation amongst the causal public observers was rife, but what they were actually witnessing was history being made. The first, and only, Leader ever to be steamed, seen outside Brighton works on the afternoon of Tuesday 21 June 1949. *H.M. Madgwick*

But why hadn't the beast moved, even shot off? Well, she was still in mid-gear but at least something had been gained: the cylinders were now pretty hot. Mr G. next found the reversing lever, and, opting NOT to go seawards towards the buffers protecting the dangerously close main signal box, pulled it towards him. Nothing happened again.

Plainly friction in the complicated system of levers, gears and splined shafts was too much for the steam reverser. Strong men with pinch bars were next called for and they inserted these in the forked ends of the shafts going, bogie-wards, in either direction. Two and then four strong men pulled mightily without the slightest effect. Not being able to stick this any longer I ventured to suggest that the two men at one end needed to pull DOWN whilst those at the other pushed UP. (This was because Leader had a power bogie at either end, each had to be 'reversed' to the same amount – or to be more accurate: one had to be in forward gear – the other reverse AND each to the same amount.) This done, there was an immediate clonk as both bogies went into full gear; depositing two men on the ground and giving the other pair an uplifting experience.

Another try was made resulting in steam shrieking from both ends; it was obvious that 36001 wanted to move, but it just didn't.

IA bystander, from Accounts I think, asked very politely if 'those wooden things with handles on' were possibly part of the problem? Whilst the four wheel scotches were being knocked out from either side of a wheel on each bogie nobody had noticed the fireman 'putting a bit on'. He was not going to be caught out. I never did like 'pop' safety valves especially with 280psi behind them, and certainly didn't now. Everyone present was startled and jumped visibly when one lifted thunderously: nerves were getting decidedly ragged.

Someone else hazarded that the handbrake was perhaps still on. 'Take the handbrake off!' shouted Mr G., adding helpfully 'it's in the fireman's cab'. The fireman found the handle and did the necessary: so could anything now prevent movement? Only perhaps if someone had, well-intentioned, put scotches in on the other side … they had!

I was suddenly glad that Bulleid was not there, because as what had started as ardent endeavour had become knockabout, a farce. Whatever next?

Up to now the power brake had not been considered at all; so that had 36001 moved off, only the handbrake or, hopefully, reverse steam in her teeth could have stopped her bounding off the 200 yards or so to the old copper shop buffers. Suppose she had demolished them and the shop walls? Far-fetched? Not really; and beyond was a drop into the road far below.

By the time the brakes had been tested, and found to work virtually first time, it was late afternoon. Sensibly it was decided to try again next day; for if nothing else, some of things not to do had been found out the hard way and some time to ponder the afternoon's events was very desirable.

Notes

(1) C.S. Cocks came to Eastleigh in 1938. It is also not true to say Bulleid brought him to the Southern or that he persuaded him to follow him. J.G. Click explains, 'In the summer of 1937 CSC took his family on holiday to Southsea and they all enjoyed it so much away from the smoke of Yorkshire that he applied to the Southern for a job in the Sunny South. As time went on and no reply came, he concluded there was nothing doing. But it is quite possible, even likely, that OVB subsequently came across this application about a year later and called him down for interview. Geoffrey Cox (his son) feels sure that until then Bulleid and his father had never met. That in itself is an interesting commentary on OVB's role under Gresley, for Cocks had been prominently involved with the design of the 'V2's and later on put forward 2-6-2 designs to Bulleid several times over the coming years. Doug Smith (Brighton draftsman) remembers CSC saying more than once that the 'V2' had been his responsibility as what would now be called 'project engineer'.

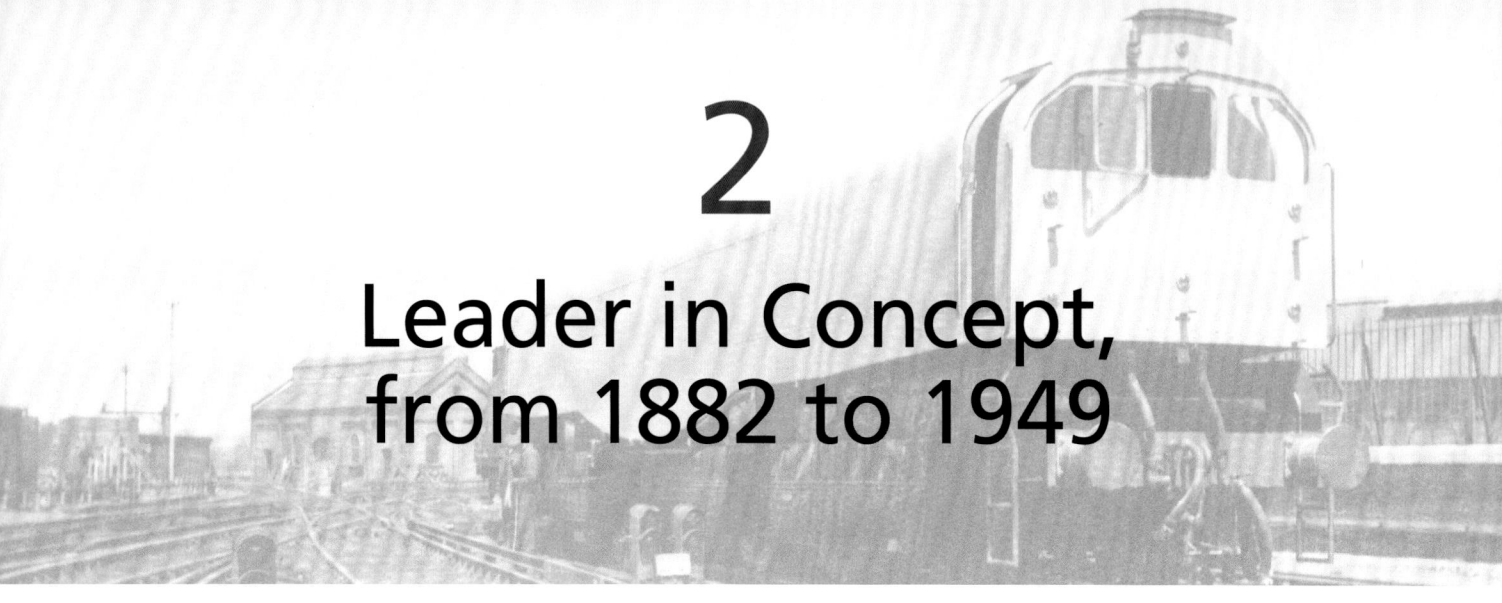

2
Leader in Concept, from 1882 to 1949

Straight away I can envisage questions being asked relative to the dates quoted in this chapter's title. The second year is easily explained; that was when No. 36001 was steamed for the first time, but 1882? Well I'm taking a slightly quizzical approach here, for 1882 was the year of Bulleid's birth and whilst quite clearly it would be sixty-seven years later before the concept of his double-bogie steam locomotive came to fruition, it was certainly sometime between those dates that the idea would first have evolved, along with the practical aspects he wished to consider.

Of course what we do not know (and this will be a question raised several times in this book), is simply, was the eventual No. 36001 what OV had envisaged, and equally, did he honestly believe it could (or might) work? Indeed, did the number of changes wrought in haste upon the design to ensure completion before British Railways came upon the scene (after nationalisation) mean the whole was a potentially flawed concept?

With the benefit of hindsight, seventy-plus years down the line, we might reasonably conclude the answer to all those points is in the affirmative but, at the time, it is similarly reasonable to conclude that both Bulleid and his design staff at Brighton were hopeful – 'confident' would be too strong a term – that somehow No. 36001 might surprise all?

So straight away why the seeds of doubt amongst the senior staff at Brighton and why the similar doubt from British Railways, not just later but even at this early stage? Well, here we have to look at Bulleid's other steam work and also at Bulleid as a man.

When OVB came to the Southern Railway in 1937 he was 55, relatively late in life to be promoted to the top tier. I have commented before and I make no excuses for repeating myself now, history was not to be kind to him; he had a lifetime of ideas to convert into practical projects in what turned out to be a very few years. Years too which would be interrupted by war, followed by shortages of materials as the country slowly rebuilt itself and, after that, railway nationalisation. Rather than condemn him, perhaps we should marvel at what he did achieve. Yet the question to be asked, and this is the one on which Leader hangs, is were those achievements the right achievements?

Certainly at the time of his move to the Southern his predecessor R.E.L. Maunsell was not in the best of health. Maunsell had retired aged 70 (he died six years later in 1944) and whilst he achieved much during his tenure, steam had become almost the forgotten element, cast aside in the Southern's ever-increasing preoccupation with electrification.

With the new man, OVB, at the helm, and as he was a committed steam man, motive power took on a new purpose, there was a fresh impetus in the drawing office and with this came what we would now refer to as a considerable morale boost. The Southern was on the way back to pre-eminence in motive power.

Part of this came from where Bulleid had previously been placed, the LNER. Indeed it was on the LNER and the LMS in the 1930s that records were being broken, culminating in the 126mph dash of *Mallard* on 3 July 1938. To have somebody at the helm who had come from such pedigree could do nothing but enhance prestige.

Accordingly, and for some years to come, when Bulleid suggested ideas that might have previously been considered radical they were driven through to become workable propositions. The use of Morse chains in the Pacifics is one obvious example; who else had even considered this for a steam engine previously, and yet they worked. Hence with the Southern Railway also building steam engines for their own use in greater quantity than had been the case for almost a decade before (20 x Merchant Navy, 70 x West Country/Battle of Britain, 40 x Q1) in the years prior to nationalisation, it is not surprising the drawing office staff literally 'followed their Leader'. It was only post-1948, when individual career prospects came to be considered on what was then the nationalised railway, and with it the ever-more-radical proposals associated with the Leader design becoming

As it transpired it did not go well. The intention for the following day was to travel the short distance to the station, reverse on to the shed, there to collect coal and so be ready for the trials to commence. However, they got as far as the station but the engine would not reverse and instead it was towed to the shed to be coaled and then towed the short distance back to the erecting shop. The saga had indeed begun. Back inside and with the 'innards' opened up, the tubular valve rod (on the left on No. 1 bogie) was found to have buckled under compression, very much as some feared it would. It was probably this damage that caused the mystery bang as the engine was pulled out. Subsequently several others failed in this same way but the problem receded when the tube walls were thickened as they needed to be replaced. Look carefully in the station view and at least one man may be seen leaning out of the office window. With the windows open it was clearly a warm summer's day. *Bluebell Railway Museum and Don Broughton Collection*

The man behind the concept. Oliver Vaughan Snell Bulleid 1882–1970. A brilliant engineer, of that there can be no doubt, but did his ambition go too far? In reality Bulleid had only worked for one CME previously, Nigel (later Sir) Gresley, firstly on the Great Northern and later with the London & North Eastern Railway. OVB often said, 'Sir Nigel told us "when you run out of ideas then copy the best."'. Bulleid as a man was considered by many to be charm personified, and he would use that same charm to win over doubters. When in charge on the Southern he might sometimes have seemed aloof to his senior staff and consequently it was quite rare for even a section leader to know Bulleid's views at first hand; although on the comparatively few occasions they were called to his office they came back up charmed and won over to his wishes; however outrageous they might appear a little later, especially after a period of quiet reflection. (The latter words, those of John Click.) What is perhaps the most amazing is that probably more ink and consequently words have been expounded on the work of Bulleid than arguably any other British UK steam designer. Something that is even more surprising when it is considered he was only in post on the Southern for not much more than a decade. Why that should be is an interesting point; unlike Gresley his engines did not achieve world records, unlike Stanier he did not revolutionise the locomotive stock of a particular company, and unlike Churchward his was not a standardisation scheme continued for decades later – even if Bulleid no doubt wished it might have been. Instead we have a man who may be described as a visionary. A 100% devotee of steam and a man who passionately believed improvements could and might be made. We should mention that Bulleid was one of the few, possibly the only man, to move from east to west from the UK to Ireland as CME; several other travelled west to east to take up similar roles; Aspinall (L&Y), Maunsell (SECR and later SR), McDonnell (NER), Robinson (GC), and Sturrock (GNR).

apparent, that some began to consider disassociation. G. Freeman Allen sums it up well in his appraisal on Leader, 'But by the spring of 1950 even Bulleid's ardent disciples on the SR's mechanical engineering staff, though their faith in the basic concept still flamed, were getting pessimistic about the amount of work and expense still needed to eliminate fallibilities in its detail.'[2]

Notes

(1) Now is not the place to go into detail about how well, or otherwise, Bulleid's chain-driven valve gear operated in practice. Higher maintenance costs and time without a doubt but on a good day an original Bulleid Pacific in good condition, with good coal and a willing crew, was without equal. But the next day under exactly the same conditions the results could be the total opposite.

(2) For the full text of G. Freeman Allen's appraisal on the engine, *see* Appendix 1.

3
History and Rationale

Years ago I recall being told by an English master, 'never cast doubt upon your own opinions or conclusions at the start of any text'. Wise words certainly but on this occasion we have little choice but to ask two questions at the start and those are simply, 'How' and 'Why'?

'How' did Bulleid come to behave the way he did when given free-rein on the Southern. 'Why' did he come to produce steam designs that were all so dramatically 'off-piste'?

This is perhaps especially strange as it has to be said he had a conventional steam upbringing. On the Great Northern there was nothing radical for him to relate to, whilst on the LNER apart from 10000 and the occasional use of poppet valves, the latter was hardly in the radical category; his physical involvement with anything other than the conventional Stephenson engine would appear to have been limited to texts within the technical and engineering journals of the day and/or perhaps possible conversation between engineers of equal standing, perhaps at meeting of the IMechE or iLoco. Eng'rs.

This in turn raises questions, was Bulleid a socialite when it came to technical interaction, or was he content to remain quietly working away in his own world? If we could answer these questions with any degree of certainty, we might be closer to understanding the brain of a man from which suddenly sprouted forth so many ideas as soon as the opportunity presented itself, that is from 1937 onwards. Radicalism and the LNER are not really two terms that sit happily together, one could hardly say the streamlining on an A4 was radical – fashionable for the time more likely – and yet there persist rumours that this external cloak was as much to do with Bulleid as anyone else.

We should also recall in attempting to analyse the man that in the 1930s on the LNER, and similarly on the Southern in the 1940s, relations between the top tiers of management and those on the lower levels were in no way similar to what the situation was like in more recent times. The words 'glass ceiling' have in the past been referred to as representing a level through which those below could never pass, although they might be able to see what was taking place. However, in earlier times that glass ceiling was a rather an opaque one, so access to and knowledge about what was happening above was simply not available, and this likely applied at several levels too. John Click possibly provides the nearest access we are likely to secure to the mind of Bulleid but even he admits he was never truly taken into confidence with O.V.S Bulleid – with his son H.A.V Bulleid more likely, and consequently the next generation down – but as Click himself recounts, he never for example met Marjorie (Mrs) Bulleid.

So from a conventional upbringing and engineering background, up to 1938 that is, what conclusions might we draw upon relative to unconventional steam locomotive development up to that time?

Firstly we should ignore the forays made into things such as compounding, feed-water heaters, poppet valves, roller bearings, oil firing, exhaust types and the like. These are ancillary features intended to improve efficiency and/or reduce maintenance, but all remain related to the conventional-designed Stephenson steam engine.

Instead it was the more radical proposals that emanated from this country that we should be looking at, principally the Paget engine(s) – there was more than one design, a 4-6-0 and a 2-6-2 but it was only the latter that was built. The high-pressure LMS Fury, the already-mentioned LNER 10000 and the LMS Turbomotive. Away from these shores there was an equal number of similar attempts to break the mould. However, not to go off at too many tangents we may conveniently ignore them – with one exception, the work of arguably the greatest steam designer the world has ever seen, André Chapelon in France. Put aside for a moment subjective aesthetics and similar partisan likes and dislikes, here was a man who produced a steam engine of conventional design which could develop 5,300 indicated horsepower whilst having an axle loading of no more than 22t. The final years of British steam in the 1950s could have been so different had more notice been taken of this remarkable man.[1]

17

The steam engine with the nearest connection to Leader has to be the Paget design of 1908, which had the use of sleeve valves and a dry back firebox in common with Leader. Whilst still junior in his career at the time, we must accept Bulleid later came to know of the history of the Paget, even if he never actually saw it. Whether he was able to grasp any technical detail of its working – limited though that was – is doubtful; this comparatively well-known image, for example, was not released until 1923, three years after the engine had been broken up. Had Bulleid been party to the full information on Paget, would he have been as keen to copy its weaknesses? But even if he was, he no doubt thought he could improve upon it. A very fair and detailed description of the engine with a rare image of the opposite, left-hand side, may be found in Philip Atkins' 2020 publication, *Edwardian Steam*, pp 151–154 published by Crécy. As an aside, the Paget design was also the first 2-6-2 tender engine until the time of the V2 design on the LNER two decades later, although tank engines with the 2-6-2 wheel arrangement had been around on the GWR for several years before. John Click admits he asked Bulleid if he ever knew Paget personally, he said no, but he of course knew of him when both were in France in WWI. 'Folklore has it that Bulleid sympathised with the French who couldn't stand Paget. Apparently, Paget's habit was to range up and down behind the front in his personal train reorganising everything in sight. He arrived at Amiens on one occasion and offered to show the French how to shunt their yard. Of course, being them, they politely agreed. After Paget eventually turned in for the night, the French made a very rough shunt onto his sleeping car. He was off next morning and was not seen for months. What a pity Paget never discussed his engine with Bulleid, the Leader might then not have incorporated some of its worst faults!'

LNER 10000, 4-6-4 with water-tube boiler. A locomotive which Bulleid would certainly have been familiar with during his time on the LNER. As is mentioned in the text, Bulleid's title as 'Assistant to Gresley' does not tell us much about his responsibilities, role and experience. The engine is seen here in its original condition, in which form it operated, albeit with some modifications, between 1929 and 1936.

The water tube boiler was removed in 1936 and substituted for a conventional boiler whilst at the same time contemporary streamlining was added. The wheel-arrangement remained unaltered as a 4-6-4. In this form, but still with its original classification of class W1, the engine is seen at Newcastle Central in 1938. As a unique engine it remained in service until 1959.

Folklore has it that whilst on the LNER Bulleid did have some input so far as the streamlined design of the famous Gresley A4 Pacifics was concerned. Whatever the truth on that score he may well have smiled when learning a Gresley A4 was to be set to work out of Waterloo during the interchange trials following nationalisation. Seen here is what is now BR No. 60033 Seagull at the head of a West of England train. Ignoring insignia and livery, the engine is in original LNER condition apart for the removal of the fairings ahead of the cylinders and which also once covered the top-half of the driving wheels.

Lord Nelson class 4-6-0 *Lord Howe* in wartime garb fitted with the experimental large boiler which was unique to this engine for a time. When Bulleid joined the Southern, the 16 locomotives in the class were the largest passenger design on the SR but their performance was mediocre. Bulleid was able to transform this with the provision of a multiple jet blastpipe and larger chimney thus proving yet again it is often the successor who improves upon his predecessors designs. (At the risk of courting controversy, might we even apply the same adage to the original Bulleid Pacific design compared with the rebuilt engines at the hands of Ron Jarvis?)

Before moving on we should conclude our comments on Chapelon and his achievements with mention that it is certainly true that in the USA especially greater tractive efforts were being obtained with locomotives that would have easily dwarfed both the homegrown and European product. Steam turbine development especially was experimented upon in America but we may confine ourselves to just two aspects of steam development on that continent, the first being the regular use of the Mallett principle and the second the 'cab-forward' design of steam locomotive, both are referred to as appropriate within the text. We should also not forget that in papers found at Eastleigh there is confirmed evidence that a Garratt 4-6-2 + 2-6-4 design was under active consideration by the Southern Railway in 1933/34. With no other excuse than the oft quoted phrase, 'I've started so I'll finish', the Garratt proposal is described in some detail within the Bradley book *Locomotives of the Southern Railway Part 1* (RCTS 1975). There we are informed that Maunsell's intended Pacific design had been rejected and, by inference, the working of the Continental express traffic unresolved. A further proposal to convert an existing Lord Nelson class to work as a compound with revised cylinders and a higher boiler pressure was similarly rejected. The compound idea based upon impressive reports then being obtained with steam working in France.

Unfortunately the proposal for a Garratt working on the South Eastern lines was rejected by George Ellson, the Southern Chief Civil Engineer, but he did offer to accept them between Basingstoke and Exeter, subject to a 75mph speed limit. The proposal as developed would then have seen goods workings restricted to night-time running whilst at the same time train lengths would increase. The trade-off was the need to lengthen various loops and sidings although there was also an estimate that just ten Garratts would replace the work of no less than seventy-seven existing engines. Why the scheme was not proceeded with is unclear as after March 1935 information simply stops. Had it been developed the engines concerned would have dwarfed anything then running, for at 209t 10cwt their size was considerably more than the LNER Garratt which weighed in at a paltry 178t. With Bulleid later in charge and no doubt appraising himself of the motive power situation, perhaps it was this knowledge of the shortcomings of the Lord Nelson class and the need for increased power on the South Eastern lines that set Bulleid his self-appointed task of designing an engine capable of averaging 60mph start to stop on these trains – the result as we know, the Merchant Navy design. But more to the point, when he took over on the Southern, Bulleid would therefore have been aware of the future locomotive requirements and was no doubt also briefed about the Garratt story. Perhaps too it was this that helped towards his idea of the double bogie loco, but not a Garratt of course, and which eventually morphed into Leader.

In might seem to the reader that even at this early stage I am also almost appearing to cast doubt on Bulleid's abilities as an engineer, calling into question his skills, his logic and his decision making. Be assured that is never the intention. O.V.S. Bulleid was a consummate professional engineer, one who through his own ability had risen up to the pinnacle of his profession. But with Leader especially, had he simply gone too far, reaching beyond what was both theoretically and practically possible? That is the question this book seeks to address.

We now need to revert to the 1930s again and his time on the LNER. To begin with let it be said that there is no evidence to suggest that Gresley and Bulleid had anything other than an excellent working relationship.

The LMS was the only one of the pre-nationalisation companies to experiment with very high steam pressures allied to a semi-compound. This was the 4-6-0 No. 6399 *Fury* which took to the rails in 1930. Unfortunately a burst tube which resulted in a fatality on the footplate effectively put an end to the engine's career almost as soon as it had begun despite remaining in this form until 1935. It had one unfortunate similarity with Leader in that despite a number of mainly unsuccessful test runs, it never earned a single penny of revenue. *Fury* was rebuilt as a conventional member of the Royal Scot class in 1935, renumbered as No. 6170 and renamed *British Legion*. It remained in service until December 1962.

Gresley was six years older than Bulleid, and as such the age difference perhaps *may* have enabled him to control his assistant carefully. What exactly Bulleid's activities were under Gresley are still not completely clear. We know of course his formal role from the title Principal Assistant, but what *did* that actually mean, and accordingly how much if any influence did Bulleid have on Gresley's locomotive designs? This is a vitally important point for apart from reference to Bulleid having been involved in aspects of carriage design, and the introduction of welding techniques, there are really only two known definite features of the Gresley steam types that may have had more than a passing reference to Bulleid.

The first was the use of poppet valves)[2] as fitted to the first of the Gresley P2 2-8-2s, and the second the addition of the side fairings on the streamlined A4s.[3] The latter were really little more than a cosmetic interlude whilst the former was not carried over to his days on the Southern. Sean Day-Lewis, Bulleid's biographer, regards the Gresley-Bulleid combination as unmatched, with Gresley sitting in firm judgement over Bulleid – the ideas man. Although perhaps somewhat quizzically, Day-Lewis does not elaborate further on the 'ideas' topic. So do we also take the term 'ideas' to mean 'initiative' as well? Well, here we have may have a clue but again we should consider that much of the design work for the LNER was undertaken at Doncaster, physically far removed from the offices occupied by Gresley and Bulleid at Kings Cross. Co- incidentally John Click also refers to being impressed by the A4s he observed as a child at Kings Cross in the 1930s.

In the 21st century it is difficult to imaging a life without the revolution in available communication that has occurred principally in the last two decades. Digital message transfer covers everything from simple word communication to images, drawings and the like, and that to say nothing of the facilities available through CAD. Back in Bulleid's days, both on the LNER and then the Southern, the most technical communication appliance available was the landline telephone.

As a result, it was physically impossible for a CME to have control over every project undertaken in his department. Having been tasked with providing – whatever – or equally having made a case for the replacement of – whichever – Bulleid (Gresley, Stanier, Collett – whoever) would set the criteria with his senior staff and they in turn would task the drawing office with turning the idea into a workable proposition. Once approved, the CME would sign/initial the drawing ready for the requisite number of tracings to be made and passed to the workshop to be translated into the actual locomotive, carriage, wagon, component – whatever. But it was to the CME that the design was credited although as seen, there were literally hundreds of others equally essential in the chain.

It was learning the requirements of his new railway (the SR) that led Bulleid down the path towards Leader and before that his previous designs. The need for a locomotive

Undoubtably the most successful of all the non-conventional steam locomotives that operated on Britain's railways was the LMS non-condensing turbine No. 6202. Introduced to the LMS in 1935, No. 6202 worked in regular service until 1939 when, because of its complicated mechanism, it was set aside. With the need for every engine available in wartime, it was restored to traffic in 1941 but was in need of heavy repairs in 1943/4. It continued to work in turbine form until 1949 when it was set aside and eventually rebuilt as a conventional engine in 1952. As BR No. 6202 *Princess Anne* (a much-improved member of the Princes Royal class), it saw only a few weeks service before being damaged beyond economic repair in the terrible accident at Harrow & Wealdstone on 8 October that year. Steam turbine operation was not unique to No. 6202 as some years earlier various other experimental engines had taken to the rails although none were particularly successful. There is no mention that Bulleid ever considered this type of propulsion for his Leader design.

The first of the two main-line Garratt types, herewith the LMS version. Massive in size, although still not quite as large as the LNER variant, the class was employed on coal trains mainly between the south Midlands and London. Unfortunately size was not all and the design was usurped with the arrival of the BR Class 9 2-10-0 type.

In terms of sheer tractive effort the solitary LNER Garratt was the largest steam locomotive to operate in the UK. It was employed primarily on banking duties on the Woodhead route and after this was trialled as a banker on the Lickey incline. It is doubtful the Southern Railway would have been looking for a machine of quite this size. There is also no reference to suggest Bulleid ever attempted to resurrect the Garratt idea during his tenure.

A medium size tank engine that John Click states an affinity for is the SECR J class 0-6-4T design. There were also no apparent restrictions relative to passenger workings either (as similarly applied to the LBSCR 'I' class family). Here J No. 1595 is recorded on a Margate to Charing Cross, via Canterbury West express, approaching Dumpton Park sometime in the late 1930s. *A.W.V. Mace/The Transport Treasury*

able to haul 600-ton trains from Victoria to the Kent Coast at an average of 60mph may have been a principle he set himself whilst in similar vein during WWII when the need arose for additional freight engines, the Q1 was the result. It is also true to say they were the last new inside-cylinder design built on a British railway; true, elsewhere Pannier tanks were being built, up to the ridiculously late date of 1956, but these were to a much earlier design than 1942, when the Q1s appeared. Now is also not the time to discuss the merits or otherwise of the Q1 class, they performed well, braking ability was, shall we say, not ideal on unfitted trains, and the fireman could often hit his head on certain of the cab fittings, but otherwise they did what was required and it was really only the external appearance that belied the unconventional approach of their designer.

Back in 1942 it would have been too much to expect a totally conventional engine, after all the Merchant Navy class had included a whole raft of novel features from their 'air-smoothed' casing to the chain-driven valve gear – and all places in between. It was almost as if Bulleid could not accept anything at face value: it had to be changed, tinkered with or altered, and at this stage, decades later, sometimes almost as if it were change for change's sake.

The same was true of the smaller design of Pacific that emerged from 1945 onwards. These were in effect a replacement for older engines now well past their steaming date, a veritable army of older 4-4-0s particularly still at work on the South Western lines and long overdue for retirement.

But what the Southern really needed, apart that is as replacements for the various Drummond 4-4-0s, was a modern efficient tank engine. Every other railway had them; on the GWR there were the 61xx type, on the LMS it was the Stanier and later Fairburn 2-6-4 design, and on the LNER the V1, V3 and later the L1. All performed well, individual company preference will rate one above the other, of course, yet it was only on the Southern where this gap in motive power occurred. (The other gap relative to motive power on the Southern was for an eight-coupled heavy freight engine. Instead the H15 and S15 shouldered the role; there was never any real need for anything having more coupled wheels, whilst the advantage of the 4-6-0 was its ability to be purloined for other tasks should that be required.)

This reluctance towards big tank engines may be traced back to the Sevenoaks disaster of 1927. Only a very basic summary need be repeated here: suffice to say a tank engine running at speed rolled over, resulting in much loss of life. Both Maunsell as CME, and George Ellson as Chief Civil Engineer, blamed each other, locomotive and track respectively. The General Manager of the time, Herbert Walker, took what was probably the only reasonable course

A design that Bulleid did have a lot of time for was the LNER P2 2-8-2 – this example No. 2001 *Cock o' the North*. It is also reasonable to assume his fondness for the principles involved was what had led him to first propose a 2-8-2 for the SR – vetoed by George Ellson the Chief Civil Engineer. This rejection was the reason a revision was made to a Pacific (4-6-2) and resulted in the Merchant Navy class. We may even ask did Ellson object as Bulleid's 2-8-2 design would have had a leading pony truck exactly as per No. 800 at Sevenoaks? Bulleid was keen to tell others something Gresley imparted, '…when you run out of ideas then copy the best'.

Maunsell River class 2-6-4T No. 793 *River Ouse*, one of 21 of the class (one was built with three instead of two cylinders). The first had taken to the rails in 1917 but the remainder were not constructed until 1925–6. They were intended to work express passenger trains on what were the main routes of the former South Eastern section but quickly gained a reputation for rolling at speed. In consequence of the Sevenoaks accident of 24 August 1927 involving No. 800 *River Cray*, all were rebuilt as tender engines.

The tragedy of Sevenoaks was when the 5pm service from Cannon Street to Folkestone, Dover and Deal, carrying 350 passengers, derailed just outside Sevenoaks. Eleven persons were killed and 20 seriously wounded. The cause was the engine rolling and falling onto its side in a cutting, resulting in the following vehicles piling up behind. Subsequent tests on the LNER main line displayed little in the way of instability at speed; on the Southern, however, it was both the ballasting of the track and the engine that were jointly considered responsible. It is widely believed that CCE George Ellson never truly recovered from his department's degree of responsibility and in consequence came to have a pathological fear of running tank engines at speed. *Alan Cobb Collection*

Notwithstanding the comments in the caption to the previous image, in 1931 Maunsell introduced the 15 members of the W class 2-6-4T design. These however were intended for freight and to see any of them coupled to passenger stock was rare. Here however we see one of the class – identity not confirmed – on the Up through line at Raynes Park, with what is almost certainly empty stock, for Clapham or Waterloo. *Bloxham/Author's Collection*

open to him, re-ballasting of the complete boat train route and at the same time the conversion of what were K-class tank engines into tender engines of the U class. But we must not leave the facts there, for running trials were carried out with a K-class engine on the LNER main line shortly afterwards and here there was no rolling.

Standardisation also was not a word we might think applies just to the GWR and later to the LMS, for under Maunsell's tenure no less than six steam classes had similarities both in proportions and also the interchangeability of major components, these were the U, U1, N, and N1 tender engines, and the K and W tank classes. The latter, the W class of 2-6-4T engines of which fifteen were built in 1932, were in reality the Southern's equivalent of the other railways' classes mentioned earlier. There was an edict though that under no circumstances must they ever be used on a passenger train[4], an instruction that was to remain in force until the very last one went for scrap in 1964. This was despite numerous requests made to BR in their last days that they might be used on enthusiasts' specials and also that by this time 2-6-4 tank engines to both the Fairburn design and later of the BR standard design had been active on passenger work on the Southern region since almost immediately after nationalisation.

George Ellson, it seemed, was almost petrified of a potential repeat of Sevenoaks and yet on the Brighton lines especially, two 4-6-2T engines survived as passenger tank engines into BR days as well as veritable army of 4-4-2T engines, the latter especially replicating some of Drummond's engine designs as being well past their 'best steamed by' date. Ellson meanwhile had retired from the Southern Railway in 1944 and as such one of the obstacles to Bulleid's more radical ideas had been removed. Concurrent with Bulleid there had also been a new General Manager in place for much of his time, (Sir) Eustace Missenden. Missenden was altogether more sympathetic to Bulleid, whilst Bulleid's known charisma also allowed him to win over others to his way of thinking. Hence the oft-quoted phrase when the traffic department first requested a replacement for the elderly M7 0-4-4T design, Bulleid's famed retort being along the lines of, 'You don't need something so restricted ... you need something capable of ...,' going on to describe what would be his go-anywhere, do-anything (well, certainly most things) machine. This is what would result in Leader although at the time it is possible even he had no idea of what he was offering to produce. Indeed, to be fair, it is very likely that was the case but having publicity in the form of well-known minutes at Board level to at least set the criteria, it would be very difficult to pull back later. Possibly then circumstances were driving him as much as he was driving what became the Leader design.

Had Bulleid simply said at that same meeting, 'I will produce you a large 2-6-4T design similar to the Stanier – or whatever – type', this would certainly have matched the criteria, but we will never know if others had similar memories akin to George Ellson's and in consequence his proposal might well have stumbled. Perhaps even Bulleid had already been warned to tread carefully when referring to large tank engines but this certainly did not seem to the case later, with the raft of drawings showing proposed engines based very much on a Q1 and Light Pacific outline. However, these were only working copies and would likely have circulated only amongst the drawing office and the CME himself.

Now we need to backtrack and ask questions about how Leader might have been formulated in Bulleid's mind. Might it have come about from something on the LNER? Here the answer is perhaps unlikely but because of the hierarchal situation that existed on the LNER and elsewhere, we just cannot be sure what the responsibilities associated with his role as 'Assistant to the CME' (Gresley) meant. The closest we can get is that Bulleid was an – take note the word 'an' is used deliberately in this context in preference to 'the' – ideas man. What little we do know is that Bulleid was a strong advocate of the use of welding whenever possible. Indeed such a technique was utilised in various aspects of the Gresley coach designs – no doubt at the then instigation of Bulleid. Similarly did Bulleid's original preference for a 2-8-2 tender locomotive for the boat trains (an idea scuppered by Ellson) originate from the P2 class on the LNER?

Equally is it interesting to consider for a moment how LNER locomotive policy might have developed if Bulleid had either remained at Kings Cross or perhaps returned to take over after Gresley's death in 1941. Movement between railways for promotion was commonplace. Maunsell, for example, had gone to the Southern from Ireland, one of his principal assistants Clayton was an ex-Midland man, another assistant Holcroft arrived via Swindon and we should also not forget perhaps the most famed move in the period 1923 to 1947 when Stanier left Swindon to take over on the LMS. Further speculation, with due acknowledgement that we have done exactly this in other areas already, relative to 'what ifs' or more prosaically 'who ifs', is perhaps best left unsaid.

We have already speculated above on the possibility of Bulleid's first proposed 2-8-2 having its origins in the LNER P2, whilst it must be almost certain that his use of welding on the Southern, not just on Leader of course, originated from his positive results with this technique on the LNER. So is there anything else we can compare that shows a direct link between the LNER and the Leader design? And indeed there is in the form of the Gresley corridor tender.

Folklore has it that at work Gresley was mulling over the problem of how to provide for non-stop running between Kings Cross and Edinburgh, 393 miles, and which was realistically beyond the capabilities of a single footplate crew. At the time there were really only two obvious solutions, a brief (working timetable) stop for an engine or crew change, or by carrying an additional crew on board. As it stood, there was also only place for the latter, on the engine footplate itself, hardly conducive to men attempting to rest before or after duty.

Then came the moment of genius: Gresley was either playing with or watching his children at play. The play involved crawling along a narrow gap between some chairs and a wall. Here was the answer – a narrow corridor along one side of the tender to allow an exchange of crews on the move. The result was the Gresley corridor

In their 25-year history, the Southern Railway built no tank engines for secondary passenger services, relying instead upon existing designs. Hence by 1948 there was an urgent need for a versatile, modern 2-6-4T locomotive which was sated when a number of former LMR tank engines were built for, or drafted onto, the various Southern lines. This included No. 42099, a Fairburn LMS design engine from 1945 but built at Brighton in 1950. It is seen here on a London Bridge to East Grinstead working, leaving the short tunnel between Oxted and Hurst Green on 21 May 1952.

tenders, attached to examples of the A3 class from 1928, and later some A4 engines. Let us state straight away there is no suggestion here that Bulleid ever intended corridor tenders on the Southern. (Water troughs were considered in 1948 but for different reasons).

Bulleid would certainly have been aware of the corridor tender principle and yet no evidence has been found to suggest these were unstable, although the first run did result in a bearing running hot. Subsequently all such corridor tenders were fitted with counterweights on the corridor side below the actual corridor to act as a balance against the otherwise unsymmetrical load distribution. This degree of counterbalance consequently added just over 6t to the weight of the actual tenders but with a fully laden weight of 62t 8cwt this was still not a problem, distributed as it was over four axles. Perhaps it was this success that evolved into the later decision to offset the boiler and bunker of Leader by 9in from the centre line to allow for the side corridor between the cabs and thus communication and access between driver and fireman. Unfortunately with Leader the later addition of extra balance weights did have a negative impact on the overall weight and consequently the axle loading of the engine. As an aside we cannot be certain if Leader as built had any balance weights provided at all! (According to Alan Rimmer in his book *Testing Times at Derby*, the LMS also possessed a single corridor tender, which was used for test purpose only. Don Broughton of Leeds confirms this was built during the time of Stanier and the corridor could be used by the dynamometer car crews to reach the locomotive footplate if required. There is no information available as to any balance or weight distribution difficulties that might have been encountered.)

To return to the design, of all the questions raised about the 'why' the one that stands out the most is over its similarity to the Paget engine of 1908. That design ranks amongst the closest to Leader's of any engine built anywhere. At a quick glance such a statement might appear strange, but aesthetics aside, the two shared two major similarities. The first was a dry back firebox, meaning a firebox without a water jacket at the sides, and secondly the use of sleeve valves – although it should be stated that in the Paget engine the sleeves were of bronze, not mechanite. Like Leader, the Paget 2-6-2 was also multi-cylindered but had eight cylinders rather than the six on Leader. Unlike Leader it did not use chains for the valve gear or final drive. Trials were run and, again like Leader, at times it was a free running and free steaming engine. Exactly how much in the way of trial running took place is uncertain, possibly not as much as the designer might have wished. We should also recall it was a private venture and Deeley who was in charge at Derby was certainly not enamoured with it, nor for that matter of Paget.

On an outing in 1912 a seizure occurred on one of the rotary sleeves, resulting in total failure and the engine blocking a main line for seven hours. Because we do not know how much trial running took place, we should not draw conclusions that failures were commonplace or disproportionate to the amount of successful running. Even so with Paget having no further funds available, No. 2299 was placed in store at Derby, allegedly sheeted over in a corner of the paint shop, and there it remained until broken up in 1918 at a time when Paget was overseas commanding the Railway Operating Division.

But before leaving the subject of similarities there are a few points to make. Firstly there is available in print a reasonable amount of factual information about the Paget design; dimensions, equipment used, etc. But what is missing is the 'why' in so far as why did Paget opt for the dry back firebox and especially sleeve valves, and do we take the term 'rotary' (which is how the action of the sleeves is described in contemporary literature) to imply he did the same as Bulleid did later when the sleeves were imparted with a degree of axial rotation (perhaps instead of fore and aft)? Was there even an earlier precedent for sleeve valves and the dry back boiler (firebox) that has somehow become lost in history?

Paget's engine appears likely to remain an enigma; one in which it would seem extremely unlikely much further information will come to light.

We should also make the point relative to the P2s that it was Bulleid who accompanied the Gresley P2 No. 2001 *Cock o' the North* to the Vitré locomotive testing station in France in 1934. Bulleid spoke fluent French so would have been able to discuss the technicalities of steam development both in the UK and France. Again the information gained would have been stored for the future. What we do not know is if he met Chapelon then, although the latter had also yet to rise to the pinnacle of his profession.

Summarising this period, we have no evidence either to suggest Bulleid was unhappy or unsettled working for Gresley. Why Bulleid was invited to apply for the top job on the Southern is also unclear whilst it appears (without confirmation from any definite source) those on the Southern who were equally qualified were either considered too old or simply unsuitable but Bulleid was no youngster either in 1937.

Having been Assistant to Gresley, did Waterloo see him as a man who would not 'rock the boat' when it came to being in charge, especially as the avowed intention of the Southern was still towards wholesale electrification? Perhaps he was indeed seen as a safe bet – someone to continue along similar lines of Maunsell. But if so, how wrong they were to be. It would be too cruel to suggest the LNER wanted to avoid a power struggle between Bulleid and Thompson as potential successors to Gresley – should the top seat on the LNER become vacant for whatever reason. Possibly something in his Waterloo appointment allowed an otherwise latent flame to burst into life. As I recounted earlier, Bulleid had a lifetime of ideas to compress into a few short years. His time in office would also be seriously affected by world conflict and then, nearer to home, political interference in the form of nationalisation. Time would not be kind to Bulleid, although what he would achieve in that timespan and under those circumstances was without equal on any railway, certainly in the UK.

The BR (Standard) version of the 2-6-4T, this example one of a number also built at Brighton but in 1951. A large number of the class remained on the Southern (eventually displacing the Fairburn engines which were transferred to the LMR) and afforded excellent service. This and the Fairburn design was exactly the sort of engine the Southern so desperately needed but as we know Bulleid was never one for convention. Within the UK the 'big-four' railway companies were also very conservative when it came to a preference for their individual designs and despite the existence of the Association of Locomotive Engineers, which would meet on a regular basis to discuss common ideals and standardisation, there was never any real similarity of product until post-nationalisation and the emergence of the standard designs. This is turn led to a very insular attitude amongst the railwaymen themselves, convinced their home-grown product was superior. The one exception was when Maunsell, convinced a 4-6-0 was required for the Southern (this after the reports of the trials between the LNER Pacific and GWR Castle became known), approached the GWR to borrow drawings of the Castle class engine for the Southern. Swindon declined but Derby were more co-operative, and drawings for the Royal Scot type were willingly provided. With due allowance for subjective preferences, there is really no reason why a design from one company might not have been eminently suitable for similar traffic on someone else's lines. The building of locomotives to the design of one company at another company's works did not occur until WWII, when a number of Stanier 2-8-0 types were constructed at both Swindon and Eastleigh.

An M7 0-4-4T, the design of which dated back to 1897, but it was performing useful work in Bulleid's time. A total of 105 of the class were built and were used in two particular roles; branch line services from Cornwall across to Sussex and empty coaching stock trains out of Waterloo. It was in the latter role that Richards and Bulleid considered them to be outmoded and in need of replacement. What was effectively needed was a 2-6-4T or 2-6-2T as indeed was provided later; how on earth Leader came to be seen, especially by Bulleid, as their natural replacement is almost beyond belief, not least as the Leader design would have occupied twice the length of an M7 at Waterloo where platform space was often at a premium. *R.C. Riley/The Transport Treasury*

One of the 'I' series of 4-4-2T engines dating back to LBSCR days, (there were three types, the I1, I2, and I3). This is an I1X class engine, originally dating from 1906 but later rebuilt with a new boiler in an attempt to improve performance. All the LBSCR 4-4-2T types were mediocre performers, which is perhaps why they were seemingly not considered for ECS or similar work out of Waterloo and where it was necessary to move as rapidly as possible to keep out of the way of the electric services.

Notes

(1) The reader is specifically referred to two books on the work of Chapelon. The first is the biography *Chapelon – Genius of French Steam* by Col H.C.B Rogers, published by Ian Allan in 1972 and reprinted by Crécy under their Goodall imprint in 2021. The second is *La Locomotive a Vapour (The Steam Locomotive)*, originally published in France, but an English translation from 2000 was also produced. The locomotive specifically referred to is Chapelon's 4-8-4 No. 242.A.1. from 1946, which showed it was able to produce *no less than 3,500hp* at the drawbar and in excess of 5,000hp at the cylinders. Against such numbers anything produced by Bulleid, or indeed any other British steam designer, looks decidedly tame.

(2) Poppet valves (often to the Lentz design) had been used to great effect both in the USA and also on locomotives of several European railways, although it must be said in the latter case usually on compound steam types. Either single or twin inlet and exhaust valves might be provided and through the usual method of operation via an oscillating shaft or rotating cam. The advantage of the poppet valve was that far less lubrication was required compared with a piston valve, whilst there was also a consequential weight reduction and the physical movement of the valve off its seat necessary for admission (or exhaust) of steam was also less. There was also a reduction in the 'throttling' of steam and consequent increased free running. As with any change, the advantages had to be weighed against the disadvantage of increased complexities and associated maintenance.

(3) According to the Wikipedia entry on O.V.S. Bulleid and referring to the Gresley designs produced whilst he and Gresley were working together, 'Bulleid had a hand in many of them, including the P1 2-8-2 freight locomotive, the U1 2-8-0+0-8-2 Garratt freight locomotive, the P2 2-8-2 express locomotive and the A4 4-6-2 express locomotive.' This is quoted without citation and the present writer believes it should also be read with caution. A more accurate version might well be 'During the time Bulleid was working with Gresley on the LNER the following types were amongst those produced....'.

(4) In his 1976 book *The Maunsell Moguls* (Oakwood Press), Peter Rowledge quotes on p.47, 'The W Class was kept off passenger work, only extremely rarely appearing on empty stock, but in May 1948 No. 31918 worked a special from Victoria to Tunbridge Wells West and easily kept to time, a couple of days after some test running between Ashford and Tonbridge.'

4
The Last Vestiges of Convention

Make no mistake about it, in Leader Bulleid set out to produce a conventional (meaning non-turbine and without compounding) steam engine but technically more advanced and efficient than any other. This was to be achieved in several ways (the present writer's bullet points with my comments in italics):

• The use of a boiler/firebox having the greatest possible surface area so allowing maximum heat transference from fire to water. *Bulleid succeeded. Leader could raise steam faster than a Terrier and even faster if an outside steam/air source were attached to the blower ring within the smokebox. Whether such a rapid raising of the temperature of the metals involved was ideal is another matter.*

• The use of sleeve valves to maintain the highest possible temperature around the cylinder and so increase efficiency in the use of steam by reducing both temperature and pressure losses of steam between the

Gresley is supposed to have had his 'eureka' moment regarding the provision of his corridor tender when watching his children playing between some chairs and the wall. With a narrow corridor running alongside the coal/water space it was perhaps not totally surprising that on the first run a bearing ran hot. Subsequently, all such tenders were built with weights below the floor. Bulleid would have known of this and yet with Leader he designed the engine with the boiler *and* water/coal space offset to one side *and with no counterbalance*. The engine here is Gresley A4 No. 60017 *Silver Fox* at Kings Cross (top shed) in 1960. *Canon Alex George/The Transport Treasury*

regulator header and the steam chest. *Fine in theory but the additional unequal rotating/reciprocating drive to the sleeves was not a success. No. 36001 performed far better once this additional complication had been removed. The greatest disadvantage was maintaining steam tightness between the piston, valves, liner and casting. Until all these had expanded and become a sufficiently tight fit, steam loss was excessive. When tried with more restricted tolerances seizures occurred. Consequential oil usage (lubrication) was also excessive.*

• An even torque through the use of chains as the final drive. *Again successful although the unequal drive on the bogies created additional stress on the crank (drive) axle and may have contributed to failure of this component.*

• Adhesion – *Excellent.*

• Visibility – *Excellent, for the driver that is. This was certainly not so for the fireman whose skill would normally include regulating the steam requirements of the boiler to suit the present location (a station for example or the anticipation of a gradient ahead) but was probably totally unaware of his surroundings due to the enclosed space where he worked in the centre of the engine. The placing of the boiler offset from the centre line to provide a corridor of sorts as means of communication between the crew meant there was excess weight on one side. Balance weights had then to be placed in the corridor to offset the unequal weight distribution. This in turn had two detrimental consequences; firstly, it made communication, and with it access between the cabs, even more restricted and secondly, it increased the overall weight so restricting the potential sphere of activity of the engine to even fewer routes.*

• The use of coal as fuel. *At the time Leader was in the design stage, the Southern along with the other railways were, upon the instructions of Government, in the process of converting steam engines to burn heavy oil. Bulleid had indeed intended for Leader to burn oil which, had this been achieved, 'might' have allowed remote control of the firing and meaning the fireman need not have been separated from the driver – a remote means of checking the boiler water level and operating the steam/water controls for the injectors would have been needed. No such provision was ever made in the driving cabs. Was this intention towards oil fuel the reason Brighton rapidly converted a Terrier to burn oil in 1946 'to gain experience'? (For full details of this and the other conversions of the time, see* Southern Way Special *No. 17:* The Southern Railway Oil-Burning Engines 1946–1951 *referred to in the bibliography.) Moving almost into the realms of fantasy, but if oil had been available might this even have allowed the boiler/firebox to be turned around [and of course then centralised] as per the American 'cab-forward' design?)*

The archetypal 'cab-forward' design as operating on the Southern Pacific railroad. The SP had 256 of these monsters of four different types, all using the Mallett principle. No. 4294, a 1944 4-8-8-2 is the sole survivor and when in service was capable of developing 6,000hp. The 'cab-forward' design came about over concerns of the risk of crew asphyxiation in tunnels and snow sheds when working backwards plus the sheer bulk, meaning otherwise poor visibility. This was one of the very few other steam designs which like Leader had the driver (and in this case consequent upon the use oil firing, the fireman as well) provided with an uninterrupted view of the line ahead. The engine would be turned at the end of each journey. *S.C. Townroe*

- The temperature on board. *120°F has been quoted – wrongly – it was actually 122°F. But what is conveniently forgotten is that on the same day a similar temperature reading in the cab of a Merchant Navy registered 140°F. The 120°F figure has oft been quoted with the fireman needing to lag his legs and even seek hospital treatment for burns. Lagging – maybe – neither confirmed nor unconfirmed, but only two regular crews ever worked the engine, [nearly] always the same men from Brighton and likewise a volunteer crew from Eastleigh. The regular fireman at Brighton denied this ever having been the case, similarly the driver at Eastleigh categorically denied hospital treatment was ever needed for his mate. A case of a misquote and what we would nowadays call 'fake news'.*

But we have jumped ahead, for behind the scenes John Click provides some interesting background to that all-important Southern Board meeting of December 1944, which has previously been quoted as when the genus of Leader first emerged. We should remember too that Bullleid's own position on the Southern was by now well assured, the Merchant Navy Pacifics – recall at the end of 1944 the West Country class were still to appear – already performing prodigious feats of haulage, the two electric locomotives were running well and the Q1s similarly taking their place high amongst among the Southern's steam stock.

Click comments, 'Bulleid, whose loyalty upwards always seemed beyond reproach, has until now been credited with

What weaknesses there were in the design were caused as much by haste as attempting to incorporate so many untried and consequently untested innovations in the one engine.

Bulleid's express passenger design emerged in 1941 as the Merchant Navy class with the 4-6-2 (Pacific type) wheel arrangement. Clearly an express passenger machine, he managed to convince the government and SR Board that continuing production of what he stated was a 'mixed traffic' design would aid the war effort. Notwithstanding the 6ft 2in wheel diameter, which was slightly less than the normal express passenger size used by other companies, the workforce at Eastleigh were not convinced and a strike was a distinct possibly based on the belief that the works should be concentrating more on genuine war work. The first of the class using Bulleid's enigmatic numbering 21C1 *Channel Packet* is seen at Salisbury on freight during WWII – one of several similar views deliberately circulated and intended to show the versatility of the class. (The type were also used on mammoth 20 coach passenger workings; the fact Waterloo could not accommodate trains of such length does not appear to have been considered.) The design was also not without its problems. Do not get the impression from the outset that the object of this book is to challenge Bulleid purely for the sake of it. But others have also clearly felt the same way in years past, witness A.F. Cook (albeit a Swindon man) who in the 1952 issue of *Trains Annual* published an article 'A Challenge to Orthodoxy: Bulleid designs of the Southern'.

Bulleid's Q1 design of 1942, certainly more conventional from a mechanical perspective, also the final 0-6-0 type built in the UK. Mechanically more conventional but such an accolade could hardly be applied to the physical appearance. Again the numbering system is to Bulleid style 'C' standing for the number of coupled axles and the '18' the engine number. It was number C21 of the class that was involved with speed trials running in reverse at 75mph and then later No. C36 that was coupled to a West Country tender for similar tests. According to the Traffic Manager neither was truly satisfactory – perhaps exactly what Bulleid had actually wanted him to say – for this then left the way open for more 'creative' thinking. It is unfortunate that despite extensive searching no views have been located showing No. C36 attached to a West Country tender but we do have this view of what was by now the renumbered BR No. 33036, appropriately at Paddock Wood but in June 1961. *A.E. Bennett/The Transport Treasury*

"writing up" the Traffic Manager's request for a locomotive to replace the "M7" into the "Leader" on his own and without much real authority.'

This statement of Click's is in itself most revealing and appears again to confirm the present writer's earlier assertions that formal meetings were held almost to 'confirm' what had been previously agreed. Whether such 'arrangements (agreements)' were something that had always occurred on the Southern, whether they were something Bulleid had brought over from the LNER, and indeed whether this was how others behaved as well, is all unknown. Even so it does tend to cast some doubt on this previously quoted statement, attributable to Bulleid, that it was in fact he who had stated what was required was not a tank engine, but a more modern, more versatile machine and associated with this would be greater efficiency in both operating, maintenance and servicing. After all, this same concept had led the design of the Pacifics; the oil bath and within the enclosed valve gear intended to require only minimal attention between works visits and consequently a reduced preparation time. Unfortunately in the case of the Merchant Navy design (and the later West Country type) his ideals and intentions, certainly so far as maintenance was concerned, were not achieved. But at least Bulleid was a realistic man and was not suggesting or attempting to produce a machine that would require no maintenance between works visits.

Rather than speculate further on origins and which would be to little effect, let us instead turn to fact. As first built, Bulleid's Q1 0-6-0 design was found to run well up to 75mph but was considered 'lively' in reverse due to the light construction of the tenders. When full with 5t of coal and 3,700gal of water, a Q1 tender weighed in 38t, but if the water and coal were removed the net weight was just less than 20t. However, putting matters in perspective, the tender of one of the Pacifics was only about 1t heavier when empty.

When it came to Bulleid's ears that crews were concerned over the behaviour of the Q1 tender when running at speed, he acted in what we may truthfully say was typical fashion. He travelled to Ashford and boarded No. C21 for a test run, tender first to Maidstone and return. Speeds of 55–66mph were reached without mishap and consequently the pre-existing fears began to fade away. (There were other crew grumbles about the Q1 class appertaining to water leaking from the tender, draughts and noise. Some of these subsequently abated but are irrelevant to the subject currently under discussion.) More pertinent was the later addition of strengthening plates, additional internal baffles and rolled U-sections internally welded to the sides to reduce vibration. Perhaps the most telling change though was the addition of 2½in of concrete to the interior base of the tank, although it is not known if this latter modification was applied to all the tenders from the class. A small reduction in water capacity would of course result, whilst there was a consequential weight increase of 1½t. No doubt others in his position when faced with a complaint such as this would have instructed a subordinate to deal with the issue, but that was not Bulleid's way and it should be recorded that he was someone who should be remembered as being prepared to lead from the front and not to hide from his detractors.

Unfortunately we have no date for this footplate venture, which is a pity regarding what follows. We can tie it down only to a two-and-a-half year period, between June 1942 when C21 was built and the December 1944 meeting. What is apparent is that on the Southern there was an amount of regular tender-first working diagrammed for the class and with a high tender and standard left-hand drive, the visibility for the driver when reading signals was not ideal.

Subsequently another member of the class, this time No. C36, was modified so as to be able to be driven from either side of the footplate and this time attached to 'Light Pacific' tender No. 3256[1] suitably painted black to match the engine. (It is Bradley who tells us No. C36 was modified, but this is then contradicted by HAV as per the next paragraph.)

The intention of providing a West Country type tender was to improve visibility for the driver when running tender first and various goods turns were worked with this combination over a protracted period from September

Bulleid's 'Light Pacific' or West Country class, a slightly smaller version of the Merchant Navy type and which would eventually number no less than 110 examples. Mechanically they were almost identical to their larger cousins and consequently shared the same attributes: on a good day without equal, but also unpredictable. Externally the design is also similar although it will be noted the front end casing has been modified, this was in an attempt to improve air flow and consequently smoke lifting. (Several engines of the earlier Merchant Navy class had been fitted with ribbons or similar soon after building in an attempt to identify air flow/currents; again a great pity no views of engines with these embellishments have been found. Q1 No. C36 was attached to a tender of the type seen here for the experiments referred to in the previous caption and in the text. The engine seen here is No. 21C133 recorded at Brighton when new and later named *Chard*.

We should not ignore Bulleid's collaboration with the SR electrical engineer Alfred Raworth in the building of two electric locomotives CC1 and CC2 in 1941. Ignoring the pantograph, the external similarity to Leader is sufficient to understand why the non-technical may have taken 36001 to be another electric locomotive. According to Michael Bonavia in his *History of the Southern Railway* (Harper Collins, 1987) 'The Leader fiasco must have been a source of quiet satisfaction to Raworth whose two prototype electric locomotives were performing very satisfactorily.'

1945 to May 1946, the duties chosen deliberately involving much tender-first running. The mention of duplication of the controls is partly contradicted by HAV who comments 'they explored electrical as well as mechanical methods of duplicating controls of regulator and brake … the result was a "double fronted" Q1 as shown in diagram W6393 … it was not liked by the running department and incidentally the drawing office failed to design a dual-control drive to their satisfaction.' Click later commented, 'The DO had been working on two competitive methods of duplicating the regulator, the reverser and the brake on either side of the engine, but the lever system was awkward to say the least. OVB was pleased he wanted feasibility proved for an electronic alternative, but in 1945 that was a term we had never heard of. But it also showed how anxious OVB would be to apply the latest technology from any other field, no matter where it originated, or how relatively undeveloped it was and potentially troublesome as a result. He was always pushing away at the frontiers of loco design.' Click adds a final rider to the last few words, '… "a habit learnt under Sir Nigel" he would have explained', the latter surely a somewhat curious comment to make as Gresley had always seemed to be more solid and conservative in his approach to radical thought.

Running with a West Country tender attached to a Q1 surprisingly reported no real advantage to visibility, which is unusual as it would have been thought the driver at least would have preferred the better view now available. Perhaps cost and complexity were the over-riding parameters rather than practicalities. But whilst there is no definite connection with Leader, the one linking parameter is the wish/need to improve visibility for either-direction working. Again we may speculate as to what followed, but we should also ask ourselves did the idea that would later evolve as the steam engine with the driver having excellent vision forward regardless of the direction of travel – and without the need to use a turntable – originate from Bulleid instructing the drawing office – or was it the drawing office

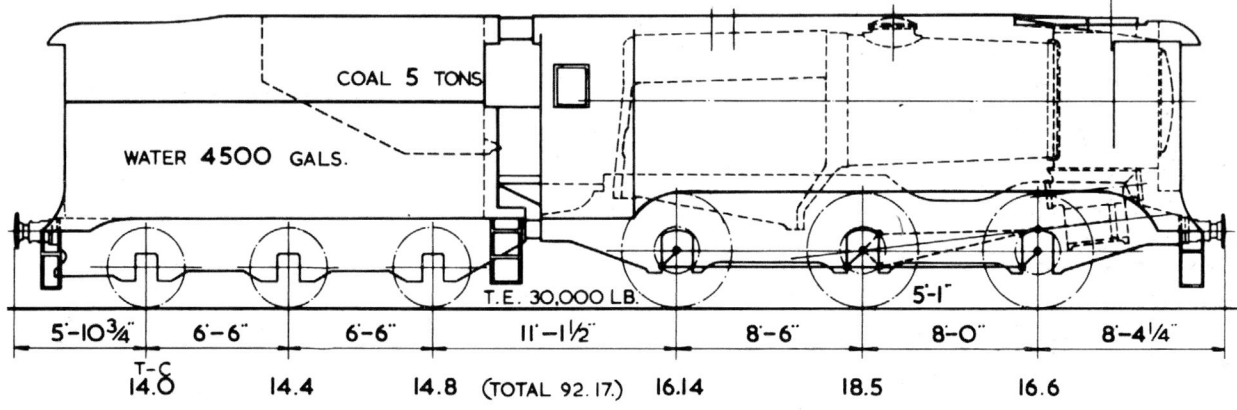

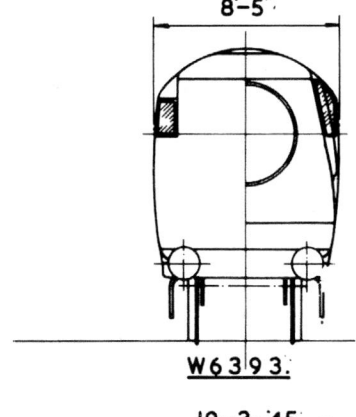

Drawing W6393: the double-ended Q1 of March 1945 and in outline similar looking to a West Country. The proposal would have had two 19in x 26in cylinders, the same as the conventional Q1 and likewise the same wheel diameter and boiler pressure, respectively 5ft 1in and 230psi giving a tractive effort of 30,000lbs. Unlike most weight (or indeed all) SR weight diagrams, this one has the engine facing right in LNER style. Perhaps an instruction from C.S. Cocks, late of the LNER.

coming up with their own 'radical' ideas based on their own belief in where development lay?

Before moving on let us remain for a moment with the Q1 proposal. One thing that is not mentioned was a cab at the rear of the tender. Visibility would certainly have been improved whilst the shorter physical distance between the tender cab and the engine would surely have meant remote operation of the regulator would have been possible. After all had not air-operated pull-push workings with the crew separated in this way been successfully operated on the Southern for many years? No one had objected to the normal view available to the driver on a Q1 when running forward and this surely would have solved the question when operating for any distance in reverse.

Perhaps left to his own devices Bulleid would have persisted with improvements to the Q1 to enable improved vision when running tender first but instead it was the Traffic Manager, R.M.T. Richards, who in effect scuppered the idea when, in December 1944, a meeting was held to 'rubber-stamp' the 1946 locomotive building programme with an agreement for ten shunting engines for Southampton Docks (these would become the USA tanks class), and twenty-five West Country type. The latter is also interesting as in December 1944 none of the class had been completed; the first, No. 21C101 *Exeter*, appeared on 21 June 1945 followed by a further nineteen by the end of the year. Curiously too it was also not twenty-five of the type that subsequently appeared in 1946 as thirty-two took to the rails! Perhaps the increase was to make up for a shortfall in 1945.

At the same December meeting a further twenty-five engines (we may say with 99% certainly 'steam') were supposed to have been approved and for these Bulleid suggested more of the Q1 class – possibly with his own belief that with a different tender attached, these would be better at reverse operation. But what Richards really wanted was a large tank engine and with Ellson recently retired as CCE we may conclude Richards felt confident in requesting something that was long overdue.

Consequently, on 15 December 1944, Richards wrote to Bulleid stating, 'With regard your suggestion that the material for the construction of (more) Q1 engines should still be used for this type instead of for passenger tanks, an opportunity has been taken of inspecting locomotive No. C1 and the conclusion has been arrived at that the lookout facilities provided on this engine are not suitable for regular tender-first running. The rear lookout on the driver's side does not give a sufficiently wide range of vision, and the absence of a lookout on the fireman's side is a serious drawback, having regard to the fact that it is necessary for the fireman to assist in looking out for signals when not otherwise necessarily engaged and this is particularly important having regard to the fact that the normal driving position for signals is on the left-hand side. Unless, therefore, the observation conditions, tender-first, can be materially improved, I am afraid they will not be suitable to traffic requirements. Another point I would like to raise is as to whether you are satisfied that these engines are suitable for maintaining necessary speeds running tender-first when light in coal and water.'

Separation of the crew on a pull-push (motor/auto) train was never an issue in steam days. A specially adapted locomotive and coaching stock used whereby turning/running-round was avoided at either end of the journey. Duplicate regular and brake controls were provided in the end compartment of the coach and the driver would remain there whilst the engine was propelling; the fireman attending to the fire/boiler and cut-off from the footplate. This practice was widespread on various branch and some cross-country routes throughout the Southern system, with similar arrangements elsewhere. Separation of the crew was never considered an issue. Likewise on an electric unit the motorman worked alone. Yet criticism was later raised about the crew being separated on No. 36001. Had safety alone been an issue it would surely not have been beyond the remit of man to design a 'dead-man' for the driver on No. 36001? This type of steam pull-push/(motor/auto working) continued almost until the demise of steam. Seen here is H class No. 31263 at the terminus at Westerham on one such working.

H.A.V. Bulleid commented in his own book that Gresley could have demolished this by a strong reply, but Bulleid instead appears to acquiesce, perhaps even deliberately.

Consider also Richards clearly appears to have prior knowledge of the reportedly lively running of the Q1 type operating tender-first as he mentions the relevant point concerning speed when the tender might weigh less when low on coal and water. But no mention ever appears on tender-first working of the Pacifics either now or indeed later, perhaps for the simple expedient that tender-first running for these engine was less, and consequently over shorter distances and at lower speeds.

So to return to late 1944, we can realistically assume regular behind-the-scenes contact between the traffic and CME departments, as emerging from the drawing office in September 1944, is the first attempt at a large tank engine in the form of an 0-6-4T. (It is believed there had also been an 0-6-2T proposal although the drawing for this has not survived.) The 0-6-4T drawing was produced by W.H. Hutchinson.

It was also to the first of what would turn out to be a mammoth amount of work undertaken by the locomotive drawing office under the charge of C.S. Cocks.[2]

that would eventually result in No. 36001. But neither of course was it the only task to occupy the locomotive team, for there was work on the Light Pacifics, the USA class, shortly after the oil burning conversions, plus any number of other regular tasks.

HAV tells us (p.125 of his book) that Cocks approved of both the 0-6-2T and the 0-6-4T, both proposals using designs already to hand from the Q1 plus having, at 30,000lb tractive effort, half as much again as an M7. No doubt also either would have proved exactly what the traffic department required and they were eminently suitable for either direction running, but to Bulleid's furtive mind they were, to quote HAV again, 'stodgy and boring'.

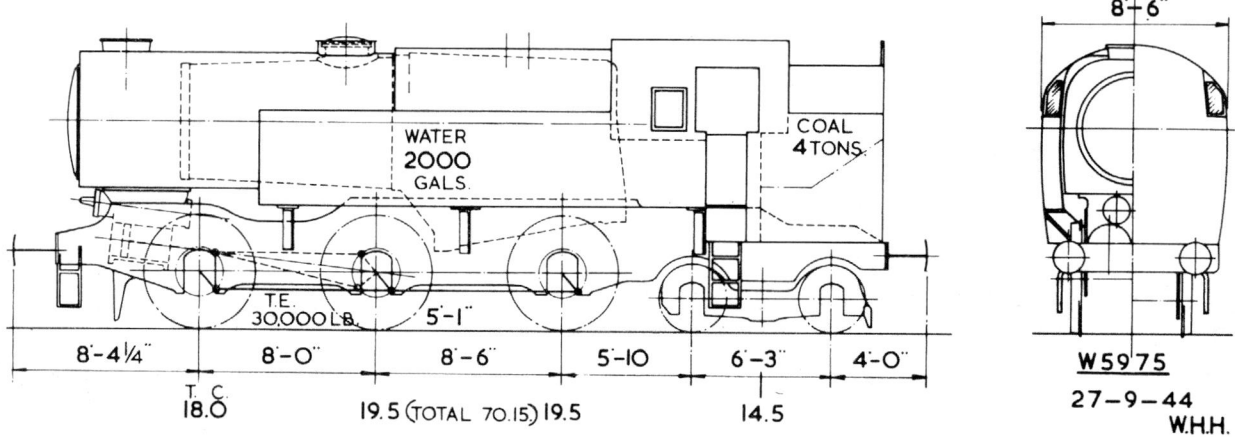

Drawing W5975, the July 1944 0-6-4T version of the SECR J class tank and the same wheel arrangement. Using this as a basis the Q1 design would have resulted in a machine with a 50% greater tractive effort than the J but with the disadvantage of having no leading pony truck. Although this and a slightly smaller 0-6-2T would have no doubt have done all that was required of a medium to large passenger tank engine, Bulleid was not impressed.

Why Bulleid felt this way is explained by HAV, 'Early in 1944 he had first seriously raised the possibility of a compact locomotive on two power bogies, and he raised it again now. Cocks again dissuaded, though with difficulty, on the grounds of excessive novelty.'

Considering the timespan involved, December 1944 when Richards declined to accept a Q1 and then Bulleid undertook trials for some nine months from September 1945 with a member of the class having a Light Pacific tender, we are left with two questions; firstly, was Bulleid simply still attempting to resolve the duplication of controls issue on the Q1 or, secondly, was this instead a step on the way towards something quite different?

At this point Click again takes up the story from where he had commented on Bulleid's loyalty – see p.38. 'That always seemed wrong if only because it was unlike the man. Now, in my own mind I am convinced I have found the truth of this riddle, thanks to the missing piece of the puzzle given me by Sir John Elliot. Bulleid was loyal, yes; and an opportunist too, fully capable of putting the two together.

'At the start OVB had suggested more Q1s; but Traffic needed a short engine if only to take up minimum space at the buffer end of Waterloo's platforms, but it had to have the range to bring stock in from outlying sidings and be much more powerful than an M7. Up went the axle weight though, compared with the Q1, because of the heavy side tanks. Several shortened versions of the Q1 boiler were also then looked at. The usual procedures got followed: wheelbase and weight diagrams were submitted to the Chief Civil Engineer and the likely route availability established for the Traffic Manager's approval, hopefully.'

Click continues, 'The fully justified niggles about the Q1 running backwards brought a predictable reaction from OVB: he pulled ever harder in its favour. I was surprised (Click was at Ashford by this time) to find a newly built West Country tender, which instead of setting off for Brighton in a freight train, was coupled to a Q1, No. C36. Curious, I watched developments. It was steamed for a trial in the Maidstone direction, an unusual route, so I hung about. After a while CSC and Jimmy Jones appeared, waved cheerily to me, climbed on and away they went, chimney first.

'At Maidstone East OVB got on for the real object of the exercise; a tender-first dash back. The view was better though the ride would have been lively and very draughty; but if the Chief was as querulous as the others on board, he certainly didn't show it, I was told.

'Then the penny dropped; I suddenly saw why three of us at Brighton had been given a couple of hours, one Saturday morning, to put an 'air-smoothed' casing onto a Q1 model. We did it with cardboard, Seccotine (a brand of refined fish glue use for gluing paper and card which remains flexible after drying), pins, Plasticine and ingenuity: OVB was said to be pleased with it when Cocks took it down to him later that same morning. A fully finished model of the air-smoothed Q1, in yellow lining, was produced but looked "cheap and nasty". Sadly it finished its life as a child's toy, in Jarvis's time, when many development models were sold to draughtsmen for their kids' Christmas presents.

'The "go-either-way" Q1 convinced nobody, and that included OVB himself that is after he had grown tired of it; it looked suitable for a tinplate O gauge version, without needing Sir William's advice about where to wind it up.' (Sir William Stanier had apparently asked 'Where do you put the key?' after seeing a photographs of the first completed Q1.)

Meanwhile back at Brighton the next diagrams produced were for conventional 2-6-2 and 2-6-4 tank classes, eventually culminating in a 4-6-4T dating from August 1945. Again all would have used the basic (or slightly extended) Q1 boiler (and by this we presume is also meant the Lord Nelson type firebox) and externally portrayed the 'austerity' perspective. Once more whilst each would no doubt have filled the role of an M7

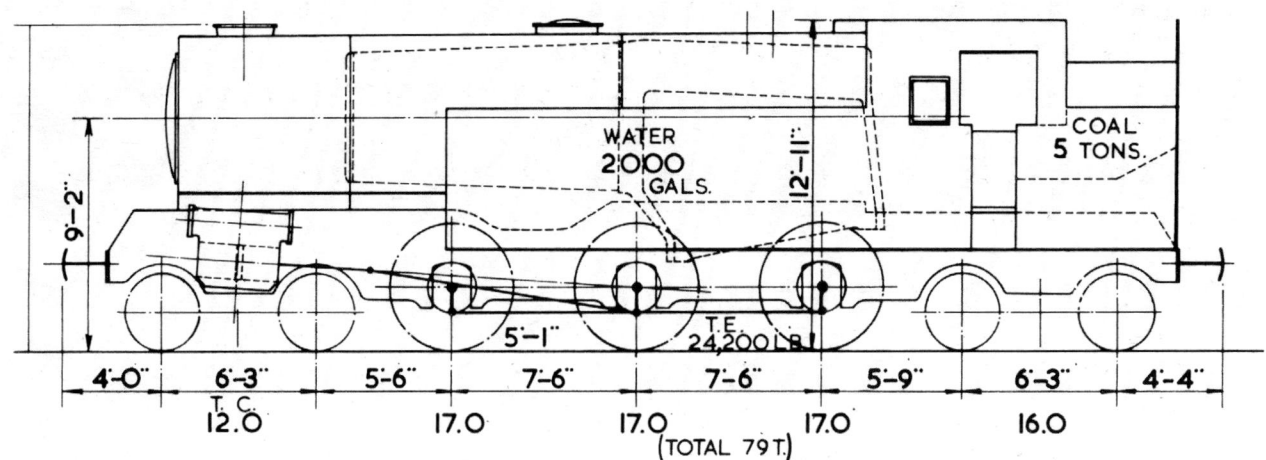

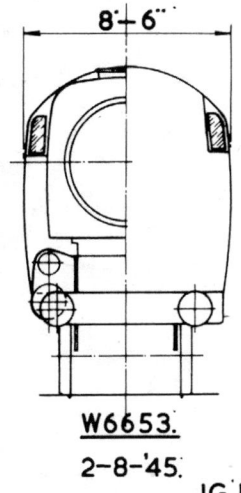

Drawing W6653 of 2 August 1945 and where progression had been made to a large 4-6-4T AKA as per the Furness Railway perhaps? Worth noting is that the 'W' prefix related to Brighton-produced drawings. A considerable number of these drawings appear to have survived and are included in a register of Southern drawings (LSWR, LBSCR, SECR and SR) held at the National Railway Museum. However, those listed are not necessarily shown in consecutive numerical or date order (800+ pages of entries). Whilst there are a considerable number of drawings for the components and details of Leader itself there are many gaps, including for example any further drawings of the proposed weight diagrams/outlines that would eventually lead to No 36001. Just in case anyone ever had the idea of attempting a 'new-build' we should say there do not appear to be any drawings of the sleeve valves – perhaps a relief! To return to W6653, it is again based on the Q1 but with smaller cylinders placed outside. The boiler is also now pressed to 250psi and extended in length by 18in. For an overall weight of 79t only 51t is available for adhesion, a far from ideal arrangement and the same issue that would prevail with the C.S. Cocks proposal dating from around December 1945. (See drawing on page 51.)

replacement, there was concern (according to HAV) over riding issues with the 4-6-4T at high speed. Justified or historic concern is not certain and then what was meant in this context by the term 'high speed' and would it have been necessary anyway? Certainly it could never be said that an M7 loaded to perhaps 400t of empty stock (or more) would have achieved anything like high speed between Clapham Junction and Waterloo and even less if venturing further afield with this type of load. Perhaps it was the operators who wanted to push these workings along a bit more and so free the running lines for the intensive suburban area service.

What is also certain is that the 4-6-4T design resulted in a disproportionate amount of weight being unavailable for adhesion, just 51t out of a total 79t. Perhaps convention in the form of tank engines with a leading/trailing bogie/pony truck had been taken as far as possible, for what was to follow after this was truly a venture into the unknown.

Notes

1 Tender No. 3256 was later attached to the new No. 21C138 *Lynton* from 5 September 1946. This also indicates that this tender at least was completed some time before the engine to which it was subsequently allocated. The then No. 34038 received a replacement tender on 31 December 1948.)

2 Clifford S. Cocks, had gone with Bulleid to the Southern from the LNER and held the role on the SR as Chief Locomotive Designer. Although similar in name, but unconnected, was C.M. Cock who, from 1945, was appointed Electrical Engineer on the Southern Railway. Clifford S. Cocks was eventually replaced at Brighton by Ron Jarvis in 1949. This was part of Riddles's 'cross-fertilisation' plan following nationalisation which saw Cocks and Jarvis exchange places. J.G. Click comments, 'Whatever the constant demands Bulleid made on him (Cocks) he always had something to show him even at the shortest notice: but at the same time he had to restrain OVB's wildest ideas, and that took its toll. He was never happy at Derby … Brighton was more adaptable, though everyone in their hearts knew how much they owed to Cocks.'

5

The (Iron) Horse Designed by a Committee

I am sure readers will have heard the phrase 'A camel is a horse designed by a committee'. It is attributable to Sir Alec Issigonis, the designer of the Mini car; he had coined the phrase to illustrate his dislike of working in teams. So far as timescales were concerned, the words would also probably date from years after Leader had been laid to rest but had they been around at the time they would surely have found their home in No. 36001. We could even take it one stage further with 'A camel is a very efficient machine but it is not a very good horse'. Where does this lead us? Well simply that left to his own devices, unconstrained by time or availability of material, Bulleid's replacement for the M7 would probably have been very different to both an M7 and Leader. It was the constraints placed upon him – *plus* the criteria he set himself – and the need to in effect rush through the process that resulted in our 'camel', although in the case of No. 36001 it was surely a camel missing certain vital components!

So with Bulleid having clearly rejected the various tank engine designs, August 1945 also saw the first of the radical proposals – the word 'radical' being used deliberately.

Forgetting aesthetics for a moment, proposal W6656 was probably unlike anything seen anywhere before. Instead of a set of coupled wheels on a conventional steam engine there were instead two separate three-axle bogies, each axle seemingly independent of the next and individually driven by gears from its own 3-cylinder engine – a total of 18 cylinders – with a cylinder size of either 7in x 10in or as an alternative 8in x 11in. Allied to a high pressure 350psi boiler, driving wheels (scaled) of just 4ft diameter, the tractive effort the 18 cylinders would between them produce was 30,500lb or 43,800lb respectively, the latter twice that of an M7. (Tractive effort is calculated at 85% boiler pressure.)

Whilst on the surface appealing, there were numerous engineering complications, not least of which would be the physical fitting of 18 cylinders into such a confined space – as HAV also points out, 'How would the rear 6-wheel bogie clear the ashpan?' HAV adds that Gresley had toyed with the idea of a multi-cylinder geared locomotive seventeen years earlier in 1928 (this date comes from HAV) but it was realised the idea presented insurmountable problems. (The Gresley concept would have been a 6-cylinder D49 4-4-0; *see* p.107 of Geoffrey Hughes' biography of Sir Nigel Gresley, Oakwood Press 2001. From this could we even say Gresley was as keen to try out 'radical' proposals as the next man. Perhaps even the other CMEs toyed with similar off-piste projects from time to time. Could this even be where Bulleid's vision to be different stemmed from? The difference, though, was that Gresley identified it was not a viable proposition and stepped back. On the Southern, Bulleid did not.)

Another point is that unlike other designers who may have had a basic precept on which to base their ideal, an enlargement of whatever, or the use of certain standard components – boiler, wheels etc. – to base their new design upon, in Leader nothing was sacrosanct. True the concept had been approved by the Board of the Southern Railway in 1946 but this approval was for five engines of 'unspecified design'. A slightly unusual approval when there appeared to be nothing actually fixed – other that is, than the Southern was seeking a replacement for the M7.

Perhaps Bulleid would have liked authority for more than five as the initial order but the motive power department at least were only too aware of the difficulties associated with the Merchant Navy class when they had first emerged and whilst the class had settled down to perform sterling service, it could not be denied the design was still heavy on coal and especially maintenance. A multitude of new engines to an untried design was a risk too far, hence the limited number. Material was also on hand, but by this we should clarify that this was raw material, steel etc., the latter in short supply post-WWII, and which had originally been earmarked for a further batch of Q1 locomotives. Do not for one moment think this was physical material made into Q1 components but not yet assembled. Indeed the only thing Leader ever had in common with the Q1 was they shared the same wheel diameter of 5ft 1in, but even then, the actual wheels were different as those for Leader had no crankpin onto which a coupling rod would attach – the final drive on Leader being by chains attached to sprockets on the outer ends of the axles.

But Brighton had to start somewhere; hence it was with the Q1 design, altered to be a tank engine, where matters commenced.

Moving on, C.S. Cocks was able to bring Bulleid back to current reality with another 4-6-4T, the principal differences from W6653 being an increase of 1ft in the coupled wheelbase, cylinders that were 1in less in diameter but with a boiler that was pressed to 350psi instead of the 250psi on No. W6653. In outline it was a West Country with a bunker instead of a tender. The higher boiler pressure also gave a greater tractive effort, 30,000lb whilst the provision of the four-wheel bogie either end would certainly have made for good riding. Visibility would have been about average for a steam engine, certainly that of a modern machine where the boiler was pitched almost to the limit of the loading gauge. But against this was still the amount of adhesive weight lost due to the presence of bogies fore and aft, whilst extreme boiler pressure would have almost guaranteed slipping would have been an issue. Lamentably this drawing is not numbered, and consequently dated, but it is believed to be from around November 1945. Why the date especially should be an issue is because for the first time the fuel referred to is '2½ tons of coal or 2,500 gallons of oil', the very first time oil as a fuel is mentioned so far as the Leader concept is concerned. The perception has always been that No. 36001 was intended to be oil-fired, indeed oil as an alternative to coal is still being shown on proposals produced in May 1946 but, and this is a very big but, we should take care not to get carried away with the belief that Leader *was* to have been oil fired. The government scheme intended to convert steam locomotives to burn oil was not confirmed until August 1946, so did the Southern even have early plans to 'go it alone' with the use of oil?

We have a possible clue in a further NRM drawing reference. This comes from drawing W10634 dated 19 October 1948, which carried the heading 'Oil Burning Conversions' and referred to the 'Arrangement of fixing lugs for firebricks on firebox backplate'. The scale of the drawing is noted as '3 inches = 1 inch'. We should also consider the date of this drawing in two other contexts: firstly, on 8 January 1948 the government had ordered that all work on further coal to oil locomotive conversions (and depot installations) should cease, and then on 2 October 1948, those locomotives already converted to burn oil should stop work. (The full story of the Southern oil burning conversions is told in *Southern Way Special No. 17* written by the present author.) So was the heading of this drawing of 19 October a simple misprint, or did the Southern Region, as it was then, really hope that Leader would run on oil even after they had been told oil would no longer be available? On this we may still speculate and it is regretted that despite much searching, there still remains no definite proof.

A modified version of the same drawing, No. W6916, appears on 15 December 1945 and is basically identical to that of October, excepting for two salient points. The first is that only oil is mentioned as the fuel and the second

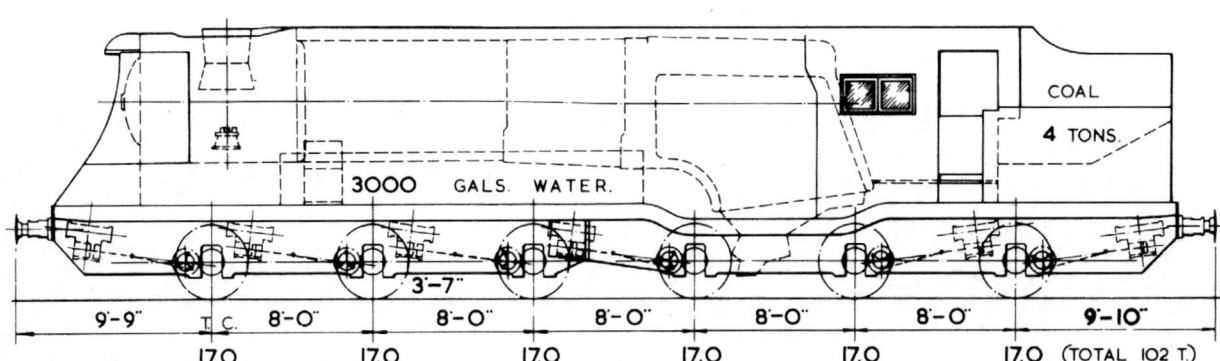

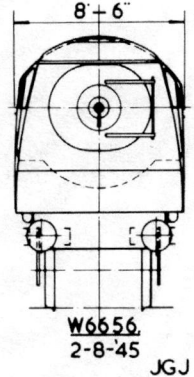

W6656 of 2 August 1945. (We would dearly like to know about the missing numbers in the series, W6654–5, etc. Only one has been located, the reference that is and not a drawing. This is W7090 which is for a wood model of a modified Q1 – we are not told in what way 'modified'. It is dated June 1947. W6656 really was a novelty for many reasons; 18 cylinders for example and a high pressure, 350psi, boiler. The small cylinders, either 7in x 10in or 8in x 11in would provide for 30,500 or 43,800lbs of tractive effort. Wheel diameter is not shown but scaled from the drawing appears to be in the order of 3ft 9in. Might this even have been the reason the Sentinel engine was rescued from the former Dyke railcar, it would certainly have needed a high speed engine? There were many unanswered questions, such as how would the rear bogie clear the ashpan, but advantages too including the total adhesion. Bulleid would surely have come up with an answer to the ashpan issue, perhaps simply oil firing although it is not mentioned on the drawing.

that now a cab at each end is shown. Water capacity is the same as before at 2,500gal but this is written on what could well be a side tank. However, we may jokingly suggest that back in 1945 the original draughtsman may well have recorded it as such to confuse any writer three-quarters of a century later for there is no alteration to any of the axle weights, hence it would appear the water tank was still in its original bunker position.

So far as the feature of a cab at each was concerned, the provision of these causes no increase to the overall length of the proposed engine and consequently when scaled from the proposal drawing the proposed drivers' cabs at each end would have been only just over 2ft wide. Whilst it is appreciated the cabs of some of the EMU sets were not much wider, in a steam locomotive this would have been 'cosy' to say the least, in addition to which the necessary driving controls would have reduced the available space even further. Add that to being next to a 'warm' smokebox door at one end it would certainly not have made for a comfortable working environment. Ash disposal was evidently not considered an issue for, as mentioned, oil was the preferred choice for fuel at this time. We should mention that an end elevation is also fortunately provided, which records a distinct similarity with a contemporary EMU. The boiler also remained on its centre line at this stage. Pity the poor fireman!

The design also incorporated an all-welded water-tube boiler with additional vertical (water) tubes either side of what H.A.V. Bulleid refers to as the 'fire area', which we take to mean the firebox. Inside cylinders are also shown with enclosed inside motion – the latter typical Bulleid and showing distinct family similarity to the Pacifics. External coupling rods *appear* to be indicated but this is not totally certain from the size of what could equally be final drive sprockets at the ends of the axles.

And despite the seemingly growing list of ever-more-complicated proposals emerging, we should not for one moment lose sight of the fact that the whole thing is straying ever further away from the twenty-five tank engines which had been the basic requirement of the Traffic Manager twelve months earlier.

It appears too that by this time Traffic may well have been exerting pressure for a definite proposal to appear and it is possible Bulleid batted off this pressure by utilising the skills of one J.G. Jones in the Brighton drawing office. Jones is a new name to our story, described by HAV as 'one of the expert design draughtsmen, able quickly to incorporate the newest idea and shrewdly to estimate the resultant axle loads – an essential for the preliminary submission to the Civil Engineer'. We should not forget that these diagrams are best described as 'the illustration on the box lid'; meaning they indicate the contents of what lies below but do not in themselves describe

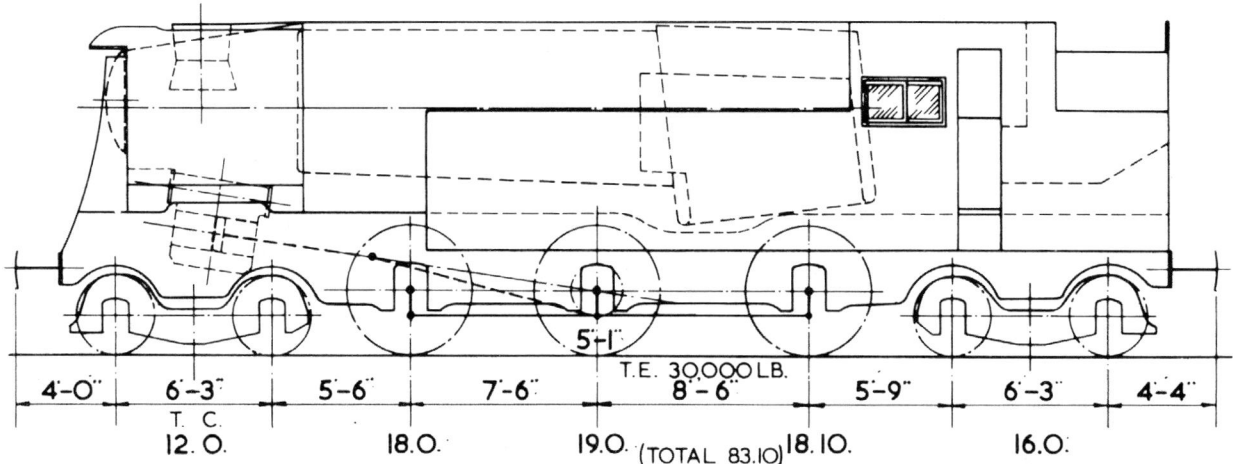

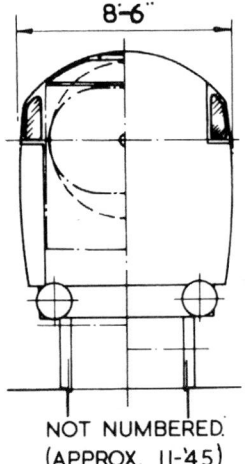

The un-numbered drawing from approximately November 1945. C.S. Cocks was trying to get Bulleid away from the totally radical but there was the unusual feature of the high pressure boiler at 350psi. Coupled to just two cylinders of 16in diameter and 24in stroke it provided for a tractive effort of 30,000lbs again with Q1 size wheels. Options were for coal and water; 3½t and 2,000 gal, or 2½t of oil and 2,500 gallons of water. It is interesting in that the oil capacity is given by weight and not liquid. Again the 4-6-4 wheel arrangement was not ideal but this time a slightly higher adhesive weight of 55t 10cwt against an overall weight of 83t 10cwt, allied to a higher maximum axle weight of 19t.

Not related to Leader but another experiment during Bulleid's time involved multiple chimneys fitted to King Arthur No. 783 *Sir Gillemere*, first in November 1940 with three chimneys and then in February 1941 with just two. We cannot lay this totally at the door of Bulleid as the work was undertaken at the instigation of the Ministry of Transport. The idea was to increase the speed at which the exhaust would dissipate and so reduce the chance of steam giving away the position of a train to enemy aircraft. Trials were carried out north from Eastleigh but the net results did not justify further engines being converted although perhaps the Chief Civil Engineer would have been able to examine the undersides of his bridges and tunnels more easily, 100-year-old soot being dislodged! The best results were obtained with the two-chimney version but at the expense of the driver's view ahead. A third experiment, not illustrated, was the provision of extra plates between the smoke deflectors and the smokebox. (Several Southern engines were damaged in consequence of enemy action in WWII including Merchant Navy class No. 21C4 *Cunard White Star* which was shot up near Whimple on 18 November 1942.) Note that in the image with the three

chimneys, the two new additions are placed ahead of the original chimney. In later years we would have seen the same results so far as dislodging ancient soot when the Crosti boiler members of the 9F class began to appear complete with their side exhaust.

Oil burning on the Southern commenced in August 1946 and basically ended in October 1948 (there was an exception when one member of the West Country class continued with this fuel until 1949 – that is until Waterloo had their wrist slapped by Marylebone!) Whether there was any serious effort made to produce Leader as an oil burner is moving slightly in favour of the affirmative and perhaps this may well have been the case if the engine had appeared on time. Instead Leader would burn coal in conditions that were hardly suitable for the crew. On an oil burner however the crew had a far easier time; the passengers perhaps not so with the inevitable all-pervading smell. Here we see King Arthur No. 740 *Merlin* one of five members of the class converted to oil, working a turn which is probably the 7.20am Eastleigh to Waterloo and 11.30am return. The service was photographed by Maurice Earley near Winchfield on 9 May 1947.

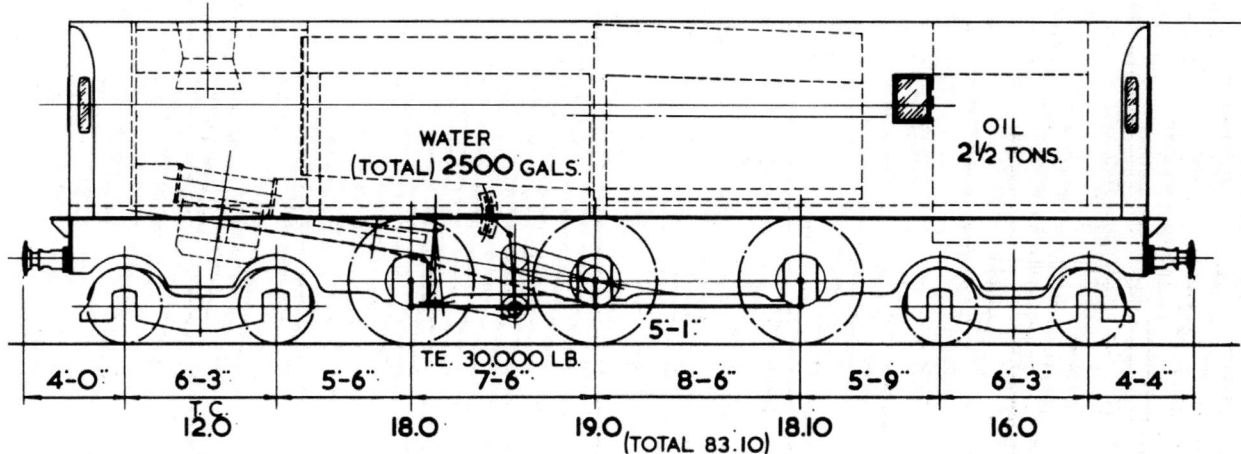

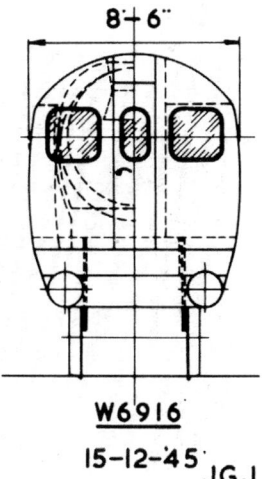

The final 4-6-4 design was from December 1945 and in many ways similar to the previous (un-numbered) drawing with the same high pressure 350psi boiler. This one appears to have two (16in x 24in) inside cylinders but otherwise weights, boiler pressure and tractive effort are identical. Where it becomes radical is as far as the driving positions are concerned: a ridiculously small cab at either end or possibly as only oil firing is shown, did this mean remote operation – as per the American 'cab-forward' arrangement? A detail from the end appears to show a connection door for multiple operation, but the rationale (or indeed need) for this is not explained. It will be noted that many of these reproductions carry the initials 'JGC' for John Gayward Click. To prepare these Click must have had access to the originals at some stage. But as stated the 'W' reference numbers even for these originals do not appear in the NRM drawings register and neither are there copies in the located JGC papers. For the present at least we can only say these remarkable proposals are the only ones that appear to have survived. JGC adds slightly more to the story of the drawings, 'Amongst the diagrams not used for HAV's book were some more conventional ones, in the Bulleid style all right, but which I couldn't place; they had no numbers either. A clue to dating them was that they were on a heavy kind of tracing paper known to have used for only a short time at Brighton; and on which, fortunately, one of the numbered Leader drawings was drawn too and so could be dated from the register. I had taken these mystery drawings to Derby with me, but neither Jim nor Dick Barnes could remember when, or why or for whom they were drawn: "after all we did so many," was Jim's comment at the time.'

the actual contents in great detail. HAV indicated Bulleid might sometimes arrive in the office at 10.00am and want a new diagram from Jones in order to catch the London train just after mid-day. It seems too that Jones was able to oblige.

Through all of this HAV tells us the new boiler design showed promise, whilst the one feature Bulleid really wanted to incorporate was the locomotive on two bogies. Cocks though was still resisting and consequently Bulleid took the somewhat sly route of waiting until Cocks was absent to instruct the drawing office to work on what is/are aptly described as 'the boiler on the well wagon'.

Two of these similar drawings have survived, respectively dated January and then February 1946. We might well imagine Bulleid arriving at the desk of perhaps Hutchinson or Jones and setting out his specification before leaving the office to let them get on with it. What Cocks must have thought is not reported and we also do not know how long he was absent from the office. 'Whenever he could OVB much preferred to work through just a few individuals. At Brighton C.S. Cocks and W. Marsh (his administrative assistant) were in and out constantly, but he also had a secretary and a personal clerk, S. Richardson, who looked after his correspondence and kept his diary as straight as possible. Richardson also made the necessary phone calls in a vain effort to keep up with each successive change of plan.' (Quote from JGC.)

This first drawing does not provide weights but does show two 4-wheel bogies having three cylinders apiece, two outside and one inside, a boiler with the same high 350psi pressure and a tractive effort not that far short of that of a West Country. Driving wheel diameter is indicated at 4ft. One certain advantage was total adhesion but the boiler was commented upon as being 'impractical' and the cylinder positioning 'optimistic'. Bulleid wrote on his copy 'Return to Brighton Drawing Office to file at present'.

The second drawing of the pair has an slight increase in wheel diameter to 4ft 3in, again with the same 6-cylinders – presumably sited as before – and with a water tube boiler, so creating greater water–heat transference. The cylinder

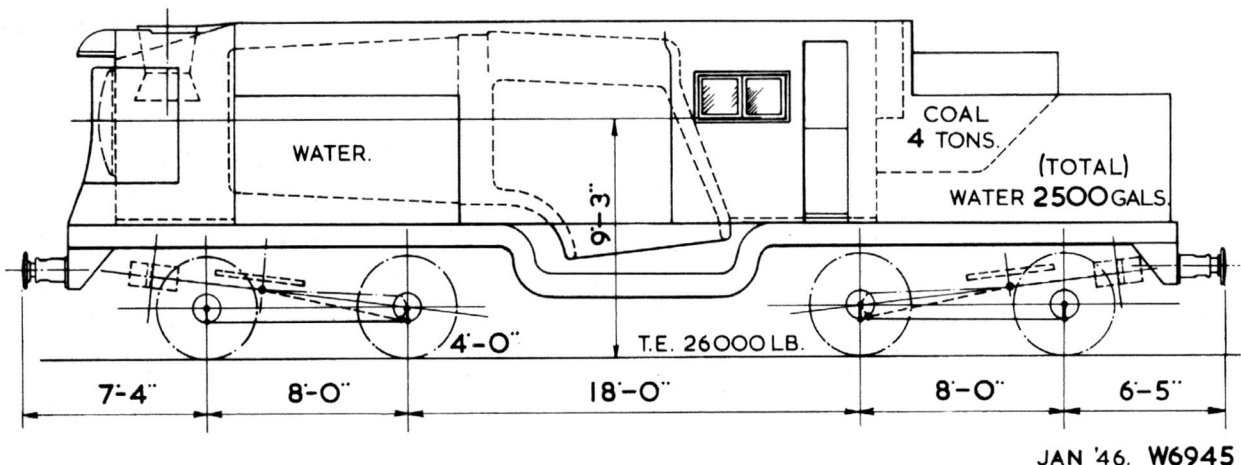

JAN '46. W6945

Referred to as 'the boiler on a well-wagon' for obvious reasons and apart from the complexities of six cylinders, 10in x 14in, and a 350psi boiler, a proposal that has the look of serous feasibility. No weights of tractive effort is shown but it does have the advantage of being a total adhesion engine. Listed at the NRM but unable to be accessed are various drawings which are a bit of a puzzle. These include 'Box 14, Roll 067' 'Misc Charts' W9844 'TE Curve double bogie engine'. Also another drawing dated 26-5-48. 'Box 306 Roll drawer 405, W8725 GA Leader class engine' – the latter possibly similar to that seen below. Slightly more obvious but showing the level of detail is a drawing for 'Lamp Shades' for No. 36001 (there were lamp shades above the electric switches in the cab and also above the outside coupling lamps), the rack for the fireman's tools, and 'chain drive for 'Hamworthy' pump'.

Hot on its heels so to speak came a similar version, the main difference being a water tube boiler; tubes forming the firebox sides, with two drums above. According to HAV, 'Welding problems in this design caused it to be abandoned.' Limited information is shown on the drawing. Six cylinders were anticipated of 14in length and depend upon the diameter, 12⅝ or 14¼in giving either 30,000 or 40,000lbs of tractive effort.

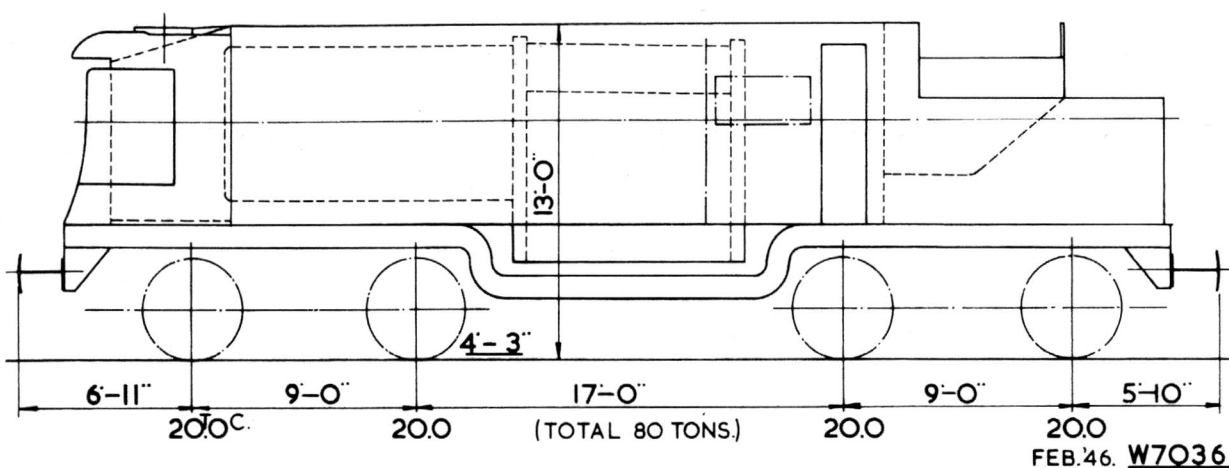

FEB.'46. W7036

diameter also increases (two options are shown) whilst the boiler pressure goes down. The result is a potentially very powerful machine but now with the unacceptable axle weight of 20t on each. They were getting close but still not quite close enough.

Closer still was drawing W7169 of 1 May 1946 – it would certainly be interesting to know what was going on between February and May of that year! Perhaps a clue comes again from HAV when he states that in an attempt to squeeze everything in, some components were even manufactured but later discarded. Unfortunately we have no further detail.

The obvious answer to reducing the axle weight below 20t was of course to spread it further and this meant a 6-wheel bogie. Unconventional certainly, but above the running plate the rest was relatively predictable, a boiler at 280psi, 6-cylinders (3 per bogie) and a conventionally positioned cab. Again oil was shown as the alternative to coal. But we should know Bulleid was never one to accept convention when he felt it could be improved upon, witness the space indicated for the possible inclusion of the Holcroft/Anderson pressure condensing system as had been fitted to 2-6-0 No. A816 between 1931 and 1935. Suffice to say it was not pursued later. (The Holcroft/Anderson

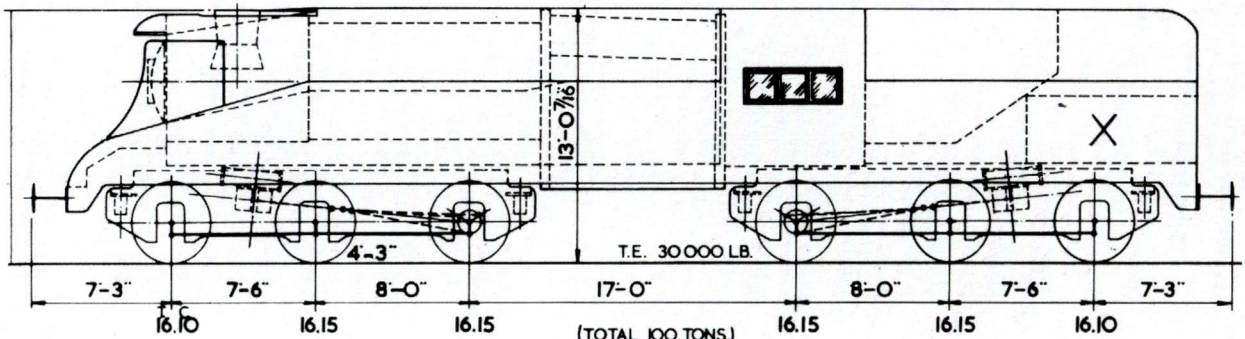

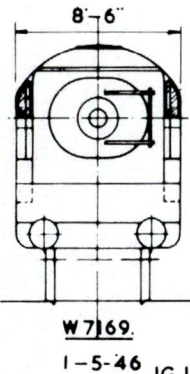

W7169 and very close to the design sanctioned – but in appearance nothing like what was eventually built! For the first time we have a locomotive on two six-wheel bogies but no mention of sleeves or firebox type. Instead we have is a 6-cylinder (12⅝in x 14in) layout, a central cab, and a space, marked with an 'X', for Holcroft/Anderson pressure condensing apparatus. This is the only time this feature is mentioned and it was not (perhaps fortunately) added to the eventual Leader design. We might also enquire how might the crew have joined the engine? This was another where differing fuels were considered; 4t of coal and 2,500 gal of water, or 2.6t of oil and 2,800 gal of water.

trials with No. A816 are described in detail in *Southern Way* Issue No. 33.)

One thing in common with the second of the 'boiler on a well-wagon' schemes was the wheel diameter, still at 4ft 3in. The arrangements for the final drive are not completely clear, but it will be noted the three cylinders drove onto the innermost axle of each bogie and then presumably by conventional external coupling rods.

Meanwhile, away from the drawing office, ideas were being considered from existing material. One of these concerned the former power unit from the Sentinel railcar formerly used on the Dyke branch. This vehicle had commenced use in 1933 and whilst reasonably successful on its own had been unable to haul a trailing load as was needed at peak times. Consequently its life on the steeply graded Dyke branch was short, lasting until 1936, after which it was tried with varying degrees of success on various other branch lines but was withdrawn in 1940. Dismantled, the body found a new purpose as a mess hut whilst the power unit somehow survived, at the time we may suspect more by luck than judgement. Knowing of the railcar's existence, enquiries were made and Hutchinson ordered the power unit be retained in case it might be useful towards the development of the 18-cylinder proposal W6656, from August 1945. In the event it was discarded and scrapped. Attwell also comments, 'The first sign of development toward the Leader emerged in 1943/4 when some preliminary design work was carried out by our F.J.R. Watts on high-speed engines. These were essentially for use on power bogies which would be replaceable units. No decision was reached on the use of these units.' This also appears to be the one and only time the name Watts is

Harold Attwell's sketch of the rejected water tube firebox proposal. That it was cast aside is partly explained by Click, 'The idea of a water tube firebox was examined and I spent some time developing a welded boiler of this type. (Unspecified) welding problems proved difficult to overcome, mainly due to access.'

mentioned and Attwell and others do not refer to the topic again. But assuming Attwell's recollections are correct as regards period, then we now have an even earlier date for the start of investigations.

One idea that did not go away was that of sleeve valves. At the time most steam railway engines were using one of two types of valve to admit and exhaust steam to and from the pistons, the piston valve or the older slide valve. A few experiments with poppet valves had taken place but these were certainly not widespread. The sleeve valve, though, had shown considerable promise both in pre-war automobile internal combustion engines and then in British aircraft engines of WWII, notably the Napier Sabre, Bristol Hercules and the Centaurus. (*https://en.wikipedia.org/wiki/Sleeve_valve*) At the forefront in the development of sleeve valves was Ricardo Engineering at Shoreham,

ABOVE A very rare view of the N class 2-6-0 No. A816 modified with the Holcroft/Anderson condensing gear seen outside the front of Eastleigh works. The engine was intended to consume its own steam and so reduce water consumption whilst draught was provided from a fan attached to the front of the smokebox. In this form the engine ran sporadic trials from Eastleigh between February 1931 and 1935 but was subsequently returned to conventional use. *The Lens of Sutton Association*

BELOW No. A816 stored outside the front of Eastleigh works. Most images depict the engine out of use in the Eastleigh paint shop so to see it here is unusual. The additional 'plumbing', oil separator etc., necessitated much external equipment and we might even wonder about how much this affected the visibility from the footplate. Perhaps a cab at each end was the answer! *The Lens of Sutton Association*.

The remains of the Sentinel steam railcar which had only a short operational life on the Dyke and Westerham branches. Hutchinson recalled – or perhaps he was advised – that this vehicle had incorporated a high-speed steam engine. Fortunately enquiries revealed it had also survived, consequently the parts were removed and taken to Brighton. Whether these were then just examined or actually run with steam is not reported. In the event they were not used but it does go to show the lengths Brighton was going to, to achieve the results Bulleid desired. The railcar is seen here, clearly out of use, at Ashford c.1946.

just 15 miles from Brighton. Although primarily involved with improvements to the efficiency of the internal combustion engine, sleeve valves were also a part of this process. Attwell comments, 'OVB had become interested in the possibility of using sleeve-valve cylinders and he obtained copies of the journal *Aircraft Production* which gave details of the valves. The journals were passed to me with instructions to develop a valve suitable for steam locos.'

When applied to the steam engine, as indeed had been the case with some stationary engines, the sleeve valve allowed for a greater efficiency having the piston totally surrounded by steam and so allowing greater heat within and consequently more efficiency in the use of steam.

But there were also disadvantages, namely difficulties in ensuring adequate lubrication and if that vital lubrication was not present, seizure would undoubtably occur. The solution at the time was to maximise oil delivery in return for reducing – but not totally eliminating – the risk of seizure. The trade-off was excess oil consumption. Both Nos 2039 and 36001 would demonstrate these characteristics in due course. Even so Bulleid was keen to try to benefit from the advantages of the increased efficiency on offer and consequently it was Hutchinson who was tasked with design work for the inclusion of sleeve valves in – whatever – final design eventually emerged.

Diagram W7169 was the turning point in the whole episode. Up to this point the various drawings had been little more than ideas, feasibility studies, of the type that occurs in almost any commercial enterprise, railway or otherwise, ideas which might well eventually morph into a new product.

Bulleid was convinced that W7169 showed a potentially feasible proposition and so it was in April 1946, or soon after, that Bulleid first proposed the Traffic Manager to set out what would go down in history as his formal statement as to the requirements for the new engine type. For whatever reason this did not arrive until July and it would certainly have been most interesting to have been the proverbial fly on the wall in the preceding three months when no doubt there was much deliberation and discussion between the parties involved. For completeness, and although well-known, Richards's requirements are set out below:

From the Traffic Manager, R.M.T. Richards; –
Routes and weights to be hauled;
Plymouth to Tavistock or Okehampton – 256 tons
Okehampton Halwill Junction and Bude – 256 tons
Barnstaple and Ilfracombe – 325 tons
Exeter and Exmouth – 384 tons
Bournemouth and Swanage – 320 tons
Brookwood (or similar outlying stabling grounds) to Waterloo – 450 tons
Speed of trains – 50 to 60 mph
Distances to be run between taking water and coal – 60 miles for water and 120 miles for coal.

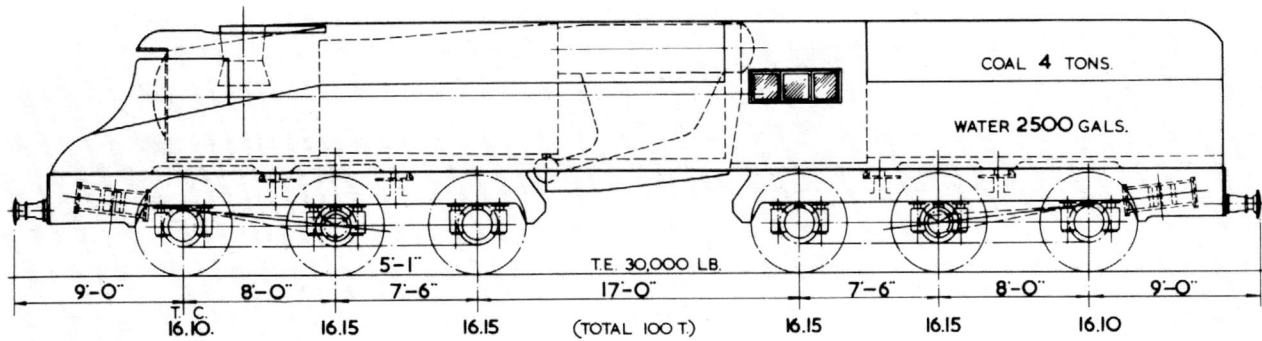

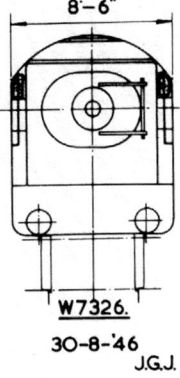

Diagram W7326 upon which the initial order for five engines was based, incorporating six 13¼in x 15in cylinders and 280lb psi boiler. Note too the firebox design incorporates syphons and for the present at least a conventional central cab. When presented with a proposal such as this it is hard to imagine the reaction it might have generated from those present on 4 September: admiration, revulsion, whatever, but remember these were professional men not used to venting their opinions publicly. Perhaps the closest we come to the true sense of concern over a totally untried concept was from G.L. Nicholson, deputising for T.E. Chrimes the Motive Power Superintendent, who commented 'They contain so many novel features that they are certain to have some initial troubles'. There spoke the voice of reason from the department which had experience of the Merchant Navy class. Regarding the diagram, some parts of the design were indeed carried forward: the thermic syphons and dry back firebox plus the use of sleeve valves. Notice there is now no mention of oil firing whilst the axle loading is shown as a paltry 16.15t maximum, if only that too had been something that survived. A considerable amount of overhang is present at the front and rear but necessary for the three cylinders per bogie which now drive onto the centre axle but again the final drive from this is not totally clear. Externally the casing certainly resembles a Pacific whilst for reverse running having the coal bunker placed centrally would afford reasonable vision to either side. No Holcroft/Anderson condensing system is shown. It was a long way from a modern tank engine replacement for the M7 and at 66ft long almost twice the length of a 34ft 8in M7. Other details are obviously from the drawing itself.

Meanwhile Bulleid had certainly not been idle, as HAV informs us 'there had been further improvements to the layout of diagram W7169'. What these were, was not specified, for the next diagram to appear is W7326 of 30 August 1946, although before this comes Bulleid's response to Richards but sent to (via) Eustace Missenden, the SR General Manager.

'In order to meet these requirements within the limits imposed by the Chief Civil Engineer as regards permanent way and bridges, I propose a locomotive in accordance with the enclosed diagram. The engine will have a maximum speed of 90mph, will be able to work goods trains which are normally taken by the Q1 and passenger trains equal to the "West Country" engines, and will carry at least sufficient water and coal to run 80 miles between taking water and 150 miles without taking coal. The engine weights are so distributed as to enable it to run over the whole of the Company's lines with the following exception; Wenford Bridge line, Hayling Island Branch, Bere Alston and Callington Line, Rye Harbour Branch, Newhaven Swing Bridge, Dover Prince of Wales Pier, Axminster and Lyme Regis Branch, Isle of Wight Lines, none of which is important. It is estimated that, if a batch of 25 engines of this class were built, cost per engine would be £17,000. If one prototype was built, the cost would obviously be greater, dependent upon the development work found to be necessary during construction and might reach £25,000. With reference to the conversation at the Progress Meeting on the 28th June 1946, I hope it will be possible to hold the proposed meeting soon as I am anxious to put in hand without delay the construction of the prototype in order to complete it by June 1947.'

Even so, it must have been clear to all that a completion date of June 1947 was hopelessly optimistic but here we need to look at conditions further afield and with a Socialist government now in charge at Westminster and whose avowed intention was nationalisation of the railways, it is not surprising that even at this early stage in the development (of what would morph into No. 36001) there was an increased degree of urgency placed upon the whole project.

The meeting to discuss W7326 (and no doubt other matters) was held on 4 September for which purpose Bulleid also provided the following description:

'This design of engine makes full and complete use of the total weight for adhesive purposes and braking. The type of bogie is similar to that introduced on the electric locomotive, the riding of which has been found to be satisfactory. The springs and gear will be above the axle boxes and under continuous lubrication. The whole of the moving parts will be enclosed and fitted with automatic lubrication, so that it will not be necessary for the driver to lubricate any part of the machine. Each engine will have three "simple" cylinders driving the intermediate axle. The load is transmitted to the leading and trailing axles by chain drive in an oil-tight casing. Roller bearing boxes will be fitted to all axles and will receive force feed lubrication. The axleboxes will be contained in an oilbath. Each axlebox guide is fitted with a "Silentbloc" bearing. The leading engine will exhaust to atmosphere, by way of the blast pipe in the smokebox, so as to provide the necessary draught in the boiler, but exhaust from the trailing engine will be used to heat the water in the tank, the hot water being pumped to the boiler by suitable hot water pumps. The boiler is a new design which will obviate the maintenance inherent in the normal type of locomotive boiler.

T.E. Chrimes, the Southern Railway Running Superintendent from 1944 onwards (later Motive Power Superintendent) whose job was to ensure locomotives were available for all traffic needs. Along with R.M.T. Richards, we know little of these men yet both would have played a significant role in the Leader story. Mr Chrimes is seen at an unrelated event. *S.C. Townroe*

The engine will also be fitted with feed water treatment incorporated in the tender. The controls of the engine will be such that both men will be able to carry out their duties seated[1] and will be duplicated where necessary, so that they can drive in either direction. The weight of water and fuel indicated should be ample for the normal requirements of the Southern Railway, especially as by condensing steam from one engine, the water consumption should be appreciably reduced. The engine is fitted with 5ft 1in wheels and this in conjunction with the short stroke, will allow the engine to run at speeds up to 90mph, without exceeding the normal piston speed. The engine will not be air-smoothed in any sense of the word, but the front end will be based on that successfully introduced on the "West Country" class engines, in order that the steam, when the engine is working lightly, is carried clear of the cab.'

The formal minute of the 4 September meeting dealing with the new engines was brief. Under the heading 'Renewals of Engines' the following appeared, 'It was noted that the CME had now produced a design of the proposed Passenger Tank engine, which was under consideration by the Traffic Manager.'

The Committee Chairman emphasised the necessity for an early decision being arrived at and the Traffic Manager was requested to submit his recommendation, together with justification[2] for the twenty-five Passenger Tank engines as quickly as possible, so that authority could be given for five of the engines to be built in order that they may be available by the summer of 1947. (The term 'tank engine' continues to be as much for historic reasons as anything else. A tank engine is defined as an engine having its boiler, fuel and water supplied being carried on a single frame. There was no separate fuel/water tender permanently coupled to the 'engine' part. The fact Bulleid's designs were in essence the size and weights of an engine and tender combination made no difference, the fact it was all on a single frame meant it was still by definition a 'tank engine'.)

So there was no formal decision to go ahead on 4 September but a week later there was. Again we may imagine a week of considerable activity between the CME and Richards. Richards for his part needed new engines, replacements for the type on carriage duties at Waterloo – whatever – Bulleid meanwhile was simply biding his time. For his part we may have some sympathy with Richards, and indeed with the motive power department – a new untried design full of innovations it could go one of two ways, but there was no substitute. There was no alternative proposal on the table, Richards had rejected the suggestion for more Q1s and this had thus led to the situation in which he now found himself. There was little choice but to proceed.

Consequently as early as 5 September Missenden wrote to Bulleid:

'Proposed Tank Engine. With reference to Minute 79 of the meeting of the Progress Committee held yesterday, the Traffic Manager informs me that he has had a further discussion with you upon the matter and he now recommends we proceed with the building of the five engines to Diagram W7326. I shall be glad if you will proceed accordingly.'

The formal order, No. 3382 was issued to O.G. Hackett, the Works Manager at Brighton, on 11 September with copies circulated all round, 'Build five tank engines to Diagram W7326'.

Leader was on the way.

Notes

(1) 'Both men seated…'. Then how could this be achieved unless some automatic means of stoking/firing was involved. Oil would thus seem to be what is being referred to for a mechanical stoker for coal is not referred to.

(2) The 'justification' referred to would be this same issue of age and ability of the design, especially as employed on ECS duties from and to Waterloo.

6

The Sacrificial Lamb: No. 2039 (and No. 1896)

Attempting to keep the Leader story in a strictly chronological sequence is not easy. So much was going on at the same time, meetings between individuals or committees in London (or perhaps Deepdene – the wartime headquarters near Dorking) plus various work in the Brighton drawing office and elsewhere. A sense of urgency was also driving progress at an accelerating rate.

We have already seen how, for example, Hutchinson purloined the engine unit from the former Sentinel railcar when the idea for a multi-cylinder engine was first mooted – *see* comment surrounding proposal W6656 on p.47 – subsequent to which it was necessary to provide some brief detail on the railcar itself, as well as its use. Similarly we have had on occasion to refer back to Bulleid's time on the LNER and the work of Gresley, and his thoughts on a multi-cylinder design, the D49 of 1928 (*see* p.46).

For the moment though, we need to move forward and conveniently skip over what was happening on the design and development of Leader and move to the two testbed engines, Nos 1896 and 2039.

The modification to U1 2-6-0 No. 31896 which we can probably safely say was almost a knee-jerk reaction to the realisation that oil would no longer be the chosen fuel for Leader. Consequently ash-disposal, remember this was in the days before self-cleaning smokeboxes were the norm, was an issue that had to be dealt with. Click is not totally clear on No. 1896; yes, he rode on it but contradicts his own comments. He states the crew were not to be told about the fitment; so, was it then permanently open in which case surely upon preparing the engine it would be noticed (check inside the smokebox and a hole would certainly be seen at the base), or was there even some kind of lever within the cab or outside to operate it remotely? An outside control would seem to have been the most likely but even so why choose a 3-cylinder engine which would certainly require a chute taking a route other than perpendicular; unless it was to identify with the same situation as would be experienced on No. 36001? *R.C. Riley/The Transport Treasury*

No. 1896 in service but after having been restored to standard condition. Unfortunately we have not been able to access the drawing of the chute (although one does exist, *see* later in this caption). The closest we can come to a date for this fitment is 16 March 1949 which refers to drawing No. 9869. So far as history is concerned this does seem very late in the development stage of Leader as No. 36001 would be in steam just three months later. Even more curious is that a similar drawing for an ash chute (Drawing No. 9523) but this time for an 'H1' (which must be No. 2039) is dated 10 September 1948. Does this mean No. 2039 had a similar ash chute? This might then appear to have been the case but any such provision is not mentioned or confirmed by anyone else. On the basis that sometimes equipment was simply put on an engine and a drawing made subsequently, we are tempted to suggest somebody suddenly realised the route of an ash chute on Leader would by necessity be convoluted and they had better try the idea out in practice first on a 3-cylinder engine. F.W. Webb had conducted similar experiments on the LNWR from Crewe in the 1870s but the real breakthrough did not come until much later into BR days with ash screens fitted into the smokebox. In this the ash as it passes through the tubes is held is suspension by the exhaust blast from the cylinders to be carried with it and ejected out of the chimney. Some small particles may still fall through the mesh but the amount of smokebox cleaning was considerably reduced albeit at the expense of an increase in the number of lineside fires. Built in March 1931, No. 1896 lasted until the great cull of Southern steam stock on 31 December 1962. *R C Riley/The Transport Treasury*

We are also assuming readers will by now already have some idea of what the final design of Leader looked like. It should also be mentioned that HAV makes no mention of the experiments on No. 1896 whilst those involving No. 2039 are covered in a single paragraph. It would be unwise to attempt to draw conclusions from this limited coverage. Instead we return to John Click who comments upon both, starting with the U class 2-6-0, No. 1896 although in this case in a series of odd notes without much, if any, elaboration.

In the Leader design, and with coal now the fuel of necessity, 'it became imperative to have some form of smokebox cleaner. OVB opted for an open chute in the bottom. Try it on a mogul. No. 31896 went back after a "general" to Redhill. Worked the "County" to Reading loading up to 13 bogies. Strict instructions not to tell the enginemen there was a six inch square hole. Working hard the air divided the exhaust in two. Dicky trips, Dorking Bank almost beat us several times. Time that was lost was made up down other side. Guildford stop then Pinks Hill. Fun with Reading men and white wipers (?). Considerable surprise that the loco steamed as well as it did. Taken off. Leader still fitted though. Very soon it was blanked off on 36001.' *(It seems rather strange for Click to comment that the crew did not know of the fitment. Part of the job of preparation as to check inside the loco smokebox and there was a b....y great hole at the bottom it would surely be noticed. Click seems to imply it was also open all the time and not covered by a sliding plate to maintain smokebox vacuum. In addition he does not mention that on No. 36001 this same chute, very necessary from a practical point of view as cleaning the smokebox of Leader in a confined space would have been difficult to say the least, did indeed adversely affect the steaming as the plate would not close properly, bits of char and ash holding it open thus allowing air to be drawn into*

LBSCR Atlantic No. 39 in original condition. Seeing the engine in its pristine state it is hard to imagine what fate would eventually befall such a graceful machine. Designed by Marsh, No. 39 was always regarded as a 'good engine' and came to be reserved for Royal and other special duties as per the next image. Even later there is reported to have been some resentment that No. 2039 was selected for conversion as it, together with No. 2038 were still highly regarded.

Continuing on from the above, in June 1913 No. 39 was specially named *La France* to haul a special train in connection with a state visit by the President of France.
Bluebell Railway Museum

In January 1926 the name *La France* was replaced for that of *Hartland Point*, a change brought about by the publicity department of the SR; the four other engines of the type were designated with similar promontory names.

the smokebox. Hardly scientific, but until authority made the decision it was to be permanently sealed – welded shut probably – the Eastleigh test crew used to bring horse dung with them and smear this around the edges to effect a seal – it worked, but we may wonder if the boffins in the dynamometer car knew what went on! Such action certainly not mentioned in any of the official reports on the engine.)

We move on now to No. 2039. This was a 4-4-2 tender engine of the H1 class originally built in 1905 as one a small class of designed for the principal services on the LB&SCR. By the late 1940s, age, electrification, and the influx of 'new-build' Light Pacifics had rendered the remaining members of the type basically redundant. Indeed two out of the original five, Nos 2040 and 2041. had already been withdrawn in 1944 leaving just three, including No. 2039, in service. Hence when Bulleid cast his net to find an engine on which to try out sleeve valves this was the one he settled upon, but it had not been his first choice. That had been for a 4-6-0 of the King Arthur class. HAV has it that adding sleeves to the existing pistons increased the width over the cylinders too much, so as to foul the loading gauge, but folklore has it the motive power department were persuasive in their argument that they could not afford to lose an efficient and reliable locomotive. Rumour again has it that it was suggested he make use of his own creations Merchant Navy, West Country or Q1, but the complications associated with modifying a 3-cylinder engine or the inside cylinders of a Q1 in an ever-more-urgent timescale were realistically one of the reasons why this particular issue was not pursued. HAV's comments though do raise a further question. With No. 2039 selected, width over the cylinders as extant was still an issue, hence the cylinder diameter was reduced from the original 19in to 14in. The length of the stroke remained unaltered at 26in. (The cylinders on Leader were 12¼in x 15in, so do not make the mistake of thinking the cylinder size and consequently the various component parts of No. 2039 and No. 36001 were interchangeable, on the basis of size alone this was not possible.) In a 'conventional' steam engine, the parts were piston (probably a cylinder liner which was a tight fit into the body of the cylinder) and then the outside casing – that was it! The valves to admit and exhaust steam were holes cut (machined) into the top/side of the casing and liner and, as mentioned before, either of the piston valve, side valve or poppet valve type.

Comparing the above, with the sleeve valve there was first the piston, then the sleeve and then a liner.[1]

Finally came the external casing which was in effect a jacket containing steam and also served as the inlet and exhaust from the cylinders. Rings were provided between the piston and the sleeve and also the sleeve and the liner, 28 per cylinder. (Differing sources conflict slightly the number of rings fitted both on No. 2039 and later on No. 36001. We believe it was 24 per cylinder/sleeve on No. 36001 and 30 per side on No. 2039.) The sleeve would slide forward and back, dependent upon the setting of the cut-off which was as usual under the control of the driver. Exactly as with other valve gears, this would then admit more or less steam as required. A long cut-off and the greater amount of steam – 40%, 50% – whatever, a short cut-off, 15% or so, and less steam is admitted. The term 'cut-off' meaning the amount of time the inlet port remains open to admit steam to the propel the piston before the supply was 'cut-off'. In theory the sleeve valve afforded greater efficiency consequent upon less loss of heat and with it pressure from when the steam had passed from the regulator header to the cylinder.

In final Southern Railway condition (livery excluded) and now as No. 2039, prior to being selected as the guinea-pig for sleeve valve experiments. It is from Harold Attwell, via John Click, that we learn the original intention had been to conduct experiments involving No. 2039 solely within Brighton Works. Bulleid however decided the engine could indeed venture out, this following satisfactory static tests. But were these tests really satisfactory? In reality, probably not always and to allow No. 2039 to travel out on the main line where she did in fact sometimes cause delays to other traffic was, in hindsight, not such a good idea. It could only have made all concerned more wary when later came the time for No. 36001 to start her own trials and may even have contributed to the need to have a 'buddy' engine either attached or following close behind No. 36001 – did this ever happen in the early days of No. 2039? (By 'following close behind' we do not mean within the same block section, but instead at least one section in the rear.)

The modified No. 2039 in a line of other engines at Brighton shed on 24 July 1948. When not in use, or undergoing repairs/modifications, she would spend a lot of time parked in a similar position. In general terms the changes wrought by Bulleid affected the engine externally ahead of the front driving wheels, plus inside the frames so far as how the valves were driven. Livery at this time was all-over black, a hangover from her last wartime overhaul in 1942. *Terry Cole*

ABOVE Work progressing at Brighton on the conversion of No. 2039. New cylinders have been added together with a new circular steam inlet pipe and fabricated exhaust pipes; the latter either end of the cylinders. Note the plating on the front framing has been removed, although part was later replaced. The drive to what will be the sleeve reciprocating mechanism at the front of the cylinder is partly in place whilst the 'ears' of a sleeve may also be seen protruding from the cylinder. Two mechanical lubricators and their associated oil reservoirs are placed on the framing immediately under the smokebox, one serving each cylinder. The mass of oil pipes is also apparent. It was hardly the ideal location to place the reservoirs but there was little space elsewhere, unless perhaps on the extremities of the buffer beam but that would then have hampered access to the sleeves if needed (and it most certainly was!). No mention is made if any of the subsequent seizures were caused by lack of lubrication as a result of blocked feed pipes. Seen from the rear, a sleeve with its corresponding connections to the oscillating gear is standing vertical, of necessity these were inserted from the front. The reader is referred to the accompanying text so far as the metal(s) that were used for the sleeves.
Mike Thorp and J.G. Click

The design of the sleeve was again the work of Hutchinson. Bulleid approved but wisely sought council from Sir Harry Ricardo. Ricardo similarly approved but made one specific suggestion which was to add a degree of rotation to the sleeves, not full rotation of course, but 15% either side of a theoretical centre line. This axial rotation was intended to improve lubrication and to even-out wear. And it was lubrication that was the essential element of successful sleeve valve operation, hence the number of oil pipes fitted was considerable – both for No. 2039 and later for No. 36001. The reader is referred to the earlier comment about the Paget engine, and where in contemporary reports there is mention of 'rotation'.

The conversion of No. 2039 into a mobile testbed for the use of sleeve valves commenced when the engine was taken into Brighton works in July 1947. Why specifically No. 2039 and not one of the other members of the class is not explained and we should not spend time digressing too far. Suffice to say of the three remaining members of the class, this was the one that had been chosen. At Brighton, the work first involved the removal of the original cylinders to be replaced as described above. In consequence a replacement bogie was also needed so that the rear bogie wheels would not foul the new fitment. This was

BELOW Sleeve and connections to the oscillating gear – compare this with the view of the sleeve end in the previous image. Bulleid's original intention had been to use a member of the King Arthur class for his experimentation but when drawn out on paper, the additional width across the cylinders fouled the loading gauge. Folklore has it such a choice was also far from popular with the motive power department at risk of using a reliable engine.
John Click/National Railway Museum

The Sacrificial Lamb: No. 2039 (and No. 1896)

sourced from a D3 0-4-4T which had wheels of 3ft diameter compared with the 3ft 6in wheels and bogie originally fitted.[2]

The physical space required by new cylinders dictated the running plate be cut back whilst the plating was also removed, for the present at least, on the front framing. Fabricated outside steam pipes for both admission and exhaust were provided. The sleeve valves were driven as before by cams attached to the axle with Stephenson's link motion. The valve rods were connected to plungers and guide bushes pressed into a fabricated steel

LEFT The completed front end, which does not exactly leave the fireman a lot of room to clean the smokebox. We must remember that in this form No. 2039 was purely an experiment: A testbed intended to prove the viability of sleeves vales for Leader. In that respect it cannot have been said to have been satisfactory. To quote John Click referring to No. 36001, 'Would the sleeve valves be better than those on 2039 – they needed to be, though in some ways the Leader's looked less good.' In consequence of the modifications the Westinghouse pump was re-sited, note also the air pipe coupling seen hanging below the buffer beam. *John Click/National Railway Museum*

RIGHT No. 2039 in steam on what was reported as its very first outing at Brighton on 5 November 1947, although current research tends to shed doubt on the date of the photograph. Mention has already been made as to how the original intention had been to test the engine solely within Brighton works but according to Click when it was steamed inside the works this turned out to be a most unpopular move. Might this also have had something to do with why Bulleid decided tests would be continued on the road? Records now tell us the engine emerged from Brighton on 3 December 1947 and was seen by Bulleid's brother in law H.G. Ivatt (of the LMS) on the same day. Apparently, it was moved up and down the yard for inspection but was also enveloped in steam as rings had yet to be fitted. Assuming then the photographer's record is simply one month out, and the image was in fact taken on 5 December, why does steam not appear to be issuing elsewhere than perhaps from one of the snifting vales; perhaps a simple answer is that the rings had been fitted in the previous 48hrs. (We might even question how might it have been possible to undertake workshop tests if rings were not present when the engine was steamed inside the works?) Note too the new paint on the smokebox etc., this was the only part of the engine that was repainted in consequence of the conversion. Finally we turn to the rather cruel enlargement of the rear wheel of the pony truck which clearly shows the first and last digits as '2' and '6' (**INSET**). This would match the contemporary RCTS correspondent's information that the wheels at least came from D3 No. 2366, one of the few occasions when Bradley appears to have been misinformed. Even so No. 2366 was officially still active for another 15 months, until February 1949: well parts of her at least! As before it is not possible to determine the wording chalked on the cabside. One interesting point comes from Harry Attwell, who comments on the lack of visible exhaust from No. 2039 and that when fitted with rings, trials within the yard on 13 December 1947 indicated that 'steam leakage had been practically eliminated'. *B.J. Miller*

stretcher bolted between the frames. This stretcher was in the space originally occupied by the inside steam chests. To transmit the drive to the outside of the frame, a rocking lever was mounted either side, each pivoted in a substantial bushed steel housing bolted to the outside face of the frame. The outer links drove rearwards and were attached to each of the sleeve crossbars where connection was made by universal ball-type joints. This was to absorb the independent oscillating drive. The latter was itself obtained from a rotating camshaft sprocket driven by a Morse inverted tooth chain from the leading coupled axle. The shaft was mounted in bearings located on both main frames, through which they protruded to terminate with an eccentric flange on either end. The flange worked in a horizontal slot providing a bearing block bolted to the outside radius of the inner sleeve hub. Thus as the sleeve was made to reciprocate and so provide the valve events, an oscillating motion as suggested by Ricardo was imparted to facilitate lubrication and even-out wear. The sleeve therefore performed a 'figure of eight' movement, which was fascinating to watch. No oil bath was provided for the Morse chain.

Inside the smokebox was a multiple jet blastpipe which exhausted through a fabricated chimney, best described as tapering in the shape of a half-barrel. The Westinghouse air brakes originally fitted were retained but the external Westinghouse pump had also to be moved and was now located further forward on the right-hand side towards the front of the chimney. Finally two mechanical lubricators on the running plate immediately below the smokebox door allied to a mass of pipes fed lubrication to the cylinders, and sleeves. The position of the lubricators exactly where they would be most likely to be covered in ash and cinders when the smokebox door was opened for clearing was not ideal, but it must be remembered No. 2039 was in effect a mobile test bed intended to prove the viability of sleeve valves in the railway context. (JGC refers to their positioning as 'just ridiculous … but with an experimental engine like this one, it just had to be tolerated.' After all sleeves had only even been used once before in a railway steam engine, Paget of course, and that was more than a quarter of a century earlier. (A sleeve valve diesel engine was fitted to an early diesel shunter operating on the LMS in the 1930s.)

In addition to the *Railway Observer*, the Stephenson Locomotive Society's journal informs us as to start and later the progress of the modifications with No. 2039. In the former context how on 29 June 1947 the 10.05am Newhaven boat train had No. 2039 as a pilot engine in place of the usual 4-4-0. Perhaps this might have been a way of assessing the performance/condition of No. 2039 before its conversion or even a way of getting the engine closer to Brighton in preparation for its conversion. Subsequent reports of society (enthusiast) visits to the works in the autumn of 1947 refer to the engine being present (amongst other goings-on, of course) but without specific mention of the changes wrought by rebuilding – indeed so far as No. 2039 was concerned it is probably more accurate to say it was a rebuilding rather than a modification.

Fortunately JGC also provides some notes as to the progress of the engine. 'When No. 2039 was first lit up and steamed it was in the Erecting Shop which as it transpired was a very unpopular move.' Shortly after this, perhaps even the same day, No. 2039 was moved, still in steam, onto the rollers at Brighton for various tests including valve setting. Evidently some 'tinkering' was still required as it was almost a month later before the engine was eventually moved outside.

Later Click elaborates on the secrecy we might have expected surrounded the project and his knowledge of what went on regarding the test runs. 'When No. 2039 was first given a stay of execution to become the sleeve valve guinea-pig locomotive, Bulleid wanted to give little away as to what was going on inside No. 2039's new cylinders. Anyone not in the know would have taken a long time climbing over and under her before finding much out[3]; especially as it was later found possible to put the foot-framing back – this refers to the front framing above the buffers and below the smokebox (ahead of the new lubricators) although its replacement is not clear from photographs. The problem was with the foot-framing back in place, it then wasn't convenient for those testing the loco to be able to see what was going on either! Doug Ellison, who started as Bulleid s sole Pupil late in 1943, remembers how he nearly caught his death perched on the front of No. 2039 in the depths of winter trying to get a close-up view of the sleeve's behaviour. He had nothing to hold on to either.'

Attwell comments that temperature and dimensional checks were made on the modified 2039 to ascertain any deformation of the sleeves, the temperatures usually being in the range 200°–250° – might this have been one of the reasons physical observations were made on the road? He continues, 'During following tests in Brighton Erecting shop with the loco on rollers, I observed the behaviour of the sleeves and on only one occasion did it appear there was likelihood of seizure; the bronze pin slightly dented.'

It is also from Attwell that we are fortunate to have a sketch and record of a sleeve and dimensions taken after a failure had occurred.

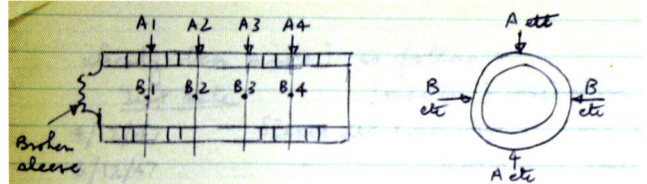

Harry Attwell's sketch of the point where dimensions were taken, with reference to the table below.

	A1 = 15.745	B1 = 15.7435	A1 = 15.751	B1 = 15.751
LH	A2 = 15.746	B2 = 15.743	A2 = 15.754	B2 = 15.749
Cyl	A3 = 15.744	B3 = 15.743	A3 = 15.751	B3 = 15.748
	A4 = 15.744	B4 = 15.742	A4 = 15.7495	B4 = 15.751
	A1 = 15.744	B1 = 15.742	A1 = 15.749	B1 = 15.7505
RH	A2 = 15.7435	B2 = 15.743	A2 = 15.749	B2 = 15.749
Cyl	A3 = 15.740	B3 = 15.740	A3 = 15.751	B3 = 15.750
	A4 = 15.741	B4 = 15.742	A4 = 15.7515	B4 = 15.749

No. 2039 on the turntable at Brighton. *J.G. Click. Colour by David Williams.*

No. 2039 would finally emerge from inside Brighton works on 3 December 1947 ready for its first running test but at this stage without any rings being fitted. Not surprisingly when movement was made there was much escaping steam, reminiscent of running with the drain cocks open at all times except this time the steam would have emerged from the front and the rear of the cylinders. Consider also for a moment, in theory with the rings in place, the sleeve would remain parallel with the sides of the cylinder and similarly with the piston fitted with rings, that would also be parallel with the sleeve. With no rings fitted not only was there going to be escaping steam but the two would be moving forward and back rather than parallel with each other. Bulleid's brother-in-law H.G. Ivatt from the LMS had been invited to view the proceedings but what he must have thought (attempting) to observe No. 2039 move through a cloud of steam is not reported. Perhaps the best comparison to be made is to consider what was going on at Derby with the first main line diesel LMS No. 10000 (presented to the Press at Euston on 18 December 1947) whilst 190 miles south of Derby was the trial of a 'modern' steam engine. Attwell comments, 'Bulleid was not amused' (of the behaviour of No. 2039) but he must have been aware of what was likely to happen as surely the same would have occurred when on roller tests in the shops. But then Click also tells us Bulleid was not a frequent visitor to the shops, perhaps the answer is simpler, no one had perhaps dared to inform 'the chief' what went on.

Two weeks then elapsed during which time the 60 rings were fitted and No. 2039 was steamed again on 15 December ready for its first run, albeit light engine. This was made to as far as Lewes together with 'E5' No. 2404, the operating authorities seemingly determined to ensure there would be no breakdowns and consequent disruption of traffic. The same would apply later on the first outings of No. 36001, a tank engine following ready to come to the rescue as necessary – the railways equivalent of a motoring breakdown service!

Without the benefit of any formal report, it is difficult to comment exactly on the results although we know from the earlier reports there were failures of the sleeves at the 'ears' but also now broken rings. It was no doubt for this reason that certain men were directed (or did they volunteer?) to travel on the front framing to observe the actual workings. Winter 1947 would also hardly be an

Getting away (or is it even reversing into the station?) at/from Brighton with a test train. As with Leader later, any available rolling stock was used, although a record was kept of the trailing load, whilst station to station working was employed to replicate realistic operating conditions. This is believed to have been a Brighton to Groombridge via Uckfield test, the route chosen due to limited line occupancy after leaving the main line at Lewes. No headcode is displayed. *P. Ransome-Wallis*

ideal time to travel this way and be so exposed to the elements. Whatever, necessary repairs were undertaken at Brighton works.

Bulleid's aim in using sleeve valves was to increase the efficiency of the steam usage by reducing losses caused by condensation. The sleeve valve allowed virtually the whole cylinder to be permanently enveloped in a hot steam jacket and as such what was in effect a circular steam chest. This steam chest also now afforded a volume some 3¼ times the cylinder capacity at maximum cut-off – 75%. With the addition of the large steam inlet and exhaust annuli a free flow for the steam was ensured and consequential free running. However any advantage gained was offset by the increases in mechanical complexity and identified difficulties due to friction losses. It would take the various test runs to establish if a steam-tight seal could indeed be maintained especially across the exhaust ports and front radial outlet slots for the extension drive lugs.

We mentioned above no formal report on the test running of No. 2039 has been located and that is indeed the case although without doubt records would have been kept. Fortunately both Attwell and the *RO* come to the rescue as between them we have some detail of the runs made from 4 December 1947 onwards; all those known of are replicated below for the sake of convenience. The trips in the Christmas period are perhaps slightly surprising as it would have been thought traffic levels might have precluded these taking place. In addition there were other runs referred to after the table.

Test Date	Detail + Condition & Temperature etc	Source
4/12/47	Sleeve with liner rings. Temp 250°C.	HA
8/12/47	Sleeve with liner rings and cover rings. Temp 275°C.	HA
10/12/47	Sleeve etc with all rings. No temperature record.	HA
13/12/47	20 trips on siding as 10/12. Temp 235°C. Steam leakage practically eliminated. Bronze drive pins on above and all subsequent tests.	HA
15/12/47	To Lewes and return in company of 'E5' No. 2404. Without chain drive from Falmer and hauled by another loco. Minor trouble not recalled.	HA/RO
20/12/47	To Lewes and return with other loco as precaution. No trouble.	HA
22 & 23/12/47	To Eastbourne then Pevensey and return. OK. Lub set a min feed.	HA
29/12/47	To Eastbourne then Pevensey and return. Lub at max feed – not satisfactory.	HA
30/12/47	To Haywards Heath and return. Lub unsatisfactory.	HA
31/12/47	To Haywards Heath and return. Lub satisfactory.	HA
1/1/48	To Three Bridges and return via Hove. Lub satisfactory.	HA
Unknown date(s)	Several tests from Brighton – Eastbourne services sometimes with SEC 3-coach set No. 597 (ECS). Stopping at all stations so as to provide information on acceleration when restarting. Other trials between Brighton and Three Bridges either light and also propelling another engine, the latter believed to have been a 'K'.	RO
Feb 1948	Light engine trials between Brighton and Hastings.	RO
11/3/48	Noted at Brighton shed.	RO
29/5/48	Two return runs scheduled between Brighton and Hastings	Special Traffic Notice
7/6/48	Two weekday trips daily (excepting Saturday) with four and five coach ECS trains between Brighton and Tunbridge Wells. In the up direction via Cowden where the engine runs round.	RO
c.Sept 1948.	Test train Brighton to Cowden, bogie utility van and two Royal Mail vans Nos s4951/2.	RO
By 16/10/48	Loco arrived at Brighton Works.	RO
Dec 1948	Sundays only, two return trips light engine between Brighton and Hastings.	RO
19/12/48	Reference the previous entry, failure at St Leonards with fracture of right hand valve rocker. Taken into Works for repair.	RO
Interest in it, and with further trials with No. 2039, seem to peter out at this point, no doubt as interest shifted towards the completion of the first Leader. There is some suggestion that Bulleid 'took pity' on the engine and it was steamed for an Officers' Special from Brighton to Ashford around this time but it disgraced itself en route.		
Sept 49	Comment that 2039 to be returned to traffic with a replacement boiler sent from Eastleigh.	RO
2/9/49	Loco in repainted condition in Brighton shed.	RO
Nov 49	Loco not believed to have worked a passenger train since last emerged from Works and appears to be in store.	RO
Note: Where a month/year only is shown, this relates to when the information appeared in the *RO*. Allowing for the time to report and publish in the next monthly issue, the actual information was a few weeks out of date.		

Paused at Uckfield, southbound – the station level crossing is just visible in the background. (Departing, or with steam issuing from the drain cocks, is it cruel to say 'attempting to depart'?) No. 2039 had been fitted with new cylinders, the outer casing of which was in the form of a fabricated steel shell, hence the horizontal line visible on several of the views. Whilst the Paget engine *Hartland Point* and later Leader might be thought to have been the only sleeve valve fitted railway engines ever to work in the UK, the LMS had also operated a standard gauge sleeve valve locomotive that performed successfully between January 1941 and May 1942. This was not steam, but instead a small 0-6-0 diesel shunter, LMS No. 7403, built by the Hunslet Engine Co. of Leeds and fitted with a 150hp Brotherhood-Ricardo sleeve valve engine. It was also briefly employed as a pilot at Eastleigh Works (no dates) and no photographs appear of it on the Southern. Why it might have ventured away from its native system is not explained and consequently it would not be appropriate to attempt to draw conclusions from this limited information. (Reference, Colin Marsden *The Diesel Shunter*. OPC, 2003.) A further view of No. 2039 on trials but at an unreported location will be found on the excellent SEMG website. *P Ransome-Wallis*

On the first day of the newly nationalised railway system, 1 January 1948, No. 2039 supposedly worked ex-SECR 3-coach set, No. 597, between Brighton and Eastbourne although Attwell comments they went to Three Bridges – perhaps there may even have been two tests on the same day? (It is believed Coach Set 597 or various other 'Birdcage' sets were used on a number of occasions behind No. 2039.) This was an empty stock working with the guard instructed to ensure that passengers were not permitted to join the train at the various station stops made. Again having stops gave information as to the acceleration characteristics of the machine in its modified form.

At this stage all was well, and no doubt buoyed by the success there followed what was an almost daily test, again north-east from Brighton, to Groombridge via Lewes, a distance of some 30 miles. The train would then turn on the Groombridge Junction–Ashurst Junction–Birchden Junction triangle before stopping to take water at Eridge and so retrace the same return route to Brighton. Again it is unfortunate that no formal records of these trials have survived although the runs would undoubtedly have been monitored by members of the Brighton test section. What is known is that the modifications appeared to bear out the hope for a free running engine with speeds of 70–80mph reached with ease.

Sometime in the same month there were also some light engine trials to Three Bridges in company with a K class mogul, which was propelled by 2039 in both directions. The presence of the extra engine again no doubt a means of insurance against breakdown on what was the main London line.

Evidently though enough confidence had been gained to find No. 2039 a more cost-effective role and from February

Comparisons at Brighton, No. 2039 alongside unmodified sister engine No. 2038 *Portland Bill*. The changes to No. 2039 have hardly enhanced its appearance, the once graceful lines of Edwardian design gone forever, but No. 2039 was not intended to be beautiful in its guinea-pig state. Creeping into view on the left is a member of the West Country class with extended smoke deflectors. 24 July 1948. *Terry Cole*

Special Traffic Notice for 29 May 1948 giving details of runs between Brighton and Hastings. The fact the trial appears in what was one of the weekly notices indicates it would have been arranged at least some days in advance. Other runs may have been organised at far less notice. Hastings was also a regular destination for the trials as there was a turntable at nearby St Leonards shed.

1948 she was therefore put to work on trains of carriage underframes between Lancing and Eastleigh. Whether these were one-way trips with the engine returning light from Hampshire is not certain.

Unfortunately by now all was not well, for despite the limited mileage actually covered, No. 2039 had developed a considerable thirst and which in turn would have led to a far greater consumption of coal whilst the consequential work for the fireman would have similarly increased. Folklore has it that No. 2039 would leave Brighton for Lancing and then Eastleigh with a full tender tank but have to stop for water at least twice en route. Usually these stops were at Chichester and Fareham, and this on a run the total distance of which was just some 65 miles. This equated to something in the order of between 53 and 87 gallons per mile, up to 3½ times what would usually have been expected. To evaporate this amount of water the equivalent coal consumption was also high, and likely to have been in the order of 60lb/mile. Not unexpectedly then, the engine was observed back in the works by the end of the same month, February 1948.

Repairs (or was it modifications?) were carried out, and between March and June there were a number of runs from Brighton to either Lewes or, it is stated, Cowden just north of Groombridge. At least one run to Hastings is also known of, as witness the attached timings sheet for Saturday 29 May 1948. Of course this relates just to the anticipated timings to be achieved and does not mean the trial either took place or was indeed completed.

Climbing out of Brighton on the way to Lewes, the youthful fireman seemingly aware of the photographer. (Whilst the official photographer was active concerning Leader, no similar record appears to have been taken of No. 2039 either whilst in the course of rebuilding or on test.) At least one member of the test section or a fitter – perhaps both - was usually present on these trials to record timings, engine performance and assist where necessary. Readers will recall from the text the comment as to the engine being put to work on a public service and perhaps even questioned 'why' when her behaviour was not always predictable. Click provides us with the answer although this only comes years later when he was in Ireland. Bulleid was asking Click about trials in burning turf and Click made the point about there being no need to risk main line failure. Bulleid agreed but said that 'politically' it had to be seen to run. 'I remembered No. 32039's misfortune at Earlswood and fully understood.'

It is not known if the other runs were all light engine or with empty stock in tow, although we know that certain of the Cowden trips involved a single bogie utility van and two Royal Mail vans, Nos s4951/2. The latter two vehicles reported as specially allocated to this working.

What is certain is that in June a 3-coach set was taken from Brighton to Tunbridge Wells West at least once, after which the same load was worked on several occasions between Brighton and Hastings – possibly to the latter location at similar timings to that seen above. As at the start of 1948 the results were again encouraging hence the load being increased to between 4–5 bogie vehicles once more to Tunbridge Wells West and which working continued twice daily until sometime in July.

Click also comments on his first experience with the engine, 'I first rode on No. 2039 when I visited Brighton on 29 July 1948 – this was to seek Cocks's advice on my future. I couldn't believe my luck when she was off to Groombridge at 2.20pm. CS came along the platform on his way back from lunch and gave me a knowing look that fell short of recognition but said "you cheeky hound!" By then No. 2039 was no longer being monitored every trip I was interested to find. Our load was an SECR three-coach "birdcage" set. She was not a strong engine because of her reduced cylinder diameter but steamed well and was very quiet when running.'

The rest of July and August 1948 are something of a mystery but it is known that in September 1948, No. 2039 was seen at the head of a train of bogie utility vans but the destination and likewise whether this was empty stock or an actual service movement is not certain.

Details for the autumn of 1948 are again cloudy but with No. 2039 known to have been in Brighton works again for much of this time. Possibly though little actual progress in the way of maintenance or repairs/ modifications was actually carried out and the length of time out of service could well be because any previous urgency had already evaporated and Brighton was of course almost running at full capacity on its Light Pacific building programme as well as the construction of 36001 and of course other normal repair projects.

December 1948 also did not seem to bother the operating department as much as the previous year in so far as using No. 2039 was concerned, for at the start of the month there were a series of light engine runs as far as Hastings, often twice each day and usually at weekends. Then on 19 December came the chance to excel, with the engine set the task of hauling an Inspection Train/Officers' Special between Ashford and Brighton (how the engine came to be at Ashford is not reported). All was well until leaving St Leonards (near Hastings) where there was a sudden fracture of the right-hand valve rod. Click adds, 'It went in to St Leonards over a wet weekend and everything rusted. I had to report and got "a rocket" for allowing evidence to get lost.' JGC's comments perhaps written with the aid of notebooks, perhaps also from memory speak of this being the last working of No. 2039, which clearly it was not. We may perhaps suspect he became slightly confused with his months/years as clearly the engine was working on occasions into 1949, that is until the onus naturally shifted towards No. 36001. All we know for certain is that the motion had to be completely taken down followed by a tow back to Brighton.

Again now, and for almost three months, nothing is known although it may be reasonable to assume No. 2039 simply languished at Brighton. However at some stage during this time it was also obviously repaired, for on 14 March 1949 the engine is reported as in charge of a revenue-earning passenger service, the three coaches of the Hastings–Birkenhead through-service which No. 2039 was booked to work on its own between Brighton and Redhill. In view of her previous unpredictable performance and the fact this was a main-line working, it was perhaps surprising that no pilot was provided and so it must have been that behind the scenes 'someone' had exerted pressure to ensure a sleeve-valve engine could be entrusted to work in a reliable fashion. It does not take a genius either to imagine who that authority probably was, although their faith was indeed rewarded for both the outward and return workings were accomplished without difficulty. If it were only known at the time, this would be the only time No. 2039 would ever work a fare-paying passenger service. (The Birkenhead through trains had only been re-instated a few months earlier on 27 September 1948 and then after a lapse of some nine years. SR/GW stock was used on alternate days with the task set to No. 2039 classified as Brighton Duty No. 530. At Redhill the Hastings portion would then be attached to that from Margate and Dover and the service then continuing towards Reading and its ultimate destination.)

Two days later the engine was set to work an empty 3-coach set north from Brighton to Redhill again, and as on 14 March, without a pilot. Click comments, 'I was booked to go on the duty but then Attwell decided perhaps he should and went instead.' As it was, it would have made no difference to what transpired. All was well until Earlswood when adverse signals were sighted; the

No. 2039 on Brighton shed. On this occasion a headcode disc is shown – but several other workings did not display this identity, indictive perhaps that the trial was not following a regular identified route. *Arthur Taylor*

train running ahead of time – the free running characteristics of No. 2039 once again. The crew stood at the signal on the up fast line waiting to cross but when the 'clear' indication was received No. 2039 stubbornly refused to move – in either direction. No amount of coaxing, opening of drain cocks, forward or reverse gear would encourage the recalcitrant machine to move. There was a long delay whilst E class 4-4-0 No. 31587 (Click refers to the assistance provided by a 'tank engine') was hastily summonsed to drag No. 2039 and her train the final short distance to Redhill. In reality it matters not what form the assistance took as the cost had been other services were delayed by almost twenty-five minutes. The return to Brighton later in the day was again with the

RIGHT Again at Brighton. Unlike with No. 36001, the reciprocating mechanism at the front of the sleeves was never removed from No. 2039 although the failures the engine suffered, including the occasions when she almost stopped 'blind' refusing to move either forward or back except with some difficulty were also destined to be repeated later on Leader.

BELOW Seemingly having one of the oil reservoirs topped up at Brighton prior to a test, Tonbridge headcode perhaps? At some stage part of the original foot-framing was put back. Click comments accordingly, 'and it was here that Doug Ellison, who started as Bulleid's sole Pupil late in 1943, remembers how he nearly caught his death perched on the front of No. 2039 in the depths of winter trying to get a close-up view of the sleeve's behaviour. He had nothing to hold on to either.' *H.M. Madgwick*

same pilot engine, clearly this time no chances were being taken. As Click aptly describes, 'A bad blot'.

Back at Brighton the next day, examination revealed the engine had stopped with the ports in a totally 'blind' position, meaning no steam could enter the cylinder regardless of the setting of the reversing gear. Whether this was a fault in design, manufacture, assembly or valve setting was never revealed. Perhaps never even investigated and established although Sean Day-Lewis puts it down to haste in design. Slightly strange considering No. 2039's valve and port openings (and closings) setting had been checked on the Brighton valve-setting rollers – but then things might have altered slightly with replacement sleeves being fitted from time to time.

Subsequently at Brighton some form of alteration was no doubt carried out as on 1 April – the date would be destined to have something of a wry irony later – No. 2039 again ventured out, this time on a three coach special from Brighton to Ashford routed via the coastway line and Hastings. Bulleid and another member of his senior staff were on the footplate as observers and were thus able to view at first hand the difficulties experienced by the driver in restarting after a signal stop near Ore. The record revealed some 7½ minutes were spent in attempting this restart.

The final confirmed run in which No. 2039 participated (although no date is given) took place a short time later and when the engine was again rostered to head what was deemed a 'works-train' between Lancing and Eastleigh and thought to have consisted of four passenger vehicles.

After this came a period of open store at Brighton until she entered the works on 14 June 1949 with the somewhat strange intention at the time to return the engine to its original form. But as referred to earlier, the class was already considered life expired and so instead she remained untouched inside the works, no doubt whilst elsewhere a decision was made as to the future.

That decision, when it came, was for overhaul but still with the sleeve valves being retained and accordingly, she was given what would be in effect a major refurbishment which even included a replacement boiler sent especially from Eastleigh. She emerged by 2 September 1949 as BR No. 32039 painted in unlined black but perhaps significantly without any ownership insignia or wording. Presumably also test running would have been involved following the overhaul but this is not reported upon.

Following overhaul – and presumably then a satisfactory period of trial (and running in?), the engine was allocated to Brighton shed and intended for normal work. How this could seriously have been anticipated must be open to question as unless some major modifications had been made, she would surely have behaved in exactly the same way as before with limited haulage capacity and a propensity for excess water consumption. Indeed her reputation was known and, possibly due to instructions from the shed management to the roster clerks, she was always ignored and it appears may never have been used as intended.

No. 2039 in steam at Eastleigh having taken a train of carriage underframes from Lancing to the carriage works here. Whether she returned light (no doubt stopping for water on several occasions) or with a similar load is not reported. In this view it can be seen the cylinders are placed at a very slight inclination compared to the horizontal as indeed they had been on the original design. The use of No. 2039 on this (or is it these?) working(s) is still the subject of some unanswered questions. For a start there are no reports of hold-ups to other traffic so clearly the operators must have felt she was capable of working. But recall particularly her thirst: stopping en-route at least at Chichester and Fareham but evidently being able to start away again and so not delay traffic. So was this simply another example of 'showing she could work' or perhaps might it have been a 'one-off' trip? We should also consider her power output (tractive effort) – in consequence of the reduced diameter of the pistons was now little more than a Terrier, in which case how much might she have even been able to pull? One final point to make is that no mention appears in the *RO* or other contemporary journals about this or indeed subsequent similar workings.
S.C. Townroe

The rest of 1949, all of 1950, and the start of 1951 were spent the same way, out of use. The engine obviously deteriorating both in store and without having been used. Finally in February 1951 official notice was received to move No. 32039 to Eastleigh for assessment but inspection at Brighton revealed she was unsuitable to make the journey under her own power (whether this was a boiler defect is not reported), and she was instead towed to Hampshire by C2X No. 32438.

Not surprisingly the inspection at Eastleigh revealed the same as had been found at Brighton, and that a further overhaul would be required in order to restore the engine to traffic, following her long period in store. This time such a lifeline was not forthcoming and No. 32039 quietly disappeared from the scene being noted on the scrap lines at the works on 24 February 1951. She was finally dismantled at Eastleigh in March 1951, although at least one of the nameplates survived. Her remaining two sisters did not survive much longer either, as both were withdrawn just five months later in July 1951 possibly also not having

Fresh from overhaul and now renumbered in the BR series but without ownership insignia of any sort. (Was there any 'running-in' following overhaul?) Why in June 1949 the decision was made to overhaul the engine remains a mystery. Euphoria at the emergence of Leader is unlikely, there was little sentiment involved especially as we know the original intention at overhaul had been to return the engine to its original condition; does this even mean the original cylinders had been retained? Perhaps instead they had been discarded or when sourced were found to be in poor condition but as approval for the work had been given it went ahead anyway. The results were a total waste of money for all concerned especially as the work included a reconditioned boiler. It is ever stranger considering the engine had been considered life-expired two years earlier. Sharp-eyed readers will note the snifting valves either side of the smokebox top have been removed. *V. Evans*

worked for some time. All three, including No. 2039, achieved more than 1 million recorded miles in service.

Sean Day-Lewis comments on her demise with the words, '... the lessons she taught were invaluable'. Sorry, but that just cannot be the case.[4]

What No. 2039 showed us was that sleeve valves, whilst fine in theory and indeed perhaps when used in some settings, were not ideally placed for a railway locomotive and this despite the best efforts of Bulleid, Ricardo, Hutchinson and others to prove otherwise. If No. 2039 did serve a purpose it was to indicate what would likely happen later with No. 36001. That prophecy sadly was also only too correct.

An objective view is also taken by JGC who refers to why, as a test engine, No. 2039 had indeed been tasked with working a passenger train. He refers to a later conversation with Bulleid when both were in Ireland and a successful trial has just taken place, reference the Turf Burner, at which point Clicks adds, 'I made the point about there being no need to risk main line failure and he (Bulleid) agreed but said that "politically" it had to be seen to run. I remembered No. 32039's misfortune at Earlswood and fully understood.' *See p.75.*

Although we know Click was an avowed disciple of Bulleid he later wrote, 'In my view the concept was not proved to be practicable on No. 2039 and going ahead with sleeves for the Leader was a mistake: I think OVB set too much store on Meehanite overcoming the problems that had been encountered. Would sleeve valves be employed (on Leader); No. 2039 was giving discouraging, or at best, inconclusive results. If sleeve valves did have to be dropped would the alternative arrangement with piston valves be feasible? Had there been time (!) a trial of a Meehanite sleeve on one side of No. 2039 would have helped the decision.' Click concludes with a slightly strange comment, 'No. 2039's application was a good deal better than on the Leader.' He probably means the sleeve valves on No. 2039 but fails to elaborate further.

So what do we conclude with reference to No. 2039? I would suggest a few things. Firstly the fact that Hutchinson and others did a remarkable job in a comparatively short space of time but in reality, the die had already been cast in September 1946 when Bulleid had made the promise to have the new engines ready for service in mid-1947. The Leader design incorporating sleeve valves was basically

Overhauled – but back in store again. Other images show the engine in similar position and with the chimney sheeted over. In theory the engine could have taken its place in a suitable link working from Brighton shed but recall she was now of very limited power due to her reduced piston diameter and as such, in tractive effort terms at least, from 20,070lbs to 11,892lbs, was only marginally more powerful than a 'Terrier' (10,695lb). Small wonder there was little or no gainful work available for her whilst her erratic reputation meant even when motive power was short, she was understandably passed over, surprising perhaps considering her use between Lancing and Eastleigh referred to earlier – unless the Lancing to Eastleigh turn(s) were deliberately intended to show up her unsuitability? *F. Foote, courtesy Mike King*

No. 32039 was officially stored in the open at Brighton from 10 September 1949. More than a year later she was steamed for a run to Eastleigh, seen prepared here with a tender full of coal. After all this time it is not surprising that she was deemed unsuitable to run under her own power – that steaming is probably seen here – and instead the fire was dropped and she was instead towed to Eastleigh. Eighteen months in the open has done little to preserve any sense of cleanliness as had been present immediately after the 1949 overhaul and repaint. *Joe Kent/Bluebell Railway Museum*

fixed from then on and, with the need to push matters along as fast as possible, any attempt at substituting a different design, piston valves for example, might well have delayed matters still further and possibly resulted in the whole concept being dropped by the newly formed British Railways. Was Bulleid wrong to try? Absolutely not. Progress in any organisation or industry will inevitably be by stages of experimentation, some will work, some will not, whilst others will work (or be used) probably in a form never at first envisaged but brought about through experimentation and experience. What Bulleid and his staff would have learnt from No. 2039 more than anything else was that were likely troubles ahead. J.G. Click was not senior enough at the time to be party to private discussion between senior staff and similarly respectful enough not to push Bulleid on the point later but we can be certain these conversations did come up, most likely of course in private.

The genius that was André Chapelon was said to have taken a particular interest in Bulleid's use of sleeve valves and according to HAV in *Master Builders of Steam* (Ian Allan, 1963) sent a congratulatory message to Bulleid. Chapelon wisely, as it turned out, decided not to modify or incorporate such a concept on his amazing rebuild, No. 242.A.1., nor indeed on his sadly further still-born steam proposals.

Notes

(1) The liner used with No 36001 was Mechanite – a fine grade cast iron. We know the same metal was used as a cylinder liner on some (all?) of the Bulleid pacifics. Mechanite was also used for a time as the material for the liner on the cylinders of No 2039.

(2) We know No. 2039 was in Brighton works for modification for over four months between July and 5 November 1947. Bradley gives just one member of the D3 class withdrawn in that year, No. 2363, which was officially taken out of service in December. 'Official' withdrawal dates do not always correspond with the date an engine actually ceased to work although we should mention there had been no other withdrawals of the class since before WWII. No. 2363 would therefore appear to have been the most likely donor. The RCTS, however, in their regular periodical *Railway Observer* for the time, suggest the wheels came from another member of the class, No. 2366. This particular engine was not withdrawn until February 1949 but of course could have been out of use beforehand. There is also some doubt as to whether it was the complete bogie that was substituted or just the wheels/axles.

(3) The secrecy referred to is in some ways understandable but we might also ask, who was he trying to keep away? Nationalisation was just around the corner, it was not as if any of the other railways was likely to be interested in stealing his ideas, indeed recall only a short time later H.G. Ivatt [Bulleid's brother in law], was invited to view 2039 in steam. This was not of course the only time Bulleid had been against anyone knowing about the steam stock on the Southern, recall 1942 when Bulleid was certainly less than pleased at a young Ian Allan producing a book of Southern engine numbers.

(4) The Day-Lewis book is close to excellent apart from a few odd comments. For its time, 1964, it was one the first books to accurately describe the work of Bulleid from an historic perspective. But what it also did, on just a very few occasions, was to stray away from an objective look at a topic, such as with these conclusions on No. 2039. I have commented on this point before and do not change my views today. Possibly this occurred because at the time it was published, OVB was still alive and there would be no desire to besmirch the reputation of a man who despite perhaps the failings of No. 2039 and 36001 still achieved much. The present author's comments about the (understandable) involvement of Bulleid in the Day-Lewis biography had previously been similarly identified by E.S. Cox at the foot of p.107 of his own 1971 work *Speaking of Steam*. Cox comments, 'The story of the Merchant Navies and their smaller brethren has been told in many publications, Day-Lewis in his book, *so clearly supervised and checked by Bulleid...*' The emphasis that of the present writer.

LEFT There was immediate condemnation at Eastleigh and No. 32039 was quickly shunted on to the scrap line where she was photographed, perhaps for the last time, on 27 February 1951. Souvenir hunting had not become the business it later was as it will be noted at least one nameplate is still attached. (The late Les Warnett had one of the plates from the engine in his collection.) The demise of No. 32039 cannot have been unexpected in 1951, more modern motive power was becoming available and inroads were being made into any number of pre-group classes. According to official records, No. 32039 ran a total of 1,116,454 miles during its lifetime, the vast majority of these prior to its conversion. So did it point the way towards Leader and were any lessons learnt? Yes, to the first part in so far as it showed what difficulties and failures were likely to occur – and of course they did. As to whether any lessons were learnt, the answer has to be no. By the time No. 2039 was running the design of Leader was too far advanced, so far as the inclusion of sleeve valves was concerned, to be changed. A major redesign of No. 36001 substituting the sleeve valves for an alternative system would have delayed the project even further. Bulleid was a clever man and would certainly have realised this, delay beyond June 1949 perhaps resulting in a 'Stop' order being sent from Marylebone. In summary, it would not have taken a genius to work out that the Leader design was potentially flawed, basically from the very first failure that occurred with No. 2039. (The Drummond tender ahead on No. 2039 was evidently for sale at just 5/- !) *A.E. West, courtesy Mike King*

7
The Race Against Time

Returning to 11 September 1946 and notwithstanding the tests and trials of No. 2039, Bulleid's twin bogie steam engine now had the go-ahead. But note, the words are used carefully and deliberately, 'double-bogie' not at this stage 'double-ended'; that would come later, and with the double-bogie concept still included of course!

From this time too we are able to follow, or at least imagine, the progress that followed. All three works would be involved, Eastleigh for the boilers, plus the manufacture and assembly of the wheels, cranks (these set at 120°), axles and sprockets; Ashford meanwhile had responsibility for at least the first of the main frames and probably the others as well; and while we do not know where the bogie frames were built, even so it was at Brighton that the final assembly took place. The engine that eventual emerged would also have only so much in common with diagram W7326 and consequently the drawing office were going to be busy with various ideas, some of which would in the end not be pursued further.

One of these *may* have been for a double-acting piston, which put simply would involve two pistons one at each end of a cylinder and which were driven by a common crank in the centre. We are not told if these pistons would have included sleeves or more conventional valves. If it all sounds complicated, it was, hence, not surprisingly, this particular idea was dropped at an early stage. Where such thoughts also originated is not confirmed but the impression throughout is that Cocks was a form of stabilising influence on Bulleid – even so, at the end of the day, it was still master and subordinate.

We can realistically assume that the Brighton drawing office (and possibly those at the other works and perhaps also at Waterloo where the CME maintained a small staff) was kept busy, whilst in the offices of the traffic and motive power departments it would seem the concept was still not one which had been totally subscribed to. We learn this from correspondence between the present writer and the late G.L. Nicholson, going back to the mid-1980s.

Brighton works plan. There are two principal sources of images that reference the construction of No. 36001, the collections of Don Broughton and John Click. So far as the former is concerned, Don acquired the images from an unknown individual but who clearly must have either worked at or been a regular visitor to Brighton. On occasions both photographers also took similar views, wherever possible we have attempted to use images not previously published.

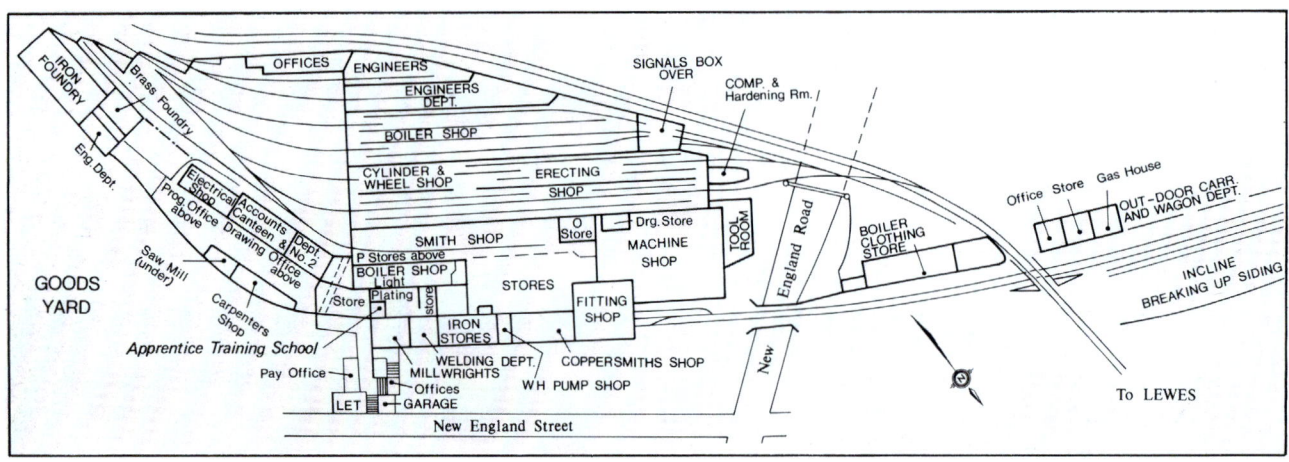

FOR THE IMAGES IN THIS SECTION WE HAVE DELIBERATELY LIMITED THE VIEWS TO THOSE SPECIFICALLY RELEVANT TO THE BUILD AND WE BELIEVE WERE RECORDED IN THE PERIOD 11 SEPTEMBER 1946 TO 21 JUNE 1949. MORE DETAIL ON THE MECHANICS WILL BE FOUND WITH THE IMAGES ACCOMPANYING 'APPENDIX 2', PAGE 262 ET.SEQ. So where to start with the images in this section, by date or by item? The choice is actually made for us as many of the views do not come with a date. Consequently we will begin with the main frames, then the boiler/firebox, wheel bogies and cylinders, assembly of the various components and finally the complete engine. Fortunately photographs are available for most of the principal items – plus some of the smaller ones. In this first image we see the main 'fish-belly' frame and nearer the camera to the left; a bogie frame. This is almost certainly inside Brighton works – as most of the views will be. Certainly the first set of main frames was built at Ashford and possibly the others as well, but this cannot be confirmed. No information has come to light on where the bogie frames may have been made. Centre is a crank axle from a Pacific and so totally unrelated. The date was recorded as 11 May 1948 and consequently one of the earliest views with definite parts present. *Don Broughton*

Nicholson, was a senior player within the Motive Power Superintendent's department at the time whilst also adding, perhaps modestly, that his own part in the Leader story was only 'marginal'. But do recall it had been Nicholson at the time deputising for Chrimes[1] who had managed to persuade Missenden and 'much to Bulleid's displeasure' that the original building order should be reduced from an initial twenty-five locomotives to just five. In one of his letters received by the present author, Nicholson also continued, 'which – as events turned out – was still four too many'. (Elsewhere in the formal notes there is a simple mention that the Southern Railway 'Superintendent of Operations' – who this was is not totally clear but it cannot have been Richards – had expressed the view that just a single prototype should be built. We do not hear from this postholder again in our story.)

Nicholson also expounded his own views on Bulleid, 'OVB was a man of extraordinarily complex character and gifts. His normal demeanor seemed quiet and almost unassuming. This concealed a quite enormous determination to have his own way. He was extremely astute and would normally pursue his ends with a combination of charm and guile, backed up by argument sometimes well-reasoned, often assertive and an almost overwhelming power of persuasion and conviction that he was right. Like many another, he could become pretty unpleasant if he thought he was being thwarted. He was a difficult man to argue with. In bad times, such as failure on his – or his Department's part – to deliver in accordance with previously declared promises, he would quite unscrupulously conceal the true position, even if this entailed further misleading undertakings he knew he could not fulfil.

It is very tempting to think of Leader as having a parallel body but this view of the frames will dispel that: instead it tapered inwards on both sides and at both ends. Nearest the camera is the top of a bogie. Slightly further distant is one of the central cross members which will later be above the middle of the bogie. There is no date for this image but a similar view shows a set of frames inside the works on 11 May 1948 was then photographed by H.C. Casserley still in the same position on 24 July 1948 and with no apparent progress towards made. *Don Broughton Collection*

'A dominant characteristic was his total devotion to the unorthodox, quite frequently merely for its own sake. It was heresy or near heresy for any member of his design staff to present him with anything that "looks like an ordinary engine". As a general rule he disliked conforming to normal practice: i.e., his own brainchildren would not only be different: they must look different, even when they were not much different. (The Q1s for example. Or what useful purpose was served by his numbering system?). This constant pursuit of the unorthodox sometimes warped his judgment with almost ludicrous results, like those awful buffet cars on the Victoria–Portsmouth main line electric m.u.s; or still more awful "Tavern" cars on the main line expresses out of Waterloo.

'The Leader saga well illustrates a rather more serious aspect of this characteristic. The OVB objective throughout was I feel sure to produce a revolutionary, powerful and all purposes steam loco, counter to emergent electric/diesel main line traction: and thereby to crown his reputation. (A perfectly laudable objective for a devoted steam man: though in the context of the times, neither the concept not its execution says much for his judgment.)

'He saw his opportunity when his management decided it wanted to replace the M7s. No one but Bulleid would have dreamt of trying to transform the humble tasks these old locos were engaged on into such a specification as that for the Leader. When – sensibly and prudently, but very likely, guilefully as well – he asked for the Traffic Manager's "exact requirements", what happened?'

Nicholson then goes on to relate the standard repeated sequence of events leading to up to the well-known memorandum. He continues,

'I fear such a mundane interpretation would have had little effect on OVB, who proceeded to mesmerize his management into thinking they needed a loco of the Leader's potential capabilities for such work. Assuming there was a case for the Leader, it certainly wasn't for the purpose set out in the Traffic Manager's note of 3 October 1946. Something like that was I fear the genesis of the "Leader" fiasco.'

Nicholson was clearly warming to his theme for he continued, 'OVB, with his really remarkable innovatory talents, his vision and his energy, was a splendid chap to have around when and as long as he was kept on a very tight rein, as he was under Nigel Gresley. But there was no such rein on the Southern – nor later, in Ireland. The tragedy was that his persuasive powers were such that for the only time is its history, the Southern found themselves provided with large numbers of modern express locomotives. Neither the MNs nor WCs could be regarded as successful. When they were in good nick, they were splendid to drive, masters of their job, comfortable to ride on, bags of steam. But they were atrociously expensive in coal and water consumption, and oil – oil all over the system! Depot maintenance staff, whether mechanical or shed, disliked them for their inaccessibility, unreliability and so on. Their casualty rate was high, and so were their operating costs. Eventually they were all rebuilt – at considerable cost – but then became, so far as I know, useful citizens indeed.'

We should perhaps pause to comment upon perhaps just one of Nicholson's comments where he says, 'The tragedy was that his persuasive powers were such that for the only time is its history, the Southern found themselves provided with large numbers of modern express locomotives.' Realistically it would be difficult to agree with the use of the word 'tragedy' in this context. Indeed, why should it be such, modern motive power was surely welcome, agreed the reliability of the Bulleid Pacific designs was perhaps not always what was desired, but part of this may well have been down to available skilled staff, depot facilities, and the time needed for a limited number of men to maintain older Southern motive power that really should have been pensioned off years earlier. Remember too these are the words of a motive power man, an individual charged with maintaining and providing enough locomotives to run the service. We really should have a balancing view from the other departments involved, design, workshop and traffic. That is not to suggest Nicholson was wrong but with only one viewpoint, a degree of bias is always a risk.

John Click meanwhile makes little mention of the politics and the progress at this time, but with his move to Brighton in 1948 his involvement with the final assembly, first steaming and trials with No. 36001 afford us, particular a little later, with a unique perspective for the time.

The Traffic Manager R.M.T Richards and his colleagues seemingly were not pinning all of their faith in the new design, for just a few weeks later at the beginning of October 1946, Richards submitted his official requirements for motive power, which was placed before the Rolling Stock (Repairs & Renewals) Progress Committee at Waterloo.

'In reply to your letter of the 5th September and referring to minute No. 79 of the Progress Committee Meeting held on the 4th September. The case justifying the construction of 25 new passenger tank engines is given below. At the present time and, indeed, for the past 45 years the most powerful passenger tank engines on the Western Section have been those of the class, 104 of which are still in existence. These engines were built between the years 1897–1911 and

A fascination small scale (non-working) model of the Leader boiler and firebox – minus the firebox sides. This was prepared for and shown to the VIP visitors at Eastleigh during the formal inspection of the locomotive at the end of June 1949. The position of the syphons from the crown to the lower part of the boiler is thus indicated. It was probably made by an apprentice; the subsequent fate of the model is not known. *David Burnett*

although the last 49 embody slight improvements, the whole class was based on a design prepared in 1897 and now, therefore, nearly 50 years old. They were originally built for L&SWR suburban traffic and were, in due course, rendered redundant by electrification. They are now being used as general utility locomotives, 25 working empty trains between Clapham Junction, or other stock berthing points and Waterloo, and the balance on local and branch line services on the Western Section. They are completely out of date and inefficient by modern standards, and their continued existence prevents any improvement on the services they operate. In the report to yourself dated 1.12.1944, upon our locomotive position in 1950, prepared by the Deputy General Manager and other Chief Officers, the whole of these 104 engines were condemned, and this recommendation was confirmed in the corresponding report upon the 1955 locomotive position submitted on 3.9.1946. The report dealing with the Engine Building Programme during the years 1947–1955 recommends the building of 60 new tank engines, diesel or steam, in addition to the 25 tanks already proposed, and I now recommend that the latter be constructed. It is understood that the five engines to be built will be a guide as to the building of the subsequent 20.'

Perhaps Richards even still held on to a vain hope that another simpler and more straightforward design might materialise but privately he probably knew this would likely never happen with Bulleid as CME. However, yet again it is interesting that nowhere does it seem anyone considers the development of or a revised use for any of the existing large stock of tank engines originating on the former SECR or LBSCR systems, types J and W, from the South Eastern, and D, E and I classes from the Brighton. That is not to say any were perfect, but the W at least would surely have been preferable to an M7.

We should also stop for a moment to consider some of Richards's comments relative to the dates and building programmes he refers to for the period 1947 to 1955. Recall this memo was penned in October 1946, the Socialist government was in power and they had promised to nationalise the railways. There may not have been a date for this to take place – yet – but was it not perhaps slightly strange to be planning ahead for up to nine years from the time of writing? Perhaps it was a case of intending to present any new organisation with a fait accompli – indeed just as Bulleid would seem to do with his five Leader engines on 1 January 1948. Remember too in October 1946 no details of how the new motive power set-up post-nationalisation had emerged; again another interesting topic to perhaps muse over at some other time (but not in this book!).

LEFT AND ABOVE The boiler/firebox for the first and subsequent Leader engines were constructed at Eastleigh, one of which is seen here – complete and on a trolley. There are several items of note. Firstly, the main boiler barrel is of all-welded construction – some rivets and some stays, yes, but these are in the 'crown' area above the firebox. All parts were of steel, no copper was used for the main construction. Next, and although not immediately obvious, it was constructed in two parts, the main barrel and then a crown, attached to the main barrel at the top of the firebox throat plate. The sides and back of the firebox are of simple steel sheet. Notice at the rear the firehole door is offset whilst two water gauges are affixed to the crown. Controls within the firing compartment were limited. At the front end, the smokebox of Leader needed merely to be functional and was fabricated at Brighton, of necessity then it did not follow the round contours of the barrel. We turn now to the four syphons (seen from the underside, the two on the outside are not immediately obvious). These were situated within the firebox, one end of each supporting the crown and at the other emerging at the base of the firebox and then attached to the underside of the barrel. These assisted in increasing water circulation and also increased the heating surface. Note also the wash-out plugs at the base of each – there were others elsewhere on the engine. (It is not thought the boiler of Leader was ever washed out all the time it was running, such was the advantage of the TIA water treatment.) Whilst this view dates from September 1948 and was presumably the first completed boiler, we cannot be certain it was the one actually used on No. 36001. The reason for this doubt is that seen here it is painted white for the benefit of the official photographer. But the boiler seen installed within the frames of No. 36001 later does not appear to be this clean – that is in the few areas where it may be viewed during assembly where lagging was not present. There could be several reasons for this. Perhaps it was later steam tested and this burnt off the paint or might it have been steam tested already – perhaps not as per John Click's comment about the test at Brighton when everyone made themselves scarce. Or was it later stored in the open at Brighton until needed? With no boiler identification numbers reported, this quandary will likely remain. Note also the steam fountain on the side, this was the take-off point for live steam for the injectors, etc. (This was on the internal corridor side of the engine and seemingly just at the right height to give anyone passing a good size whack on the head should they fail to notice it!) Lastly, we come to the circular flange high up on the front. We should point out that this image came from the collection of Reg Curl who has made a pencil comment on the reverse of the print asking what it is? We see it again but with a fitment attached in other views – and it is for the regular linkage. However, other boiler only views do not show this ring although the fitment is later seen added. Might it have simply been that with the ring present the loading gauge was compromised for travel? Finally, near the base of the syphons it is possible to see the fitment for blowing down the boiler. The photographs were believed taken on 7 September 1948. *Reg Curl Collection*

Two views of what is probably the same boiler on wagon No. 61169 in Brighton works yard on 28 September 1948. The previous views of the boiler at Eastleigh have a pencil note on the rear 'around 7 September 1948', but it would be unfair to suggest it had taken three weeks to move the 60-odd miles to Brighton as we cannot be certain when the move took place or indeed how long the boiler had stood on the wagon seen here. From the rear we get a good view of the firebox and its strange angular shape. *Don Broughton Collection*

At this point Bulleid's undoubted enthusiasm can surely have known no bounds. Whether he had secretly always hankered after a steam engine that was 'different' we cannot be certain. Certainly we can doubt he had ever envisaged something like Leader during his tenure on the LNER but it was his quest to prove steam was not a spent force that probably continued to drive him on now. At this stage he had the backing, although perhaps not quite the full support, of the Southern management. But most importantly he had the support of Missenden as General Manager. He now had to prove his case and rapidly, and from the perspective of a totally new and untried design incorporating so many novel features, a timescale of two years and eight months from approval in September 1946 to first steaming in June 1949 was probably very commendable. It might have even been sooner had not so many changes been made along the way. Day-Lewis comments there were so many design changes, bits were being removed and alternatives welded on at an ever-increasing rate. (This statement has been made before but without detail. Regretfully too and despite extensive searching, we can still give no detail of the physical changes that affected the actual build as it progressed.)

But there were still dark clouds on the horizon. Bulleid was well aware of the limited time he had left him before nationalisation would occur. As mentioned, at this stage there was no actual date, that would come later although just a few weeks after on 26 November 1946 the Transport Bill had been published by Parliament. That morphed into the Transport Act on 6 August 1947 and, as we know, nationalisation of the railways would occur less than four months later on 1 January 1948. There was an awful lot to do and so little time, in which it appears too that Bulleid had once again set himself a brief as only he might, and in reality, only loosely based upon the original agreed specification.

This was a further example of how he had previously set himself the task of providing the Merchant Navy class with greater power than the traffic department had requested, so this time too he set himself a further goal of enshrining into a steam design the advantage of total adhesion allied to capturing as many of the potential advantages of contemporary early diesel and electric locomotives as then existed. (According to 'A.F.C' [might this be A.F. Cook – a former Swindon man?] in the SLS Journal for October 1965, Bulleid intended the new design to equal the performance of the SR electric locomotives, later BR Nos 20001/2. This conjoined perspective is referred to in similar, although not identical fashion, by E.S. Cox later.)

As also mentioned above, it cannot be believed that such ideas – perhaps it might be fairer to call it inspiration – would have appeared overnight. More likely what Bulleid had in his mind was the culmination of a lifetime of ideals, his vision of a steam engine for the future. Now was probably the very first time he had dared to allow these ideas to develop. Moving back a few years to 1940, and for as long as there are steam enthusiasts, so will there be debate as to how Bulleid had managed to get not only the Southern Railway Board, but also the Ministry of Supply to agree to the construction of what were clearly express engines in 1940/41. Forget the hype that with a wheel diameter of just 6ft 2ins the Merchant Navy class were intended for mixed traffic – rubbish – this was an out-and-out express design exactly as Bulleid had envisaged the Southern Railway needed to operate their peacetime boat trains and similar workings. Had wartime restrictions not interfered either, the valves of the Merchant Navy class could well have been very different also, but such subjects have been well covered already by others elsewhere and it is not necessary to repeat the exact history of that class here.

Nicholson also alludes in part as to how Bulleid managed to get approval for his various steam ideas, especially from a railway whose avowed aim was eventual wholesale electrification. In short, he cultivated individuals who he considered were either on his side, might be successfully lobbied, or who might also be useful to him with their own contacts. We should not forget that several of the Southern Railway directors held similar positions in other companies. As an individual he was also often regarded as 'rather clever' by certain members of the SR Board as well as a number of other senior non-technical officers. Cruel facts perhaps but given the circumstances of the time we have to say who could blame him for using contacts and reputation to best advantage, whilst his backing came from the fact that he had also put the Southern back on the map. From an engineering perspective the SR was now up with the others again, indeed to some it seemed Bulleid could do little that was wrong.

The December 1944 Board meeting however was thus not completely clear as regards the 'Passenger Tank Engines'. But behind the scenes a meeting is known to have taken place between the Traffic Manager R.M.T. Richards, Sir Eustace Missenden and Bulleid. Whether this preceded the Board meeting is not clear. What is known is that it was one of the regular senior officers' meetings that were held. Amongst the items discussed was the projected 1946 locomotive-building programme, out of which two items of particular note emerged. The first was again a request by Richards for this replacement for the tank engines, which were even then considered out of date for branch, secondary, and also empty stock duties, mainly between Waterloo and Clapham Junction. Richards's comments on the class could almost be said to be the impetus to Bulleid pushing ahead with the 'Leader' concept.

Either at the same or another meeting between Bulleid and Richards the subject of suitable locomotives for the cross-London freight workings was discussed. At the time these were ably handled by Maunsell's W class tank engines, a further batch of which would no doubt have sufficed. But Bulleid, fresh from his work with the drawing office team, was insistent that a more flexible approach was required and after apparently listening to the request in silence is reported to have exclaimed, ' … you don't really want them, because they are confined to one class of duty. What you need is a substantially more powerful mixed traffic tank locomotive with full route availability.' (In practice, and according to Townroe, the cross-London freight turns were a nightmare for the operators. Any engine diagrammed for the duty would spend most of its time waiting either for pathways or loads to be made up. It was very unlikely in the 1940s and 1950s railway scene that such engines could practically have been used for much else.)

Away from the Southern briefly and at this stage the plot definitely thickens, for in 1945 Bulleid presented a paper entitled 'Locomotives I have known' (the same title was used by the late J.H. Maskelyn in a totally unrelated book) to the proceedings of the Institution of Mechanical Engineers. The content of this may well be summarised by

The Leader boiler now within Brighton works. At least three other boilers were completed and moved to Brighton, later being installed within engines 36002, 36003 and what would have been 36004 although as is depicted later, this was merely a set of main frames and boiler. The fifth engine which had been destined to have been No. 36005 is probably best described as a 'kit of parts' – possibly a less than complete kit as it is possible parts were cannibalised from Nos. 36004/5 to keep No. 36001 running. We may reasonably assume as well that all these boilers were completed at Eastleigh. (When the order came to cease work on Nos. 36002–5 did this also mean the final boiler was perhaps not even completed?)
Don Broughton Collection

K.P. Jones as 'An unusual paper in that it selects a number of locomotive types for detailed consideration. Three are obvious, "Lord Nelson" – modifications, "Merchant Navy" and "Q1" classes – in that they were his own designs. The others considered were the Gresley A1, A4, O1 and P2 designs, the Ivatt Atlantics and a French design. From the choice of LNER types it would appear then that Bulleid agreed with much of Gresley's design policy.'

In public at least it would appear Bulleid was a man who was not only justifiably proud of his own achievements but he also appeared to admire the work of his former chiefs. The paper contained nothing unknown either, radicalism, it seemed, was not quite ready to be revealed yet.

We should also consider for a moment how Bulleid carried his staff with him, especially the senior men who were often professionally trained engineers. Again it is appropriate to quote Day-Lewis: <<QUERY: indent this 6 par quote? Quotes left on incases too short for an indent>

'Bulleid's attitude to his professional staff was (rather) different. The workmen received the courtesy and consideration due to outsiders, his (*professional*–KJR) staff he treated more roughly as though they were his brothers: and with the departure of Holcroft, younger brothers. His ideas were sufficiently revolutionary to give offence to the more conventional of his own department as well as the professional employees of other departments, and as an

The first 'Leader' boiler is ready to be pushed outside for its first steam test – seemingly at Eastleigh for what follows later. When it was given its hydraulic (water) test the Boiler Shop Foreman, Charlie Soare, rang Bulleid to say he had just achieved the first completely dry test (meaning no water seeping anywhere) he had ever seen; which was just as well, since the whole pressure vessel was welded, all staying included. Any moisture around the boiler would have been through a weld – a very serious matter – as opposed to a slight weep at a caulked joint or round a screwed stay in a conventional boiler. The story was that as the boiler made steam on this first test all but the lighter-up and Charlie melted away, effectively evacuating the area. JGC adds his own comments, 'When I asked Charlie Soare in his ninety-sixth year (and very shortly before he passed away) what he thought of this boiler, he replied "I wasn't struck", but whenever I mentioned Bulleid's name he smiled warmly, remembering his old Chief with whom he had had such a unique rapport. Dugald Drummond had employed Charlie at Nine Elms, before the transfer to Eastleigh, and he retained the clearest recollection of every word that passed between them all those years before. The whole of the firebox plating that can be seen was "dry" and lined with very carefully designed firebricks which were all ingeniously fitted together in model form in the D.O. but quite another when fused together, damaged by flame action, cracked by distortion of the plating and by the use of fireirons to break up clinker during disposal. The four thermic syphons, on the other hand gave no trouble, and together with the rest of the firebox heating surface (the crown and the tubeplate) produced a great deal of steam. The closely spaced syphons, especially in the centre of the box, did tend to quench flames prematurely and caused a lot of smoke to be produced; though on the other hand the brickwork, once up to temperature, materially assisted combustion.' Pressure testing was to 350psi hydraulic and 290psi steam, notice the blanking plate fitted where the take-off for the steam fountain was located. Which boiler and for which engine we cannot tell, but certainly not in 'photographic grey/white'. *S C Nash/Stephenson Locomotive Society*

individualist he found it impossible to work with some of the men he inherited from Maunsell. But he was respected by all and inspired a fanatical enthusiasm in many. If greatness can be measured by the reaction set up in those who meet it then Bulleid was, with Gresley, the greatest British locomotive engineer of the century.

'It got so that nobody thought he could do any wrong, particularly himself. "I think we would have given him square wheels if he had asked for them," dryly commented one such admirer.

'The Brighton drawing office, whatever it did to Bulleid's locomotives after his departure, remembers his regime with gratitude and glowing pleasure. Many of his notions seemed outrageous and they sometimes came to nothing, but the effect was to keep the staff constantly on the alert. They learnt that everything should be constantly re-examined and nothing done simply because it was the traditional practice of the past.

'We never knew when he might call. Sometimes he would be on the phone asking for some drawings to be ready by 9.30 p.m. And we happily worked through the evening for him.

'His confidence was boundless, but he was never satisfied with anything. No two locomotives were exactly the same and even an order for twenty-five coaches might be stopped half-way through because some improvement had suddenly

It is likely the bogie frames were erected at Brighton. Once the 'shell' was completed they were then transferred to a motorised rotating jig 'welding manipulator' principally so that the cylinder casting could be incorporated. This jig allowed the cylinder assembly to be welded into place with access for the welder made as easy as possible. The concept of the rotating jig is believed to have been copied from U-Boat construction during WWII – note the jig could only accommodate a single bogie frame at a time and not the complete main-frame assembly. We see here the bogie assembly from one end and then from the top looking from the rear. This, the 'engine' part of the design is the one thing Bulleid admitted he would have liked to have made removable. (He does not appear to have been similarly self-critical concerning the other major issues that would later show up, namely the use of sleeve valves, the weight distribution, the welded boiler or the working conditions for the crew.) When looking for reasons for failure later, questions were asked concerning the actual welding of the cylinders to the frame in so far as was there distortion created within the cylinders due to localised heat – almost certainly yes and *see* later. In more general terms, the alignment of the cylinders also needed to be 100% accurate although it would be unfair to suggest this too may have been an issue affecting later failure. Finally, note in the first image, the main frames alongside and three sets of wheels behind. This view we know was taken on 1 October 1948. *Don Broughton Collection*

come to mind. This gave much discomfort to his Works Managers at Eastleigh and Brighton, A.E.W. Turbett and L.J. Granshaw respectively, and when the first "Leader" class locomotive was nearing completion new ideas were being welded on right up to the first test, and after.

'Sometimes it seemed that Bulleid would never come to the point of saying: "Yes, go ahead". He was restless and impatient, but if his Chief Locomotive Designer, the loyal and admirable Clifford Cocks, turned down a proposition as completely unworkable he was quite capable of waiting until that official had gone on holiday and then getting his deputy to work out a plan.'

We have no clear timeframe for progress on the Leader build but some indication can be gained from a study of dates of certain photographs, therefore here are progress dates, taken from dates of photographs and information in the 'RO' (again in the case of the latter the dates quoted are when the information was published and as such is likely to be a few weeks old):

April 1948: (*RO*) Brighton is soon to build five high-pressure steam engines of unconventional design to be known as the Leader class. ….. After the first five engines have been tested a further 31 will be constructed, A set of cylinders and valve gear of the pattern to be used were, until recently, on test at Brighton.

26 June 1948: Leader boiler seen in an advanced state of construction at Eastleigh.

24 July 1948: Main frames seen laid out at Brighton having arrived from Ashford.

6 September 1948: By this date first boiler had arrived at Brighton. And from the RO: at Eastleigh work is proceeding on other components including further wheels and axles and outside roller bearings.

1 October 1948: Bogie frames seen held in a rotating jig for welding. On the same date wheels and axles (at least five axles with their outside sprockets protected) noted in Brighton works. As previously indicated, the wheelsets were assembled at Eastleigh and also constructed/machined/assembled there.

24 November 1949: Leader not yet finally fitted with boiler although this has been tested in the frames.

19 February 1949. Enthusiasts visit to Eastleigh reports wheels, boilers and other parts on view.

19 March 1949: Bunker noted as added to main frames, also mantle shelf tank.

April 1949 (RO): Second Leader class bogie frames have been set up in the shops and work has begun on the fitting of the frame stretchers. First Leader is approaching completion.

May 1949 (RO): Main frames of second Leader are now in the shops and work has begun on the frames of the third.

2 May 1949: Wheels, cylinders, sleeves and oscillating gear fitted to at least one bogie.

13 June 1949: One bogie at least almost complete although lower chain case to protect chain drive/sprockets still to be added, also to be added is the front cover to the sleeve valve oscillating gear.

14 June 1949: Loco recorded on its bogies in Brighton erecting shop, amongst work still to be completed are the addition of a roof panel and vacuum pipes still to be added from body to the front of the bogie.

20 June 1949: Complete and painted black inside the works. (See p.114/5.)

(The John Click listing of Leader photographs do not assist with dates.)

Progress, with the wheels added. In addition other parts visible include the springs with two of these already fitted plus their external covers, the top casing that will fit over the final drive chains, the steam turbine driven oil pump, and the driving cab access steps. Although not confirmed, the centre and rear axle wheels do not appear to be on the ground so might this have been around the time of the ill-fated steam test on No. 1 bogie? *Don Broughton Collection*

An almost complete bogie from the leading end, 13 June 1949, just eight days from the first steaming. In addition to the components mentioned earlier, the principal addition this time is the oscillating gear attached to the front of the sleeves. Both bogies would have been placed on the valve setting rollers whilst later and when virtually complete, No. 1 was set up on blocks at the south end of the shop and run in under steam – supplied from an E4 0-6-2 tank engine outside. The CME invited his friend André Chapelon over to see the bogie running at this stage. John Click continues, 'I saw the two of them walk over and become totally absorbed by the spectacle, to which they returned several times … fascinated, before going back to the offices.' Left to right, notice between No. 1 and No. 2 cylinders the drive for the oscillating gear emerging from the top. This single lever between two of the ball-and-socket joints at the ends of the valve rods is the one providing the oscillating movement to all three of the sleeve valves. Oscillation was included on the advice of Sir Harry Ricardo to help spread the lubrication, so that any point on the surface of the sleeve performed a figure of eight in relation to the cylinder liner. The whole of this front area would later be covered by a casing intended to keep dirt out. Due to the number of sleeve difficulties later experienced during the trials, No. 36001 later ran several (if not all subsequent) trials with the oscillating gear still in place but with the cover missing. This in turn allowed the ingress of foreign matter and may have then contributed to further failures. (The proverbial 'Catch-22' situation.) When the oscillating gear was later removed, the sleeves fractured far less frequently but the rate of wear become unacceptable before a useful mileage had been accumulated. Finally note the large lifting brackets on the frames above the buffers. *Don Broughton Collection.*

So, from the above we have the first signs of physical progress visible from June 1948. Recall this was already a year on from when the first engine had been planned to be in service and similarly a year behind when the first engine would indeed actually steam. It was also six months into the British Railways era.

JGC takes up the story, 'In the spring of 1948 the Southern Motive Power Officers saw clearly the way the "Leader" wind was blowing, found their worst fears confirmed, went to Rudguard[2] at the Kremlin and came home with a promise of two of the latest LMS 2-6-4 tanks for trial. This loan came at the time of the more famous Interchange Trials, of which I saw nothing, and involved Nos 42198 and 42199. The first one came to Ashford and worked on duties usually allocated to my beloved Wainwright 'J' class 0-6-4 tanks.' *(JGC does not elaborate why he had such feeling for the 'J' type.)*

We can only imagine the relief that must have been felt by perhaps both the motive power and traffic departments at last having a modern tank engine at their disposal. Even so the second engine was seemingly tried not on shunting and ECS duties but instead on stopping train working between Waterloo and Basingstoke. History also tells us they were an instant success and Brighton would eventually build forty-one of this Fairburn design for use in the region in 1950/51. However, they would still not replace the M7s and instead superseded some of the work being done by the earlier Brighton tank types, mainly in the 'I' classes. Numbered in the BR series as 42066 through to 42106 the Southern Region had originally allocated numbers in the 38xxx series. Later, between 1952 and 1954 seven were exchanged with the North Eastern Region for a like number of BR Standard Class 4 tank engines, whilst the remaining thirty-four were the subject of a similar exchange with the LMR at the end of 1959.

From the rear an almost complete bogie and this time showing the two large vacuum reservoirs that were placed on each bogie; these were fed by further vacuum reservoirs located on the flattened area above the smokebox. From the position of the shaft that will lead to the reversing cylinder, we can tell this is No. 2 end bogie. (No. 1 was the smokebox end of the engine.) Notice that it is only on the front and centre axles that drive sprockets are provided.
Don Broughton Collection

Click again, 'The "Leader", though I knew I then had grave doubts about it, still pulled like a magnet; C.S. Cocks wanted me back in the Drawing Office, and the prospect of a shed was also exciting. Rugby Testing Station was about to open – I'm surprised I didn't try for that and get in on the ground floor, though I'm glad I didn't. I went to ask Cocks' advice. Canny as he was, he offered me a compromise he knew I couldn't refuse, "Come back to us and you can go into the Testing Section under Attwell – you'll be in sheds every day and out on footplate too". With five "Leaders" on the stocks it was quite likely that I'd even have one of my own to live with and keep out of trouble! What a challenge.' *(What a hope! – KJR)*

Elsewhere in his memoires JGC, who was also clearly a steam man in the mould of Bulleid, comments, '…. when I was *(later)* offered the chance of going to the Locomotive Testing Station at Rugby it seemed by far my best, and possibly my last, opportunity of doing something for steam. No consideration had been given to putting the "Leader" on test there; and, even if it had, only one bogie could have been run for the Plant hadn't been designed for anything so unconventional or for six driving axles over a long wheelbase.'

'So back, to Brighton I went; in time to see the "Leader" being built and to photograph as much of it as possible on the days when I was there. Film was almost impossible to get but if one was lucky some very fast, very high contrast ex–RAF stuff could sometimes be had – the worst possible film to put into my old camera because it could only be made reasonably light-tight by swathing it in insulating tape. Spies from the Drawing Office were not welcome in Brighton Shops, so my photos were all taken very furtively. Works Manager Granshaw was in the habit of having a lunchtime prowl and he had to be avoided at all costs; and financially costly it was to me. My method was to present the camera, make a first pass of the target to select a viewpoint and only return if the coast looked completely clear. Then I'd adjust the camera level with a pile of coins and shoot. More than once I had to bolt without scooping up the loose change and I've often wondered what their finders made of it – in Ireland it would surely have been thought a gift from the "little people".'

Jumping ahead now to June 1949, Click adds, 'As the Leader neared completion the painters swarmed all over it painting it black – after all this one really was a mixed traffic locomotive. When done end to end OVB must have come down to have a look for before that paint was properly dry, they set to again doing the whole of the upperworks a light battleship grey.' *(Possibly more like the order had come down from Marylebone that the engine needed to prove itself on test before being painted in its formal black livery. Hence the reversion to 'photographic grey'.)*

However, moving back slightly now to the year 1947, the centenary year for the Institute of Mechanical Engineers (recall JGC was still at Ashford at this time), the occasion was marked by contributions from each of the reigning

CMEs: Ivatt, Peppercorn and Hawksworth. The meeting was held under Bulleid's chairmanship, with each CME summarising the 'state-of-the-art', as they saw it. In addition, M. Armand (then Deputy Director General of the SNCF) spoke on 'Motive Power Trends on European Railways', as well as P.W. Kiefer, Chief Engineer, New York Central System, who gave a masterly review of 'Railway Power Plant from the United States Point of View'.

Bulleid started, as well he might, referring to the responsibilities of a Chief Mechanical Engineer being '…to keep in service the largest possible percentage of the stock of locomotives, and to see that whilst in service the locomotives require as little maintenance as possible and that no defects occur that would affect their time-keeping whilst working trains. His ability to do this depends upon the quality of the staff and equipment at his disposal.' Just these few sentences are at odds with Nicholson's views of the same period recounted earlier. (Around this period Nicholson's principal role was as Assistant in Charge on the Isle of Wight, the same role A.B. MacLeod had held earlier, but clearly he was at Waterloo for various meetings.)

After the pronouncement of various figures and statistics, Bulleid continued, at the same time ever warming to what would follow; 'When it is remembered that the figures quoted and the observations I have made follow from many years of sustained effort to obtain better results, it will inevitably be suggested that the accepted methods of design or construction cannot be expected to give substantially better results. That is to say the results were as good as could be expected from the designs, materials, finish and methods of operation which were used. Consequently if we are to reach the higher level of achievement in continuity of service which is now required, a new conception of the steam locomotive is needed. Such thoughts caused us to question accepted ideas and forced us to investigate the locomotive as regards design, use and servicing. The very age of the steam locomotive has acted against its further development for its bad features have come to be accepted as inherent and inevitable. It is these bad features which enable other forms of traction to compete with it, and consequently such bad features must be eliminated if the steam locomotive is to survive.'

This is the rear view of 36001's No.2 bogie. Vacuum braking demanded very large brake cylinders, as can be seen. Designers using air brakes today need far less space. The opening to the oil bath is visible but the cover for this has yet to added. The reversing shaft, which rotated, waits to be coupled up to the splined shaft from the loco body. The reverser, as 'standard' as possible with the Pacifics, was on the corridor side of the locomotive but to make the bogies truly interchangeable between ends, as well as between others of the class, certain details were repeated on both sides of each bogie but served no purpose; the example here being the 'dummy' oil bath around the reversing shaft bearing that is repeated on the far side.

The wheels for Leader were of typical 'BFB' design and at 5ft 1in the same diameter as the earlier Q1 type. Here though the similarity ended, for with Leader there was no crankpin. The drive sprockets, wheels and axles, including the crank axle, were all manufactured and assembled at Eastleigh (which drawing office was responsible for the various items is not certain but it would have been most likely that everything was done at Brighton – not least so that all the information was available in one place. The original drawing would then have been traced, copies made and these passed to the appropriate manufacturing works). The centre crank axle was the only one with drive sprockets on either end of the axle, whilst the front and rear axles each have a drive sprocket on one side only and were interchangeable. Also visible in the views is the pedestal guides, in the centre of which were roller bearings. For movement from Eastleigh to Brighton the drive sprockets were encased in wooden packing. Accordingly to Bradley, the Works Manager at Eastleigh (A.E.W. Turbett) had 'very wisely avoided involvement with the Leaders'. 1 October 1948. *Don Broughton Collection*

E.S. Cox upon quoting the above also gives his own analysis:

Bulleid was not perhaps as clear as might have been expected about these bad features, for when he listed in his Address the improvements which he thought were badly needed, five of them were perfectly well attainable within the ordinary Stephenson format. These were:

• To be capable of running over the majority of the company's lines.

• To be capable of working all classes of traffic up to 90mph.

• Suitable for complete common user.

• To run not less than 100,000 miles between general repairs with little or no attention at sheds.
To cause minimum wear and tear on the track.

The sixth improvement – to use substantially less fuel and water per DBHP hour – had certainly not been attained on his Pacifics, nor was it likely to be attained on any more novel machines working between substantially the same inlet and exhaust temperatures and pressures. His four remaining points did admittedly call for something new: to have its whole weight available for braking and the highest percentage thereof for adhesion; to be equally capable of running in both directions with unobstructed look-out; ready for service at short notice and to be almost continuously available.

At this point we need to bring back John Click who adds, 'I requested and got permission to attend (the lecture) from the Works Manager at Ashford and sat spellbound when OVB at last got to the exciting part of the lecture and what was going on now at Brighton.

'The slight figure, his head lit by the light over his papers, he read quietly what we had all come to hear. When he reached the "heavy mixed traffic tank engine" there was an electric tension in the hall as, in exactly the same quiet matter-of-fact way, he described his forthcoming Leader:

"A new type of heavy, mixed traffic tank engine is under construction and these engines embody further developments of the innovations introduced in the tender engines, all with the object of developing a steam engine as easy to maintain and operate as possible. As the locomotive is carried on two six-wheel bogies, the whole weight is available for adhesion and braking and the engine can run over 97 percent of the company's lines."'

Later in the same year more details emerged, again from Bulleid himself when he said, 'SR traffic requirements could be met by two classes of tender engine and two classes of tank engine, the former for longer distance services and the latter for all local and short distance working.' (The Q1 was regarded by then as a wartime necessity not to be perpetuated, and the second tank engine [Leader was evidently the first and the larger of the tank engines] never got looked at very seriously – we would love to know about this proposal as well but it is not mentioned again by Click and no weight diagram or other information has been located.)

Bulleid continued, 'A new type of heavy mixed traffic tank engine is under construction and these engines embody further developments of the innovations introduced in the tender engines, all with the object of developing a steam locomotive as easy to maintain and operate as possible. As the locomotive is carried on two six-wheeled bogies, the whole weight is available for adhesion and braking, and the engine can run over 97per cent of the company's system. Each six-wheeled bogie has a three-cylinder simple expansion engine driving the middle axle, which is coupled to the leading and trailing axles by chains. A new design of engine has been adopted completely eliminating all piston or valve glands subject to steam pressure. Roller bearing axle boxes are fitted throughout and the usual horn guides suppressed. A new design of boiler has been introduced without the usual water legs so that stay trouble has been eliminated. The engines will carry water treatment equipment, so that there should be no longer any trouble resulting from the failure or absence of water treatment plants. Automatic lubrication has been carried a stage further so that it is nearly complete. It is expected that the availability of the locomotive will reach a percentage comparable with that of any other form of traction, i.e. be determined by traffic conditions rather than by locomotive requirements.'

Click summarises his experience in a few words previously quoted but reading these seventy-plus years on, we cannot be totally certain they were truly objective for he says, 'At the conclusion Bulleid gave his closing remarks. With almost complete impartiality his summary showed the lucid and far-reaching overview he would take towards a situation; whilst within it, vigorously promoting his own ideas. He really did see the whole wood, despite the trees, from his position bang in the middle.'

Recall too this was at the start of June 1947, the very month when the first locomotive had been due to be complete. It is also clear from his comments that JGC is clearly a disciple and consequently a fan of Bulleid, nothing wrong with that of course, but we know now Bulleid's comments were not strictly accurate. In June 1947 the design was still not finalised as regards the comment over construction – well artistic licence perhaps but physical progress made with only a limited number of parts could hardly be considered as 'construction'.

We now return to 1947/8 when despite the railways having passed into public ownership, Bulleid was still very much involved with his utopian project. Design detail however was still changing almost daily at this stage, all within the unwavering aim which was to go for a cab-each-end general purpose steam locomotive able to equal or improve on the performance being obtained with the two electric locomotives designed between Raworth and

As an interlude from both mechanics and politics, we might use this moment to discuss the names that had been proposed to be fitted to what was now officially the Leader class – *see* note later in this caption. H.A.V Bulleid has suggested his father sketched name suggestions for the engines on an old envelope including; 'MISSENDEN Sir Eustace, General Manager Southern Railway Co.' and 'CHURCHILL Winston P.C.O.M. Prime Minister of Britain 1939–45', the annotation to be carried over three lines of text. (Stephen Townroe later recounted to the writer, two other names were likely, 'MONTGOMERY, Field Marshall', and 'WALKER, Sir Herbert' were considered. The use of capitals for the surname of each recipient was as per the original suggestion. Some of the unofficial names suggested in the works for the engine, including 'Fred Carno' were somewhat less polite. *Fred Carno – sometimes spelt 'Karno' was a music hall impresario. His 'circus' being a travelling comic opera troupe. The period in which he was a performer predated that of Charlie Chaplin's movie career, but at the time of Leader's existence, the synonym 'Fred Carno Circus' was still in regular use as indicative of a poor quality product.*) In the event the delay in the completion of Leader meant a Battle of Britain class engine No. 21C151 had already carried the name Winston Churchill for nearly a year before No. 36001 would finally emerge from Brighton (not the first time a steam engine had been named after a Prime Minster either, witness *Gladstone, Disraeli, Rosebery,* etc, but all of these were some years before Bulleid came upon the scene. If we really want to digress, we could add that on the LNWR there were: (another) *Disraeli, Gladstone, Palmerston* [also on the Festiniog!], *Peel* and *Stanley* [family name of the Earl of Derby]. The GWR too were represented by *Stanley Baldwin* [who was a GWR Director and subsequently PM}, *Gladstone, Beaconsfield, Disraeli*, and *Wellington* [the Duke not the aircraft or the place.] Finally the name *Iron Duke* used by the LNWR, GWR and BR all referring to the Duke of Wellington. In the words of JGC, who takes up the story: 'Bulleid eventually opted for the name Sir Eustace Missenden to appear on another new Pacific, No. 34090 which received a special nameplate arrangement plus: green wheels and yellow tyres – but in so doing it overdid the whole effect. The naming ceremony was at Waterloo on 15 February 1949. Sir Eustace seldom showed any emotion, perhaps he was regretting letting OVB have a free hand with "Leader".' (A further illustration of this particular naming ceremony appeared opposite page 76 of the March 1949 issue of the *RO – see* also page 283). Click continues, 'The Brighton record book of nameplate drawings (full of detail for all the Light Pacifics built at the Sussex works) has no information on "Leader" type plates ever having been drawn and therefore cast, certainly they were never fitted.' Finally we should mention that the name Leader class was probably derived around this time in consequence of the choice for names, although it must be said names was surely a minor detail in the scheme of things. Whatever, the Leader class was sometimes in the early years corrupted to 'Leading' class although as time passed, failures mounted and costs grew, a corruption to the 'Bleeder' or 'Bleeding' class was also used. This time a reference to the conditions on board and once again to the costs involved. In the images we see an unsmiling Sir Eustace Missenden in the cab of No. 34090 (and a rather concerned looking fireman). The engine was also seen on display at the Ashford works open day a few months later; aesthetically the position of the large nameplate was less than ideal. *Spence Collection and Arthur Taylor*

At this stage we should bring in this mock-up produced by Brighton pattern-maker Dick Martin. It gives a guide as to the operation of the valve gear, sleeve and oscillating motion. The connecting rod is driven by a crank which pushes and pulls the cylinder as usual. At the same time the valve is driven in conventional form. A separate drive outside of the cylinder then taken it to the front of the cylinder where is basic terms it imparts a degree of axial rotation to the sleeves. Chain connections (of course!), the whole here shown in mid-gear. The subsequent fate of this model is not known. *John Click/ National Railway Museum*

himself. (Again comment attributable to JGC.) We should also repeat Bulleid's twin aims which were to return steam to favour and so save his Company the high initial costs associated with electrification.

For the sake of Leader, it was also fortunate that the Ministry of Labour had failed a few years earlier in late 1941 to sequestrate all Bulleid's designers to the Supermarine office at Hursley Park near Winchester for work on Spitfire modifications. Click again, 'They would have been used to mods all right, but making them fly? Yes: they'd have done well, but that would have been curtains for OVB's locos. He successfully resisted the Ministry somehow; on "Q1 design" and war work generally.' As an aside we might mention that three of Bulleid's senior draughtmen, Jim Allott, Dick Barnes, and Doug Smith – the last named taught maths at Southampton University by the great R.J. Mitchell himself – had all seen the maiden flight of the first Spitfire, K5054, from the Eastleigh drawing office in 1936. Doug Smith recalled being with the foreman in the erecting shop late at Eastleigh one evening investigating a broken rocking shaft on 'a "Merchant Navy" as yet another production "Spit", its Merlin throttled back, came in over the works from its first flight. "There are no b.... rocking shafts in that," the Foreman commented, pointing upwards!'

Certainly from late 1946 and then into 1947 onwards the major problems with the new design (not to be read as being in importance/date order) were:

1. Would sleeve valves be employed; No. 2039 was giving discouraging, or at best, inconclusive results. If sleeve valves did have to be dropped would the alternative arrangement with piston valves be feasible?
2. Could a stressed superstructure be devised – for this had been assumed since it had first been shown on W7169 (see p.53): the problems being adequate strength, getting the boiler in and out, lifting the superstructure with the boiler in position in the works;
and, worse, having to lift the loco complete with bogies following a derailment.
3. The boiler was fairly well settled, though nobody was happy with it yet.
4. Weight was getting critical and risked getting (or already was) out of control.
5. Costs were bound to be escalating frighteningly.
6. Time was running away.

Options couldn't be kept open indefinitely if only because of the time factor.

Click again, 'OVB must have come as close as he did to worrying in private. He never seemed to be a worrier, though. Cocks, brave man that he was, must have realised he would sooner or later have to go to his Chief with something like an ultimatum. He must have done so not much later than the end of 1947/start of 1948, saying that firm decisions could be delayed no longer on the above and many other details.

'Bulleid would have seen Cocks was right, without any rancour. The time had come all too quickly to steel himself and take the plunge, for better or for worse. The meeting must have been a long one, and on the sleeve valve issue OVB must have dug in pretty hard. He would also have analysed the causes of No. 2039's failures. *(Nowhere does JGC refer to a formal report having been compiled by the test section on the performance of No. 2039, and which as has been mentioned elsewhere, is certainly baffling, the nearest we have is that noted from Harry Attwell).* At the same time nobody was happy with the alternative "engine", except that it shortened the loco and would undoubtably result in less total weight.'

By this, do we take the word 'alternative' to mean a complete locomotive or an alternative to using sleeve valves? Probably the former but in which case 'which one' and the only conclusion has to be a reversion to one of the earlier 4-6-4T proposals.

Assembly, the date is 25 January 1949, leaving an awful lot to be done in less than five months. Here we have No. 2 (bunker) end with the side plating for the water tank yet to be added – to be welded, of course. The cross bracing within the water space is apparent as is the actual part that will given over to coal. The circular hole in the right end will later accommodate a water gauge. At Brighton Norman Dunster was the man who did the original General Arrangement drawing for the engine. *Don Broughton Collection*

JGC: 'I am sure that the one thing that made Bulleid feel confident in going ahead with sleeve valves was that a new material was going to be used: Meehanite, a cast iron in which the free carbon was distributed, not as random flakes of graphite, but as more concentrated nodules. In this way the valuable self-lubricating property of all cast irons was retained without the brittleness of cylinder iron. Sold as "high tensile" cast iron it was going to perform far better. Had there been time (!) a trial of a Meehanite sleeve on one side of No. 2039 would have helped the decision. Meehanite has come widely into use for motor-car crankshafts, where its performance has been excellent, Bulleid himself used it latterly in the valve gear three-throw shafts in his "Pacifics" where the cost saving compared with steel forgings was also very valuable indeed.'

Meanwhile the design of the oscillating gear had by then also come out right, at the start a seemingly almost impossible problem solved by Doug Smith. A point on each valve, seen from above, was required to perform a figure of eight; a need prescribed by Sir Harry Ricardo as a means of distributing lubricating oil and keeping wear within bounds. Hence it was a 'go' for sleeve valves.

The load bearing, stressed body, familiar enough nowadays (monocoque) was a pretty tall order then, inviting the most dreadful stress concentrations at many points and an enormous welding manipulator to do it well. OVB seems to have given way without too much struggle, though if it could have been done weight could again have been saved. As things turned out the alternative conventional frame was worryingly close to being overloaded, and barely stiff enough.

The boiler was already proportioned very much as it was to be built but originally there were only three syphons, so the firebox heating surface was rather less. During construction, three individual drums were run together into one crown and an extra syphon was then worked in. Their necks were later turned up into the barrel instead of entering a collector drum which might have rather invited an accumulation of dirt and also been difficult to wash out.

Notwithstanding what from an outsider's perspective may have appeared a long timescale, in engineering terms the period between 1946 and 1949 passed all too quickly. We know there were umpteen detail problems but with pressure mounting all the time to proceed at an ever-faster rate, many of these were dreadfully rushed so that quite simple mistakes made at this time caused annoying stoppages later on. Day-Lewis comments on the second engine, No. 36002, that with the lessons learnt from the first engine, No. 36002 would surely have been a better engine. Unlikely. Maybe the manufacturing process was no longer so rushed and so some failures could well have been eliminated, plus certain changes made to lessen failure in light of the experience of the first trials but, even so, one fundamental fact remains: No. 36002 and the other three from the initial build were to the same design; they would have displayed the same basic characteristics. It is absurd to suggest No. 36002 or her sisters might have performed any differently. (Perhaps this comment by Day-Lewis is another of the type Cox comments about.)

Interestingly but equally frustratingly, from mid-1948 the woodwork shop at Brighton was being more and more taken over by what looked like, 'a wooden whale washed up above the water line' (the words of JGC). This had started as a part mock-up of the Leader's centre section but ended being extended fore and aft to include the whole superstructure, also built to full size. Bulleid was known to like having a full-size mock-up of a favourite project that was currently on the go. Another was the third electric locomotive No. 20003, whilst earlier it had been a Merchant Navy cab, complete with fittings. *(What a great shame none of these survived, 36001 especially.)*

Click was shown the wooden Leader mock-up by Len Cox, with the former again taking up the story of what happened next: 'There was a sudden shout "Bulleid's coming" and taking the lead from Len, we both beat a hasty retreat by a devised escape route – why? I wish so much we had stayed; what could he have said, or done. This attitude came from somewhere – I think it was manufactured by those who interposed themselves between him and the lower ranks; left to himself OVB was a friendly, rather shy, man; willing, even anxious to know the points of view of others and not just his chief clerk.'

Perhaps some at Brighton may also have begun to have slight personal reservations. Admittedly the design ideology was admirable, but would the execution be good enough? Would the radical boiler brick walls hold up? It was vital that they did. Would the sleeve valves be better than those on 2039 – they needed to be, though in some ways the Leader's looked less good. (The latter JGC again.) Above all would everything, tried and untried, work 'with little or no attention at the sheds.' JGC amongst others – although he does not mention names – thought not. Click then adds a damming statement even at this stage, 'So did Motive Power as, little by little, they learned what was afoot.'

The fireman's cab seen from ground level. The fireman worked within a sunken well hence the firehole door is low to the ground. The gauge on the backhead was a recorder for when the TIA blowdown was operated. Almost directly ahead are the wheel controls for the two injectors; live steam and water. To the right of this is the coal chute from the bunker; this was to the side of the actual bunker and in service it is quite likely that jams would have occurred at some stage. Above the coal chute and to the right is the access door to the coal bunker. Many items have yet to be added including the Ajax firehole door. *John Click/National Railway Museum*

RIGHT This is a most unusual angle as it is looking out from where the firebox will later sit with the fire grate visible. Beyond is the bunker and several of the parts mentioned in the previous view. *John Click/National Railway Museum*

BELOW Exterior framing is now being added. The large oblong opening is where the side window will be located; originally drawn as having just two sliding panels as per the original Light Pacifics (*see* drawing on page 117), which were fitted with two windows. Leader however had three. *John Click/National Railway Museum*

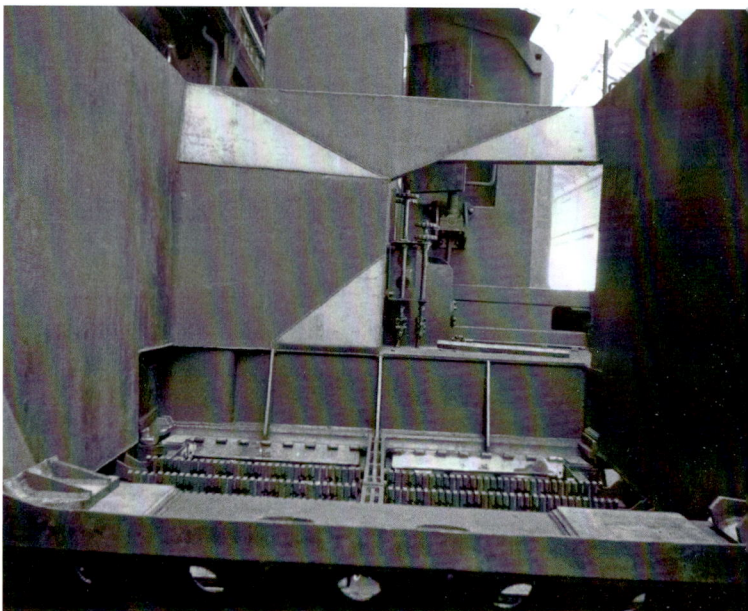

'He certainly kept everybody on their toes, but the frequent changes were very time-consuming. It has been described less kindly as "keeping everyone dancing on hot bricks" by one anonymous critic. Some would have agreed, but it also meant that alternatives were given every consideration, and that is what good design is about. U-turns can be part of the process too, and our Chief made plenty of those as well. It could be very frustrating and very stimulating too but the most serious aspect of it all was the time factor.

'In the early days at Eastleigh OVB was in and out of the drawing office like a cuckoo clock, never standing on ceremony, but talking freely to everyone including the most junior lads who benefitted enormously. He positively revelled in getting involved at the detail design level. His predecessor Maunsell had done the same thing but always through his Chief Draughtsman, careful never to infringe protocol. Bulleid was less careful, it seems, for he by no means always followed what long custom had decreed were "the proper channels". There can be no doubt that he unwittingly caused some hostility in some of the older and more senior men who had got very set in their ways. Equally he fired the enthusiasm of the up and coming generation whose loyalty was never afterwards in doubt.'

We have already mentioned the frustration at not being able to report a specific timeline so in general terms suffice it to say, draughtmen drew, welder's welded, and fitters fitted, subject to the changes that took place on the way, for as already stated, the detail design was also changed several times. As an example we need to look again at W7457, of September 1946, *see* page opposite, not seemingly shown to the Traffic Committee, and where the major change now is to the double-ended locomotive but also with corridor connections as per the latest design of the Southern electric, the 4COR family.

Interestingly perhaps, nowhere is there a mention of axle weights relative to W7457 although it cannot be assumed it was similar to the 16.15t on the earlier W7169 as on the former the boiler is now clearly seen to be offset. Had the original weights been maintained then the route availability envisaged by Bulleid could well have been achieved although could it also have been that the weights were deliberately left off W7457 owing the offset boiler and no one had yet calculated (or dared to calculate) the effect this could have had? Do not forget too than having an offset boiler in a steam engine was not unique to Leader. In America, there had already been a design where the boiler was offset from the centre line and without ever any difficulty over total engine weight or weight distribution. Indeed it is believed between 2,000 and 3,000 steam engines with an offset boiler were successfully worked in America. These were of course the Shay type. In this concept a balance between the offset boiler was created by having vertical cylinders and a solitary geared drive on one side only, the latter really only suitable for slow speed operation. Shays were used almost entirely for slow speed haulage on lightly laid track, invariably also involving timber haulage. But the offset boiler did work – it just had to be counterbalanced!

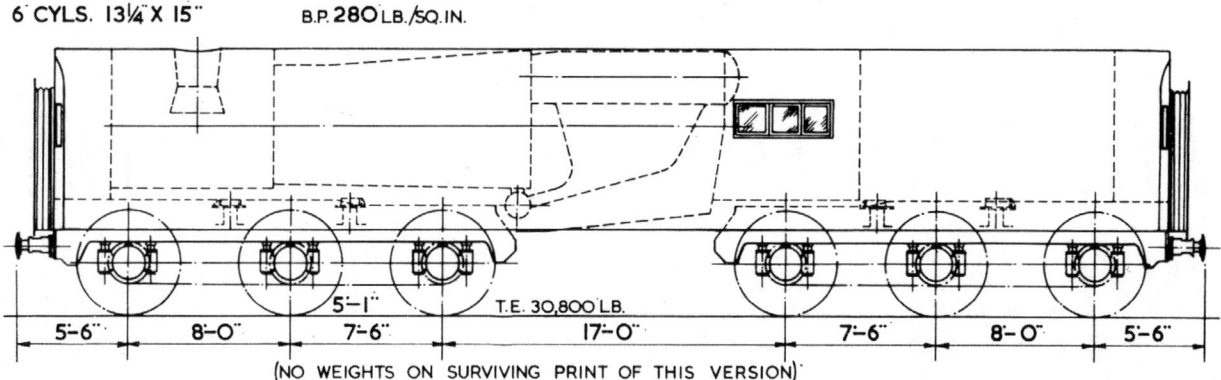

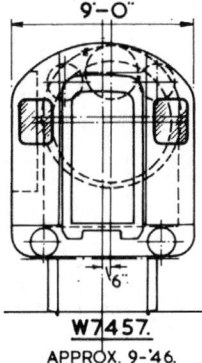

ABOVE Drawing 7457 from approximately September 1946. The concept has now morphed into a double-ended engine although the need for a corridor connection at either end is questionable. Certain of the principal items at least do appear fixed: the wheel diameter, boiler pressure and the offset boiler, but not as yet the engine length or cylinder diameter. There were several variations of this drawing.

Although not perhaps originally anticipated, at some stage too the dry back firebox had become part of the design, as mentioned by Bulleid at varying stages previously. We have already referred to the first steam test for this design of boiler and it is reasonable to assume at least four of the five boilers built were similarly tested. (The first four had been installed within their respective frames so would have been tested before this took place, progress on No. 36005 though at the time the order was received to curtail work was such that this was little more than an (incomplete) kit of parts and as such it is quite possible boiler No. 5 may never even have received a steam test. Bulleid also applied for a patent to cover the new boiler design. In the event the patent was not actually issued until 21 January 1949 – No. 616.445, which was formally stated as covering 'Improvements relating to locomotive and like steam boilers'. We can probably say, perhaps slightly sadly too, that he was never likely to have received any royalties in consequence of someone else using the design.

Bulleid's previously stated aims for the new design also now need to be referred to again: 'both men will be able to carry out their duties seated' but how, unless oil firing was to be used surely this was an impossible task? Click suggest it was the traffic department that vetoed that idea and in the event, history would also prove them right as '… soon after the government scheme fell through'. These few words also then give us a useful clue as to the timescale at this point; the Summer–Autumn of 1948. Summertime for

Moving forward we come to the front of the boiler and the fabricated smokebox. The flange previously referred to has now been boxed in and will form part of the regulator assembly – the two control rods (front cab regulator and ditto for the rear) combine here to the actual regulator which was within the smokebox. (*See also the boiler views in the shops from Reg Curl.*) This in No. 36001 and yet on the barrel of the boiler there is no 'photographic grey' paint: proof perhaps that the first boiler was not the one used with No. 36001. *John Click/National Railway Museum*

when the order came through to suspend further work on the depot infrastructure and locomotive oil conversions, and the start of October for when the last regular turns with oil-fired engines came to an end. There was one exception to this, West Country No. 34036 which was still at work burning oil until September 1949 and for which Waterloo received a smack on the wrist from Marylebone. The Southern had got away with it on the basis it had been 'to try out a different type of burner and so gain experience if oil were ever to be used again in the future.' Really? I think it would be just as safe to say this was Bulleid still hoping! (Again the reader is referred to *Southern Way Special No. 17* mentioned in the bibliography.)

With this plea from the traffic department for coal burning no doubt ringing in his ears (probably so as not to restrict the sphere of operation to depots where oil would have been available), we can also begin to understand why the boiler is now offset – a communication channel between the driver and fireman. A practical asset? Doubtful, and although lagged it would take a brave man to want to venture between the firing and driving cabs whilst moving at speed. (John Click refers to several trips on Leader whilst on test later but only once does he mention progressing down the corridor when the engine was in motion – *see* p.182). Not mentioned anywhere is the possibility a mechanical stoker for coal firing using an Archimedean screw. Was it considered a complication or was there simply no way of sourcing the requisite equipment at the time in the late 1940s? (One had been fitted to No. 35005 since March 1948, albeit second-hand.)

Recall too that back with diagram W7169 of 1 May 1946 – in chronological terms that date seems an awfully long time ago – we see mention of space for the Holcroft/Anderson condensing system. Holcroft himself makes little mention of this addition in the biography and similarly talks little of work with Bulleid, but again care must be taken not to attempt to draw conclusions just because individuals fail to mention each other.

What we do have though is another definite reference to feed water heating, an idea that was not in the end carried forward to the prototype. This particular aspect was not in itself unduly complicated and would have given the added advantage that perhaps less water might have been needed to be carried – less weight of water also equals less overall weight. It is perhaps likely that feed water heating facility was, in the end, not included as greater benefit could be achieved with TIA water treatment and which would be more beneficial to an engine working in the south of England where much of the feed water itself was hard – recall the tall water softening plants at Brighton and Eastleigh for example. Unfortunately TIA water treatment is also not compatible with feed water containing any globules of oil and which would inevitably have been the case with the Holcroft/Anderson system. Yes, an oil separator could have been incorporated and similarly hot water pumps instead of injectors fitted if required, but each added a new level of complexity and for only a marginal improvement more than offset by the cost of the fittings and maintenance thereof. For once Bulleid wisely decided to play safe and conventional cold water injectors and TIA water treatment were provided.

Around this time, 1948 onwards, it was also perhaps quite natural that rumour would start to circulate outside and amongst the enthusiast fraternity – although certainly at this stage no actual images of the construction seem to have been published. From the enthusiasts' perspective this might be considered strange as certainly there were society visits and even an official Open Day at Brighton works, later held on 24 November 1949, when nearly 1,000 visitors attended. Might it have been as simple as photography was discouraged – Click's example of his own experiences – although we certainly know the official photographer visited on occasions. But even if photography was discouraged, who was against it? The obvious candidate is the Works Manager, Mr Granshaw, with his instructions perhaps vicariously passed down to the shop floor. However, the present writer has nothing to substantiate this particular hypothesis, except for the known behaviour during that interval, as described by John Click, although we should take care to explain this may equally have been drawing office versus workshop rivalry.

But even if photography were prohibited in some form or other, some individuals managed to evade that prohibition. John Click took pictures, as we know, but there are also those taken by an unknown individual and which form part of the Don Broughton Collection. Examples from both form part of the photo selection contained within this work. In addition there are contemporary reports within the *Railway Observer* of works visits and mention made of the construction. These same reports must have been read with some amazement by others, for not only was there nothing to compare the design with, but mere words are hard to find to describe what was such a novel machine.

Outside of the enthusiast circle, murmurings were starting to circulate as to how the Leader design might operate in service – with the first concerns raised over the potential isolation of the crew. We may take this to mean from a safety perspective but it must be recalled that no such reservations appear to have been raised over 'pull-push' operation and where the fireman might spend half his shift, or on occasions even more time, separated from his driver. If the reservation was instead related to the driver being on his own, then clearly the situation as applied to the motorman of an electric train had also been forgotten. More serious but seemingly not reported at the time was the potential for injury to a member of the crew separate from his mate, but again could not the same thing again also be said reference 'pull-push' trains?

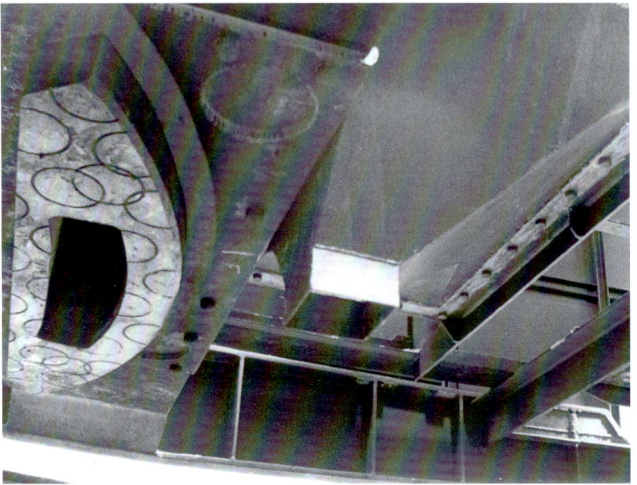

Another unusual angle. We are looking up from ground level with the rectangular opening seeing the ash chute from the smokebox. On the left is the part of the Mintex pads that will rub on a similar pad on top of the bogie; no centre pivots for the bogies. Consequently this is No. 1 end. *John Click/National Railway Museum*

The Race Against Time

The first of the more technical journals to pick up on what was happening at Brighton was *Modern Transport*, which included what was almost a resume of the design ambitions. As such it was thus made 'public' but remember *MT* was not widely circulated outside the technical engineering field and in consequence the masses would still have to wait awhile yet. Much that was reported was also similar to Bulleid's earlier presidential address.

Modern Transport comments (and it is almost a re-write of Bulleid's earlier lecture):

> In the early days of railways the locomotives were purchased from outside builders and the railway company was content to operate them and allow them to be maintained by the builder … In order that the repairs could be done economically the necessary machine tools and other equipment were provided gradually and it was soon appreciated that this equipment was equally suited in manufacturing new locomotives … it will inevitably be suggested that the accepted methods of design or construction cannot be expected to give substantially better results. That is to say, the results were as good as could be expected with the designs, materials, finish, and methods of operation which were used. Consequently if we are to reach the higher level of achievement in continuity of service, which is now required, a new conception of the steam locomotive is also needed. Such thoughts caused us to question the accepted ideas and forced us to investigate the locomotive as regards, (1) design, (2) use and (3) servicing. The very age of the steam locomotive has acted against its further development for its bad features have come to be accepted as inherent and inevitable. It is these bad features which enable other forms of transport to compete with it and consequently such features must be eliminated if the steam locomotive is to survive. Our investigations soon satisfied us there that was room for improvement under all three heads …
>
> What sort of locomotive may we expect to see if it is to meet the majority of our future requirements? …
>
> The locomotive should be built
> (1) to be run over the majority of the company lines;
> (2) to be capable of working all classes of train up to 90mph;
> (3) to have its whole weight available for braking and the highest percentage thereof for adhesion;
> (4) to be equally suited for running in both directions without turning with unobstructed look-out;
> (5) to be ready for service at short notice;
> (6) to be almost continually available;
> (7) to be suited for complete 'common use';
> (8) to run not less than 100 000 miles between general overhauls with little or no attention at the running sheds;
> (9) to cause minimum wear and tear to the track; and
> (10) to use substantially less fuel and water per drawbar horsepower developed. …

Assembly is progressing in this undated overhead view taken from one of the shop cranes. A quick glance might almost appear to show Leader as a conventional machine: a boiler and firebox with a tender behind. There are several points to note in the image. Firstly, the smokebox/boiler being offset to the left; next the (Idaglass) lagging that has been applied, including to the front of the smokebox door; this as much intended to retain heat as to keep the front (No. 1) cab from becoming excessively hot – something that did not work in practice. (We can also appreciate why it was not always easy to confirm the smokebox door was fully closed covered as it was in lagging.) Turn now to the shape of the smokebox top. As mentioned before this only needed to be functional and by flattening the top there was a place for the 25in of vacuum reservoirs – *see* the mechanical description later in Appendix 2. The shape of the smokebox door; very much-à-la Gresley A4 as illustrated in the next image is apparent. Finally observe the length of the frame ahead of the smokebox. No. 1 cab was considerably longer than No. 2, the metal framing later covered by wooden boards. A limited amount of asbestos packing was also used, but we are not told where or in what context.
John Click/National Railway Museum

The Gresley A4, the external cloak purportedly one of Bulleid's responsibilities whilst he was on the LNER. The basic smokebox door design was very similar to that on Leader although here the reason was not due to overhead vacuum cylinders but the shape of the top casing. (The engine depicted is No. 60008 *Dwight D. Eisenhower,* appropriately at Southampton being prepared for shipment to the USA and preservation. The front external cover of the casing ahead of the smoke door has also been temporarily removed.)

Side view of boiler and smokebox, lagged and this time with the pipework taking live steam from the steam fountain to the injectors shown. Ribs to support the casing have also been added. Of particular note is the 'mantle-tank' seen on the side of the firebox. This was a late addition to the design and was intended as much as a buffer against heat alongside the corridor and around the rear of the boiler/firebox. It added little to the overall water capacity of the engine and sadly failed in its intended purpose of dissipating heat in the area of the fireman's cab. The mantle tank also acted as a useful shelf for the fire-irons (and keeping the fireman's tea can warm.)

A new type of Southern engine has been designed, the construction of five has been authorised. The engine will incorporate the following features and it is hoped will satisfy the design criteria given above. The locomotive is carried on two six wheeled bogies the general design of which follows that of the bogies designed for use under the company's electric locomotives. ... The engine develops a torque the uniformity of which is comparable with that of a nose suspended electric traction motor but has a higher speed range and the unsprung weight is less. The capacity of the boiler has been made greater, relative to the cylinder horsepower than in the case of any previous Southern locomotive. The cabs at the ends will give an improved lookout. The engines are intended for working fast passenger trains of 480 tons weight over the difficult Southern Railway main line, and goods and mineral trains of up to 1,200 tons; that is to say, something aboove the heaviest trains that would be required on the system. They carry sufficient fuel for 200 miles....

It could almost have seemed as if the Southern Railway would end its days as a private company and enter public ownership as the one company which had pushed modern steam locomotive design further than any other. Perhaps even privately this was the bequest that certain staff and officials might also have wished for, certainly some of those at Brighton. Regardless too of the reservations that might persist over the new design, eventual success was taken for granted and it mattered not that there still issued a stream of both ideas and ideals that should – and perhaps more importantly – would be incorporated.

One of these was for the idea of an interchangeable power bogie, a laudable concept and one which was perfectly easy to achieve and feasible from an engineering perspective – simply lift the engine at one end, disconnect the necessary steam inlet and exhaust pipes together with lubrication and vacuum pipes, and wheel the bogie out. From a cost perspective a far greater fleet than the initial five engines would be needed to both justify maintaining such major spares and, more importantly perhaps, incorporating them in the design. This very concept – the interchange of bogies – was in the end never undertaken with 36001 but, as mentioned in what follows later, it might well have made a difference if it had! The idea of a removeable engine unit was another ideal but not

ABOVE From the internal corridor looking towards the cab at No. 1 end. Much fitting our remains to be undertaken but some indication of the inside view is apparent along with the curvature of the base of the smokebox and the prominent regulator handle. Aside from sliding access doors on either side of the cab, the central window could also outward opening. Notice the cross bracing at the front – the external sheeting being just 22swg thick. *John Click/National Railway Museum*

RIGHT Within the side corridor, this time we are looking from the front cab (No. 1 end) towards the firing compartment and beyond to No. 2 cab. No floor has yet been added. *John Click/National Railway Museum*

proceeded with, it would be with 'Leader Mk2' later. (Spare boilers were available for certain steam classes so it was not much of a step forward. In addition certain diesel and electric locomotives and units did in later years under BR and the privatised operators, adopt the removable bogie and indeed engine, policy.)

Possibly the concept of a fleet of engines based on the Leader design would have been the thing to justify on cost grounds, spare bogies, etc., came nearest as a result of a Southern Railway Board minute from November 1947 at which a further thirty-one Leader class engines were authorised for construction – this again before the first had ever turned a wheel. It would seem neither Richards nor any of his more sceptical colleagues would appear to have objected much either. Perhaps the fight had gone – after all nationalisation loomed and consequently, for now at least,

From the side on 19 April 1949, we see the massive timber trestles which are presently supporting the upper works. These trestles would later be transported to Eastleigh at the time of the failure of the crank axle. Note the general colour of the engine being an overall grey; this being the colour of the unpainted metal.
Don Broughton Collection

The front cab has now been added to which a sliding roof vent and the whistle have been attached. Holes have also been cut in the plating for what will be the marker lights. Alongside the rotating frame is also visible with a bogie/cylinders undergoing attention and beyond on the right the sides of a bogie frame seemingly painted white/grey.

Very nearly complete: engine and bogies in the process of being united. We have no indication that as the design developed there was ever a time when Bulleid returned to the various senior officers' meeting with updated/revised drawings. He certainly would have been back to further meetings between 1946 and 31 December 1947 and likely later too as the Southern Region began to sort itself out under a unified British Railways. It would also be naïve to suggest the topic of the new design was never mentioned again – questions would surely have been asked as to progress – more likely it was seemingly not reported. Still to be added are the Alton flexible corrugated steam pipes between the main structure and the cylinders. Within the text we have mentioned the secrecy that surrounded the project in certain quarters although as we know occasional open days and society visits took place at Brighton and Eastleigh where it was clear to many that something very different was going on. (RCTS records show official visits to Brighton during the first six months of 1949 to have taken place on 26 February and 28 May, and to Eastleigh on 19 February and 14 May.) Even so not all were party to the technical papers/general periodicals but the *Railways Gazette* did, sometime in early 1949, reproduce a 'snapshot obtained by stealth' which was the first indication most people had of the appearance of Leader. (Quote from *Rail Centres Brighton* by B.J. Cooper.) We regret that with the majority of this text being written whilst the UK was under lockdown in 2020/2021 the opportunity to clarify exactly which issue of the *Railway Gazette* was involved is simply not possible. *British Railways*

it appeared that no less than thirty-six Leaders were to be built – and straight off the drawing board.

According to G. Freeman Allen (*see* Appendix 1), the effect of ordering the additional engines was to display an almost 'hands off' notice to the newly nationalised system. But it would backfire. This was simply too much for what was then still a totally untried design. Accordingly one of the first decisions of the newly formed Railway Executive was to rescind the building approval for the additional thirty-one engines. Bulleid might still have an ally at headquarters in the form of Missenden but perhaps even he could now see the need for a degree of caution. Possibly if the order had been for a lesser number, six for example, it might have been approved. As it was in the short space of time between November 1947 when the thirty-one were approved, and the cancellation in the early part of 1948 (the actual date is not known), no material was ever ordered and consequently no work started.

The year 1948 at the new British Railways was also a testing time. The huge new organisation would take some time to settle, and very wisely the man in charge of Mechanical Engineering at the Railway Executive, Robin Riddles, decided to allow the now four 'regions' autonomy – whilst the dust settled. That is not to say he did not keep a watching brief on progress at Brighton, regular reports being expected – likely too a similar eye on the output of the other regions.

One of the concerns relative to Brighton was the spiralling costs. Quoted in July 1948 as being £87,000 for the five engines, this was increased by 15% just two months later to £100,000. It would eventually rise still further, which at the time was double the cost of producing

Painting in progress and a black undercoat applied. We can be certain of this as the time taken to reverse the process was literally one day and yet here much in the way of detail, but essentials components still need to be added. This includes pipework from the loco to the front buffer beam, the lower covers to the chain drive, and the dustcover on the front oscillating gear. We are looking at No. 2 (bunker) end. *Don Broughton Collection*

ABOVE AND RIGHT The remarkable images of the first and only Leader to appear in glossy black, recorded inside Brighton works on 20 June 1949. The views are not retouched or altered in any way. Despite the passage of time these must remain two of the most amazing images of the engine; what a great pity she did not run in this condition complete with lining and insignia. Doubt remains but could No. 36001 actually be in steam as well? The black paint had been applied on the instructions of the drawing office but it was Bulleid who had it changed to 'workshop grey' in a tradition going back into the mists of time. (Grey was used as it showed up better in photographs.) *Don Broughton Collection*

a comparable size and power steam engine to an existing conventional design. Small wonder then that the project was unofficially referred to as 'Bleeder' within the offices at Waterloo and Marylebone – a somewhat cruel reference to its escalating cost base. Indeed one unnamed official when asked if there was concern over the cost of the project is reported to have replied, 'worried is not the word'.

Overall it still appears as if it was a close-run thing in presenting the new British Railways with a project already sufficiently advanced that it was worthy of continuing. Had construction work not actually started, and the design only existed on paper, it is quite probable 36001 would never have materialised. Therein perhaps lies some of the reasons for failure, which are discussed in far greater detail in a subsequent chapter – the whole thing was a rush job! Under Bulleid, his unique series of numbering (not favoured by Nicholson!) was also to have been applied and appropriately because of the six-wheeled bogies, the engines would have become CC101–5.

So it was to be under British Railways and not the independent Southern Railway that Leader No. 36001 was eventually completed. The finished design was very different indeed, both mechanically and aesthetically, from Diagram W7326. At least the idea of a corridor connection had not been pursued from some of the earlier proposals! But in its place the host of technical innovations almost invited difficulty. Never before had a steam engine of such avowed complexity, novelty and with so many untried features succeeded. Indeed many of the design features had never been tried either, and those that had had been attempted by Paget and on the two guinea-pig engines had not always worked particularly well either.

Bulleid though and his team still appear to have been charged with optimism even if the messages from 2039 were disappointing. So much depended upon success for the project. Leader needed to succeed if only to justify all the effort that had been put in. There was so much to aim for and so little time to do it in.[3]

Notes

(1) *See also* the full correspondence between Nicholson and the present writer at Appendix 3.

(2) Lt.-Col Harold Rudgard OBE TD MIME (c.1885–1958) was Chief Officer (Motive Power) at the nationalised Railway Executive and a former Superintendent of Motive Power on the LMS. Rudgard will again feature later at the time of No. 36001's abortive attempt to haul a train to London.

(3) Sir Eustace Missenden relinquished the role of General Manager in October 1947 and instead took a post on the new Railway Executive. He was succeeded at Waterloo by John (later Sir John) Elliot. Bulleid would then have had dealings with the new General Manager after October 1947 and it is believed both men enjoyed an excellent working relationship. Bulleid also now had the advantage of a useful ally on the newly formed Executive. In his published autobiography, Sir John Elliot makes no mention of the Leader project.

8
From Brighton to Eastleigh
(More than Once) and Back to Brighton Again

Following on from the 'entertainment' within the works the previous day, the first Leader, No. 36001, finally emerged into public gaze on Tuesday 21 June 1949, a full two years later than had been intended for the prototype. One of the reasons she had been so reluctant to leave the comparative safety of 'inside' was also now revealed, the whole engine being so much longer than anything seen before. It had in fact struck, and then stuck, on the curved exit road leading from the erecting shop; the timber framing to the workshop doors had to be removed to allow her to emerge. Likely one of the reasons this occurred was simply that nothing as long as this had ever been in the works before – conventional steam engines were built around a shorter wheelbase.

In what was a smart and clean grey livery, No. 36001 remained where she stood outside the works throughout the day, simmering quietly. She would remain in steam in the same place overnight; presumably a fireman was sent over from the running shed to tend to her needs.

The *Railway Observer* for July 1949 reported on her appearance outside the works on that day with an unnamed correspondent adding: 'Very similar externally to the electric locomotive No. 20003 … although the larger wheels do create a somewhat top-heavy appearance'. At the same time the uninitiated were commenting about appearance of 'the new diesel locomotive'. To match the grey-painted body, no lining or insignia was present, the bogies were black, whilst numberplates were yet to be fitted. John Click adds his own comment to the subject of appearances, 'OVB was in two minds at least, as to whether he wanted an electric loco to look like a steam one or the other way about; but as we know he eventually settled, quite rightly, for the latter.'

Wednesday 22 June was when she would move again, the short distance to the station and then to reverse to the shed coaling road – or that was the plan. She arrived in the middle road on the west side of the station without much fuss but then would not reverse again. With live conductor rails everywhere, this was no place for pinch bars so she was picked up and towed on to the shed where she was indeed coaled and but then taken back to the works……*the saga had begun*.

Had this disappointment not occurred, the plan had been to leave No. 36001 on the running shed overnight and then to run the first trial the next day from Brighton Station, in similar way to the earlier tests with 2039, where the trials would replicate normal station-to-station working.

John Click comments that back inside the works the fault that was preventing a reversal was traced to the

No. 36001 At Brighton in the days between her first public appearance on 21 June and her move to Eastleigh five days later. In the interim she made one light engine trip (in company with an E4 for 'insurance') to Falmer and Groombridge. This was achieved without incident. Notice the lack of numberplates. Midnight oil was burned to get No. 36001 ready for her public (official) unveiling at Eastleigh on 28 June. With its offset chimney, Leader would have had the same effect on decades of soot and smoke quietly languishing under bridges and on the roof of tunnels as did No. 783 a few years earlier. *V. Evans*

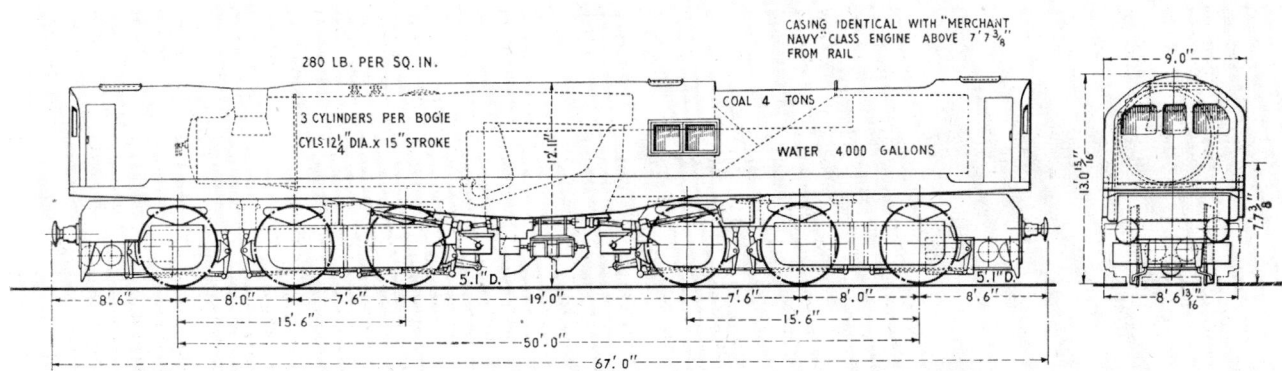

This drawing of the new design appeared in the January/February 1949 issue of *Railway Magazine*, accompanying a brief article on the type which described the design but also placed great emphasis on TIA treatment generally. Note the slight differences in design of the windows for the fireman's cab and the driver's doors, the fireman's compartment having no obvious point of entry/exit. The comment concerning the casing being identical with that of a Merchant Navy above the specified height is not explained further. There were no side windows in the sliding doors although fixed ones were shown in one diagram. At the time there was a belief that the driver might be affected by a form of strobe effect from seeing scenery rushing past the corner of his eye when travelling at speed. Why it should be thought of now is not clear, as such an effect was evidently not considered an issue in EMU cabs. It was for the same reason that several of the early main line diesel classes were built with a bonnet at the front; but not the Bulleid/English Electric diesels Nos. 10201–3. A case of 'do as I say rather than as I do' perhaps?

The final design of the engine. Note the differences compared with the above drawing but, also that no steps are shown leading to the fireman's compartment from outside – these were provided on the actual engine. A particular point of interest is how on this drawing the lining panels together with the number decals at the ends (as per the actual livery from July 1949 onwards) are shown. Might this drawing have been prepared retrospectively? The axle weights have also increased somewhat from the originally planned 16.15t. In all, a might different from W7326, (*see* page 57) upon which original approval had been given.

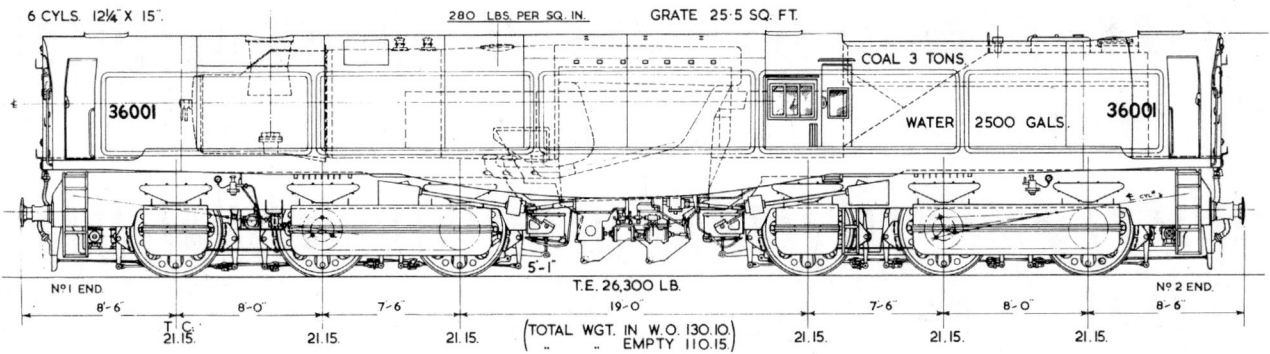

tubular valve operating rod for the middle sleeve on No. 1 bogie (smokebox end) being broken, whilst at the same time the oscillating gear associated with the sleeve to the same cylinder was bent. Click adds, 'it had buckled under compression very much as many of us had feared it would. It was probably this damage that caused the mystery bang as she was pulled out. Subsequently there were several other similar failures but the problem receded when the tube walls were thickened as they needed to be replaced.' Click does not go on to explain how it was that the sleeve mechanism had any direct relation to the reversing problem, unless he may in fact be referring to the position of the cut-off. The defective items were repaired/replaced, in the case of the latter parts possibly taken from one of the other engines of the type under construction or even stored as stock in hand. (Again in the RO for July 1949, the same correspondent reported that work was progressing on the next two engines, which would be Nos 36002 and 36003.)

Interestingly this failure was only the first problem to affect No. 1 bogie (No. 1 bogie was under No. 1 end, the smokebox end of the locomotive). Indeed some time earlier when this bogie at least was complete inside the works, Granshaw had the wheels and axles raised off the ground and steam supplied to the sleeves and consequently the pistons from a stationary source. At a low pressure of just 8psi it ran 'smoothly and sweetly – like a sewing machine' (quote from H.A.V. Bulleid, p.142), that is to say the sleeves, pistons, oscillating gear, crank-axle and chains moved without hesitation or difficulty. He then instructed a similar trial be carried out in reverse but, perhaps in a hurry or simply not noticing, failed to wait for the forward movement to cease. The effect of steam working against the existing mechanism was to cause the bent or broken components. Bulleid was evidently none the wiser.

Returning briefly to that first experience at Brighton Station, this failure to reverse was destined to become a not uncommon problem later but for other reasons, the steam cylinder mounted centrally underneath the main frames and intended to reverse the direction of both bogies simultaneously being notoriously unreliable. Again whether this was design failure, manufacturing fault or anything else was never established. Similar criticism – design/manufacture, etc., was later applied to other components, all of which issues could well have been overcome if desired. We should also recall 'reversing' did not just mean a change of direction, a functioning reversing gear was essential to ensure the economic use of steam when moving. But to be safe, a large crowbar was regularly carried on the engine soon after – and of course at least one extra man, a fitter.

Three days, from 22 to 25 June, were spent in the works but on the latter date No. 36001 emerged for her first main line trial. This was 'light' to Oxted and Groombridge via Lewes and coupled to an E4 tank. Leader though was doing the work and no mechanical problems were encountered, a record of the day showing that the steep 1:60 gradient out of Lewes was accomplished with ease, although to be fair it should have been anyway, as this was running (almost) light engine.

Another Comic Stage

At Groombridge a stop was made for water, and now it was discovered that the station water column would not reach out and over the high profile of the engine to where the filler cap was located – atop the roof. This was no fault of the design, purely a simple oversight that no one had considered the means of replenishment. By this stage on the day water was urgently required, which left two options – either drop the fire, or attempt some other means of refilling. The latter was the choice, by means of a small hose attached to a tap in the porters' office, but it took a very long time. It was obvious the rest of the run could not be completed in this fashion as the same problems would have occurred at Oxted, consequently there was no choice but to abandon the trial for the day and return to Brighton. A quick 'Heath Robinson' compromise of a copper chute and extension leather bag was carried on all later tests and so, in effect, extending the reach of the Central section water columns. (Another solution would have been to have water filler locations 'amidships' as per some of the first-generation main line diesel locomotives, which still needed to take on water for what was the steam heat boilers although this would probably have reduced the amount of water able to be carried.)

Meanwhile arrangements had been made (perhaps instructions issued?) that No. 36001 was to travel to Eastleigh the next day to be ready for inspection by the Association of Locomotive Engineers two days later on 28 June.

Leader, having travelled from Brighton, this time with a K for company, arrived at Eastleigh shed without issue on the way. (Click perhaps gives a clue here as he states No. 36001 had been keeping 'just a wisp of steam on all the way'. Are we perhaps a bit cruel to suggest this was deliberate in the hope she might arrive without incident?) Then Leader was shunted the short distance from the shed to the works yard by a D15. The contrast could not have been greater; the clean and latest 'modern' engine against the 37 year old 4-4-0. Even so the old stalwart would have the last laugh, outliving its young interloper by four years. Bulleid's choice for 'photographic grey' was hardly conducive to a working steam engine as per the accumulation of soot and smoke stains around the chimney.

The engine has now been shunted into the works yard and is stabled in front of the office block. She is yet to receive the attention of the painters. An illustration of Leader also appeared on p206 of the August 1949 edition of the *RO*.

Subsequently, upon its return to Brighton, Leader was taken back into the works again to be prepared. JGC adds a note, 'It was touch and go … and a team of foremen and fitters worked all night. Bulleid had got the canteen ladies to lay on a midnight supper and a local agency photographer to record the event. On an occasion like this, OVB was completely without "side" – for want of a better word. Everyone present would have treasured the rare personal contact they made that night…'.

Click's comments are interesting as they could be taken two ways. Where he says '…touch and go', this implies there were problems to resolve. But what were these, as aside from the water issue there is no mention of any difficulties on that first Groombridge trip? Unfortunately despite much searching we have been unable to locate the Agency/Press photographer, and consequently the image(s) involved.

With cast number plates proclaiming 36001 (there were two – one at either end) now fitted but still with no other insignia or identification, the engine set off on 26 June bound for Eastleigh and this time accompanied by a K class 2-6-0, No. 32343. Originally it was believed No. 36001 was again doing all the work but JGC tends to imply otherwise: 'No. 36001 keeping just a wisp of her own steam on all the way,' perhaps caution was the word. However, the journey along the coast route via Worthing, Chichester, and Botley to Eastleigh passed without incident. At the running shed she was serviced as necessary and retained in light steam.

Inspection was due two days later on 28 June and we know she was cleaned and repainted in the works yard before the VIP visit – but on what day, 26, 27 or even the 28th of June? When complete she was moved around to stand in front of the works offices although, as stated, on what day is not certain. What we do know is that when this move took place it was a shunt move undertaken by a somewhat grimy D15, No. (30)464. The contrast between Leader, still at this time in relativly clean 'shop grey', and the somewhat sad-looking Drummond engine was accentuated by the contrasting liveries. To be fair, almost forty years also separated the designs.

A repaint/retouch once more to grey in the open air outside the works (or was it just a clean?) was unusual on two counts, firstly because only a few days before the engine had been painted in grey inside Brighton (we know it was only a few days previous because she had been seen complete but in black inside Brighton on 21 June) and secondly because this was being done out in the open air, fortunately the weather gods were smiling. Perhaps it was the combination of a 'touch-up' and a clean as certainly the grime around the area of the chimney appears to have been removed by the time the official images of 28 June were taken, whilst in addition the engine was also now sporting the first BR 'cycling lion' emblem mid-way along either side, plus the identification 36001 in transfers immediately underneath. There was no lining out, although to enhance the overall appearance the wheel tyres were painted white – for which purpose and to cover the whole circumference, she would have had to have been moved at some time.

It was also during this time that the official photographer was active (as indeed he had been during the build process at Brighton) whilst various unofficial images were also recorded, including what remain the only two known colour views of the engine, both from the camera of Stephen Townroe. (Some unofficial black-and-white views were taken the same day by works staff who ventured out to see what the engine was, this after the official party had gone to luncheon.)

For the formal inspection, the VIPs had travelled down in reserved accommodation on the 8.30am from Waterloo. Upon arrival at Eastleigh they were taken by bus from the station to the works.

Whether the visit was just to see the new engine is not clear, but we do know those present included at least Messrs (Robin) Riddles and (Roland) Bond from Marylebone Road, plus former company CMEs, Messrs Stanier, Ivatt,

Peppercorn and Hawksworth (although Click remarked he could never find the GWR man). Bulleid would also have been present but nowhere is he specifically mentioned or indeed identified. For the benefit of the 'great and the good' she was in light steam and was moved up and down the yard, which was achieved without incident. Riddles also drove her in the yard and was said (by Click) to have described the engine as 'an unqualified success'. Click adds further, '… this was told me by someone who should have been reliable and claimed to have heard him (Riddles) say so.' But tantalisingly nowhere does Click identify who this person was! The party later travelled back to Waterloo late that afternoon from Southampton, courtesy of the Up *Bournemouth Belle*.

Until now the astute reader will no doubt have noticed that the name of Bulleid has rarely been mentioned relative to the first runs of Leader and it can only be conjecture as to the whereabouts of the designer at this time. Certainly he would have been appraised on a regular basis as to progress and this would continue for some time. Interestingly a contemporary note gives the impression that Bulleid had, in the last few months at least, become somewhat impatient with the (lack of) progress in completing the first engine. This supports an alleged comment that at the time 36001 first emerged from Brighton, he had impatiently decided Eastleigh should fit the multiple valve rings as Brighton had complained of difficulty with this task. In any case, Brighton must have managed the task as there is no record, written or photographic, of the engine enveloped in steam as would certainly have been the case on these first trips either on the way to Groombridge or at Eastleigh.

The great and the good (52 in total) posed in front of No. 36001, which has been moved back close to her original stabling point. (JGC adds, '…the most important VIPS had positioned themselves in the centre.') The group included the other former company CMEs as well as the hierarchy from Marylebone with JGC in his notes referring to the gathering as 'a conference'. This is perhaps not quite correct due to the limited time the group would actually be together but he goes on to add 'Everyone of note was invited and most turned up…. "Leader" plainly the *piece de resistance*.' The engine was in light steam and at some point was moved up and down the works yard – perhaps on more than one occasion. Riddles also drove her in the yard and was said (by Click) to have described the engine as 'an unqualified success'. Click adds further, 'this was told me by someone who should have been reliable and claimed to have heard him (Riddles) say so.' But tantalisingly nowhere in his memories does Click identify who this person was.

Photographing the photographer: On the extreme left is the bus that had brought the party from the station to the works and would later be used to return them to Southampton for the up 'Bournemouth Belle'.

John Click was also present at Eastleigh for part of the time and has recorded his own view of No. 1 end which also gives a good idea of the front cab handrails, the rain strip above the front windows and the six lamp brackets/marker lights. In the centre of the right hand group – presumably the man with the cap – is Alf Woods, the Eastleigh works driver.

THE LEADER LOCOMOTIVE

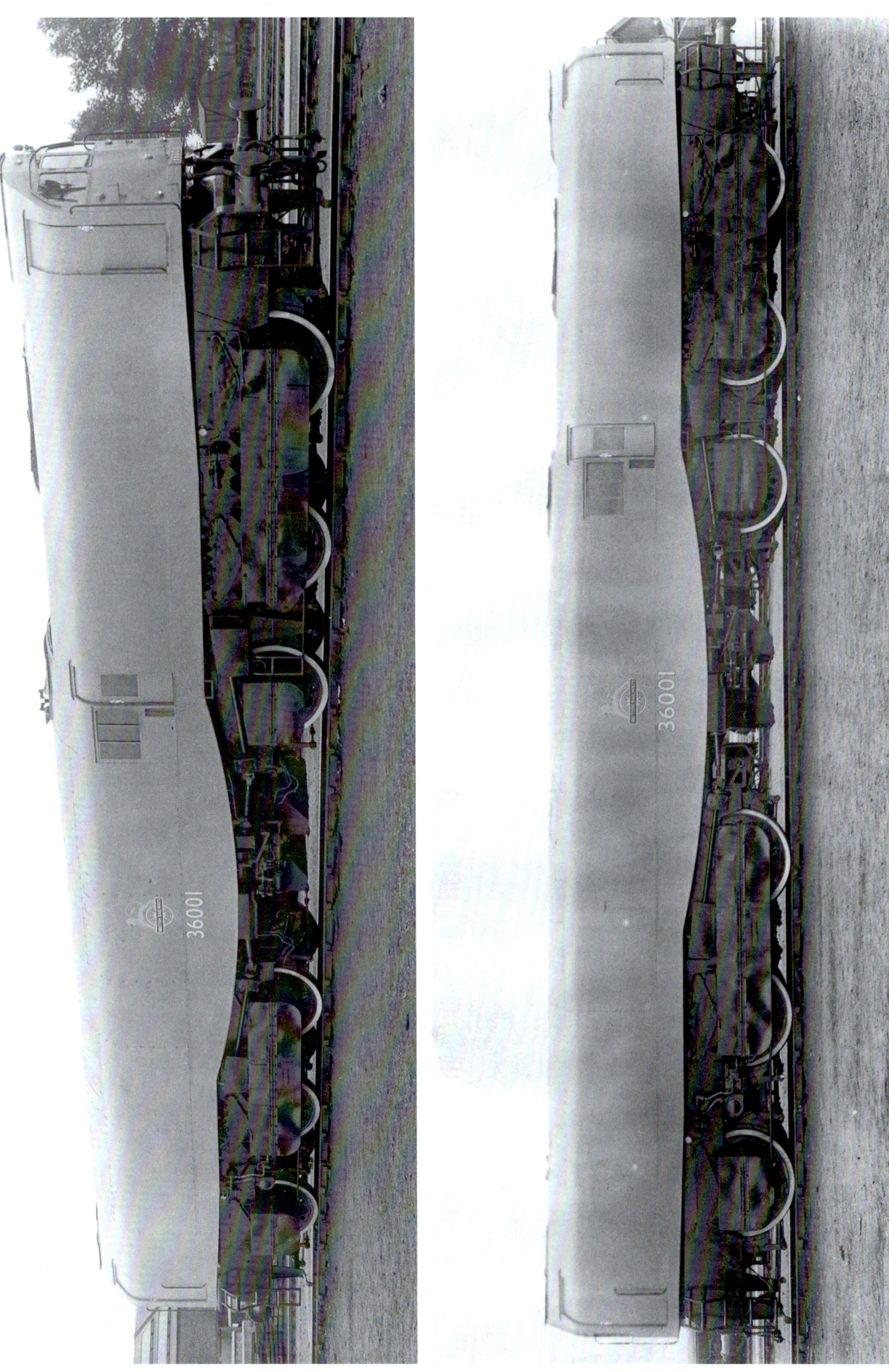

The official BR views of the engine from both sides and No. 1 end. Mention might also conveniently be made of the front and rear cab steps at this point which are seen to commence vertically from the ground before becoming convex. This was necessary to allow for ease of access/egress if the engine were stopped on a curve – the unfortunate side effect being it was also all too easy to bang one's shins in the process. No lining is applied to the sides or ends. *British Railways*

ABOVE After the VIPs had departed, No. 36001 was the subject of some scrutiny by perhaps 'lesser mortals' from the works, whilst in the background an even older veteran, 0395 No. 30571 stands ready – perhaps to move No. 36001 around to the shed to prepare for the return to Brighton. The 0-6-0 was 68 years old and yet would outlive Leader, surviving until 1953. It was around this time that a young Eastleigh apprentice by the name of David Burnett happened to venture out and was admiring the engine from ground level. He recounted that a tall man in a well-cut suit approached and asked if he would like to look inside. David replied he would and spend several minutes looking around. When he emerged the same man was waiting for him and asked his opinion. David responded that he was impressed and hoped he would see more of a similar type. As he made to move off, he noticed the Assistant Works Manager come rushing up and address the tall man as 'Sir'. The well-suited man was Bulleid, who after having dealt with the manager turned to the crowd that has assembled with the words, 'This young man has seen it first, now you can all have a look if you like'. Not surprisingly for one young Eastleigh apprentice this left an indelible impression. *Reg Curl*

RIGHT Stephen Townroe's classic original colour view of No. 36001 being made ready for inspection – number decals etc., have yet to be added although some cleaning on the roof line has taken place whilst the man on the ladder has a paint pot in hand. The engine has also been moved to a different part of the works yard. At some point during her few days at Eastleigh the steam heat hose connection from the body to the bogie was added. It is not believed she actually went inside the works for any purpose on this occasion and consequently was not weighed. This may then be an appropriate time to refer to a conversation at Brighton between G.L. Nicholson and L. Granshaw. When Nicholson asked, 'How are you going to balance the offset boiler?', the reply from Granshaw was: 'That is a good question, we are still trying to find the answer'. (Surely Brighton must have already known the weight of the engine was unbalanced?) Had the engine been weighed at Eastleigh the truth would have been revealed that no answer had by been found or indeed ever would be found. (Stephen Townroe later commented to the author he was present when Leader was eventually weighed and witnessed the needles going beyond the marked measurements, the only time he ever saw this happen. (*See* also page 36 re the LNER corridor tenders.) Townroe recorded the engine in this position with both colour and B&W film, his latter image having the men in slightly different positions. *S.C. Townroe*

Leader left Eastleigh again to return to her Brighton home the following day, Wednesday 29 June, and this time 'light' in the true sense of the word, meaning without any accompanying engine. We do not know the reason for her solitary procession: had sufficient faith been generated, or was it simply no assisting engine was available, might it even have been at Bulleid's insistence and in so doing attempting to prove a point, that she could indeed make this 60+ mile journey without incident? At the same time we might also ask if it was that Bulleid was still the real decision-maker in the process? Instead that would surely have been Robin Riddles, in his position as the member of the Railway Executive in charge of mechanical engineering who was really in control, but who also for the present was content to allow progress to continue. Why the return to Brighton? Well, in many respects this may have been something to do with the plethora of secondary and cross-country routes available from Brighton, whilst in addition Brighton had the experience and the knowledge of the class with the actual design staff based there as well as being involved in the building of the remaining engines. Returning to routes again for a moment, the thought of No. 36001 venturing from Eastleigh to Andover via Romsey, or Bournemouth via Ringwood, is still an interesting perspective but it was not to be.

Departure from Eastleigh back to Brighton, No. 1 end leading which likely explains the open centre window, as well as the cab doors and the roof ventilator. No 'buddy' assistance was provided. She is seen on the Portsmouth line which runs parallel with the northern boundary of the works. Unfortunately it was not to be the jubilant homecoming some might have anticipated for the engine had developed a knock by the time Barnham was reached and which later transpired to be damage to the sleeve and operating mechanism of the middle cylinder of No. 1 bogie. *David Burnett*

Accordingly No. 36001 left Eastleigh eastwards, travelling via Botley to Fareham and again along the coast line. Unfortunately the confidence now demonstrated was doomed to be misplaced, as although the engine did still reach Brighton alone, a considerable amount of knocking was heard by the time Barnham was reached and clearly emanating from No. 1 bogie. The engine was also sounding decidedly 'off-beat'. Click and Attwell viewed her return, as it transpired running on five and not six cylinders, from the stairs leading to the works boiler shop.

Examination at Brighton revealed the operating rod, but this time to the middle cylinder of No. 1 bogie, had fractured whilst at the same time the associated sleeve of the same cylinder was broken in four places. The left-hand operating rod and sleeve was also displaying evidence of seizure. (Did the broken sleeve cause damage to the cylinder as well? We are not told.) The dilemma now was had it been the sleeves that were contributing to the operating rod failure, or vice-versa? Bulleid was of the opinion that the sleeves were simply too tight with insufficient room for expansion and consequently all three sleeves then fitted to No. 1 bogie were reduced in diameter by 18 thou–0.0018in. but only on No. 1 bogie. (It is possible this work involved sending the actual components to Eastleigh, which may then go some way also

Back at Brighton and seen during the short time the engine retained its BR emblem and central number before these were superseded – *see* Appendix 5. From the images that follow for the remainder of this book, it is perhaps doubtful if the engine was also ever physically cleaned again, or if so, certainly not thoroughly. The *RO* provides for another snippet of news from a visit made by members to Brighton Works on 22 July when it was reported painting was being finished and the engine was 'undergoing modifications as a result of the trials which are believed to have proven generally satisfactory'. Why it was never repainted into BR mixed-traffic (black) livery is not explained. *John Click/ National Railway Museum*

to explaining why it was not until 7 July that the engine was ready for its next trial.) Why the same change was not made to those on No. 2 bogie is not explained, neither is there any mention of damage to the cylinder liners or pistons.

With the new/replacement parts in place, on 7 July two runs were made the short distance from Brighton to Falmer and also on to Groombridge – the records are not clear if this meant the engine travelled to Groombridge via Falmer or if there was just one trip to each location, or if it had even been two runs to each location! Whatever the eventuality, a repeat was made the next day. No issues were reported.

Nothing was done over the weekend. The next trial over the same route was booked for Monday 11 July but for some reason was cancelled at short notice. Such a cancellation should not always be seen as due to a fault with the engine and it could well have been a simple traffic or operating difficulty that precluded the engine working. In the event the run was instead made, without incident, on 12 July.

At this point too we should also talk about the crew involved. As would be the case at Eastleigh the following year, it would appear (mostly) just one crew worked the engine from Brighton: Bill Long as driver and Ted Forder as fireman. This pairing was the trials crew at Brighton meaning they would take new and repaired engines on the relevant test circuit as well as being involved in most, if not all, of the actual runs wherever she went. (An image on the Southern email group at *https://sremg.org.uk/steam/h1-h2_02.html* depicts a different pair of men alongside No. 2039 on a trial run, hence there may well have been more than one trials crew or spare men were borrowed from the running shed as necessary.)

Nothing was scheduled for 13 July but on 14 July, a light engine trial was made to Crowborough, with both Bulleid and Granshaw on board. As if to typify what would later be described as the occasional 'impish' behaviour of the designer himself, Leader performed faultlessly whilst its creator was on the footplate but a repeat of the same run in the afternoon witnessed another failure to No. 1 bogie at Barcombe Mills, and this time with all three valve rods fractured. It was stated there was also some consequential damage to other (unspecified) components, perhaps implying the failure was both sudden and dramatic and possibly even at some speed. (Trial working would, out of practice, have involved cut-offs not normally associated with normal working – viz 45% and more for long periods. This was a necessary measure although by its very action would place additional strain on the associated valve and cylinder components.) A tow back to Brighton ensued, the cumulative score at this point being three failures out of nine runs, and with just 360 miles covered, hardly an auspicious start, and destined to get worse.

Back at Brighton it was thus to the works for repair, the body having to be lifted sufficiently for the offending bogie to be rolled out and in the interim the locomotive supported on substantial wooden trestles. No thought

A young Ted Forder, the Brighton fireman who worked on Leader for most of the trials. We do not know if he was also on board for the various trips the engine made to Eastleigh. When interviewed 30+ years later, Ted was proud to have been involved with the trials and was not at all happy when misquoted over any comments he made concerning the heat of the engine.

seems to have been given to a straight replacement with a completed bogie from one of the other engines, although perhaps none was complete. As previously stated, with a fleet of Leaders the idea of having interchangeable/replacement bogies would have been a valid concept. At this point we should also repeat the earlier quote from Sean Day-Lewis where he mentions that with the lessons learnt from No. 36001, No. 36002 would surely have been a better engine. Ahead in time slightly, Click later adds a rider to this himself, 'No. 36002 was very nearly completed on the day that worked was stopped on her and the other three. I got the news at lunchtime from an apprentice I knew and although not altogether surprised I clearly remember the dismay that I felt. No. 36001 was in a lot of

No. 36001, halted at Lewes whilst running light on 17 August, and then seen at Brighton on the same day. (We cannot be certain in which order the two views were taken.) Although the run(s) that day were classified as failures, it has not been possible to determine if any problems occurred whilst away from Brighton, or if the day itself was considered a failure due to the connecting rod issue with No. 2 bogie preventing a third run taking place. *Roger Carpenter/Don Broughton Collection*

trouble at the time, which was felt (by whom exactly?) was due to manufacturing problems that had been overcome in the second locomotive, and a plea was made from works level to let testing go on with No. 36002 in place of the first loco.' From this it implies the assertion by Day-Lewis had been right all along, No. 36002 would have been better, but then Click adds a final damning indictment, 'I don't think the overall result would have been much different myself.'

Returning to the episode of 14 July, the necessary repairs took nine days during which time the opportunity was also taken to paint the outline of panels along both sides, in red and black, the standard BR lining for mixed-traffic classes (there was a third colour – white – but this would not have shown up against the background grey.) Probably at the same time, although certainly by 17 August, the BR insignia and number were removed from the centre of the engine and instead replaced by numerals only to both sides and at each end. Curiously No. 36001 had now carried her number in six separate locations: twice on each side and also via two cast plates (we can hardly refer to both as a 'smokebox' plate, more accurately a 'smokebox' plate and a 'bunker' plate). With the repaint, no BR emblem was re-applied, and none would ever again be carried – perhaps a slightly naïve way of believing this was one way to avoid potential embarrassment.

No. 36001 next ventured forth on 23 July, again bound for Crowborough, and this time no problems were encountered on the two trips made. Next day it was the turn of a new destination, Seaford, and again intended to be visited twice. But as had occurred before, on the first run there were no reported difficulties but approaching the destination for a second time the valve gear on No. 1 bogie again developed trouble (this time it was just the right-hand valve rod and associated sleeve), resulting in another slow return to Brighton.

It was later revealed that at the time of the Seaford failure, No. 36001 had indeed been running at a higher speed than would otherwise have been expected and in full forward gear – 75% cut-off. Presumably as this was a light engine trial, it was on the direct orders of the testing staff on board and certainly something that would not normally have been a regular procedure in traffic but, as mentioned, it was necessary to attempt to replicate all possible conditions that would likely be required/encountered in traffic.

Even so there must have been a number of quizzical expressions, as 100 miles had been completed over the previous three runs without incident whilst a failure to the right-hand valve rod and sleeve alone was both a new and worrying development.

Additionally whilst the official reports have so far only detailed the failures associated with the reversing of the engine and those involving No. 1 bogie, there were in fact other ongoing problems as well. In particular this involved the dry (brick) lining of the firebox which from an early stage had displayed a tendency to collapse into the grate. (We are not told what other additional problems existed apart those already mentioned although the official paperwork is clear there were indeed other issues.)

Consequently repairs at this stage are now known to have involved not just No. 1 bogie but also relining both sides and part of the back of the firebox, again the necessary components probably 'borrowed' from those earmarked from another engine in the series. At this stage too, July 1949, work on the next two engines, Nos 36002–36003, was progressing slowly. Perhaps mindful of what fate may befall these if No. 36001 did not start to show signs of promise an all-out effort to submit the pair as complete machines would lead to a delay of about five months in completing other outstanding build orders at Brighton, which included West Country Pacifics Nos. 34091–4 and in turn also led to a similar consequential delays in all the other build dates for the Light Pacifics right up to what would be 34109.

Meanwhile it was to be almost three weeks before No. 36001 ventured out again, on what was destined to be the commencement of a six-day series of runs, all light engine, these commencing on 12 August.

The destinations were stated to be Crowborough, Seaford, and Lewes. As the first and second named locations are in opposite directions geographically, it is not exactly clear if the reference then refers to Brighton–Crowborough–Brighton–Seaford–Brighton, or some other alternative. What is known is that Crowborough was actually visited on no less than seven occasions during the six days. More importantly these were also the most successful trials to date with just one failure at Seaford on 15 August due to a securing pin working loose and then falling out of the valve gear. (The actual pin location is not detailed further.) Even so running repairs were successfully completed and the engine was able to resume the rest of its run without incident. Indeed as with 2039 beforehand, it was stated Leader was both free-steaming and free running, 70mph being attained without difficulty.

Whilst in the previous paragraph it would appear as if Leader was at last starting to show promise, the newer problem with the firebox lining (recall this was vertical to both sides and the back of the firebox) was starting to cause concern. Already this had begun to show signs of detaching itself from the small securing clips intended to hold the firebricks in position, with the obvious result that the firebricks would fall into the grate. This problem was noted in the official record of the run together with a reference to 'control of the regulator and reverser erratic', which referred to problems in maintaining the desired pressure within the steam chest whilst the reverser was difficult to 'notch-up'. Difficulty with the reversing gear had, of course, been spoken of before but that concerning the regulator is another new obstacle, indeed it almost appeared as if when one problem was controlled a new one was developing. Even so there is some common ground in the difficulties now being discussed, as what was clearly an ongoing problem with the sleeves could likewise well have affected accurate steam distribution to the steam chests.

No. 36001 attempting to return from a weighing at Eastleigh but seen here failed at Barnham on 20 August 1949 and being examined (two men are on the ground). Although No. 2 end is seen, the failure had been to a sleeve at the opposite, No. 1, end. It had been at Eastleigh that the excess and uneven weight of the engine had finally been confirmed – this despite Brighton having its own weight table alongside the shed. The shading along the sides is not different shades of paint, although it must be admitted that at Brighton when the BR emblem and centre number were painted out, a slightly different tone of 'photographic grey' was used in this location. We are not informed if the engine later made its way back under its own power or was subject to a tow. *W.N.J. Jackson*

Exactly who was 'in charge' of running the trials, determining the destination and if a load might be hauled, is not totally certain but it is likely it was Harry Attwell of the testing section. Assuming such and with the general success of the past few days, Leader was charged with its most strenuous test to date, to take ten bogie vehicles weighing 248t from Brighton to Eastleigh on 18 August. At an average of 24.8t each this was not likely to have been particularly modern stock, besides the traffic department would hardly want to take the latest vehicles out of traffic. There was a second reason to visit Eastleigh, and that was to enable the engine to at last be weighed at Eastleigh works. (Why this had not been done before in June is not clear – perhaps it was simply nothing more than the Eastleigh weight table was not available at the time.)

Granshaw was on-board for the Eastleigh run, although Bulleid was not. Instead he was on holiday in Perthshire with fellow members of the Association of Railway Locomotive Engineers who were thus using the final funds of the Association, consequent upon Riddle's decision to terminate the body's existence. Such foreclosure was an understandable reaction to nationalisation. There was no longer any need for regular interaction between individuals in similar roles from the different companies, however, it would certainly have been interesting to have been a 'fly on the wall' during discussion between the eminent participants.

Day-Lewis tells us Granshaw sent a succession of telegrams to the Gleneagles Hotel although the Day-Lewis text is more likely to have a been a precis of bits from several. Two of these may be quoted (likely in part only), 'Successful trial trip of 100 miles on Saturday, taking engine to Eastleigh tomorrow', and 'Successful Brighton to Eastleigh on Sunday, arrived on time, no trouble during trip, reverser much improved'. On the surface these telegrams would appear to refer to the Crowborough and Eastleigh runs although it should be said they do not correspond exactly with known actual running days for 1949. What we can be certain of is that progress report telegrams were being sent, although it might now be mentioned their content is perhaps open to slight doubt, could this even have been the sender looking for the best and deliberately not quoting the worst? (In all instances within this work the dates and records of trials are taken from the official reports held at the National Railway Museum.)

Indeed further doubt may be cast as the Eastleigh run was not in fact without incident, with part of the firebox lining collapsing en route. This run was thus officially classified as a failure.

At Eastleigh further repairs were carried out to the firebrick lining whilst additionally the ash duct in the smoke box was now also welded shut – improvised remedies of dung or similar to form a seal would no longer be required! But the down side to this was that recourse would now have to be made to the traditional method of smokebox cleaning involving a man and a shovel, a none too easy, or indeed pleasant experience within the confines of the enclosed body.

Far more serious were the results discovered when the engine was taken into works and weighed. For this purpose the engine would be in light steam with coal and water – basic running condition.

Stephen Townroe was present for the weighing and I well remember his expression when he recalled the event, probably similar to anyone else who was also there – simultaneous amazement and disbelief. Indeed, instead of the design estimate of 110t spread over six axles with a maximum of 18.33t per axle, the actual result was 130.5t or 21.75t per axle, fully 2t more and so immediately restricting the engine compared with its originally intended wide sphere of operation. But this was nothing compared with the side-to-side variation – recall the conversation between Nicholson and Granshaw? Here the additional weight on the side where the boiler was located caused the pointers of the weight table to travel off the scale and beyond their maximum range of 25t. (It has not been possible to ascertain the weight proportioned to the opposite side.)

Whilst this was undoubtedly a shock to those present, it could not really have been unexpected. What is perhaps more surprising is that no mention of this obvious weight differential had arisen before. Had there been no experience of the engine 'lurching' at any time – certainly this was to be noted on at least one run from Eastleigh later. (Conversely the later improvements to the oil supply to the pedestal guides – referred to on p.154 – were reported as having had a marked effect on the quality of the ride. Any previous harshness then having given way to a smoothness, stated to have been more akin to that of a passenger carriage.) With a 'conventional' engine some disparity between one side and the other might occur due to the tightness or otherwise of the springs, these would then be adjusted to compensate. But 25+t vis-à-vis 21.75to was far too great a differential to be compensated for by simply adjusting a few bolts. At that precise moment there must have been some who considered any future running movement of No. 36001 to have been seriously in doubt.

Such a result could also not be kept away from the hierarchy and so we have every reason to believe that at some stage Riddles, the Southern Region Chief Civil Engineer, and Bulleid were informed. We can certainly believe correspondence would have passed between the first two named. What is altogether more surprising is that No. 36001 simply departed the scene, returning light engine from Eastleigh to Brighton on 20 August, although again not without incident as at least one further sleeve valve failure occurred, again on No. 1 bogie, and the engine was failed at Barnham – possibly being later towed back to Brighton. The same return trip had also seen a further collapse of the firebox lining. (Is it too cruel to suggest that perhaps Eastleigh were just glad it was off their hands?)

When 36001 eventually reached Brighton again (it is not confirmed if this was on the 20 August, but at least at Brighton she could be hidden away rather than seen as a failure), there was another works visit for repairs. The firebox lining obviously needed to be attended to whilst in addition in an attempt to reduce the incidence of sleeve failure, the maximum cut-offwas reduced from 75% to 65% – although a side disadvantage was that this in turn led to poor starting.

Another Lewes view, No. 1 end leading. The point made earlier is also proven here as the dustcover to the oscillating gear has been removed allowing the ingress of undesirable elements, especially at No. 1 end where the cab was commodious and floorboards might be lifted to allow observation of the valve gear and sleeves. As with No. 2039, Leader rarely if even ran with just the driver and fireman on board, there would be at least a fitter and either someone from the test staff or from the drawing office. *S C Nash/Stephenson Locomotive Society*

According to official records the opportunity was also taken to fit a spark arrestor, but it may be questioned whether this was the actual device provided or if it was in some way a sort of alternative to the aforementioned ash-chute, possibly a form of self-cleaning smokebox, like a mesh designed to hold ash and ciders in suspension in the blast and so eject these from the chimney rather than allowing them to fall to the base of the smokebox.

Leader was in works, or at least out of service, for a further ten days. Whether remedying the latest round of defects actually took the whole period or she was laid aside pending repairs, or even set aside pending the opportunity for further trials to take place is not certain.

What we do know is that on 30 August she was in steam again and ran light engine between Brighton and Crowborough on the start of a new series of tests, performing (almost) faultlessly, well, for the first three days at least, as on the fourth a single fire-brick dislodged itself on the last day of working – 2 September. Officially then this last 2 September trial was once more a failure.

We now have to bring Bulleid back into the equation, as history tells us that on Monday 4 September 1949 No. 36001 was made ready for a loaded run from Brighton to Victoria, running via Lewes and Oxted (260t were to be taken), the whole thing, we may well suspect, at the behest of Bulleid who needed to prove the engine to what must have been various sceptics. Indeed this assertion is backed up by John Clicks's later comment on p.251 '"politically" it had to be seen to run'.

Just in case at this stage the reader is starting to believe success might have been achieved, do note that the present writer knows of very few instances in which a new design intended for general (or indeed specific) service had taken so long to prove itself, especially one where the multitude of failings likely to occur were really readily apparent from the outset. Most new designs might require a bit of 'tinkering' or adjustment, or might not even perform as the designer had intended – but they did at least perform. In the Southern area Drummond's 4-6-0s were not his best but they did do some useful work for a time; but were far better when subsequently rebuilt by Urie years later. Even Swindon got it wrong sometimes, witness Dean's 4-2-4T design that 'fell off' every time it moved and the first 56xx where the valve gear was assembled the wrong way round – in the latter case staff were threatened with dismissal if this story was ever mentioned around, hence it remained secret for many years. (*See: The GWR Exposed*, where it is referred to in the Bibliography.) Other engines were deliberately built as experiments and despite this worked normal services, the

At, and then setting off from, Brighton – Platform 5 – (empty coaching stock, of course). Bulleid's office at Brighton faced away from the station with its constant noise but the corridor outside did overlook the platform. John Click recalls 'I think he stood with us, with the window open, as we watched No. 36001 start off on her first (as it turned out, abortive) Victoria trip, via Lewes, East Grinstead and Oxted. Ted Forder was the fireman as the last few staff climb aboard and then quickly "puts a bit on".' Did anyone even consider letting the engine have a free run up the main line to London? Unlikely, and even if they had done, they were wise to change their mind. *John Click/National Railway Museum*

LMS Turbomotive and LNER 'Hush-Hush' are two examples in this category. Similarly and not wishing to add controversy, recall Nicholson's correspondence with the present writer on the subject of the Bulleid Pacific breed, 'Eventually they were all rebuilt – at considerable cost – but then became, so far as I know, useful citizens indeed.'

But perhaps 5 September was to be that time – to prove itself. Eight bogies of somewhat heavier stock were also involved and weighing 260t. Fortuitously a full account from E. Walton, a Head Office Inspector who clearly travelled with the service, was sent to the 'Chief Trains Clerk' and this has survived. It makes for interesting reading.

Test Trip with "Leader" Class Engine No. 36001 with 8 coaches, Brighton to Victoria via Uckfield and Oxted and return, Monday 5 September. 1949.

The result of the above Test trip was most unsatisfactory. The train left Brighton 9.50 am, Right Time, stopped at

Fiasco at Oxted: Harry Attwell was on board to record this unique moment, necessary as the water filler on the design had been found to be too high for the Central Section water columns. Improvisation was required and Brighton fashioned a form of copper chute and extended leather bag. Very much a 'Heath-Robinson' arrangement, it nevertheless worded after a fashion – the disadvantage being that taking water could mean an hour's delay (and a soaking). The adaptor was carried on the engine for the trials, certainly those from Brighton. The height of the mogul tender alongside forms a useful comparison. (Access to the tank top was via a set of steps on the rear end of the tank in No. 2 cab and then through the cab roof vent.) Another reason for testing Leader on this route was the hope that the design might be suitable to take over and improve the service between London and Brighton via Oxted – no turning of the engine needed in London. Examination also revealed just five water columns would need to be modified on this route. *Harry Attwell*

Buxted, short of steam. Stopped again at Edenbridge Town short of steam and train was shunted to yard for 10.18am Brighton to Victoria to pass. In view of the bad running I decided not to risk a run in the London Area and arranged for the trip to terminate at Oxted and return to Brighton. Left Edenbridge Town with full head of steam but stopped on Hurst Green Junction Up Inner Home signal, again short of steam. After a stop to "Blow Up" it just managed to crawl into Oxted. Here our troubles really started. The engine was short of water. It was run to a water column but to my amazement was unable to take water owing to the fact that the only water inlet is on the top of the engine casing and the only suitable columns are those with a high "Swan Necked" jib or a hanging leather hose. Decided to berth stock at Oxted and run engine light to Brighton. Oxted could not hold the stock so decided to take stock to East Grinstead to berth calling at Lingfield to take some water from tap on down platform with Cattle Dock hosepipe. Took sufficient water at Lingfield to get to East Grinstead and left. Stopped at Dormans short of steam. Eventually arrived at East Grinstead and berthed stock. Again unable to take water at crane. Connected Fire Hose to Hydrant and took enough water to get to Brighton. Would not trust engine on Main line so travelled via Sheffield Park. Arrived at Sheffield Park and shunted for traffic. Again unable to get water from water column so shunted to Up siding, borrowed garden hose from timber yard and connected to tap in Pump House. Got enough water to take engine to Lewes. Phoned Brighton to send assisting engine to Lewes to tow engine home. Arrived at Lewes found Water Crane at Lewes had a "Swan Neck" jib and by bending leather hose was able to get enough water to take engine to Brighton. Stopped assisting engine at Falmer and travelled under own power to Brighton arriving 6.25pm after leaving Oxted 1.17pm. Engine berthed in workshops at Brighton and as far as I am concerned have no desire to see it again.

Possibly on 5 September 1949, but definably at Dormans, where all are resting (engine included) after running short of steam. This was the first attempt to reach Victoria with a trailing load of 260t. No. 1 end is leading and it will be noted the train crew comprises at least 10 people (one on the top of the bunker) including the photographer and possibly even more as there is no obvious driver and fireman (there may be two more from shadows on the ground.) We know Doug Smith and W.H. 'Joe' Hutchinson are in the group but they are not positively identified. No. 36001 still has the front oscillating gear in place whilst in addition two vertical 'markers' have been attached to the buffer beam. These were provided in an attempt to measure the degree of movement of the reciprocal motion and sleeves relative to known parameters – presumably by observation once some of the cab floorboards had been removed. It was not successful and the 'markers' were later removed. This comment was personally reported by Ken Briggs formerly of the Brighton test section but by then at Croydon, to another Croydon employee, Tony Francis. *Harry Attwell/colourisation by David Williams*

In the event of further Trial Trips of this engine under traffic conditions, I suggest that the load should be restricted to 3 coaches and suitable arrangements made for a water supply to be available on the route chosen.'

Particulars of Test Trip as follows;–
Engine No. 36001. Driver Capelin, Guard Giles.
(The Fireman's name is not reported.)
Load – 8 coaches. 260 Tons.

Timings	Booked	Actual	
Brighton	9.50 am	9.50 am	
Lewes	10.7	10.11½	4½ mins Signals Kemp Town Jct.
Culver Junction	10.12	10.17½	1 minute loss by engine
Uckfield	10.19	10.27	2½ minutes loss by engine
Crowborough	10.33	11.6	25 minutes loss by engine Short of steam
Reigate Mill Jct.	10.38	11.10	1 minute regained by engine
Eridge	10.40	11.12	
Ashurst Jct.	10.44	11.14½	1½ minutes Regained by engine
Edenbridge Town.	10.58	11.30 – 11.54	25½ minutes loss by engine short of steam
Hurst Green Jct.	11.7	12.5 – 12.20	17 minutes loss by engine short of steam
Oxted	11.10	12.26	3 minutes loss by engine short of steam
Oxted		1.17 pm	
Lingfield		1.30 – 1.58	Engine taking water
Dormans		2.9 – 2.22	Engine short of steam
East Grinstead		2.31	
East Grinstead		3.31	Engine taking water
Sheffield Park		4.12 – 5.24	Shunted for traffic
Lewes		5.48 – 6.7	Engine taking water
Brighton		6.25	

No. 36001 waiting to head south again at Oxted after what was either the first or second (failed) attempt at reach London. On the second trial, ice-creams brought for the crew on board ended up going to waste – *see* page 138. It was a coincidence that the date of the first London trial was also the third anniversary of approval for the design to go ahead. Looking back those three years to 1946, it is unlikely anyone could have seen ahead to this date being only the first attempt that a Leader might reach London. As we know, it was not to be. To add insult to injury, for the run of 5 September the water column adapter was not on board, probably someone simply forgot it. Without wishing to infer any lack of ability, for the two failed London trips a different man was also in change; instead of Driver Long it was now Driver Capelin – but possibly for no more than the simple reason of route knowledge.

In addition to the above report is a comment to the author from the late H.W. Attwell, who was onboard, that on the climb back to Dormans, just north of East Grinstead, and following the decision to terminate the trial, Leader had almost stalled on the 1 in 210 gradient approaching the station. It can only have been a relief that Bulleid was probably was not travelling to witness the sad spectacle. The whole day might also be considered to be the nadir of the test runs to date; things could hardly get worse.

John Click also adds some comments of his own. 'On that day I was at Warlingham and learned of the trip having been cancelled from the signalman there. I sped down to Oxted and found 36001 standing in the up platform whilst vain efforts were being made to get the short "Brighton" water crane bag up to the filling hole. A traffic inspector was vociferating.'

Before progressing further (no pun intended) we also need to consider briefly the route taken as described in the report, for it confirms that on at least this one occasion No. 36001 ran the length of the Bluebell line. In view of the difficulties encountered this was no real surprise, the operating authorities intent on keeping Leader away from the main lines as much as possible and for no other reasons than to avoid any risk of associated delays to ordinary traffic consequent upon a breakdown or need to stop for a 'blow-up'. Bulleid's modifications to No. 2039 had unfortunately also paved the way in this respect, his 'experiments' had hardly experienced a good press!

One other question needs to be asked and that is – did the engine start off with its water tank full anyway? Additionally, had not the problem with the water supply already been identified and the adaptor made up? It appears that for whatever reason – and surely cannot have been other than forgetfulness, the said water column 'adaptor' was not being carried on board.

Back at Brighton and again inside the works, the view was coming round that the spark arrestor type device may have contributed to the poor steaming. If it were an actual spark arrestor why had it been considered necessary anyway? We have had no mention of excessive fire throwing being evident unless this had been aggravated by the use of long cut-offs or inferior coal.

Whatever, the device was removed and a second London trial arranged for three days later on Thursday 8 September. Thanks to John Click the events of that day also unfold almost as a three-act play: Anticipation at the start, a crescendo that could not have been considered by any imagination, and a conclusion again of disappointment or almost foreboding.

We start though with the anticipation. No. 36001 left Brighton at 9.51am (one minute late departure due to signals) intending to travel to Victoria via Uckfield and Oxted. Inspector Walton takes up the story, 'The train came to a stand at Buxted. Engine short of steam. After passing Crowborough, it was running well but got signal delays from Birchden Junction onwards, having lost its path over Ashchurch Jct. due to the delay at Buxted. The train was shunted at Edenbridge Town for 10.18am Brighton to Victoria to pass and then proceeded to Oxted…'

As we will see later, Inspector Walton next words were, 'where the trip was terminated'. But it so nearly wasn't. John Click takes up the story of the same run, 'The next day it was decided to go to Victoria again, on the same timing and with the same load, eight bogies. This time I decided I'd ride straight to Oxted, find out how she was doing and choose a good spot. "She's to stop here," I was told, without understanding the significance. She duly arrived, having done a good deal better than the day before and, blowing off, hooked off and ran round. It was only years later in 1960 did I find out what had really happened that day. Wallace (a man from Brighton who is mentioned here for the first time), had occasion to ring "The Kremlin" *(meaning the headquarters of the Railway Executive at 222 Marylebone Road)* to speak to "our man there", H.W. Butler, (ex-Brighton drawing office man). Wallace said to him, "by the way if you could nip over to Victoria you might just be in time to see the Leader arrive … goodbye". Butler rushed out, straight into R.C. Bond: who said, "I'll come too". Fate then took a hand, because in the corridors of power they overtook Rudguard, the Chief Motive Power Officer. "I'm not having that THING coming to London," he cried and disappeared rapidly whence he had come.' *(No doubt the telephone wires were rather hot rather quickly.)* Butler always felt guilty about the incident.'

John Click also adds some light-hearted comments on this second attempted London trip. 'I was on holiday that day and cycled from Lee to Woldingham where the signalman told me she was returning to Brighton from Oxted having been "short of steam". I got there in the nick of time to find everyone very hot and dejected; and on impulse, shot out and bought a dozen ice-creams down the road. I was only gone a few minutes, but in that time so had the "Leader". I got very funny looks walking back trying to give these rapidly melting things away, and most got dumped in the gutter. 36001's troubles weren't over then, for there was a pantomime getting water for her further down the line. They could have done with the ices!'

So why had Rudguard acted in such a fervent fashion? The short answer is we just do not know but it does beg the question was Leader in fact already condemned – in the mind of one man at least? It seems to have been. It also goes to show the power and influence exerted by one individual, clearly senior. It appears to R.C. Bond. What Riddles may have thought or said when he learned what had occurred, as he undoubtably would have done, is not reported. It is the opinion of the present writer that approaching two years into nationalisation some of the senior SR staff were only too acutely aware that the reputation and therefore the future for 36001 already hung in the balance. A failure on a busy commuter route somewhere in the London area may well have sealed the end for 36001 there and then. Consequently, in reality, there was no choice. No. 36001 returned to Brighton light engine and where, if anything, the future was now even more uncertain than three months earlier. Click comments. 'Butler had said Bulleid – who had also watched from the corridor outside his office as the first abortive

In disgrace at Uckfield on 20 September 1949. Again Harry Attwell took the image and with four others present this indicates driver and fireman plus two others. On the extreme right is believed to the regular Brighton trials driver, Bill Long. It was as a result of this failure that the decision was made to remove the oscillating gear for the sleeves to No. 1 bogie. One slightly later light-hearted 'failure' occurred when three distinct 'cracks' were heard with those on board immediately of the opinion three sleeves had failed, so the engine was immediately brought to a standstill. Examination revealed all to be well; it turned out the engine had run over three detonators (fog signals, but it does give an indication of how loud such a failure was when it did occur. Three such detonators usually meant an obstruction immediately ahead – fortunately no collision occurred and so it may well have been simply detonators previous placed and which someone later forgot to remove. We are not informed where, what or when this might have been.
Harry Attwell

London departure left the station – was furious about the whole (cancellation) thing and he (Butler) had always felt guilty about the way in which he had unwittingly been the cause of having the one and only London bound trip nipped in the bud.' Click concludes with these words, (his or those of Butler?), 'The whole episode must be typical of the way – the extremely high-handed way – in which the Railway Executive people dealt with the Leader experiment from beginning to end.'

Those on board No. 36001 would of course have known nothing of the rapidly developing political situation until they had reached the point when the message was ready to be relayed: Rudguard contacting the Southern Region headquarters, who in turn would pass it on to the Central Division control office, (probably Redhill) who in turn would have contacted various strategic points (control would have had prior knowledge of the route and timings) and consequently, dependent upon the time the message was received, the appropriate signal box would have been notified, in this case Oxted.

Despite the subsequent comments of Inspector Walton, one can also only imagine the likely bitter disappointment of others on board. No. 36001 would never reach London but, as we know, two other members of the class Nos 36002/3 did later, although not exactly in the way that it might have been anticipated.

In disgrace again, this time at Crowborough on 9 October 1949. Bill Long and Ted Forder at left and centre respectively plus a works fitter. The photo was again taken by Harry Attwell. This was the first day of resumed testing after a five-day hiatus. The engine had taken just 150t at the drawbar but was declared a failure as a result of what were now cast iron firebricks having melted into the fire. After cooling off the engine returned to Brighton 'light'. Despite the accumulating number of failures, any enquiry from a member of the public to the crew on board was met with a positive response as to its performance, 'will be in service soon', as the usual verbal riposte. On such occasions could this be said to simply have been the crew not wanting to answer difficult questions, or might it even have been an instruction from higher up? Certainly later BR admitted they had no wish to wash their dirty linen in public. *Harry Attwell*

Returning from Seaford to Brighton on the reverse side of Falmer bank. This photograph first appeared in *The Times* on 4 November 1949 under the heading 'A new type of British Locomotive'. Aside from the build details, the information given was almost all correct. It showed a test train running between Lewes and Seaford. 'A new and unusual type of locomotive, the Leader class 0-6-6-0 six-cylinder tank engine driving two power bogies, undergoing tests near Lewes. Making a departure from British locomotive design, it has a driving cab at each end connected by a corridor, to obviate the turn-round. The fireman's cab is in the middle. Five of these locomotives are being completed at the Eastleigh works of British Railways.' The article appears not to have provoked any comment at the time, being merely a news story, but later in 1953 the same photograph would be used in the *Sunday Despatch* complete with exaggerated and inaccurate reporting. Sensationalism and factual distortion is not limited to late 20th and 21st century news and television media either, for the same view reproduced in another book states 'The fireman is having a breather' (referring to the heat within). Certainly at first glance it does appear as if someone is leaning from the centre cab; closer examination however reveals it is in fact an elbow, with the body of the individual facing inbound. The sliding centre door is partly open – No. 1 end is leading. *Colour by David Williams*

Inspector Walton meanwhile continues with details of the 6 September run, (At Oxted) '… the trip was terminated with the intention to return to Brighton. The engine had to take water at Oxted for the return trip to Brighton and whilst this was being done it was found that the fire box brick lining was damaged and the engine became a partial failure and could not take the stock back to Brighton. Oxted could not berth the stock and it was taken to Edenbridge Town by the "Leader" class engine and berthed there. Arrangements were made to take the stock from Edenbridge Town to Eastbourne where it was required for the weekend working. An adaptor was carried on the engine to enable water to be taken from an ordinary water crane but even so, it took almost an hour to top up the engine water tank. The result of the above Test Trip, the second, was again unsatisfactory.'

Ironically, the intended destination at Victoria was just a further 20 miles further on from Oxted. One other thought concerns what the arrangements might have been upon arrival in London? An immediately turn around and return is perhaps unlikely. The test crew would probably want to examine the engine to ensure all was well before the return so a trip to Stewarts Lane depot. Any return working from Victoria itself would also be interesting to see how the engine performed under load on the steep climb from the terminus up Grosvenor bank. After this it is probably safe to say the route back would have been cross-country again, somehow the thought of No. 36001 galloping away down the Brighton main line was unlikely to have been worth the risk – indeed No. 36001 only rarely ventured on to any part of the 'Brighton line' and then only in crossing from one cross-country route to another.

From Inspector Walton's report:
Engine No. 36001: Driver Capelin: Guard Twigley.
(Again no Fireman is named.)
Load – 8 coaches 260 tons.

Timings	Booked	Actual	
Brighton	9.50 am	9.51 am	1 min. Sigs.
Lewes	10.7	10.8	
Culver Junction	10.12	10.13	
Buxted		10.26 10.39	
Crowborough	10.33	10.55	21 mins. Loss by Eng, short of steam
Eridge	10.40	10.59½	2½ mins. Regained by ENGINE
Birchden Jc.	10.42	11.1 11.7	7 Sigs.
Ashurst Jc.	10.44	11.10	
Edenbridge Tn.	10.58	11.26 11.51	Shunted for Traffic.
Hurst Green Jc.	11.7	12.2	
Oxted	11.10	12.4	Terminated.
Oxted		2.5 pm	
Hurst Green Jct.		2.8	
Edenbridge Tn.		2.14	Stock berthed.
Lt Engine			
Edenbridge Tn.		2.49pm	
Ashurst Jct.		3.19	
Birchden Jct.		3.20	
Eridg4725/86		3.22	
Redgate Mill Jct.		3.24	
Crowborough		3.28	
Uckfield		3.40	
Isfield		3.46 4.0	Shunted for Traffic.
Culver Jct.		4.6	
Lewes		4.13 4.25	Waiting Traffic.
Brighton		4.44	

Click's writings indicate he was not involved directly with the Brighton trials, which he describes as 'a bitter blow'. He also adds that as the failures began to accumulate it was decided not to involve the testing section (although we know Attwell at least had been involved at times) and instead to send out draughtsmen on the engine 'after all they had done the design work, and it would be very good for them to see life out in the raw, for the first time in too many cases. It brought some of them down to earth with a bump long overdue.' As to who might have made that decision, it is not reported.

Digressing slightly on the subject of draughtsman, John Click gives an insight into one individual who was perhaps not quite as might have been expected. '… a new gentleman was recruited though I must say I thought he was more trouble than he was worth. Long experience and exposure to the sun in Africa had wrought irreversible

Another Oxted view with the test train waiting to head back towards Brighton. Observe the driver (?) standing at the cab door and from his position being clearly foul of the loading gauge. Of necessity during shunt movements the cab door had to be open but then if he looked outside, he risked being dangerously close to lineside structures.
J.G. Click/National Railway Museum

changes in him. Before he could work, he had to have his board altered to an almost vertical position, universal now but very eccentric then. He began by making drawings of brackets, pulleys, and weights he required, and of the special square. The toolroom obliged, and he fussed about for a week before declaring himself satisfied. He prepared to work but before that happy development there was a slithering sound as the tee-square rushed up his board, bounded over the top and crashed on to the floor scattering instruments everywhere. He swore in what most took to be an African tribal dialect though I must say I thought it was French. He only ever did one drawing – the main vacuum pipes. *(For what engine is not mentioned but it cannot have been No. 36001 or her sisters.)* After he had left we found that as drawn the pipe had to pass through both the inner and outer fireboxes en route from one end of the engine to the other; we concluded that was not a complication worth incorporating.'

But away from the flippancy there was also the serious. On another unreported test run and whilst the engine was undergoing the trials from Brighton, six draughtsmen were travelling in the rear cab. Passing through Crowborough tunnel a freak vacuum was created and it was only perhaps by good fortune that tragedy was avoided for these men, who were on the point suffocating. Having three cabs and a connecting corridor, even if that was alongside the boiler, was hardly ideal to stand in – whilst the fireman's cab was, to say the least, 'cosy' – did mean the engine could carry a considerable number: the record was actually eighteen crew and fitters/observers on one occasion (no date given). In addition we know Bulleid and other distinguished guests and senior staff similarly travelled, one of these being André Chapelon.

A Leader would of course later reach London, two members of the class in fact, Nos 36002 and 36003, but neither would be in steam, and the engines were instead quietly just hauled to store at New Cross Gate pending (the inevitable) decision as to their future.

No. 36001's return to Brighton on the afternoon of 8 September might thus be viewed from two opposing standpoints. The first, one of sympathy and disappointment, the second a realisation that the future was bleak. It would also be reasonable to assume there were individuals around who were surprised the trials were still being continued, but recommence they did with two runs from Brighton to Crowborough on 16 September with loads of 180 and then 271t. We should also not lose sight of the fact that this was still less than three months from when No. 36001 had first turned a wheel.

What is also interesting to note is that there appear to have been no more comments over difficulties with the sleeve valves, instead it is the steaming that is being erratic. We have to believe this was also more a locomotive issue and not due to the fuel provided or the ability or otherwise of the fireman. The 16 September trial was reported as displaying no difficulties as regards the sleeves or firebox lining but again it was the erratic steaming that resulted in this, as with so many runs, being deemed an official failure.

In general terms it must be admitted that the modifications being made to the engine were very much on the basis of trial and error. Individuals from the drawing office and the testing section, men such as, W.H. 'Joe' Hutchinson and Harry Attwell, doing their level best on the trials but often restricted due to the lack of any scientific test equipment being available. Brighton, or indeed the Southern Region (Railway), had nothing like the sophisticated measuring and monitoring equipment that had been available to the other three companies, although of course Leader would benefit (?) from dynamometer car trials later.

This BR view recorded at Oxted, a favoured location for several views, shows the engine in the midst of four successful days of running from Brighton to Oxted and Polegate with loads of between 153 and 255t. To the present writer this is perhaps one of the most depressing images, captured between 21 and 24 November 1949, because Leader's progress was all downhill thereafter. The official record is not clear which load was taken when and where but most probably an 'a.m.' then a 'p.m.' trial, the engine running round at each destination. The grey day and the grey locomotive accentuate the gloom of the occasion whilst it may be noted the oscillating gear has been removed from No. 1 end, although the vertical 'markers' are still present. *British Railways*

Light engine; near Lewes and stopped for signals. As we know, load trials, and with so many ending in failures, resulted in what was a string of almost continuous repairs and modifications, which were then tested in the form of light engine working before No. 36001 was entrusted with a load again. For those who had belief in the concept, including John Click, it must have been thoroughly disheartening, especially as the order to suspend further work on the rest of the build was hardly a good omen. No. 36001 is seen here with the oscillating gear dustcover removed but the actual oscillating gear intact on No. 2 bogie. One point to note is the engine had a tendency to prime, caused on occasions by over enthusiastic firing but also a desire on the part of fireman to always have enough steam and water should the testing staff demand a maximum effort. In this respect being separated from the driver was a disadvantage. Built with a maximum 280psi boiler pressure, unlike as occurred to the Pacific type later, this maximum pressure was never reduced. *C.C.B. Herbert*

No. 2 end this time with the oscillating gear removed. Whether running the engine in this condition contributed further to additional wear is a rumour that cannot be confirmed either way. Notice the lampshade cover over the coupling light. We might also mention the steam heat pipe is still connected, although likely this and the vacuum pipe would have had to be disconnected to access the sleeves, and when it had been in place, the oscillating gear. By reconnecting the steam heat, perhaps the works staff were considering the comfort of the guard in the train during the autumn and winter trials.
John Click/National Railway Museum

In so far as the poor steaming, or perhaps we should say more accurately erratic steaming, was concerned, Bulleid was of the opinion that the difficulties were traceable to the front-end design and accordingly the size of the chokes was reduced within the multiple jet blast pipe, although this resulted in fire-throwing. (We have to careful here as to dates, as fire throwing had been mentioned once before with the spark arrestor.) Instead what we can be certain of is that a new and more resilient' type of firebrick lining was installed – whether this was the cast iron bricks known to have been fitted later, is not certain.

Further modifications to the blast pipe orifices meant another three days without work, but when venturing out next on 19 September, there were again similar problems. There was then another modification to the blast-pipe and the engine was programmed to work a further two trips with varying trailing loads the next day – 20 September. Clearly these modifications were relatively simple and indeed possible to achieve with the engine still 'warm', as proven by the limited time available for work to be conducted at Brighton between successive test runs. Alterations of this type were most likely made in the works rather than the running shed.

Unfortunately Tuesday 20 September was not a good day. Although destined for Crowborough, in the area of Uckfield a distinctive 'crack' announced the failure of one of the sleeve valves, this affecting the middle cylinder on No. 1 bogie (again), at a point where the forward extensions were attached to the oscillating gear. Dismantling of the associated parts by the fitter who accompanied every trial allowed the engine to return to Brighton, the subsequent return light engine.

Reference to the fitter is also of interest, as at least one artisan would accompany the engine on each trial – often it appears there were two – together with the other observers from either the test section or design office. No special tools were carried, necessary repairs (or dismantling) was undertaken with basic tools, no doubt including various size hammers, a crowbar or two – accompanied most likely by a few expletives from time to time.

Here, if it were needed, was also proof that the poor steaming was still not the only problem. The sleeve valves were still not 100% reliable and in consequence the bold step was taken (by whom – Bulleid perhaps?) to remove the oscillating gear completely from No. 1 bogie whilst at the same time the Mechanite 'valve guides' were replaced by an identical component made of steel. (The reference to the 'valve guides' being replaced in this way is taken from one of the official reports on the engine although it must also be said this is the first time such a component has been referred to. Could it actually mean the cylinder liners? Whatever the part, it would have been thought that time would also have been needed to manufacture such components and yet 36001 was out of service for just two days before she was steamed again, complete with modifications. It would likewise appear the oscillating gear associated with No. 2 bogie was left intact at this stage – proof again of the earlier comments associated with the sleeve failures seemingly only affecting the one end. A second comment from the same time referred to necessary patching of some of the lower fire-bricks consequent upon them being badly worn – but how exactly do you 'patch a fire-brick'?

Meanwhile the traffic department log of the run of 20 September was as follows:

Trial trip of Leader Class Engine, Tuesday 20 September, 1949.
The arrangements shown in L.C.D. (London Central Division) Notice No. 952 for the above were quite satisfactory. The train was formed as under:–
Engine 36001 – Driver Long
10 vehicles – 271 tons – Guard Morris, Brighton.
Running was as under:–

	Booked	Actual	
Brighton	9.50	9.50	
Kemp Town Junction	9.53	9.54	Signals
Falmer	9.58	9.59	
Lewes	10. 7	10.8	
Culver Junction	10.12	10.14	
Uckfield	10.19	10.21	
Crowborough	10.33		

Owing to trouble developing in the valve gear of the engine the train terminated at Uckfield where it was shunted without causing delay to other traffic.
An engine was requested to haul the stock back to Brighton, this left at 11.58 am.
The Leader engine after receiving attention of fitters left under its own power for Brighton at 1.20pm, running at reduced speed as under: –

	Arrive pm	Depart/Pass pm	
Uckfield		1.20	
Culver Junction		1.34	
Lewes Home Signal	1.41	2.5	
Lewes		2.7	
Falmer		2.18	
Kemp Town Junction		2.25	
Brighton	2.28		To Loco Works at 2.34 pm

It is possible the 1.12pm Ore to Brighton was delayed by this engine.
Redhill Control were kept advised of the position at Uckfield.'
A different Inspector was also involved – A.E. Gayland.

Leaving the question of how to patch fire-bricks unanswered for the moment, let us instead turn to Bulleid's own part in the continuing saga. Retained by the Railway Executive to oversee the trials and hopefully intended commissioning into service of Leader, his control over the whole project appears to have been lessening, although it should be stated this may well have been at his own insistence. It is the opinion of the present author that outside forces were involved, one engineer, Ron Jarvis, at least, was placed in a senior position by the Railway Executive and was now in effective control of the project and reporting directly back to Riddles. Bulleid had been originally due to retire from BR – he received a presentation set of cutlery at Waterloo on 23 September – with effect from the end of that month. He could be said to be occupying a dual role as he had been consulting engineer to the Irish National Railway system from 26 April 1949 but with the caveat. 'The appointment to the "CIE" ...to take effect as soon as Mr Bulleid can become available'. Most surprising of all was that in September 1949 he was passed an olive branch in the form of a request from Riddles to extend his tenure with British Railways, which allowed for him to remain in theoretical control of the Leader project until the end of 1949.

Away from the thought of any allegation of political interference, No. 36001 was made ready to test the repairs and sleeve modifications in the form of a series of light engine runs between Brighton and Crowborough from 23 to 25 September. A total of five runs were made amounting to some 235 miles, all of which were successful in so far as the sleeves were concerned, although again the firebricks were reported as needing 'slight attention' following the final run. For this latter reason the later official report on the engine deemed the Sunday 25 September run as a 'failure'.

Possibly the staff now took the opportunity for a belated day off, as the next series of trials commenced on Tuesday 27 September and ran until Friday 30 September and involved a relatively light load of just five bogie vehicles to Lewes, Crowborough, and as far afield as Oxted. Over four days, a total of 447 miles was covered with no mechanical difficulties encountered but still the steaming was being erratic.

What changes if any ('tinkering' perhaps?) was undertaken next is not reported, and possibly nothing at all. Despite the previous steaming problems, the same type of trial was scheduled to recommence on 3 October, although restricted to Crowborough only. As might well have been expected, the same difficulties occurred as before.

Additionally, and for the first time, both drive chains feeding the oil circulation pumps became detached and whilst these were relatively easy to replace, when the same defect threatened on the second day, the governor valve to the pumps was immediately suspect. Clearly with lubrication such a crucial issue, this sequence of tests was again terminated. The firebricks were also found to be in poor condition after the last run.

It is at this stage in the official records that the first mention is made of the provision of cast-iron firebricks, although, as stated earlier, it may well have been that these had been in use beforehand.

Testing resumed again on 9 October, the destination now to be Groombridge, and the load again a paltry 150t. Four men were on board: Brighton driver Bill Long and fireman Ted Forder, a works fitter, and test engineer Harry Attwell. At Crowborough, however, the engine failed again and this time in spectacular fashion with the cast iron firebricks having melted into the fire on one side of the firebox – the other side threatening to do the same. The consequential heat for the fireman within the firing compartment can only be imagined, although ironically approaching the point of failure there had still been difficulties with poor steaming.

These were not circumstances under which the test could continue so after allowing a suitable 'cooling off period' (probably for all concerned), it was once again light engine to Brighton.

At this stage it may be appropriate to consider the actual steaming qualities of the engine itself. Leader's boiler was without doubt a superbly designed steam-producing vessel. Bulleid was a master at boiler design and this was also probably his best ever. Indeed, even allowing for the lack of a water jacket around the sides and rear of the firebox – normally one of the hottest parts and in consequence where most steam will be generated –, the provision of the thermic siphons, allied to excellent water circulation, more than compensated for this omission. Let there be no doubt, Leader's firebox and boiler could certainly generate steam – the trouble is that it was not being used efficiently. Indeed the heat involved on that fateful day can only be imagined, as a temperature in the order of 2,700°F was needed to melt the cast iron! Do not though fall into the trap that so many others have in the past, this was an exception with regards to heat, agreed, even if it was an unacceptable exception.

Indeed Click confirms the boiler's capability by saying, 'No. 36001 didn't take long to make steam because the grate area was large compared with the volume of water in the boiler. Full pressure could be got from cold in not much over two hours but a lot of smoke would result and damage to the brick lining of the firebox occurred due to differential expansion.' (We should read the term 'bricks' to mean in general terms regardless as being of conventional fired clay or cast iron.) Going forward but continuing on the same theme and once more from Click, 'Jarvis said he had tried to get Riddles to try a Leader boiler in one of the Garratts but without any success.' Folklore also has it that there had been suggestions to put a Merchant Navy boiler on a Britannia but that idea was shelved for no other reason than weight.

Returning to 1949, the central firing compartment of Leader was often cooler than the cab of other steam engines due to air from outside being drawn in towards the firehole, although condensation and consequential humidity was a separate issue and one that was never

Oxted, again, with No. 36001 seemingly in the process of having run round and now being coupled to its train. The lack of any headcode discs and the 'wrong road' positioning would tend to confirm this. Again note how far out of the cab the driver is forced to stand. *G.E.S. Parker/Kidderminster Railway museum. Colour by David Williams*

Another *Times* image probably taken around the same time and in the same vicinity. (The Press photographer would most likely have made contact with British Railways to ascertain when the engine was – hopefully – running and on which lines.) No other newspapers appear to have shown any images of the engine around this period. Folklore has it that when the signalman was alerted, in consequence of a special traffic weekly or daily notice that the engine was running, they would advise nearby residents in advance to take in any washing as Leader was known to throw sparks and cinders over a wide area. *Colour by David Williams*

An all too frequent occurrence: No. 36001 being shunted at Brighton works and again in the course of repair/modification. Notice the lower half of the drive casing is missing from No. 1 bogie, along with two of the spring covers. Having failed to distinguish itself it is not surprising that there is no further mention of the type working Oxted line trains or the Brighton–Bournemouth services. Indeed it might even be said that some of the urgency seemed to go out of the project as soon as the first 2-6-4T locos based on the Fairburn design began to appear on the Southern. From this time on it was more a case of 'proving Leader' rather than preparing it for service – whatever that might then have been.

resolved. Indeed the oft-quoted comment that the temperature of the central cab of Leader would reach 120° was wrong – it was actually measured at 122° BUT on the same day a reading in the cab of a Merchant Navy Pacific revealed 140°. This is proof, if it were needed, that by being deliberately economical with the truth and when used out of context, the incorrect information will abound. This was just one of the many aspects used by 'authority' and supposedly informed journalism, to condemn a project out of hand. Yes, Leader was hot – but others were hotter. (According to Antony Bulleid, by March 1950, '… the firebox was stokeable by an asbestos-clad fireman'. This somewhat sweeping comment has not been borne out anywhere else and was never mentioned in interviews with the author personally by any of the crews who worked the engine at the time, nor any of those he spoke to who travelled on Leader, or were associated with the trials. The again-ambiguous statement that the men wore sacking around their legs to protect themselves from the heat is similar.)

Around this time as an alternative to the cast-iron, conventional, albeit thicker, firebricks were introduced. These amounted to some 3½in thickness and were attached using larger, and thus supposedly stronger, securing hooks. Another problem was that the firebricks were multi-functional. Their main role was of course to retain the heat of the fire itself and radiate this back into the firebox whilst a secondary task was to protect the plain sheet sides of the firebox from what would otherwise be severe heat distortion and at the same time reduce the heat that would otherwise be present at the corridor side of the firebox. With the bricks themselves having fallen or become dislodged on a number of previous occasions, the side walls were thus distorted by the radiant heat of the fire and this in turn this altered the position of the securing hooks. It was a no-win situation – the more heat, the greater the distortion, and the greater the distortion, the more chance of the firebricks falling – consequently, greater heat again. To reduce the heat along the side of the firebox, a subsidiary water tank (known as the mantle tank) was installed around part of the exterior side of the firebox. This was never intended to be a steam-producing tank, merely an additional water storage unit and which, it appears, was a somewhat late addition to the design. Its purpose was hardly to increase the water capacity as a few gallons there would make little difference (the exact capacity is not known), but instead was suggested as being necessary to afford some form of 'insulation' between the potentially hot firebox sides and the man working in the compartment. Unfortunately, as the same tank was also part of the feedwater supply, the water generally became hotter than desirable for the efficient working of the injectors – and which would then not work.

Fitting the new firebricks occupied almost fourteen days and it was not until Saturday 22 October that the engine was ready for another trial run. Now testing would often continue over a weekend and likely for several reasons. Firstly, and perhaps most obviously, there was a degree of urgency over the whole project. Bulleid himself was only to be around for a further two months, and in similar fashion to a few months earlier when wanting to complete the build as soon as possible, so it was again very much a race to produce a workable engine. In addition, line occupancy, as well as stock and staff availability, was sometimes best achieved at weekends. The various wages-grade men involved were no doubt also glad of the overtime the project generated. But to be fair, there were also other side-benefits from working with Leader and with Bulleid in particular. Recall him laying on the canteen supper the night before the engine made its first trip to Eastleigh? Well, now he regularly gave a £1 tip to the crew every time he travelled on the engine.[1] (It has been suggested that officially Bulleid had to seek permission from Marylebone Road if he wanted to travel on No. 36001, but as he was notionally still in charge of the project this is perhaps unlikely.) Harry Attwell was likewise recalled for his generosity and would share bars of chocolate with the driver and fireman at a time when such confectionary was difficult to obtain and still on ration.

With all eyes now on this latest medication to the firebox, No. 36001 successfully took another featherweight train of just 150t from Brighton to, it was said, 'Oxted and Crowborough'. (Does this again mean two separate tests or were the destination names simply written in reverse order?) Regardless of the locations visited, all was well on 22 October, and likewise for a similar performance the following day. The plan was then to repeat the same on Monday 24 October.

But now the gremlins again showed their hand with what is believed to have been the first major failure to affect No. 2 bogie and the fracture of the middle sleeve. This took place near Lewes, although the direction of travel at the time, outward or return, was not stated.

Investigation at Brighton revealed the cause was probably simple metal fatigue affecting the extensions 'ears' of the sleeve valves and as a result the oscillating gear was similarly removed from this bogie as well.

With the complicated oscillating gear now no longer a feature of either bogie, testing recommenced again on 29 October with the engine visiting what was then new ground, as the destination was Tunbridge Wells via Crowborough. For the first two days in this series of runs, the trips were understandably 'light engine' and to the same destination. Subsequently, however, and continuing through until 13 December, varying loads of between 153 and 255t were taken daily and again either to the same or similar destinations. Two trips per day might also be involved and perhaps involving a different trailing load in the morning and afternoon. (This was again purely for operational convenience and would sometimes simply depend upon what stock was available at the time.) As had been the case with No. 2039, the trials would usually commence from Brighton Station, which would then enable a realistic comparison to be made with actual operating times.

Without doubt this period of running, an aggregate of 27 days working over the period, would probably also witness what was the most consistent success of Leader at any time in its short life. True, there still some difficulties with the steaming as well as the firebox lining, whilst occasional mechanical defects in the form of broken valve rods and circlips still occurred but compared with what had occurred in the past it was more success than failure.

Bulleid was on board on a number of occasions, one memorable run with him recalled by the crew relative to a comment from the designer when the engine was just about to start the 4¾ mile climb from Buxted to Crowborough. 'come on let's get to the top as quickly as possible … then if anything is going to fail at least we will find out what and why.' The crew of course diligently obliged, even if the unexpected demands for steam had meant the fireman was ill-prepared for the effort and in consequence the engine surmounted the summit with just 120psi showing on the gauge. Even so the distance had been accomplished in the astonishing time of just 4½ minutes, less than half of the normal timetable allowance of 10 minutes and at an average of more than 60mph on a rising gradient. Nothing untoward occurred; unfortunately the date of the occasion in question is not recorded. Whether as a result of stress created during the first run, or some other cause, a second trial over the same route later the same day, but this time without the presence of Bulleid, resulted in failure.

On another occasion Harry Attwell was riding alone in the rear cab when there was a sudden 'crack-crack'. At first impression, this implied the immediate failure of two of the sleeve valves – it transpires the noise was no more than the engine passing over two fog signals!

But despite the apparent success now being enjoyed, there was considerable gloom at Brighton on 19 November 1949 when information was received that a directive had been issued by Riddles at Marylebone instructing that all work on the other engines in the series, Nos 36002–5, was to cease immediately. Bulleid's thoughts at this time were not recorded, but it must have been disheartening for so many of the others who had all worked so hard up to now.

Click explains that behind the scenes much had been going on, and this despite assurances given to Bulleid concerning him overseeing the whole project. Click is not totally clear on some of his dates, nor for that matter the order of events (the J.G. Click notes are a series of typed pages NOT a complete manuscript and some pages are missing whilst others have clearly been drafted and then re-drafted with no way of knowing which is the most up-to-date).

Part of the correspondence also indicates that Riddles himself may not always have been quite up to speed with progress. For example on 22 November 1948, a full eight

In temporary store, again at Brighton, on 8 February 1960, having made another visit to Eastleigh six days earlier. This view gives a good indication of the placement of the access steps to the central cab, hardly ideal but necessary due to the position of the innermost axlebox cover on the rear bogie. At the front someone is about to mount the front cab. Leader is immediately adjacent to a WD 2-8-0, several of which were being repaired at Brighton around this time.

months before the first engine turned a wheel, Riddles wrote to John Elliot, the Chief Regional Officer at Waterloo. (The CRO was in the equivalent post as had been the former General Manager.) 'My dear Elliot', then under the heading 'New 0-6-6-0 Steam Tank Locomotives' Riddles makes 'one or two points which I consider important and on which I should like to have your views'. Pointing out that individual costing of locomotives had not been a Southern practice, he went on ask the CRO to arrange for:

(1) A daily log for each of the five engines showing work performed and the mileage run.

(2) A daily record of running shed attention and repairs carried out with information regarding issues of lubricating oil.

(3) A record of running shed repairs and examinations.

(4) Individual records of costs of repairs or alterations in Main Works.

'Coal consumption will, of course, be an important point but this aspect of the matter will be covered by dynamometer car tests in due course'. (*This is the first time we hear mention of these, so also clearly planned very early on*). Possibly also with visions of OVB doing something exotically non-standard over names and painting, he reminded Elliot that 'in accordance with R.E. Memo. M.137' (of 3.5.48), proposals for the names of new locomotives are required to be submitted to The Railway Executive. 'A Committee is dealing with this matter in a general way and will shortly be making recommendations but as these engines are at the moment known as the "Leader" class, you will no doubt have some particular names in mind and I shall be glad if you will submit your proposals as soon as possible.' This letter concluded, 'As these engines are mixed traffic types I presume you are arranging for them to be painted black and lined in accordance with the decision conveyed in my letter of 26 April 1948, to Mr Bulleid, copy of which was sent to you.' All a bit heavy-handed by today's standards but very much in the idiom of the time.

The CRO acted as postman at once, and replied to Riddles agreeing about the proposed costing, promising to write 'shortly' about names and saying, cheerfully, 'As these are Mixed Traffic Engines they will of course be painted black and suitably lined and I think they will look very well.'

Riddles wrote personally to Bulleid a fortnight later and was sent the following reply, with Bulleid clearly a little irked at having to write to confirm a conversation. 'Dear Riddles, I informed you verbally that this locomotive is not yet in service. Your request for records has not been overlooked and as soon as the locomotive is delivered to traffic they will be kept and sent to you.' It was signed 'Oliver Bulleid'.

We move now to sometime in 1949, at a guess around October, with Riddles clearly not a happy man. We say this for he sent a 'tight' letter (JGC's word) to S.B. Warder at Brighton. Click recalls: 'Warder though was not there – but Smeddle (ex LNER) was. *(Robert Alfred Smeddle had been appointed Assistant Mechanical and Electrical Engineer for the Southern Region in 1949. In 1951 he moved as MEE to the Western Region at Swindon.)* Warder somehow (but that was what clerks are for) endorsed the letter for Smeddle's attention A.S.A.P.! Riddles had said, "The interpretation which Mr Bulleid has put on my requests ... is not quite what I had in mind ... and it is essential that I should have a full account of its (meaning No. 36001's) performance and history since it was first turned out of the erecting shop. Will you, therefore, please gather together the information which you will have available ... and sent it to me at your early convenience." The first report was to be from day one to the end of September with monthly information "thereafter". On expenditure he asked for a "brief note" showing what No. 36001 had cost up to the time it emerged, what had been spent on the remaining four, and how much "alterations etc." had so far cost on the first locomotive. It was perfectly plain that Riddles (wise man?) was going to have chapter and verse on this one.' *(The words 'wise man' and the question mark are again those of JGC.)*

Click again, 'Eight days later Warder sent off a summary of the 'experience with the first "Leader"' engine from the time of her initial trip on the 22 June up to 30 September last.' The engine had run 2,200 miles. Regretfully we do not have a copy of the Warder report but we may assume it was eventually incorporated into the (Jarvis) Riddles' final report on the engine.

There is an amount in the previous paragraphs that we cannot leave without making further comment. Firstly the behaviour of Bulleid, where I don't think we can do other than say he was being evasive. Riddles had every right to ask as he did and not having received the response he expected, he was probably left with little alternative than to go behind Bulleid's back. But this was not an easy thing to do, as likely it would create difficulty both at the time and subsequently. It also put Warder – and/or his clerk – in a difficult position, Smeddle perhaps as well. We are not party to any discussions that might have taken place subsequently between the named individuals but what becomes ever-more clear is Bulleid's attempts at fending off questions over 'his Leader', fearful perhaps that the truth would out. We are left with the inescapable conclusion that already Bulleid must have known that in the design of No. 36001 he had gone a step too far and yet who can blame the man for wanting to prove it had all been worthwhile. Success, it must have seemed to Bulleid, was always, 'just around the corner'. This is also almost the only reference to R.A. Smeddle's time on the Southern Region and other perhaps than being aware of what was going on he does not appear to have played any significant part in SR motive power during his short tenure. Finally we should mention that at intervals throughout the JGC text there are references he makes to having copies of correspondence. If this still survives it has not been found,

so we are left with the quotes made both here and elsewhere in this text by JGC and not unfortunately the complete draft.

Any trials post 19 November might then almost seem to be a bit of a surprise but, as described already, these continued and indeed as we know, would continue to do so into the following year. It was almost as if Riddles was determined to make good on his promise regarding dynamometer working but it will also be noted that nowhere else does JGC mention this and we might wonder how and where on the Central Section lines this could have been accomplished without major disruption to traffic – one of the criteria for accurate testing being sustained periods of continuous steaming, hardly possible on the secondary lines the engine had so far mainly worked upon. There is also no further mention of whoever it was attempted to get No. 36002 substituted. (Again refer to p.172.)

During the first week of December six days out of seven were occupied with test runs. The official report showed two differing load figures per day, so indicating there were two runs each day. We have no details as to what may have occurred – if anything – on these occasions except to say the final day, 6 December, was classified as another failure but, as mentioned, for reasons we are not told.

There was then a gap from 6 December through to 12 December on which latter date started two days of runs, again without detail. That of 13 December also classified as a failure. Although unknown at the time, 13 December would also turn out to be final time No. 36001 would ever haul a load of any sort on the Central Division lines.

It had been planned to commence a new series of runs soon after, but instead, these were cancelled by the operating authorities for the simple reason of the build-up of traffic due to the Christmas peak. Instead on 16 December, Leader successfully ran light to Eastleigh for weighing. We are not told if a 'buddy' was involved but at this stage that would seem unlikely. What we can be certain of is that again the 'coastway' route via Chichester, Fareham and Botley would have been taken.

At Eastleigh the measurements taken involved weighing just one end at a time, which information could then be used by Brighton for any further modifications to come. We know the return journey was likewise completed without incident. Back at Brighton the fire was dropped and the engine was stored either inside or certainly in the vicinity of the works. Here she would remain, cold, until 27 January 1950 when a light engine run was made to Tunbridge Wells. This was followed by another light engine run to Eastleigh, likely under the same conditions as in December and probably for a further weighing. Bulleid, in the meantime, had departed for his new post in Ireland, although his BR consultancy enabling him to advise further on the engine was also additionally extended until 31 March 1950. Even so, much of Bulleid's time was now spent in Dublin and it is possible that after December 1949 he would only rarely set eyes on his creation again. One other point is that with Bulleid now

Inside the weigh house at Brighton on 28 March 1950. As will seen from the accompanying list of runs (page 287 et seq.) of No. 36001 whilst at Brighton, the engines movements between 16 December 1949 and when she moved permanently to Eastleigh were limited to just two, the remaining time spent out of the way seemingly at a few different locations within the Brighton complex. Whether the Brighton weigh table was able to accurately record the weights of the engine would seem doubtful considering the trips she made to Eastleigh for that purpose, unless it was to simply confirm the awful truth that had by now emerged. *R.K. Kirkland/Lens of Sutton Association*

absent, was the impetus for further trials removed, or did this decision to generate a lull come from another source? There is no implication or inference here, just a question being asked.

The weighing visit(s) at Eastleigh would have revealed exactly the same findings as previously and, in consequence, there were now two specific issues to address. The first was, was it was vital to attempt to balance the weights either side to a state nearer equilibrium, although an equal balance between the two sides was impossible with the boiler where it stood. Just as important was the need to comply with an instruction from the Southern Region Chief Civil Engineer at Waterloo that he would not tolerate an even heavier engine on the routes out of Brighton. The only option was to seek another location and in reality, the only place available was by basing the engine at Eastleigh, where there were the facilities of a major running shed, a main line, cross-country routes (although as mentioned these were never used) and perhaps most importantly considering her chequered history, the facilities of a main works alongside.

Indeed possibly around this time Bulleid is alleged to have expounded – seemingly in exasperation, 'send it to Eastleigh … Townroe will get it working'. (A reference to Stephen Townroe the Shed Master at Eastleigh whom Bulleid obviously held in the highest regard. Asked about the comment later, Townroe – perhaps modestly – believes the comment was misplaced and should have been, 'end it to Eastleigh … Turbett will get it working', a reference instead to the name of the Works Manager at Eastleigh and who for a time also acted as the deputy to Bulleid.) According to HAV, and in the chapter penned by Mrs Bulleid likely relevant to this period, (referring to O.V.S. Bulleid), she said: 'he was very worried and "put-out" when the Civil Engineer of the Southern Railway was difficult about the weight of Oliver's engines – thought them too heavy and demanded drastic lowering of weight which Oliver said was unnecessary, and almost impossible to achieve in keeping with his designs.'

Why with the weight issue now paramount the decision was made to return the engine to Brighton instead of attempting to make what adjustments as were possible at Eastleigh is not explained. Perhaps it was simply a capacity issue, although one is also tempted to say, without – it must be said – any foundation whatsoever, perhaps Eastleigh did not want it and Brighton were even of similar mind!

Whatever the why and the wherefore, we know the modifications were in the end made at Brighton, which included two complete changes of springs – presumably the first set were not satisfactory but of course we now ask how was it known that the first set was unsatisfactory? After this, the engine was weighed again. This time, like at Eastleigh, just one end at a time at Brighton – which of course begs the question had she been weighed like this before …. and if so, had the engine's true weight been known of for months? We can also ask where did these springs come from? The immediate answer could be to say from parts intended for Nos 36004/5 but in reality, this must be considered unlikely as the springs for these engines would have been exactly as per Nos 36001–3. Consequently we can say with certainty if weight adjustments were being made, they must have been with new springs especially manufactured for the purpose, hence the time delay in completing the work. Possibly at the same time more clearance was also given to the axlebox pedestal guides whilst the type of oil supply to the pedestal guides was similarly changed. All this undoubtedly helped but the most effective method of (counter) balancing was simply the obvious, adding pig or scrap iron, along the corridor side. (This is believed to have been little more than old brake blocks and firebars which were used.) The total amount of scrap so added eventually weighed at least 5t and has been suggested as having encroached to a height of 2ft within the corridor. Additionally recourse had to be made to pieces of slab steel both underneath the floor and vertically against the casing. The weight of scrap thus added is not absolutely confirmed although when finally accepted for test the axle-weights were subsequently known to be in the order of 24½t. Presumably too the adding of additional weight continued along the corridor running the side of the bunker? This is not confirmed anywhere but would seem to be the logical conclusion.

In the previous edition we quoted, 'The corridor obstructions meant the driver and fireman would now also be basically marooned from each other and so unable to assist each other in an emergency.'. That appears not to have been totally the case and will be confirmed in the next chapter by John Click, although it is certainly true to say access was never easy anyway.

Other modifications including further work on the valve gear, brakes, lubricators and even, it was reported, on the whistle. Whatever the defect or modification to this component was that took place, it is not recorded.

Another major change that affected the engine, whether at this time, previous or indeed subsequently is not certain, but involved the firebrick lining which was increased to a staggering 9in thick. This combination of larger bricks certainly cured the problem of the instability of the brick sides but if also effectively reduced the grate area from the original 43^{2}ft to just 25.5^{2}ft (Coincidentally the same as an M7, the very design Leader had been intended to replace.) Even so Leader would still generate steam in volume and this is a vital point to make in advance of the next chapter. We never do get figures for pounds of steam per hour from the boiler but what Leader would achieve with various trailing loads on an ascending gradient still speaks volumes for the ability of the boiler to generate steam. Make no mistake, in the boiler design (not necessarily its manufacture), Bulleid produced one of the most efficient steam-producing vessels ever run on a railway.

With the work completed, 36001 was steamed again on 27 January 1950 for a light engine trial to Tunbridge Wells. All was well. Further slight spring adjustments were then made in Brighton works together with weighing in the workshops – Brighton had been unable to accurately weigh the whole engine originally although with some figures now known it is certain one end at a time was measured but still surprising any weighing at Brighton is simply not mentioned.

Almost the final point in this the 'opening chapter' of tests, took place on 2 February when Leader made another light engine run to Eastleigh, again we may assume unaccompanied, and for a further weighing. This time we know the outwards from, and a later in the day return to, Brighton were both completed without incident.

So what next? Well as regards the engine itself the concern of the CCE was understandable. After all Leader now weighed in at something just less than 150t, the equivalent to almost 25t per axle – considerably greater than an original Merchant Navy of the time, which exposed a maximum axle weight of just 21t. (To be fair any engineer will confirm axle weights were in reality a notional figure and even engines within the same class could and would display marked variations dependent upon spring adjustment and settings. Additionally certain classes could be far more punishing to both trackwork and bridges consequent upon hammer-blow.)

But the CCE had spoken, 25t cannot be exceeded under any circumstances, and in order to remain within this figure there was now a restriction on the amount of coal and water that could be carried, meaning 3t of coal and 2,600gal of water only were all that could be on board – this compared with the design capacity of 4t and 4,000gal. There were allegations around that 36001 in both her original and subsequent heavier form had spread the track. Where and when were not stated, and certainly never proven, but by inference might rumours such as this have contributed to her later demise?

Returned to Brighton, Leader was parked in a works siding whilst her fate was considered elsewhere. Leaders 36002 and 36003 had in the meanwhile been first taken into store at the electric car sheds at Brighton but subsequently moved to Bognor for store again, pending a decision. Under cover and out of sight in the car sheds would certainly have been preferable but the Bognor move (no date is given) was likely to have been caused by space constraints.

Decisions rested with Marylebone Road and ultimately with Robin Riddles. Had he sought counsel from others, there is unlikely to have been any doubt which way Rudguard would have voted but as regards the other

In her last resting place, at Brighton at least, unloved and outside the works, 29 March 1950. Reading between the lines the impression is given that Brighton, the Chief Civil Engineer especially, would be glad to see the back of the engine; she is certainly no longer the gleaming machine of just nine months earlier. *Terry Cole*

perhaps key players, Roland Bond and E.S. Cox, we cannot be certain. Whether Bulleid's one-time ally Missenden was ever consulted, or indeed Elliot at Waterloo, is not known. Somehow we may doubt Bulleid was also involved. Perhaps because of this Bulleid, despite being occupied at Inchicore, attempted to procure a meeting with Missenden and Riddles at which no doubt he would have attempted to use his persuasive skills to best effect, but for reasons that are not clear this was not possible to achieve. In all probability the other parties were far from keen on such a meeting as it could have resulted in definite decisions having to made there and then. Even Missenden, Bulleid's former ally, privately at least might well have had an 'out of sight out of mind' perspective.

Having failed in his attempt to have a face-to-face discussion over the engine, Bulleid's next shot was in a letter to both men, in which it almost appeared as if he was admitting defeat. He writes, 'I am quite satisfied the engine can be made a useful and valuable locomotive and Mr Granshaw, the Locomotive Manager at Brighton, with the help he is receiving from Mr Jarvis, the Chief Draughtsman, can be relied upon to see that this is done.

'I shall always appreciate deeply having been permitted to follow the development of the "Leader" engine so far, *as it has given me much valuable information for future work.*

'I would like to add my acknowledgment of the help I have had from everyone concerned and especially the courtesy I have always had from Mr Riddles.

'As I do not think my services are necessary any longer and as I feel I may well be an embarrassment, I shall be obliged if I can be released from the arrangement made last September. I shall be available for consultation if desired and if I can be of any help at any time I shall always be only too pleased to give it.'

But could this have been a double bluff? (The words shown emphasised above are shown as such by the present writer.) Might Bulleid have been trying to shame/warn Riddles he intended to learn from Leader and then succeed in the future? In which case Riddles had better be sure in whatever decision was made.

Elsewhere a somewhat more critical appraisal had been prepared by R.G. Jarvis and which was submitted to Riddles, 'I have been asked by Mr Warder to express my views on this experiment as the Regional Chief Technical Assistant responsible for design. No personal criticism is inferred in the remarks which follow, and the views expressed represent my views which may well be at variance with those of the designers of the locomotive, on the basis that if doctors can differ, so may engineers.'

Jarvis continued by repeating the aims Bulleid had first set himself to achieve and then compared these with the actual results in practice. In particular,

(1) The weight will restrict route availability.

(2) The enclosure and lubrication of engines, axle boxes and springs is very unsatisfactory.

(3) The increased steam chest volume and port areas, and the reduced clearance volumes, may only have a minimal effect on thermal efficiency judging by recent tests at Rugby Test Plant. (The Rugby test results referred to related to other steam engines tested there and not Leader.)

(4) Replacement of firebox water-legs by firebricks is not successful.

Jarvis continued, 'the disappointing progress made with the locomotive to date is to a much greater extent attributable to the detail design than to the broad conception.' He stated that there was an essential need for self-aligning axle bearings, that the fireman's confined space was very unsatisfactory and dangerous in the event of a blow-back on entering a tunnel, and that the valve gear was unsatisfactory on three counts: the out-rigger drive to the valves, the bad effects as wear developed, and the fear of thermal distortion in the fabricated cylinders. He would also have preferred smaller wheels.

Jarvis concluded, 'The design has certain attractive features, it has many problems to solve, and it has some fundamental defects. That the locomotive could be made to work I have no doubt, but a great deal of experimental work will be necessary. It all depends upon how much money can be permitted for the modifications which will entail virtually a complete re-arrangement.'

It would be quite reasonable to suppose that in view of the above, Leader would be condemned there and then but not so. Instead, after some deliberation, Riddles finally decided to accede to Bulleid's original comment that the engine should be sent to Eastleigh. There it would be subject not just to testing, but to those full-scale dynamometer car trials previously mentioned.

Accordingly 36001 steamed away quietly from Brighton on Thursday 13 April 1950 bound for Hampshire. The feelings of the staff at Brighton at this departure were not recorded, some no doubt sad, others probably glad to see it go. Leader was like that, there were never any half-measures, it was like it or loath it. Time would tell which way the men at Eastleigh would respond.

Notes

(1) Allowing for inflation, £1 in 1949 was the equivalent of £34.49 in 2020.

The final view of the engine at Brighton was taken a few days later, indeed probably one of the last photographs to be taken of the engine on the central section. The door to the fireman's compartment is open, the latter sometimes referred to as the 'central' firing cab. As seen, it was nowhere near the centre point of the longitudinal axis and was instead located at the end of the boiler/smokebox and ahead of the coal/water bunker. Leader would move to Eastleigh a few days later on 13 April – no images of this move had been uncovered. Just visible on the right in this and the previous view, the sheeted over item could well be the frames and boiler of the incomplete No. 36004. It might even seem as if an effort has been made to smarten the front at least, it certainly appears a little bit cleaner than a few days earlier. Considerably more than a clean engine would be needed to impress those at her new home.
Terry Cole

9

'The Great Grey Galloping Sausage'
(vis-à-vis the Trials from Eastleigh)

Upon arrival at Eastleigh, No. 36001 was literally on her own. Bulleid had moved on to his new role at Inchicore and Leader was thus left to prove the viability of the design. With hindsight we can probably admit the die was already cast and, even if not spoken of publicly, the eventual outcome must have been fairly obvious. Leader would have to produce something beyond extraordinary to change that – and yet in October and November 1950, she almost did!

So with her creator now ensconced in Ireland it was Riddles who was in directional control, whilst Laurie Granshaw was also brought over from Brighton to take overall change of the latest trials, with Ron Jarvis tasked with issues relative to the dynamometer car trials.

As the engine had already visited Eastleigh on four previous occasions, between June 1949 and February 1950, in consequence it was only to be expected that some footplatemen had already ventured to look at ('admire' would be the wrong word to use) her and had formed their own opinion. Consequently it cannot really have come as much of a surprise when representatives from ASLEF approached the shed management to announce that ASLEF staff would not work the engine for fear of danger to the fireman in the event of the engine turning over onto its corridor side, meaning any escape from the central compartment would be nigh on impossible.

In many respects this was a logical comment to make because the firing compartment had just the single means of access and egress, and any alternative along the side corridor would be difficult, to say the least, due to the presence of the additional weight. In addition, if the engine had turned over, the crumple factor of the thin sheet metal forming the external sides would probably have rendered even this means of escape impossible. That said, with the weight still favouring the opposite side, it was perhaps less likely. Fortunately no such eventuality ever arose; there is no record that No. 36001 ever derailed even one pair of wheels. (But we should not forget the failure of the crank-axle when under steam later; this could have, but fortunately did not, result in a derailment. Recall the dramatic failure of the crank-axle of No. 35020 at Crewkerne just a few years later.)

The matter was left in the hands of Stephen Townroe, then the Assistant District Motive Power Superintendent, based at Eastleigh, and whose responsibility also included Eastleigh shed itself. Townroe admits he was more a devotee of Maunsell rather than Bulleid. This was the logic of an operating man, although he would admit a Bulleid Pacific was excellent, on some occasions indeed without equal, but the performance was also erratic and so difficult to maintain with the engines in their original form. (This was of course some little way before the rebuilding of so many of the Bulleid breed, although the erratic behaviour of the class had already raised discussion amongst the higher echelons at Marylebone, and the subsequent rebuilding was intended to produce a more reliable machine.) Thus Leader was compared with the simpler Maunsell designs, the King Arthur type in particular, which were both predictable, reliable and simpler to maintain. (The Lord Nelson class were perhaps a little more difficult, but with coaxing Townroe, through his Inspectors, was able to educate both driver and fireman to achieve the best possible. Mr Townroe's preference also comes through a little in his masterful work *'Arthurs, Nelsons and Schools at work'*.[1] We have already mentioned how the original choice by Bulleid when wishing to secure a locomotive on which to experiment with sleeve valves was indeed a King Arthur, but this was vetoed not only because the extra width across the cylinders would have fouled the loading gauge but also by the SR traffic department as being potentially too useful a machine to lose – might Townroe have a hand in that decision as well?

It must be said, a man like Stephen Townroe did not rise to his present role and indeed later as District Motive Power Superintendent without both knowledge and guile. Accordingly so far as the ASLEF complaint was concerned, an effective compromise was reached (one where it could be said neither side 'lost face') and it was agreed with ASLEF that their members would only work

On 13 April Leader has arrived at Eastleigh (we assume running light under her own power) and, after having the fire dropped at the shed, now sits in the works yard. The last time she had been in a similar position for any length of time previously was ten months earlier during the June 1949 inspection, other visits to Eastleigh in the interim being of very short duration before returning east again. Now she was here to stay with little movement, apart perhaps from being shunted at times, to take place for another seven weeks. What hopes had been aroused back in June and what disappointment had occurred since. Bulleid's comment, 'Take it to Eastleigh, Townroe will get it going' has perhaps been misheard over the years for perhaps he meant 'Turbett will get it going', references to the Eastleigh Shed Master and Works Manager respectively. Unfortunately Leader's reputation had preceded its arrival and it would also be necessary to resolve an ASLEF issue over manning the engine.

Inside Eastleigh works on Saturday 20 May 1950 and seemingly also the day of a society visit. It has not been possible to trace and speak to anyone who might have seen and climbed aboard her on this or a similar occasion hence we cannot comment on the impression she made. All we can say for certain is she was 'different'. The light painted panel where Brighton covered over the original emblem and number midships is still apparent. Why the delay in commencing trials at Eastleigh is not totally explained. Perhaps it was simply that the urgency had gone out of the situation and Eastleigh were waiting the time when the dynamometer car would arrive. Agreement with ASLEF for a trials crew to work the engine under test also had to be sought.
Bluebell Railway Museum.

the engine on the basis of trials alone and that a major redesign would be necessary before it would be accepted into general service. This might even be said to have given Riddles even more ammunition for the engine's future but society in post-war Britain was very different to how it had been years before, whilst we may even ponder briefly on the attitude of somebody like Dugald Drummond under similar circumstances. (It is believed Alf Smith, the regular driver of Leader on its trials from Eastleigh, was in fact nothing to do with ASLEF anyway, being instead a member of the alternative National Union of Railwayman!)

So whilst the subject was discussed – probably at length – at Eastleigh, Brighton, Waterloo and Marylebone, the engine itself, No. 36001, stood quiet and cold either in the confines of the shed or inside the neighbouring works. A correspondent (perhaps it was more than one?) reported in the July 1950 issue of the *RO* that '…transverse strips fixed by welding across corridor floor to allow steel ballast to be laid on the floor space. At present about two feet deep of ballast has been installed…', however, as we have stated earlier, the depth figure given may be open to some question.

For this work to be carried out, clearly instructions had been received as to what was to occur next and this was on 5 June when following a lull of just under two months from 13 April, she was steamed and made ready for trials to Fratton commencing the next day, Tuesday 6 June.

It was just more than seven weeks since No. 36001 had ventured out onto a running line. She was in the hands of the works trial crew (not Alf Smith and Ted Forder who were based at the running shed) and was attached to her heaviest load yet, ten vehicles weighing 332t. The speed limit of 50mph still applied whilst the restrictions on coal and water content also remained – recall this was now 3t and 2,600gal. (As an aside a BR Class 4 2-6-4T held 3.5t of coal and 2,000gal of water whilst for an M7 the figures were 3.25t and 1,300gal respectively.) The 50mph speed limit had been already been advised to Brighton previously and was in force certainly for the latter part of the testing from Brighton, although we suggest that on occasions compliance may have been doubtful.

The Fratton run and the ones that followed were what might well be described as 'shakedown' trials prior to the intended soon-to-commence dynamometer car tests – the later actual recorded runs using the former LNER vehicle to start soon afterwards although it was already known the test car would not arrive at Eastleigh until 29 June. It is easy to come to the conclusion that a dynamometer car was primarily used to accurately measure high speed and indeed that was sometimes the case. But with measuring equipment placed on board the trial locomotive, a dynamometer car was also an accurate means of ascertaining efficiency through the use of steam allied to measurements of coal and water both before and after a test run. The same test car had

No. 36001 smokebox leading, about to set off on a ten-coach test train to Fratton in advance of the formal tests – so likely to be around 6–8 June 1950. The presence of a tail lamp in addition to the three-disc route code Brighton–Salisbury via Southampton Central, and reverse direction – although Leader never went anywhere near Southampton in its life – probably means the engine has just buffered up to its test train, empty stock again of course and, as like at Brighton, any available stock being used. There are certainly no crew members around. Notice in the cab a wooden bench has found its way inside, as built there was never more than one seat in the driving cabs and the fireman's compartment was not provide with any formal seating. All the visible doors are open, plus the cab window and some of the small square vents on the roof, add this to the general heat inside and it would have been a bit 'warm' the average daytime June temperature for the year being in the low 70°Fs. *Collection of Mrs Talbot*

The only located image of the engine at Fratton, again probably on the same dates. Records show exactly the same weight of train, 332t, was taken on each day but it will also be noted the first vehicle behind the engine is different compared with the previous view. Consequently we may assume then that Leader has now run-round at Fratton and is coupled to the opposite end of the train ready for the return to Eastleigh. But No. 1 is again leading, so it appears the engine too was turned. The height of the engine is also greater than the vehicles behind. Crew wise, Eastleigh had found a pair of NUR men, Driver Alf Smith and Fireman Sam Talbot prepared to work the engine for tests. Even so, ASLEF were adamant that the type would only be accepted into service following a major re-design to allow better escape provision for the fireman in the event of the engine overturning. At some stage a mirror was fitted, in at least No. 1 cab, allowing the driver to look up and glance into the corridor (*see* image on page 109) alongside the boiler. Folklore has it that a rudimentary system of bell codes may also have been provided between the cabs; this is not confirmed. *D.R. Yarney*

also run behind *Mallard* on 3 July 1938 when a world record for steam traction was achieved. This time it was not speed that was to be measured, but the efficiency of the engine and, as stated, something remarkable had to be produced by No. 36001 in order to convince the Railway Executive that here indeed was something worth pursuing; it was in effect nothing short of a justification for survival.

No. 36001 left Eastleigh for the 21-mile journey to Fratton on 6 June 1950 with No. 2 end leading and in addition to the works crew (ASLEF or NUR men is not reported), a number of other observers were also on board.

One of those present was Eastleigh fitter Reg Rowde, who recalled the engine gave a considerable left-hand lurch just south of Botley coming within what appeared to be a hairsbreadth of wiping out a signal post. 'We all held our breath,' he later commented. To be fair the fault here was as much the track and unstable formation, the area in the vicinity of Botley consisting of much unstable subsoil and the cause of much subsidence – and consequential remedial work, over the years. (With No. 2 end leading, this would be bunker end and where the driver would be on the right-hand side. The corridor ran the whole length of the engine on the same side so meaning the additional weight of the engine was on the left. Hence a bad spot would cause the excess weight to lurch left and explain the movement Reg comments upon.) Aside from this, the journey was otherwise without incident.

At Fratton we are not informed whether the engine was turned or a simple run-round sufficed. Whichever it was, a return was made to Eastleigh and the same journey and load repeated in the afternoon. Indeed on the afternoon return No. 36001 was brought to a stand near to what was Eastleigh South Signal Box and pulled away again without hesitation or slip. The day had been a success with similar progress made on the next two days, again each morning and afternoon. These must also have been short-notice trips as there is no mention of them in the weekly Special Traffic Notices.

We hesitate to use the term 'successful' runs on 7/8 June as after the second run on the latter date No. 36001 re-entered the works again for what was stated to be attention to the main steam pipes and also the grate. What was involved with the former is not known, although the latter resulted in the removal of the rocking grate and its substitution with a drop grate. On the subject of the grate itself, it may similarly be mentioned that one of the items it was necessary to modify to compensate for the decrease in grate area was reducing the size of the blast pipe nozzles. But this in turn resulted in excessive fire-throwing, exactly the same issue as had occurred some time earlier when working from Brighton. The considered solution was to add a brick arch inside the firebox, not easy with four syphons present but strange perhaps that in what was a conventional (the word is used in its loosest 'Stephenson' sense) coal-burning engine, it was not something that had apparently been present before. Strangely too, Click makes no mention of this item at any stage and whilst he was certainly involved with the dynamometer trials later, he may not even have been seconded to Eastleigh at this stage. Whilst the new fitment may have assisted in reducing fire throwing to the outside, flames from the fire now became more of a problem inside, meaning there was a tendency for the fire to creep backwards with flames licking around the fire-hole door. In turn this then led to a more difficult situation for the fireman and meaning on occasions he would wrap hessian sacking around his legs. Perhaps this is what H.A.V. Bulleid had meant in his biography by the engine being able to (be) '… stokeable by an asbestos-clad fireman'. (p.145 of *Bulleid of the Southern*.)

Of course with judicious use of the blower, and which control was indeed situated within the firing compartment, the fire could well be sucked the other way. The trouble was that from his hidden position, the fireman would often have little knowledge of his actual location on the line, the only alternative being to have the blower operating for the majority of the time and this would not assist in controlling steam production when demand was lessened.

Heat was also a problem within the cab at No. 1 end of the engine and where the smokebox protruded into the driver's working environment. This was despite the presence of 'Magnesia' or similar lagging covering the whole of the smokebox with just the smokebox door handles protruding through this. This lagging also made it difficult to confirm when the smokebox was properly closed, a point of some relevance later. Accordingly for crew's comfort during the trials a timber partition was installed to separate the driving compartment from the smokebox, although its very presence again made life still more difficult so far as smokebox cleaning was concerned, the very aspect that Bulleid had originally 'designed-out' with his ash disposal chute. (The task of smokebox cleaning was often given to the younger fireman at Eastleigh who would thus become involved in various aspects of the preparation and disposal of the engine.)

With the dynamometer car due to arrive at the end of June it was anticipated the actual trials would occupy the first two weeks of July 1950, and again as a preliminary test to this, a further run was arranged over what was to be the selected test route for all the runs, Eastleigh–Woking–Guildford, to take place on Monday 12 June 1950. This was also seen as an opportunity to assess the recent modifications to the grate and steam-pipes. The formal trials were Eastleigh to Woking, where the stock would be stabled. The engine would then propel the car to Guildford where the engine and car would both be turned on the shed turntable, and after recoupling, No. 36001 would propel the car back to Woking ready for the return load test back to Eastleigh. At Eastleigh the stock was deposited in the yard and 36001 would be serviced. Obviously during the actual servicing, the dynamometer car would be stabled – likely outside the shed – although both were turned again, this time on the shed triangle, before being reconnected and made ready for the next test. The dynamometer car test crew were also primarily from the Eastern Region and so, with Laurie Granshaw and Ron Jarvis, were no doubt billeted locally when working from Eastleigh.

The one problem of running trials from Eastleigh was line capacity. Eastleigh through to either Portsmouth (Fratton) or perhaps even in the opposite direction towards Romsey would have been reasonable but to test the engine thoroughly a longer distance and varying gradients were required. The Bournemouth line provided just this – northwards from Eastleigh that is – a steady climb from Eastleigh for nearly 18 miles on gradients of between 1 in 249 to 1 in 258, followed by an almost continuous descent for 30 miles to Woking. In the reverse direction the 30-mile climb from Woking to Litchfield summit started at a gentle 1 in 326 although there was also 5 miles of 1 in 249 in the Basingstoke area. After the summit, it was downhill all the way to Eastleigh. Ironically, Woking was also only 25 miles from Waterloo but No. 36001 would never go there.

Bournemouth line capacity also had to allow for any amount of Q paths often used for boat trains, the weekly Special Traffic Notices for the period featuring numerous of these every week. Consequently the only pathway available (or perhaps the only pathway the operators were prepared to give) was to leave Eastleigh immediately after the 5.05pm Bournemouth West to Waterloo train had departed, and which, on 12 June, was hauled by Lord Nelson 30850. (This was invariably a standard Lord Nelson class turn, and the very service which would later come to grief at Shawford some two years later on 29 July 1952, when the driver of the engine involved forgot he had been routed along on 'up local' instead of the more normal 'up through' route – caused ironically by a boat train special using the through line. The result was an undignified falling over at the bottom of the embankment, made worse by the fact that Stephen Townroe lived very close by and was then quickly on the scene.)

On 12 June No. 36001 had a new record load of 337t, again of ten vehicles, 5t more than its earlier Fratton working, the few tons extra explained by the use of different stock. (Eastleigh did not keep a regular set of stock to hand for 'test' purposes.) In charge were a shed crew, driver Alf Smith

'The Great Grey Galloping Sausage'

In 1950 Henry Meyer was a teenager living in Winchester before later moving to Yorkshire where he had a career as a professional photographer. How he found out about the potential workings of Leader – as indeed did others – is not certain, especially in those pre-social media days and when telephone use was certainly not widespread. An 'inside' contact is the likely the answer. We can be certain there were also several abortive trips to the lineside for a 'no-show'; Leader might have been predictable so far as her failures were concerned but she was also very unpredictable when it came to putting in an appearance! Here though patience was rewarded as we see the engine, probably either on 12 or 15 June 1950 heading north near Otterbourne (between Eastleigh and Shawford) bound for Woking with ten vehicles, 300+ tons in tow, including, at the front, two coach pull-push set No. 2! (Was there a wooden bench at this end of the engine as well, or was it simply moved, assuming there was even room in No. 2 cab?) Note too a few other interested individuals just creeping into shot on the extreme right hand side.

The two U class moguls that feature in the story. Both are seen in BR service some years after their involvement with Leader. No 31618 is the engine it was hoped would steam better after testing, although she was considered so poor dynamometer car trials were regarded as pointless and instead, she received a general overhaul, emerging greatly improved. The engine is seen here at Nursling on 30 May 1957 with a train of Western Region stock bound for the MSWJ route and Cheltenham. No. 31830 was the second choice and under test proved to be 71% more efficient than Leader. It is seen here northbound on a parcels duty at Shawford with a Lord Nelson just creeping into view on a southbound working. Both U class engines survived into the 1960s, No. 31618 being withdrawn in January 1964 and No. 31630 in November 1962. No. 31618 is now preserved by the Maunsell Locomotive Society. *Tony Molyneaux*

In anticipation of the dynamometer car trials, Leader was prepared inside Eastleigh works with various items of test equipment added – to measure pressures, smokebox vacuum, etc. These test pieces would in turn need to be connected to the dynamometer car and with the decision made that Leader would run when under test with No. 2 end leading at all times, a circular hole was cut in the base of No. 1 end cab through which to pass the cables. This was done inside Eastleigh works although the engine is seen here in its stored condition alongside the running shed some months later. Folklore has it than when the man tasked with cutting the circular hole was so engaged, he was asked what he was doing, provoking the ribald comment, 'Bu****ed if I know…I was just told to do it', before continuing with his task. *A.E. West/Mike King*

Engine/trial preparation at Eastleigh shed. No. 36001 has steam and the volunteer crew, Driver Alf Smith and Fireman Sam Talbot, have taken over and moved her up to the water column. As we know, there had been severe problems getting water at many points over the lines from Brighton, so some months earlier, when another proposal was made to use the Leader engines on the Brighton to Bournemouth through service, JGC found himself tasked with measuring every water column between those points. Most were found wanting except, that is, the one at Southampton Central. No such water difficulties were reported on at Eastleigh, Basingstoke or Guildford which were likely places the engine would take water whilst on test. Sam Talbot is seen on top supervising the filling whilst alongside is King Arthur 4-6-0 No. 784 *Sir Nerovens*. John Click/National Railway Museum

and fireman Sam Talbot the regular volunteer crew who were also to be involved with all the subsequent trials of the engine. One obvious advantage of this was that Alf, especially, would quickly become familiar with the No. 36001 and so work the engine in similar fashion on each occasion – unless instructed to do otherwise by the test crew – in that way consistency could be best achieved.

For the 12 June run, and exactly as had occurred when No. 36001 had been halted at the stop signal on her return from Fratton a week earlier, the engine pulled away without hesitation, with a correspondent for the RO reporting it to be going as well as No. 30850 by the time Shawford was passed 4 miles later. Indeed there was some comment from those on board that they would next encounter a signal check as they were undoubtedly catching-up! But just a mile later, around Shawford Junction and despite the efforts of Sam Talbot, steam pressure was noted as falling. First to 240psi (the Leader boiler was pressed to 280psi but we are not told what it had fallen from) and then fairly quickly to 190psi at which point it stabilised. With the thought of a further 14

miles of uphill climb before Litchfield summit was reached, the decision was reluctantly taken to come to a halt at Micheldever for a 'blow-up'. (It may well have been the halt was made just before Micheldever in the Wallers Ash loops although distance wise there is little difference.)

Here boiler pressure was restored and a further successful restart made. Most if not all of the later trials were scheduled to pause at Basingstoke for water and to check around the engine, although this is not mentioned on this occasion. Instead at Woking the engine ran-round, no doubt took water (again perhaps) and was inspected there, being generally made ready for the return working. We may suspect, but do not know with absolute certainty, whether No. 36001 was running bunker first on these 'pre-trials' north from Eastleigh. Certainly this was the condition later on with driver Alf Smith insisting this be the case so he was not exposed to the heat radiating from the smokebox – this despite the insulation around this item. There was of course some smokebox-first running later when the dynamometer car was being propelled

Almost ready for the road and with Sam clearly building up the fire in anticipation. No. 36001 didn't take long to make steam as the grate area was large compared with the volume of water in the boiler. Full pressure could be got from cold in not much over two hours but a lot of smoke would result and damage to the brick lining of the firebox occurred due to differential expansion. Careful observation and some of cable connections previously mentioned may be seen. The dynamometer car used was from the North Eastern Region and later gained its place in preservation, having been attached to *Mallard* on 3 July 1938 when the world record speed for steam of 126mph was achieved. As was quoted in the first book on Leader, 'Now it was not speed that was the issue, but instead the very survival of the engine being tested.'

between Woking and Guildford in each direction but that at least was almost light engine and so the demands for steam were less. On 12 June there was no turning at Guildford (and no turntable at Woking) consequently even if it had been so on the up journey, the down was likely smokebox end first; the smokebox end of the engine also always referred to as 'No. 1 end', 'No. 1 bogie', etc.

The stop to regain steam at Micheldever also meant the test train had lost its path for the return run and consequently it was not until some hours had elapsed before Control could allow the test train back out onto the main line. Eastleigh was reached again at 2.30am, the fact the Control Office not allowing it to proceed back home again until much later is another indication of how busy this route was, even late at night. (The return runs were always under the jurisdiction of the Woking Control Office. Leader's generally unreliable performance meaning it could have been the cause of a number of delays to other services over the course of the subsequent tests.)

Back at Eastleigh investigation quickly revealed the reason for the sudden dropping off in steam pressure, a buckled flange plate which was allowing the smokebox to draw air. It was but a straightforward matter to effect a suitable repair. The fact the smokebox and door were shrouded in lagging – and not to keep heat in but more to try and stop it radiating out – also had its down side for, as mentioned, it was not easy to see if the door or other items were securely in place and creating the proper seal.

A further test over the same route, although this time with the slightly reduced load of 320t, was arranged for 15 June and almost certainly to the same schedule. With the previous defect now rectified, it would have been expected that the engine would have behaved in a predictable manner – it did but in totally the wrong sense as again they were short of steam en route! This time the cause was not reported, nor if an unscheduled stop was made and/or the time of their return.

Speaking to Alf Smith for the original edition of the Leader book nearly 40 years ago, he recalled especially the heat, whilst the conditions endured by Sam Talbot were akin to a 'Chinese laundry' so far as the firing compartment was concerned. This was exacerbated within the latter location by steam leakage from the injectors which were located under this compartment. Add to this, steam seeming to leak from a number of fittings and flanges in the same area, and the result was an almost steady stream of condensation. Interesting to note too that aside from heat, the condensation and other 'on-board' issues are not mentioned at any time, possibly they were considered to be of little consequence.

After a weekend of rest, trials had been due to recommence on Monday 19 June, but instead this was cancelled to allow 36001 to again enter the works. Here the valve events were checked, the blast pipe cap changed and a start made towards some of the fittings that would be necessary for the dynamometer car tests. It was also reported the welding of the boiler was examined, although this is the very first time there had been mention of such verification after construction and by implication it was a sinister development. (More will be mentioned on this topic in the next chapter.)

However checking the valve events of a machine fitted with sleeve valves was not straightforward and Eastleigh had no jigs available for the task. (Presumably Brighton must have had something but recall the difficulty on 14 March 1949 at Redhill with No. 2039.) Accordingly at Eastleigh it was necessary to move the engine slightly forward or back using a pinch-bar. A fascinating feature of this was that this task could be accomplished with ease by just one man – *almost 150 tons being moved in this way* – such was the advantage of having roller-bearings in the design.

Leader was released from the works towards the end of June and ready for what was likely intended to be perhaps the final trial before the full assessment with the dynamometer car. Eight coaches were in tow and again the route taken was north from Eastleigh bound for Woking.

But on this occasion, 29 June, the gremlins were at work big time and also right from the start, for as the train pulled out of the yard at Eastleigh (clearly not all trials commenced from the platform) there was a distinct knocking noise from No. 1 bogie, more pronounced as steam was applied but increasing in intensity as the engine accelerated. Nothing like this had ever been heard before and there were no doubt some puzzled faces on board.

It had also long been practice, both at Eastleigh and previously at Brighton, to remove sections of the floor of the end cabs to observe the movement or otherwise (!) of the oscillating gear attached to the sleeves and after this aspect had been removed, to study just the sleeves themselves – the ends of which still protruded beyond the end of the bogie. Observation thus revealed no immediate sign of distress from any of the components and so possibly on the basis of 'perhaps if we ignore it, it will go away' or even 'if it is important it will get worse', the engine continued north. It would be interesting to know who besides Smith and Talbot was on board. John Click, no, Granshaw and Jarvis likely not, possibly then perhaps just a works or shed fitter. But the sound did not go away and the same knock could be heard fully for 9 miles until in the area of Winchester Junction the knock changed to what was described as a deep hammering sound and this time definitely corresponding with each revolution of the wheels. Under the circumstances, and no doubt justifiably in fear of what had or indeed might next develop, the engine was immediately eased and the trial halted at Micheldever, which was the first available location where the stock could be suitably deposited.

Upon arrival there the engine was examined as best as possible. In the light of what would transpire it would be fascinating to learn what was perhaps found – or even not found, but nothing of this has come to light.

No trial could continue in that form and the engine was worked back to Eastleigh 'light' and at slow speed. Again there is no report on this return run but it would no doubt have been accompanied by similar painful metallic sounds.

Safe in the confines of the depot, the fire was dropped and the engine towed to the nearby works for examination. Regardless of the unplanned events of the day this visit

Two remarkable images from Reg Curl showing the failed crank axle of No. 1 bogie inside Eastleigh works on 7 July 1950. Rubbing has also occurred on the crank caused by the axle continuing to rotate whilst out of alignment. Had the extent of the failure been known at the time, it is very unlikely the engine would have been allowed to run any distance at all in this condition. Recall too this failure had occurred after less than 6,000 miles running whilst examination showed fatigue cracks developing in the crank axle of No. 2 bogie. As we know replacement axles were fitted but where did they come from? Manufactured at Eastleigh is unlikely, consequently we have to look to Brighton and the incomplete engines. It cannot have been Nos 36002/3 as these were running – well being towed – to various outstations for store, so it has to be parts intended for Nos 36004/5. Of the other engines alongside, only one can be positively identified, No. 34046 *Braunton,* which was in the process of a Light Intermediate repair.

was in fact pre-planned as it was still necessary to complete some further connections necessary for the dynamometer car trials.

But more interestingly of course was the investigation into the noises that had been heard. This at first centred on a possible fracture to the right-hand sleeve and cylinder of No. 1 bogie but these were found to be intact. Opinion shifted to suggest the fault lay in the vicinity of the right-hand axlebox of the centre axle. Examination of this would mean the bogie would need to be rolled out and despite Eastleigh being able to lift the body, the works seemingly excused themselves from immediately undertaking the task on the basis they would have no means of supporting the body once the bogie was removed.

The previous comment may perhaps be a slightly inconsequential statement as with a will surely conventional sleepers could have been used, after all engine frames under repair were often supported in this way. However for whatever reason, it was decided to send for the two wooden supporting trestles that existed at Brighton and which had been used during the construction process. These also appear in several of the build photographs.

Brighton arranged to forward the necessary items – similar in appearance to carpenters sawhorses although of course larger and more substantial, with, it was stated, an assortment of spares. The latter no doubt intended to cover every eventuality that might be found. Again these were no doubt purloined from the parts intended to complete 36004/5.

On 3 July 1950 the all-important pair of trestles arrived and two days later the body was lifted and supported on the trestle after the suspect bogie had been rolled out.

After this No. 1 bogie could itself then be lifted. The result was a worst-case scenario, complete failure of the centre axle which had fractured near to where the axle was pressed into the driving wheel.

Not unnaturally an immediate check was made on the crank-axle of No. 2 bogie and which despite not displaying similar audible sounds, was upon examination shown as likely to fail in the future with fatigue cracks showing up when examined using both mechanical and X-ray techniques. The only conclusion was that with a similar defect on both axles this could only be a design fault although dark murmurings over defective manufacture contributing towards the failures would also be made later. At the time it was a devastating blow and another risk to any actual trials for the future.

This sort of information could hardly be kept within the Eastleigh complex but even when informed at the Railway Executive, Riddled instructed repairs be made and the trials continued. Accordingly replacement crank-axles together with any other necessary repairs were undertaken. Almost certainly these again came from parts intended for Nos 36004/5 but once more with hindsight it would surely have been better to substitute replacement bogies with those perhaps from 36002, which were of course complete. Whether it was even considered we cannot be certain but in the event it was not done. Perhaps the excuse was that Nos 36002/3 were now longer at Brighton. (The movement of these two engines is discussed on p.217 et seq.)

Meanwhile the expense of having a full complement of engineers standing by awaiting to undertake trials with the dynamometer car had not gone unnoticed either, and it was decided that they could be gainfully employed in securing information which would in effect be used as a 'benchmark' against which Leader would subsequently be measured. In view of its size and notional power output – on paper at least – it would have been reasonable to expect something like a King Arthur or even a Light Pacific to be used for this purpose, but no, and instead the choice made was to use a U class Mogul, No. 31618.

Previous rumour as regards No. 31618 is confirmed in the RO for August 1950 in that the choice of No. 31618 was deliberate as it had long been regarded as the 'black sheep' of the class. Consequently on 9 July 1950 No. 31618 was seen having weighed coal being added to the tender having presumably had the necessary dynamometer car fittings previously added. The same route was also to be used; Eastleigh–(Woking)–Guildford and again the plan was to increase the loads as the test continued.

Rumour also has it that this particular choice was made as No. 31618 (then a Salisbury-based engine) had for long been regarded as shy for steam and regardless of the test results against which Leader would then be measured, it might well afford an opportunity to assess the previous poor reputation of the engine.

Even so No. 31618 still had to be made ready with various fixings made and accordingly it was not until 10 July that the first dynamometer car trial was actually made. It was quickly realised that this particular engine had been a bad choice, the engine in 'a poor condition' according to the test crew whilst additionally the left-hand trailing axle box ran hot and accordingly the test was terminated at Basingstoke. Following repair No. 31618 did eventually emerge as a far more reliable engine although it would take no more part in the comparison trials.

Within the works at Eastleigh it appears slightly strange but there is no record of any progress in the replacement crank-axles for Leader and indeed the same situation would exist until the second week in August. Of course, the first week of August was the annual holiday shutdown. So was it simply due to pressure of work in other areas in the works or was it that there was no urgency over what was seemingly now fast becoming a foregone conclusion? Do not be deceived either over any idea that the time delay was due to tests being made on all the Leader-type axles that existed in order to find a pair that were suitable – that was not done. If it had, it would not explain why the so-nearly-complete 36002 remained intact and untouched (save for dismantling the valve gear for subsequent towing movements) from the

John Click described this as a rather 'naughty' view. John is riding inside No.1 cab as M7 No. 30027 shunts its 'replacement' around the triangle at the back of Eastleigh shed, Leader being too long to use the turntable at the front of the shed. Inside the cab, the twin vacuum gauges and the brake pedestal are visible. Speaking of naughty views, BR, or certainly locally at least one un-named senior member of staff, is known to have confiscated film from the camera of one individual attempting to take images of Leader whilst in the neighbouring works. *John Click/National Railway Museum*

moment work had been suspended on 19 November 1949 until scrapped. This lack of progress is even more surprising when it is recalled Marylebone would have been aware of the ongoing situation and likewise the probable 'standing time' of the engineers associated with the dynamometer car. (As an aside, did these men perhaps even go back to Doncaster in the meanwhile?)

Hierarchy then decided (who and when are not known and not really important either), that the next stage would be further 'benchmark' trials with another U, this time No. 31630. Again it took time to prepare the engine and the first test with this engine was not until the end of July 1950. In all three runs were made between Eastleigh and Woking, No. 31630 performing faultlessly on each occasion with varying loads and burning 'South Kirby Hards No. 1' weighed into 1cwt bags. The tests with No. 31630 concluded on 2 August.

It will be recalled that due to its weight, the Chief Civil Engineer had also set a maximum speed of 50mph for Leader and consequently this was also the maximum speed set for No. 31630, relative, it was stated, to an average of 45–50 mph. The differential between the stated average and the maximum was therefore minimal.

No. 36001 meanwhile was eventually released from the works on Monday 14 August, and a short trial made to Botley and return the next day – presumably light engine. The same run was repeated on 15 August. The distance covered was in the order of 5 miles each way daily, a total of 10 miles per round trip and yet, according to a note in the official records, Leader used something in the order of 2,000gal of water in each direction. We have to careful in accepting the 'each direction' wording here not least for the simple fact no water column was provided at Botley. Recall too Leader was now limited to carrying 2,600gal, consequently the 'each direction' term would appear to be in doubt. We should instead read as 'per round trip' but even so, 2,000gal for 10 miles was still excessive.

Even so there is some similarity over water usage when No. 2039 was running between Lancing and Eastleigh. Finally we should also consider that even if it was 1,000gal in each direction, how much coal and consequently effort by the fireman was involved? It still speaks volumes for the ability of the boiler to evaporate that amount of water from a grate area now reduced to just 25.5 sq ft.

Suspicion then must now be centred upon the sleeve valves. Possibly the pistons and valves had been removed or disturbed during the replacement of the crank-axles. The wastage of steam past these was of course what had affected No. 2039 and seemingly now affected No. 36001 as well. But unanswered in the question is how does the engine enter works on 29 June *without* any previous mention of appreciable steam loss or excess water consumption – surely these would have been referred to in official records had this been the case – but then emerge in this condition? Over the years rumour has suggested there were darker forces involved, we have absolutely no evidence to support this and we repeat this as purely rumour based on nothing at all, but there still remain unanswered questions.

Another 'inside the works' view and possibly taken at the same time as that seen earlier. This time though the observers have clearly become more adventurous and climbed up from inside No. 2 cab on to the top where the water filler and TIA tanks were located. At least nine are present and, as has been mentioned elsewhere with similar railway images of the period, little concern as to health and safety was being shown. We may also wonder why prior to the failure of the crank axle reports of the runs mention little about the excess water consumption of the engine.

A third test had been planned for 17 August but was cancelled as a connecting rod, this time from No. 2 bogie, was striking the casing of the oil bath. Perhaps the casing had been disturbed when the replacement crank-axle to this bogie had been fitted. Indeed aside from the one failure of 24 September 1949, and as detailed previously, this was the first reported failing to affect No. 2 bogie. (Other problems associated with the oil bath although on unreported dates included corrosion of the motion pins, caused – it was stated – by water finding its way into the oil bath and not being drained away. As with the Pacifics too, there was a tendency for the chains to stretch and although a modification in the form of 'skid' was prepared, this was never fitted. Broken circlips were another common problem and which in turn allowed the motion pins to fall out. This was not the fault of Bulleid or the design and was instead attributable to the outside manufacturer of the circlips. Again it may not have assisted in the necessary working of the oscillating gear.)

Repairs to No. 2 bogie were quickly completed and a further light engine trial was arranged to Fratton on

We cannot admit other than Leader's behaviour under test had not been good. Indeed the amount of steam leakage past the sleeves when working was so bad as to lead to a report being sent to Marylebone to the effect that further testing with the engine in this condition was pointless. We learn from Townroe that Riddles paid a visit to Eastleigh, probably in the last week of August 1950, and witnessed for himself the engine running up and down the shed yard – blowing excess steam perhaps? His decision was that repairs would be carried out and consequently the engine entered Eastleigh works soon after and would remain inside for almost four weeks. Here we see the engine and dynamometer car outside the front of the shed on 26 August, perhaps awaiting that decision. *K.G. Carr, courtesy Peter Pfidzuk*

18 August. As before, the works trials crew were in charge – so it is not believed to have been Messrs Smith and Talbot this time who were in one of the spare gangs based at the running shed. This time too there is no mention of excess water consumption. So again it is very strange that only a few days earlier we have excess consumption and then without any mentioned remedial repair or adjustment, all is now well. Might it have been as simple as the water feed to one (or both) of the injectors had been left on?

Instead it was recorded that that the engine was now ready for its long-awaited dynamometer car tests, which would commence on Monday 21 August. This lack of mention over water use is even more surprising by its omission.

We also believe from comments made by him that John Click was likely at Eastleigh around this time, and we know he took part as an observer/assistant on the engine during the trials. Whilst telling us much that is new and included later in this chapter, he also includes the following taster of things we shall now never know and can instead only guess at; 'A book could be written of Leader stories but I especially recall one tranquil summer's night slipping down through Winchester under a brilliant moon and going a good deal faster than we were allowed. The ride was perfect, just the diddly-dum of the rail, perfect visibility; one could be forgiven for thinking the dream was a reality.'

Leader was made ready for the actual tests on No. 1 road at Eastleigh running shed. The dynamometer car was also attached there and the necessary cable connections made in order that various instrument readings could be taken. After this and with its compliment of observers, engineers and of course Messrs Smith and Talbot, the engine left the confines of the shed ready to collect its train of empty stock from the carriage sidings alongside the station.

The load at this stage behind the drawbar, including the dynamometer car, was 231½t, the plan being to increase this progressively for each daily test. Just one run per day was planned and as before, the schedule would see the trials being made at the same time of day, and continuing to Woking. Here engine and dynamometer car would detach and propel to Guildford, 6 miles, for turning. In theory of course Leader, having a cab at each end, would have accomplished the task without this added complication. But recall Alf Smith had deemed he would only undertake the work if he could drive on the trials from the bunker, No. 2 end, and it was for this reason and the need to turn the test car that the operation was undertaken.

In addition to the driver and fireman, a fitter was also booked to work the same turns of duty and his principal duty was to assist in the preparation of the engine. However in this area there was not much for the driver to attend to, Bulleid having achieved in the Leader design more of his ideal and the inherent advantages of the internal combustion engine, so as such, there was little in the way of preparation that was required. All the important components were designed to be either pressure or flood lubricated. Indeed it was stated there were only two oiling points on the whole engine which the driver needed to attend to. (Having made the preceding statement it is now somewhat embarrassing to admit we cannot confirm where these two lubrication points actually were! With the ever-increasing passage of time it is unlikely also that this information is available either. An assessment – confirmed in conversation with former Eastleigh fitter Eric Best, reveals it *may* have been that the two were identical and in fact referred to confirming the actual oil level within a holding tank which fed the Wakefield mechanical lubricators, three of which were mounted on each bogie.)

To return though to that first dynamometer car test of 21 August, incidentally also reported as being a wonderful summer's evening, perhaps at last this was a good omen and the gods of steam would look kindly on the project. The official report of the run would reveal the answer:

'The start from Eastleigh (just after the 5.05pm service train) was slow, and the boiler pressure fell quickly from 270 to 210lb in 6 minutes, although the regulator was only partly open with 170lb in the steam inlet pipes. Exhaust pressures of 12 and 12½lb, and exhaust temperatures of

Inside the works on 2 September 1950. During this time attention was given to the sleeves of No. 1 bogie whilst all the rings, 24 per sleeve; 72 per bogie – a grand total of 144 rings – were replaced. (Townroe quotes a slightly different figure.) Other unspecified work was also undertaken. Here we see the engine inside the works on 2 September 1950 part way through the work. Careful examination will reveal the body-to-bogie connecting hoses have been removed to allow access to the sleeves, which have also been removed, whilst on the roof a canvas cover has been secured over part of the bunker. 'On the road', a member of the test crew – sometimes John Click – would travel in the bunker emptying weighed bags of coal as required. In this way coal consumption could later be calculated. The canvas 'roof' protected him from standing up and coming into contact with overhead structures, even so, it was hardly a convivial working environment. *T.J. Edgington*

Revitalised and leaving the exit road from the shed for a trial. As the dynamometer car is not attached, this 'may' be the light engine run to Fratton of 21 September 1950. Even in workaday grime the lighter centre panel is still visible. Certainly not between Eastleigh and Fratton and probably more likely whilst working from Brighton, but John Click also talks of the speed of Leader with the words, 'On occasions some very high speed was achieved, but this was not something regularly undertaken and for the simple reason the stopping power was limited.' It was for this reason that even when Gresley was conducting his high speed trials on the LNER in 1938, which culminated in the world speed record with *Mallard*, it was always with a minimum number of coaches so that these too could provide braking power. Leader's brakes were good but even so finding a signal on at 90mph, might not have been welcome. Bulleid was very hot on brakes and not deterred by the many novelties already aboard the Leader, had required Gresham and Craven's Augmented Vacuum Brake to be fitted. The ejector, by the smokebox, was not under the driver's control but, once the steam valve on the manifold down the corridor had been opened (and left open during normal running), it charged the system and then cut in and out to maintain a high vacuum in the storage cylinders. A proportioning valve ensured normal train pipe and brake cylinder topside vacuum; and the whole system, besides giving quicker brake release, avoided steampipes in either cab, two simple horizontal banjo-type brake valves being fitted. He continues, 'A disadvantage was that the ejector made a loud and harsh noise up the chimney, seemingly 'going off' unpredictably, and certainly when least expected. There was only a hint of the raspberry-like sound made by some GWR ejectors, originally supplied by the same manufacturer.'

244° and 246° Fahrenheit were noted, also a high smokebox vacuum of 5½in was recorded. Two minutes later, although the steam chest pressure had fallen to 140lb psi, the exhaust temperatures continued to rise to 256° and 280° Fahrenheit and the smokebox vacuum to 7in. of water. The regulator was eased to give 100psi in the steam chest and allow the pressure to rise in the boiler. The drawbar arm, in the dynamometer car indicated unusual vibrations and as the exhaust temperatures continued to rise it was soon evident that all was not well with the engine working. Due to very hard work by the fireman the boiler pressure rose and was maintained at about 240psi for the remainder of the journey. Under these conditions the temperature in the fireman's cab was abnormal.' (But was not recorded – KJR)

The test continued as had been intended as far as Woking with arrival as scheduled at 8.15pm. Just over 3 hours for a 49 mile journey was excessive even for Leader standards and so we may reasonably conclude there had been a lengthy stop at Basingstoke – incidentally not a single view of the engine at Basingstoke or Woking has been discovered.

The Great Grey Galloping Sausage

John Click takes up the story of that first run; 'After we arrived in the Woking reception sidings the loco and car were detached and moved forward to await an opportunity to cross over and propel the car down to Guildford where both would be turned. In the dark we shot through Worplesdon very swiftly indeed, driving from No.1 end now and looking over the dynamometer car roof and beside the clerestory. The joke was on us because when we stopped just into the tunnel beyond Guildford station and got the dummy (ground-signal) to reverse out, and into the loco depot, she wouldn't go over – this time not due to a fault in the reversing gear but instead a more basic issue, shortage of steam – we had used it all on that mad dash from Woking. There was nothing for it but to put more coal on and wait for the blower to get pressure up again. I remember thinking on the way down let's cut our losses and go on towards Portsmouth: what would the chain of events have been … the idea of 130 tons of great grey galloping sausage "running away on right line" and propelling the terror struck E.& NE. Regional crew in their Dynamometer Car hardly bears contemplation. Several of us would certainly have been looking for new employment.' Returning to reality he adds, 'After about five long and very hot minutes we succeeded in reversing. Then a look round the loco on shed showed that the mechanical lubricator driving gear at No.1 end had broken at a weld in a way that did neither its designer nor welder any credit. The return test was cancelled and No. 36001 was left behind but the stock was worked back with us aboard. Ken Briggs, Doug Yarney and I went back next day to fit new parts sent from Brighton.' (This time a very fast turnaround from Brighton!) 'We worked back light and Ken very generously let me ride 'up front'. It was an unforgettable trip in bright moonlight made very quietly and altogether without incident at a steady 50mph with a faster burst through Winchester. The ride was superb, with every wheel beat audible from end to end: as clear an indication of what might have been…'

John Clicks recollections are slightly at odds with the official record which refers to the fault having been on No. 2 bogie. Whatever, we know engine and dynamometer car returned light to Eastleigh the next day, the schedule being 8.30pm off Guildford.

Upon return to Eastleigh some new rings were fitted whilst it was stated also certain of the sleeves were also given lathe attention.

With repairs effected, a further trial was arranged for Wednesday 23 August. As planned the load this time had also been increased by one vehicle, so making for 264½t. Again the official commentary is somewhat revealing:

'Prior to starting the up journey from Eastleigh … steam was blowing from the safety valves, but the boiler pressure fell to 185psi after 16 minutes. The exhaust pressures were again high and the exhaust temperatures gradually rose to 350° Fahrenheit which is the limit of the working range of temperature for the indicator in the dynamometer car for this purpose. In order to reduce the coal and water

Manual coaling, a thankless task, using the same derrick as had been used when coal consumption trials were undertaken with a mechanical stoker on No. 35005. No evidence has been found to suggest the fitting of a mechanical stoker to No. 36001 was ever considered. John Click, who was also involved on the trials with No. 35005 comments, 'At least this time I did not have the job of filling the sacks!'. The coal used was the same as with the earlier tests on No. 31630; 'South Kirby Hards No. 1'. Each bag weighted 1 cwt.

consumption the engine was worked in 20% cut-off instead of 30% used on the previous test runs. Although this had the effect of reducing the smokebox vacuum the engine continued to throw burning char from the chimney top. The actual running time was spoilt by a number of signal checks, seven in all, and four signal stops, they assisted in keeping up the boiler pressure. On the return journey from Woking, steam was again blowing from the safety valves and a thicker fire was put on the grate before starting away. The regulator was adjusted to give a maximum steam chest pressure and the engine tried in

15% cut-off on the easier sections of route. This resulted in maintaining a higher boiler pressure and reduced the exhaust steam temperatures within the range of measurement, but there was no improvement in either coal or water consumption. The engine refused to start on one or two occasions and had to reverse before a drawbar pull of about 5 tons necessary to start the train could be exerted. All the figures and evidence collected at this stage was ample proof that a considerable amount of the steam produced was being wasted, either by leakage past the piston, or sleeve vales of both engine units.'

Damning evidence indeed, but before discussing these comments, a few of the points raised are in need of elaboration. Indeed what had been witnessed was no more than could have been expected. The evidence for this having been laid bare on 14 and 15 August when the excess water consumption on the Botley trial was noted. Remember too on the 14 and 15 August the engine had been running light.

On the basis then that Leader was still only loaded with the officially permitted figure of 2,600gal of water, there are several options to consider for the most recent runs whilst again, and although not stated, we can assume a scheduled stop was made at Basingstoke (in both directions) where examination could be made – and water could be taken.

So assuming then the Chief Civil Engineer's dictate was being complied with as regards the water onboard at the start of the trial, and with a number of professional engineers riding with the dynamometer car, this can only be the outcome: Leader appears to have managed – *with a train this time* – to travel almost 26 miles from Eastleigh to Basingstoke without running out of water. If the converse had applied this would surely have been mentioned in the official reports. The only intermediate water stop was at Winchester, but again this is not spoken of.

The conclusion then, yet again, is that the runs of 14 and 15 August (running as a light engine trial without the

Raring to go, engine and test car soon to leave the shed and head towards the carriage sidings to pick up the test train. The headcode seen was used between the shed and the carriage sidings only. The number of persons on board the engine and the test car during the runs is not known but likely varied as various VIP observers would also occasionally travel. L.J. Granshaw from Brighton is believed to been on board for many, if not all, the runs. Townroe does not comment that he ever travelled on the engine although as we know he certainly photographed it. At Brighton Leader had achieved a record with no less than 14 on board, spread out between the three cabs.

An undated and somewhat poor quality but nevertheless rare view of the engine running though Eastleigh station on the way to collect its test train. In its wake is a considerable trail of steam, almost the only view that gives an impression of the amount of steam leakage that used to occur past the sleeves (it cannot be the cylinder cocks that are open or else a similar cloud would be seen at the front). This escaping steam would also have been obvious to the test crew behind. *Reg Curl*

dynamometer car) present an inaccurate record. We can only trust these inaccuracies would have been picked up by Riddles later – although it would likely not have made much difference to the final outcome – but it was of course upon these very reports, and not just the dynamometer car results, that Riddles would later base his conclusions. .

Do not however start to believe any conspiracy theory. The bare facts are that Leader was not performing well, far from it. The extremes in exhaust temperature allied in particular to the exhaust pressure within the smokebox clearly showed that the high temperatures – and pressures – indicated steam being fed to the cylinders from the boiler via the regulator and steam chests, was instead exhausting straight into the smokebox without performing any useful work. This would account for the decreasing boiler pressure unless the cut-off were so severely reduced that the boiler, grate (and fireman) could accommodate the demands for steam. Leader was wasting almost as much steam as it could produce. It would also go some way to perhaps explaining the difficulties in restarting the train although this was also 'helped' by the fitter assisting the reversing gear to the required position with judicious use of the crowbar. Whether Bulleid was still being kept informed of developments is a moot point as he is singularly not mentioned.

What was not widely known, and perhaps had been deliberately kept from the dynamometer car engineers, is that at Eastleigh this problem with steam leakage was already well known and an unofficial method of attempting to 'tighten everything up' when the engine was cold had been arrived at. This was simply to run light (or with the dynamometer car attached but not recording) up and down any convenient siding, the idea being that steam passing through the sleeves and therefore into the cylinders would expand the various components until they formed a better fit. Who it was had come to this conclusion is not reported; it would have been an interesting question to have put to John Click!

Perhaps this should be taken more in spirit than in fact as the same 'tightening' results would surely have been achieved within perhaps a few miles of normal running and if that had been the case then the engine would have started to perform better as the runs progressed. This was simply not the case. More likely running up and down did take place and did perhaps help a little, but not as much as those who instigated it would have wished. (In the opinion of the present author only, this 'help' given to 36001 was at the instigation of one Bulleid devotee – no name this time – who was determined to assist in the success of the project generally and especially in view of the fact that the designer was now no longer on the scene. Whilst no doubt well-intended, it did little to achieve the desired object and we can hardly ignore the fact the dynamometer car test crew could not have been

MONDAY (Night) 25th, until FRIDAY (Morning) 29th, SEPTEMBER
No. 79.—Train Alterations and Additions.

Time	From	To	Remarks	Service No.
p.m. 6 45 (F.X.)	Eastleigh	Woking	Special Train (For Testing Purposes) Hauled by 'Leader Class' Engine. **Eastleigh** to form train of dynamometer car No. 101 A and 7 corrs.	80
10 20 (Freight)	Feltham	Southampton Docks	Pass Worting Jct. 12.18 a.m. (Tuesday to Friday mornings inclusive), and run correspondingly later to Eastleigh East Yard	—
11 35	Woking	Eastleigh	Special Train (For Testing Purposes). Hauled by 'Leader Class' Engine	81

No.		80 Special Train (for testing purposes)	
		arr. p.m.	dep. p.m.
Eastleigh	..	A	6 45
Winchester Jct.	..	6	59
Worting Jct.	..	7	19L
		D	N
Basingstoke	..	7 24	7T30
Woking	..	8 5	..

A—Monday to Thursday night inclusive.
F—Tuesday to Friday morning inclusive.

No.		81 Special Train (for testing purposes)	
		arr. a.m.	dep. p.m.
Woking	..	A	11 35
Basingstoke	..	12 5	12 9
		D	N
Worting Jct.	..	F12	14
Winchester Jct.	..	12	35
Eastleigh	..	12 50	..

Extract from the weekly Special Traffic Notice covering the period 23 to 29 September 1950. This is the only advance record found covering any of the Eastleigh trials.

aware especially if visually excess steam was continually blowing back against the car from No. 1 end when running. The fact Bulleid had designed the engine and he was former LNER was hardly likely to have had any bearing on these professionals' objective views either.) Associated difficulties with the operation of the cylinder cocks, and which equally could have been the cause of excess steam being used especially if these could not be closed properly, were successfully dealt with.

The return run from Woking to Eastleigh was accomplished in the night hours, again with the probable stop at Basingstoke. The engine and dynamometer car then turned and stabled once more at Eastleigh for a further trial scheduled later the same day. Once again, the load was increased, this time ten coaches and quoted as 290½t.

Again too we have an official report of the run. 'A fourth test run was made on 24.8.1949. When running between Eastleigh motive power depot to the reception sidings to pick up the trainload the cylinder cocks were open to get rid of the condensation. The cylinders of No. 1 end can be seen from the dynamometer car and it was observed that an abnormal amount of water was issuing from the sleeve valves. The condensed steam was white and oily from the lubrication supply. When attached to the train, the boiler pressure was 275psi, and again a good thickness of fire was on the fire grate. The weight of the train for this test run was 290½ tons, a light load for an engine of this size. Working in 30% cut-off with 140psi in the steam chest the boiler pressure fell rapidly to 200lb. Good work by the fireman got the pressure back to 225lb but the pressure fell to 140lb approaching Winchester City, 7½ miles from the starting point and in a running time of 19 minutes. A stop had to be made to regain the boiler pressure but as this so upset the booked path, the test run was abandoned at Micheldever. On arrival back at Eastleigh depot a standing test very clearly showed that steam was blowing to waste and further tests with the engine in this condition was useless.'

So the conclusion, 'further tests are pointless' and here yet again we might be expected to simply say, 'The End'. But before jumping to any conclusions let us examine the report and some of its comments more closely. Firstly the time taken between Eastleigh and Winchester. Nineteen minutes relates to an average speed of only just over 23½mph, and which for '…an engine of this size' with a '…light load' is hardly a commendable achievement – even allowing for the figures relating to start to stop times. What is not mentioned either concerns the amount of water used, (or should it even be lost?), as there were definite shades of déjà-vu, as at Micheldever, recourse having to be made to replenishing the tank of the engine from a ½in hose connected to a standpipe on Micheldever Station cattle dock. The whole episode is worthy of a Will Hay comedy but one which was also reminiscent of the experience at Groombridge on 25 June the previous year.

Keeping with the water situation. It was of concern that Leader was considered to have insufficient water on board at Micheldever for a return to Eastleigh. Possibly even insufficient to reach Winchester on the return run where a proper water column was located. What we do not know is if water was taken at Winchester on the way up (or indeed on the return) and where the stop was made to rally the boiler. Even so No. 36001 had evaporated something approaching 2,600gal of water in something like 15½ miles – and still lost time in the process.

Perhaps even more amazing is that this is the first mention of the emission of steam from the cylinder cocks in the way described. None of the photographs depicting Leader on trial give any indication of steam leakage from the cylinders, although to be fair the warm air associated with the time of year when the tests were run may have make this more difficult to observe.

With the conclusion from the engineers that further testing would be non-productive, the ball was again in the court of Riddles and his colleagues at Marylebone. This would also be the third time the future of Leader was in the balance, the previous occasions being the weight issue and more recently at the time of the crank-axle failure. Surprisingly Marylebone's response was swift and succinct, 'repair and continue'.

Accordingly just three days after what some could well have thought to have been the final run, Leader re-entered the works, where it was basically given every attention it required. No. 1 bogie had a completely new sleeve fitted to the left-hand cylinder and score marks smoothed over on the other sleeves. In addition all 24 rings were replaced on each piston and sleeve, amounting to 72 per bogie, a total of 144 rings for the complete engine. These new rings were stated to be of Wellworthy manufacture. Additionally other non-specified work was carried out on No. 2 bogie and elsewhere. (According to Townroe, Riddles and Bond paid a visit to Eastleigh sometime in August 1950 and witnessed the engine running up and down the shed yard. This could well have been around this time.)

No. 36001 finally emerged again on 20 September and was steamed ready for a light engine trial to Fratton the next day. Alf Smith and Sam Talbot were on board as usual and whether it was their words that were subsequently quoted in the official reports or those of an observer on board is not certain, however, the engine performed, 'better than at any time in the past'. Most promising of all was that at the return to Eastleigh close examination revealed that for the very first time there was absolutely nothing in need of attention.

But the engine now had a considerable amount of ground to make up. An interim report prepared by the testing staff during the time the engine had spent in the works was hardly complimentary – much of which we have already quoted above. Indeed there was little other way the facts could be presented, even if, and as proven above, on at least one occasion, they veered a little from the truth.

What Bulleid's views were in Ireland at this stage are not known, although in view of what was to come later it is evident he was being kept informed, although perhaps not through official BR channels. If we had to make a guess it would be via Laurie Granshaw – Click was still too junior at this stage – but we must emphasise that is conjecture on the part of the present writer.

Back at Eastleigh, 36001 was being made ready for what would also be the final series of formal dynamometer car trials and once more over the same route, Eastleigh–Woking (Guildford) and return, to commence on Monday 25 September 1950.

The test trains left Eastleigh at 6.45pm immediately after the section was clear and following the departure of the Bournemouth West–Waterloo service. On this first

Taken from the fireman's cab of Leader, at first a slight puzzle giving the impression the engine is standing in the platform at Eastleigh. However, it is in reality a situation where the engine and dynamometer car are on the up platform road (then numbered Platform 2) to allow the up through line to be kept clear for No. 30853 *Sir Richard Grenville* on what may well be an ocean liner special. John Click recounts, 'Had I waited a split second I would have recorded the Nelson's driver giving what I construed as a rude sign indicative of the general feeling there.' Most Lord Nelson turns were worked by Eastleigh men so we may assume he meant towards the Leader design by Eastleigh men generally. *John Click/National Railway Museum*

evening, 241½t were attached and which, although less than had been handled previously, was deliberately set almost as a 'running-in' load to allow the various components to bed-in after the latest repairs.

Again the official report is quoted and which now for the first time, and almost three months from the end of June when trials had originally been planned to start, gives a record of a true test in both directions;

'Eastleigh–Woking: The engine was worked mainly in 30% cut-off and partial regulator to give 110 to 120lb in the steam chest. As a result, the train speed rose gradually to 46mph on the rising gradients to Litchfield Signal Box … on the falling gradients from Basingstoke to Woking, the booked time was maintained, the maximum speed being 55½mph.

'Woking–Eastleigh: The engine was worked in 25% cut-off with higher steam chest pressures. Signal checks spoilt the running to Brookwood, but with clear signals the steam chest pressure was put up to 200lb and this gave a drawbar pull of 3.38 tons which accelerated the train from 20 to 41mph in 1½ miles. The regulator was eased at the 31½ mile post, the speed was 50.2mph. The maximum speed was 54mph at mile post 44.'

Back at Eastleigh the engine was again examined and despite the previous evening's efforts, nothing untoward was found. Accordingly for the next day an extra vehicle was added so making the load 275t comprising nine bogie vehicles. As before the same crew were in charge, fireman Sam Talbot assisted to an extent by one of the many observers on board who would access the weighed coal bags when required, although the cramped conditions for more than one man in the firing compartment thus made the work somewhat more onerous. Despite being totally familiar with the route, it was still a new experience for the fireman being unable to confirm where he was by sight and as such it was not always easy to adjust the firing rate to compensate for changes in gradients.

John Click adds his own recollections at this point, although he does not recount which of the runs this applied to. 'For the dynamometer car tests at Eastleigh I rode on No. 36001, in the fireman's cab usually, and kept darting into the bunker to tip weighed bags of coal out on to the shovelling plate as required. R.G. Jarvis rode with us later in the week and came into the fireman's cab to show willing. However unaware of the strict rota we had established for cooling our backs in the open door he occupied that position continuously so we were even hotter than usual. We listened for sounds of possible mechanical failure; particularly after the crank-axle had fractured. Near Fleet one night there was a sudden crescendo of new sound. I made my way along the corridor to report, only to find that we had just overtaken a T14 'Paddle box' 4-6-0 which had attempted to have a race with us on the slow line. What a sight that would have been in the half-light! With only half a central cab we were blind to the "double-breaster"!' (This also tells us Leader was therefore running on the slow line.)

On 26 September there was another trial to the same timings but with a heavier load. This from the official report, 'Eastleigh–Woking: Working mainly in 25% cut-off to Shawford Junction, the speed rose to 42mph and the exhaust pressure was up to 14lb with the result that a good amount of burning char was thrown from the chimney. The gear was changed to 20% cut-off, but the exhaust pressure rose again to 14lb when the speed was 53mph. When passing through Wallers Ash Tunnel at 53mph there was a shower of large pieces of burning char from the chimney top. Sectional running time was maintained to Basingstoke. During the downhill running to Woking, a maximum speed of 56mph was noted near Farnborough; this speed could have been exceeded if it had been desirable.'

For the return, 'Woking–Eastleigh: The engine put up a good performance by passing Brookwood at 42mph a

In the evening sun No. 36001 awaits the off from the carriage sidings. The single disc headcode is 'Waterloo–Southampton Docks' (although Leader will not traverse the whole route) has replaced the twin discs previously seen. For the runs, Sam Talbot used a shovel with a shorter shaft, this was to avoid hitting his hand on the window frame of the cab and which implies he was also partly in the corridor when firing. *John Click/National Railway Museum*

The test trains ran north from the carriage sidings through the 'east yard' (heading north all the while) to finally gain the main line at Allbrook. Here Les Elsey has captured the engine and its motley load; again the canvas (or was it tarpaulin?) cover to the bunker is visible, this was only put in place after the bunker had been filled. The test runs of 12 and 15 June both involved 10 coaches but a different make-up resulted in slightly different weights.
Les Elsey/Colour by David Williams

drawbar pull of 2.4 tons was maintained and the train speed rose to 50mph at mile post 31.'

Once back at Eastleigh it is not believed any defects were found and accordingly for Wednesday 27 September a heavier set of nine vehicles were provided, equal to 294½tons. 'Eastleigh–Woking: The load was again increased to test the engine when working with higher steam chest pressures. There was some difficulty in obtaining suitable conditions owing to steam blows from the cylinder release valves when the pressure in the cylinders was above 210psi. At 21mph with a steam chest pressure of 195lb, the drawbar pull was 3.48 tons, drawbar horsepower 872 and the exhaust pressure 15lb. The boiler pressure gradually fell to 200lb. The regulator was eased to 130lb in the steam chest and the boiler pressure rose to 225lb in three minutes. At this point the speed was 51mph…'

'Woking to Eastleigh: A relatively good performance was made on the continuously rising gradient of 1 in 389 during which speed rose to 50 mph in 12 minutes…'

Again back at Eastleigh an examination would have taken place and once more there is no record of any adverse comment. Even so the record from the last run was again revealing areas of concern. The tendency for the cylinder release valves to blow at the relatively low pressure of 210psi meant that these were not operating correctly – they should only have responded at the same rate as the boiler pressure – 280psi. It is believed the issue was dealt with by simply blanking off this component although no one could be bothered to replace what were later discovered to be a set of weak springs. The high exhaust pressures though forewarned yet again of boiler steam bypassing the sleeves.

The final detailed run with the dynamometer car was scheduled for Thursday 28 September, a fine and dry evening (the weather had alternated between showery and dry over the four days from when this final series of tests had commenced.)

'Eastleigh–Woking: After passing onto the main line at Allbrook, the gear was set at 25% cut-off. The speed rose to 50mph in 12 minutes and the exhaust pressure rose to 12lb with a pressure of 195lb in the steam chest.'

'Woking–Eastleigh: Special attention is drawn to the particulars of the engine performance from Woking when a speed of 50mph was attained in 12 minutes 44 seconds. There was no difficulty in maintaining adequate boiler pressure. During this period 9cwts of coal were put in the firebox…'.

But what was not stated in the official records is that on this final run the engine was allowed to travel somewhat faster than before with the descent from Litchfield Summit to Eastleigh taken at far more than the officially stipulated 50 maximum speed. (Although no figures are given, when interviewed years later, driver Alf Smith commented he believed this could well have been in the order of 70mph. So was the engine not fitted with a speedometer?)

Back at Eastleigh, engine and dynamometer car were first uncoupled and Leader then had its fire disposed of. Either under its own power or perhaps shunted later, it eventually arrived on one of the sidings to the east of the running shed cold and lifeless. Chains and padlocks were attached around all the various cab doors, why is not certain, but for whatever reason authority was determined no one was to venture inside.

As far as most were concerned this was probably anticipated as the end of Leader and her sisters. Rumour was no doubt rife but with the words of ASLEF still ringing in their ears and the obvious common knowledge that the engine had been stopped on numerous occasions as well as having been in and out of works, it cannot have boded well. Politically the way ahead was seen with a range of standard steam designs as an interim measure, followed by later electrification or dieselisation according to technology and finance. (According to *Steam Index* and the entry on C.S. Cocks (*https://www.steamindex.com/people/engrs.htm#cocks*); he would have been happy to see Bulleid Pacifics on every region – such then was the respect he had for Bulleid, with support for this former LNER man. Indeed at this stage in history only a limited number of engines to pre-nationalisation steam designs remained to be built and it would surely take a small miracle to resurrect not only a non-standard design but one which was, to say the least and obvious to all, erratic.

It must have come then as a considerable surprise when just a few days after the completion of the last dynamometer car trial, and indeed subsequent to when the dynamometer vehicle had returned north to its more usual haunts, arrangements were set in hand for a further series of tests. The first of these was set for October but despite extensive searching we cannot be certain when it was actually proposed – or if said timetable was complied with! We should also remember that by this time Leader had been out of service for at least five weeks and a thorough examination was needed first.

Before going on the discuss this test, we should also ask 'why'? The simple answer is we do not know. Similarly we do not know by whom and how this was authorised and who might have also been on board – although we do know John Click was not involved on this or the later test. Click adds his own comment about 'A big engine needing a big train' but without explanation.

For the first time also the 'Fixing the erstwhile Chinese laundry' term might also be said to fit, as repairs were now carried out to a number of flange joints, one of these affecting the blower, whilst various flexible steam pipes to the generators were also replaced.

No. 36001 was steamed again for a light engine trial between Eastleigh and Cosham on Saturday 14 October. Again the regular crew were on board – no doubt with others – all was well and a full test was then set for Tuesday 17 October.

Notwithstanding Click's comments, exactly what purpose this test served is not certain and as just stated, neither has it been possible to ascertain under exactly what authorisation it was carried out. Folklore has it that there were those amongst Bulleid's devotees who felt the

Stephen Townroe's images of the engine and train accelerating away on the up through line from Allbrook towards Shawford – recorded from a conveniently placed signal gantry. Most of the empty coaching stock being used as load appears to be former LSWR stock but one test train at least is known to have appropriately included a single Bulleid coach in early BR 'blood and custard' (or similar) colours – *see* rear cover. Comment has been made many times both in this work and elsewhere concentrating on the heat the fireman had to endure. John Click comments that the 'central' firing compartment was at its hottest when the engine was not being worked hard. 'This may sound strange at first, but when it was working hard a lot of air went through the cab and into the firedoor so creating a draught although conversely whenever the firedoor was open the radiant heat was far worse than on a Pacific fired with a similar thin bright fire. When coasting the firedoors, if shut, would often glow red and throw out a lot of heat on to the fireman's legs which were that much closer than on a Pacific so that, with the airflow into the cab largely stopped, it could really become stiflingly hot.'

Henry Meyer also recorded two images of the dynamometer trials from his preferred location at Otterbourne. We see the test train approaching and a moment later Sam Talbot has 'put a bit on'. It would also be interesting to speculate on the 'sound' of Leader. A three-cylinder bogie with cranks set at 120° would probably sound much as a Bulleid Pacific; but were the beats uniform – probably not. Then add into the equation the second bogie and we have to ask did the two condescend to get in sync with each other as was often the case with a Mallett and Garratt type? Moving footage of Leader is conspicuous by its absence, except the very brief footage of the sleeve valve oscillating gear under test at Brighton – *see* page 206 – otherwise no actual sound footage of the engine has been located. John Click writes, 'The trials proved interesting and for those involved incorporated such highs as exhilarating high speed runs or lows such as sitting and watching for malfunction of the valve rods.' There seems to be no evidence that a cab window washer was ever fitted (the Pacifics all had them, worked off the injector) nor was a heater fitted at No. 2 end; it would certainly have been needed in cold weather, running No. 2 end first. A point to note is that the driver had no control of the blower, according to JGC this was essential and could have been done fairly simply. JGC again, 'The driver also had no information on the water level in the boiler. Some experiments were done (or have I in mind something we did at Rugby Test Plant?) on a method of providing repeaters from a water level indicator fitted with a number of electrical contacts lighting lamps. Wherever it was thought about it was *not* done!'

engine had still not had to chance to show its capabilities, especially with the type of load the designer had intended, indeed all the dynamometer car trials had been with only a limited weight, the most the engine had ever hauled being 337t back on 12 June.

For this 'big engine' trial the load was 13 coaches weighing 430t. Despite the fact there would no dynamometer car, the route and schedule were also to be the same as before with the engine turned at Guildford so as to always be working under load with No. 2 end leading. Aside from the usual crew a fitter was on board, so was Bulleid as well plus Roland C. Bond of the Railway Executive; no chance then that this was simply a local affair. As it transpired this would also be the final time the designer would witness his creation.

Leaving Eastleigh one unnamed observer described the start as 'effortless' although the engine did not behave totally as intended for at Basingstoke some six minutes were wasted whilst 36001 stubbornly refused to move either forward or back in order to reach the water column.

A (semi) official summary of the run also fortunately survives; 'The engine ran satisfactorily and whilst some time was lost on the easier sections, this could well have been avoided by slightly heavier working. The steam pressure and water level were fairly well maintained, but steaming was not entirely satisfactory during the heaviest conditions. The performance of the locomotive was such, however, as to indicate that a trial could be attempted with 480 tons.'

But why was the trial undertaken in the first place? What information could now be obtained that could not have been achieved with the benefit of the expertise of the dynamometer car? To run a test of this nature obviously took the will of at least one – probably several – senior officials and again for what purpose?

Regardless of the behaviour of the engine, Leader was made ready for what would also be its very last outing, scheduled for Thursday 2 November 1950. This time no less than fifteen coaches were attached weighing 480t, the only concession for the increased weight at the drawbar being that five minutes more had been allowed in the passing time for reaching Winchester Junction. Who was on board is unknown, although we know for certain it was not the two VIPs mentioned just now.

Even so with this colossal weight attached No. 36001 showed herself to be the master of the task set, with 50mph maintained almost throughout and now with a load greater than that given to a Merchant Navy on the *Bournemouth Belle* Pullman service – and this latter service did not have the disadvantage of a standing start from cold from Eastleigh directly on to a rising gradient. Indeed every Bulleid driver I have ever spoken to has confirmed that even with a larger Merchant Navy Pacific, 50mph was perfectly acceptable throughout the climb north to Litchfield Summit. If there was a down side already known to those on board, it was this had been achieved at the expense of a considerable coal consumption. Exactly how much is not reported as coal was no longer being weighed. Likewise was Sam Talbot still the only one involved or might he have had help, especially considering the load the engine was to face? We can also assume this was achieved still with No. 2 end leading.

En route to Micheldever it was even reported that the safety valves on 36001 lifted, there was so much steam available. A truly remarkable performance especially considering the load and the reduced size fire grate. No. 36001 was even half-a-minute early at Worting Junction which may then have contributed to a signal stop – which it pulled away from without difficulty, but then resulted in a slightly delayed arrival at Basingstoke.

There must have been jubilation on board, although this was soon to be trounced when examination of the engine at Basingstoke revealed that the smokebox door had not been properly fastened when leaving Eastleigh and in consequence had 'sprung' at the bottom edge so allowing hot ash and char to drop onto the wooden flooring of the cab. This in turn was threatening to burn the floorboards and the reluctant decision was thus made to abandon the test and return again to Eastleigh light engine. So, 50mph – 480 tons – on schedule – safety valves lifting – a grate area of just 25.5^2ft – *and* drawing air at the smokebox. That alone has to be recorded as a success.

No. 36001 had one final trick up its sleeve(s) – the pun is 100% deliberate! Running light on the return to Eastleigh and accordingly with little demand for excess steam, Leader was allowed to fly. It has been suggested she reached 90mph near Winchester, still riding as smoothly as a coach.

Back at her home depot, the fire was again dropped and the smokebox examined. All that was needed for a further trial was a replacement smokebox door – and four of these were of course available on Nos 36002–5. But it was not to be, whoever had authorised this final series of tests either cancelled anything further, or perhaps it was cancelled by others, or indeed this was all that was ever intended. There never would be any more. Once again 36001 found herself either amongst out-of-use engines or stabled alongside the shed, her access doors again chained shut. A decision was now awaited from Marylebone, it would arrive just eighteen days later.

On that day, 20 November 1950, Robin Riddles as the member of the Railway Executive responsible for Mechanical Engineering, submitted his report on the Leader project. (ironically too I am writing this very piece within a week of the 70th anniversary of that report – KJR.)

The Executive had already been made aware of the goings-on at Eastleigh so far as the weighing was concerned through the earlier preliminary report of 24 March 1950, but now would come the final reconning. This from Riddles:

Since my report dated 24.3.1950 was submitted, further trial runs have been made including two series of dynamometer car tests to determine the performance of this locomotive in comparison with a conventional locomotive of comparable power characteristics.

... It was originally hoped that adjustment to the axlebox pedestals and slides would improve the weight

Leader at Shawford and with a relatively clean exhaust. Apart from one indifferent quality image of the engine entering Winchester (not reproduced) this is as far north as we have illustrations of the engine. On the engine's final run of 2 November 1950, John Click made a last comment, 'The rockets put up that night must have been the first objects into orbit.' 1950. *Reg Curl*

distribution, but it is now evident that extensive redesign of the locomotive would be necessary in order to obtain a distribution which could be considered satisfactory for running in normal service.

It was therefore necessary in order that further trials might be run, to overcome the unsatisfactory weight distribution temporarily by the addition of 5¼ tons of ballast located on the locomotive in such a way as to produce a more uniform distribution of weight between the left and right sides ...

Renewed running of the locomotive revealed a number of minor (minor ?) defects which culminated on 29 June after a total mileage of only 6,103, in the crank-axle of No. 1 bogie fracturing and breaking in two pieces. Examination of the crank-axle of No. 2 bogie revealed a number of small fatigue cracks and this axle would ultimately have failed in similar manner.

... The locomotive had to be sent into the works and new driving wheels and crank-axles were fitted on both bogies. With the locomotive as at present built it is very probable that these replaced axles would also fail.

... In view of the very high coal and water consumption, it was suspected that steam leakage was occurring and the pistons, sleeve valves and rings, were renewed and examined. Evidence of leakage was apparent and a number of new sleeve rings were fitted and all rings on pistons and valves were renewed ... Such a marked deterioration in performance for a locomotive after only approximately 6,000 miles is exceptional and the trials have indicated that, with the present design, this rapid deterioration could only be corrected by frequently stopping the locomotive for examination and repairs to the valves and pistons ... compared with that of modern main line locomotives of more conventional design where the valves and pistons are normally only examined at intervals of 20–36,000 miles ...

... In the course of the trials, attention was given to the operating conditions as far as the engine crews are concerned ... Men have complained of the high temperature in the fireman's cab ... .the fireman's position becomes intolerable if attempts are made to run the engine chimney first, owing to the very hot air which

Repairs at Guildford on 22 August following failure of the oil pump. Normally the engine would only ever have been seen there during the hours of darkness when both engine and dynamometer car would be turned ready to be propelled back to Woking. Hence this failure gave the opportunity for the only Guildford view ever seen. We might wonder about the reaction of early morning passengers on the platforms opposite. Ken Briggs is seen kneeling next to the engine. Unfortunately we have no definite images of some of the senior staff, draughtsmen etc., who were also involved with Leader and previously other Bulleid projects, men such as Jim Allott, Dick Barnes, 'Jimmy' Jones and Doug Smith, to name but a few. JGC again, 'In his favour Bulleid did achieve success in several areas; the welded steel firebox for the Light Pacifics was a very elegant piece of design indeed. Inner and outer firebox plates were welded to a U-shaped "foundation ring", itself fabricated from pressings. By the end of Bulleid's time on the Southern he had dramatically advanced the state of the art of welding in locomotive, carriage and wagon design and production, and was at least a decade ahead of his nearest rivals. He disliked presswork and considered it an anachronism from an earlier age and had a version of this firebox drawn out with all corners welded at right-angles! Nobody liked it though, least of all Cocks and Allott, who urged making haste less quickly than the Chief wished. They successfully got him away from this kind of thing, which was in the first version of the Leader firebox drawn for his Patent. His argument was that staying took care of all direct loads and that welds did no more than act as water seals. Only in Dublin did he get his way in the extraordinary boiler for the Turf Burner. (Click and others shared a general apprehension about it.) Of those mentioned, 'Jimmy' Jones was the one who drew so many loco diagrams, he later went to Swindon where he had a lot to do with the Class 52 'Westerns' but finished up as Project Engineer for the HST Power Car at Derby. Dick Barnes worked with Jim Allott for years on Bulleid's boilers but he didn't think everything he was asked to do was necessarily the best way, in fact he thought that OVB's 3:8 miniature valve gear in an oil bath was an example of 'how not to do it' when saying so was still very unfashionable; he too went to Derby. Another Brighton Section Leader, Doug Smith refused to go to the Technical Centre and he became Chief Draughtsman at Croydon.'
John Click/National Railway Museum

emerges from the corridor when running in this direction. With the present arrangement one of the aims of the locomotive is thus defeated and it would be necessary for turning to take place at the end of each journey.

There are only two alternatives which now present themselves in respect of the future of this class of locomotive. They are;

(a) To make a number of major modifications to the present design with a view to overcoming the difficulties which have been experienced and the difficulties which have been revealed;

(b) To scrap the locomotive so far completed and the other four in varying stages of construction.

The former course would involve the following in respect of the matters referred to above;–

The high coal and water consumption is due, to a large extent, to steam leakage past the sleeve valves, pistons and rings. It is also due to the high rate of combustion made necessary by the reduction in grate area, resulting from the thicker firebrick walls which experience shows to be essential.

To correct these deficiencies would, in my opinion, involve a major redesign of the cylinders, eliminating the sleeve valves and replacing them with piston valves

(2) To reduce the total weight of the locomotive by 20 tons, thus bringing it into conformity with the original diagram ... would be virtually impossible ...

(3). ... At present the boiler is offset from the longitudinal centre line of the locomotive. The weight distribution could be corrected only by placing the boiler on the centre line, which would involve major alterations to the design of the locomotive or by a complete redistribution of the water tanks which also would involve extensive modifications.

In either case it is doubtful whether the present access which exists between the driver's cab and fireman could be retained. This would involve an automatic device in the driver's cab on similar principle to a 'dead-mans' handle on electric stock, (which would be an undesirable though essential complication) or three men would always be required on the locomotive when on the main line.

(4) The present axlebox assembly would require to be completely redesigned to give sufficient freedom to ensure the safety of the locomotive as a vehicle on the track, and to provide the necessary flexibility to eliminate breakage of the crank-axle.

It is not possible to say at this stage whether such redesign might not involve the elimination of the chains

Back at Eastleigh following a trial. The engine is alongside the coaling stage but recall she was rarely coaled in this fashion, certainly not for the official test runs. Ash disposal from the smokebox – the chute having been sealed by now – was hampered even more by the provision of a wooden screen added across part of the cab ahead of the smokebox another attempt at trapping heat. The unpleasant task of ash disposal was left to many of the junior fireman booked for 'P &D' (Preparation and Disposal') duty. Aside from passing by it, seeing it, or talking to others (the rumour mill again), many Eastleigh men thus became acquainted with the engine and as will be gathered, were singularly unimpressed. *J.H. Aston*

Following the conclusion of the trials on 28 September, the dynamometer car departed north to its more usual haunts. It is seen here at Banbury as part of the normal trailing load of a train probably bound for Woodford Halse and beyond. *Steve Banks Collection*

connecting the coupled axles and their replacement by coupling rods.

(5) It is difficult at this stage to suggest anything that could be done to ensure tolerable conditions for the fireman …

(6) The defects which are known to exist in the welding of part of the boiler of this locomotive would require to be rectified. Part of the welding of the boiler in the completed locomotive was subjected to X-Ray examination … The completed boilers for the other four locomotives, however, were not subject to any kind of X-Ray examination and I should not be prepared to allow them to go out into service until this precaution has been duly carried out.

Expenditure amounting to £178,865 has already been incurred. So far it has not been possible, nor will it be possible, to place the locomotive in revenue earning service without further heavy expense. I have not estimated what this further expense might be because, even were it incurred and all the defects eliminated the locomotive, as modified, would offer no advantages compared with one of the conventional well-tried design.

I am compelled therefore to RECOMMEND that the second alternative namely, the completed Locomotive and the other four in various stages of construction, should be scrapped and that the authority for their construction as part of the 1948 Locomotive Building Programme should be cancelled.

(Sgd) R.A. Riddles.

Notes

(1) Townroe completed more than one book on the classes mentioned, as well as a joint work with Cecil J. Allen on the Bulleid Pacifics – 1951 and 1976. All are recommended reading. Townroe was also the author of an authorative account on bicycle repairing although this is, understandably perhaps, hardly known of by the majority of railway scholars.

10
The Final Reckoning

In just forty-four words (being the final paragraph from the preceding chapter), the first engine, No. 36001, together with her incomplete sisters, were thus condemned and this time there would be no reprieve.

It was now just a matter of time before something that had taken more than four years of work was consigned to scrap. All that would be left would be the documentary and photographic records and after what was still to come later, BR might even have wished that both of the last named could be similarly buried.

In the meantime the almost-complete 36002 with the less-complete 36003 had been towed away from Brighton to store within the confines of the under-used steam shed at Bognor. There is no definite date for this transfer but from *RO* correspondents, it is believed to have been sometime soon after March 1950. (Both engines were at Bognor at least by 1 July 1950.) Why move them away from Brighton? Well, simply put, they were probably a bit of an embarrassment. The phrase 'out of sight – out of mind', could well have applied. Additionally it is very likely Brighton works were short of space, just as most works often were, hence the logical thing was to move the two engines away, for at the time there was no likelihood of permission being given for their completion anyway.

However, when it became known they were at Bognor the number of curious visitors caused another move, this time on a date we know, 11 September 1950, to be stored at New Cross Gate (in company with sixteen other stored

No. 36001 lifeless at Eastleigh. The technical people may have been dispersed but Leader's greatest achievement so far as load haulage still lay in the future. As reported in the text, on **2 November** No. **36001** took its intended **480t** from a dead start at Eastleigh and comfortably maintained **50mph** up the long **1 in 252 climb** north. All this with a reduced grate area of just **25.5^{2}ft**. So what actual **horse power** might Leader have been developing on this occasion? To answer this question the writer turned to mathematician Sean Price. Sean has calculated that the actual power output was no less than **2,067hp**, a truly **outstanding performance,** but sadly one which despite its promise was simply outweighed by too many other factors.
A.E. West/Mike King

Marylebone decision makers. L – R: seated: Robert (Robin) Riddles, E.S. (Ernest) Cox and R.C. (Roland) Bond.

locos of varying types) and also where the railway police soon became involved when brass work and copper piping started to disappear, although because Nos 36002/3 were not complete nobody could say precisely what was there in the first place!

New Cross Gate on the former Brighton lines in South London, was just 7 miles 3 chains from Victoria – which location 36001 had so vainly tried but been thwarted from reaching twice in September 1949. A Leader, or to more precise two of the class, had at last reached London – but now not in steam, and of course totally for the wrong reasons.

A final move was back from New Cross to Brighton (for No. 36002 this was on 24 June 1951 but we do not know at what time of day or night) and where what was probably the final view of No. 36002 in the process of being dismantled was recorded on 30 June 1951. By a matter of days or weeks she was destined to be the last survivor.

Meanwhile at Eastleigh No. 36001 had stood for the most part alongside the shed – cold, lifeless and again with all access doors chained. There was now no doubt as to the outcome so with no chance of No. 36001 steaming again, was the secrecy of what went on inside really necessary? Did the authorities seriously believe someone might come along in the dead of night and spirit it away? The decision to abandon the project had come with Riddles's final report of 20 November, and yet No. 36001 would remain intact for just over six months, a cruel irony as she waited for that final call. It came on 25 April when she was shunted into the neighbouring works and the process of dismantling begun. There does not appear to have been any specific instruction given appertaining to the destruction of the engine – because let us be fair, in reality that is what it was – with the central section of the casing first removed after which the boiler of Leader was lifted off the frame. This took place within the works rather than outside and so indicating more of a dismantling process took place rather than actual cutting. Even so the whole process occupied a number of weeks (it was the practice to work on any number of engines at the same time, whilst men would also be called away to assist on other more urgent work when required.) Again according to folklore certain parts, possibly the roller bearings from the bogies, remained by the oil store until at least 1959–60. *Hartland Point* meanwhile had also been reduced to scrap at Eastleigh, although for this engine it had been dealt with in the more usual scrapping position, in the open air at the rear of the works.

It should also be remembered that even then the whole Leader episode was the proverbial 'hot potato', many former Southern Railway staff at all levels (like John Click of course), having a strong affinity and consequent sympathy with the man who they had perceived as having put (or tried) to place the Southern at the forefront of modern steam engine development and consequent technology. But conversely, we should also not ignore the opposing views of Gordon Nicholson and similarly Stephen Townroe. It is rumoured Bulleid's followers did not take kindly to the curtailment of the project – although again much of this murmured comment is based on hearsay rather than fact. It should also be recalled that sixty years ago the movement of the other engines to what were then outlying locations – Bognor/New Cross Gate was carefully considered and deliberately chosen so as to make it difficult to track their locations. The communications revolution we have today was something that could not then have been dreamed of.

As to what remains, well at least one number-plate from both No. 36001 and also 36002 survived, with one of the brass whistle from 36001 – the latter for many years in the hands of the redoubtable Harry Frith from Eastleigh. (When I spoke to him at his home about the project, the whistle was mounted on a wooden stand on the hearth.) In addition there is the unfitted works plate referred to previously. At least one nameplate from *Hartland Point* lasted and was for a time in the care of the late Les Warnett whose unfailing help was invaluable in the compilation of the very first edition of this book.

Having now summarily consigned 36001–5 to history, it may now be time to return to perhaps one of the more puzzling questions of the final days of the design. This refers to the rumour, although to be precise it is really far more than rumour, that Bulleid – ensconced as he was by the spring of 1950 in his seat at Inchicore – contacted BR (on an unreported date) *with a view to the purchase of the whole class for shipment to Ireland*.

This was confirmed to the author in correspondence with the late Don Bradley, although unfortunately 'anno-domini' occurred before further discussion on the subject could occur. Click adds slightly more in his notes but when asked in person he was unwilling to discuss the matter. Consequently it is from the Click notes we learn that 'Paddy' Mulvany (Chief Draughtsman of CIE) from Inchicore (and possibly others) did visit Brighton and it

One of the very few views showing No. 36001 and her half-sister, No. 32039, together at Brighton. Taken around August 1949, the emphasis had now shifted from the Atlantic to Leader itself. Did No. 2039 materially help in the development of No. 36001? In reality probably not. What it did show is the complexities of sleeve valves were such that any benefit gained relative to heat efficiency at the cylinders were outweighed by the complications involved and commensurate increased maintenance costs. What has never been located is a breakdown of build/running/maintenance-repair costs for No. 36001 (and her sisters), nor indeed any figures applicable to No. 2039.
Lens of Sutton Association, Ref: 60251

was there – according to Click – that he spoke to both Cocks and Granshaw. (But: according to *Steam Index* again, Cocks moved to Derby in 1949. At that time Bulleid had not been appointed in Eire whilst in addition Leader had only started trials in the same year. Conclusion: either Mulvany spoke to Cocks later – we might more likely assume 1950/51 or any meeting between the two men may not have been at Brighton). Might this potential sale to Ireland have also contributed to why the engines were left stored for six months rather than being cut up earlier? Certainly by the time of the visit by the Irish delegation Bulleid's overseas appointment had been confirmed although Bulleid was clearly not very well known of, yet at least, at Inchicore. Consequently Mulvany is alleged to have asked the Brighton men, 'What kind of a man is this Mr Bulleid?' Cocks supposedly responded, 'He'll probably want you to put the chimney on the back of the tender.' Recalling the conversation in later years Mulvany, used to say, 'By George, t'ats the very forst t'ing he wanted when he got here as well' – and a reference to the experiments on the first Turf Burning engine – see p.239.

Attempting to analyse further, and assuming the Inchicore people arrived sometime after August 1950 – if they were looking for Nos 36002/3, they had of course gone from Brighton by that time but perhaps the delegation also went to Bognor/New Cross or even Eastleigh; on this Click does not comment.

Why this visit occurred in the first place is easy to understand, Bulleid was in Ireland and already working toward what might very loosely and perhaps a bit unfairly be described as 'Leader Mk2' (the 'Turf Burner'). Perhaps he thought he could adapt or modify the existing engines rather than start from scratch. At least he would also have had a complete class to start with as well, rather than end up with a single example as of course occurred! Make no mistake about it, the Irish 'Turf Burner' was a success. Whether Bulleid would have wished to have the prototype No. 36001 as well is unclear, although probably not. The fact the visiting delegation went to Brighton is also interesting, possibly because there they could have direct contact with individuals with sufficient knowledge and in sufficient authority at that location. That is assuming of course such contact was in fact allowed.

RIGHT A complete sleeve with the protruding 'ears' at the end. We cannot be 100% certain if this example was from No. 2039 or No. 36001, probably the latter, but for the purpose of the present discussion, it is of no consequence. Whilst we know the sleeves for Leader were manufactured at Eastleigh, we also cannot confirm if the same applied to No. 2039. Inlet and exhaust ports are shown, the latter being the larger.

BELOW Sleeves inserted into the front of a Leader bogie; the latter need to remove the body-to-bogie vacuum and steam heat hoses to facilitate this operation is also now obvious.

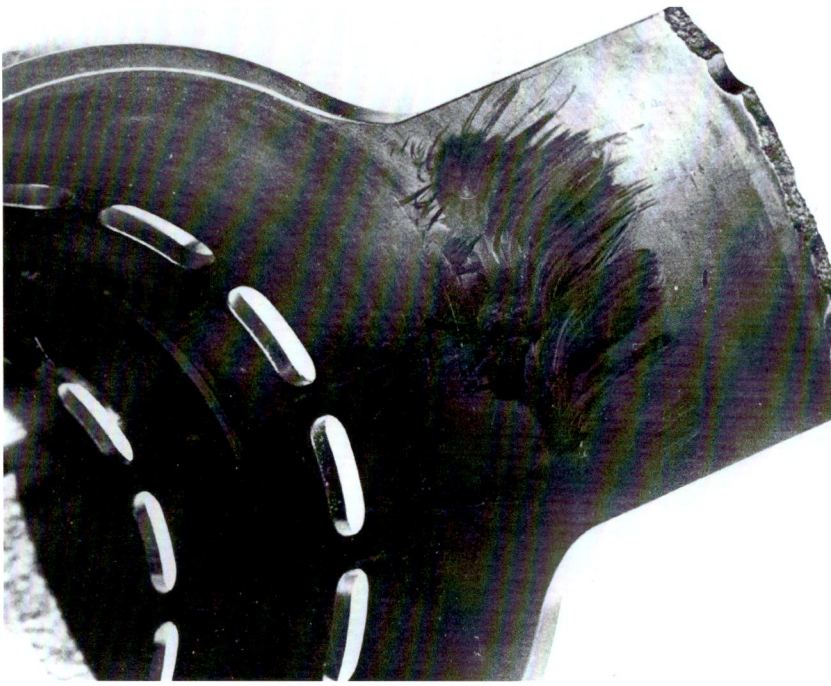

BELOW LEFT A scored and broken sleeve, again we cannot be certain from which loco and indeed on what occasion. The cause of such failures was never really established and John Click makes a valid point when he comments that the removal of the oscillating gear at the front may well have reduced some incidents of sleeve failure but it may well have contributed to others as the front of the sleeve was now no longer supported. Townroe in his written comments to the present writer – *see* page 284 et seq. – speaks of the clearances for the sleeves. But as referred to in the text there is some suggestion the two cylinder blocks for the original engine were noted to have warped slightly after final welding. The result was that as originally designed and built sleeve valve failures were inevitable and may have been why the decision was later made to increase clearances as well as having the rearmost ring removed. A bogie change between 36001 and one of her sisters, assuming No. 36002 '& Co' were not assembled in quite so much of a hurry, might well have made all the difference. Sean Day-Lewis in *Bulleid of the Southern*, refers to the same point but without great detail. We may wonder just who amongst officialdom might have been party to this information, for had the necessary action been taken it is another aspect which might have made a difference to the final report.

In the event no deal was struck. It would be unfair to state if this was because BR would not sell, it might equally have been that Dublin would not pay the price. Or it could have been the engines were simply deemed unsuitable and requiring too much modification. It could have been any one then of several reasons. Unfortunately without the finding of a record in either contemporary BR or CIE papers, it is unlikely any more light will ever be cast on the account.

Bulleid, as will have been gathered, had not of course given up on the theory of this type of double-bogie engine having many of the same theoretical advantages of the diesel and electric. Indeed this was the theme he developed at a lecture to the American Society of Mechanical Engineers in New York in October 1949.

'The first of these new engines has run about 4,000 miles. Steam locomotive development has always been handicapped (Bulleid was referring to the UK) by the absence of proper testing facilities. We have to build the complete locomotive before we can try it and the trials can only be made out on the road. As is to be expected some troubles have arisen, such as broken ends to the sleeve valves and spalling of the firebrick casing of the firebox, troubles which are being overcome. The engine has shown already the advantage of a double bogie locomotive as regards freedom of running, ease in taking curves, and the great value of having the total weight available for traction and braking.'

As might be expected he similarly ignored or glossed the numerous other difficulties encountered but recall too October 1949 was a bad time for No. 36001 and, as we have seen, destined also to get a whole lot worse. Understandably this information was not being made public at the time and certainly the *Railway Gazette* as the recognised and worldwide technical journal certainly makes no mention of the problems being encountered. Indeed the complete truth about the engine – its design, build, trials and modifications – was probably only known to a select few at this stage: Granshaw most likely, Attwell probably and likewise Cocks, and it would probably be safe to say even Bulleid and Riddles were not party to all.

The fact that he was pushing ahead at Inchicore should really be enough proof of his beliefs, as Bulleid despite his years, (he was 68 in 1950), was determined that the message of continued steam locomotive development would remain to be heralded to as wide an audience as possible. This was confirmed in an article by him which appeared in the American journal *Mechanical Engineering* in 1950 under the title 'Locomotive and Rolling Stock developments in Great Britain' and as a follow up to his 1949 lecture.

In all probability the draft had been submitted sometime in 1949 as the article was accompanied by a photograph of 36001 supposedly in service on a train at Brighton station – on a train, yes, but more correctly a test run. The caption accompanying the view – presumably also prepared by Bulleid, was deliberately misleading, as it stated, 'Leader class engine in service.' A clear inference then that the class was in service. (Even so we may forgive the man this inaccuracy as at the time the article was prepared, it was expected the class would enter service. Indeed nowhere has it been found that Bulleid acted other than in an honest and straightforward way.)

Perhaps even more interesting within the article were two sections of text describing both the Leader design and also the way Bulleid hoped to see steam traction being taken forward. 'While in American eyes this is a small engine, its horsepower will be about 1,700 and consequently it will give as good results as a Diesel-Electric locomotive with a 2,000hp engine. How successful we have been in the new design remains to be seen, but the new features in the engine should give us better service, help to improve the performance of the steam locomotive and restore steam traction to favour.'

In view of what was already happening on the railways of America at this time, Bulleid's comments are slightly strange. Perhaps he was seen and indeed received in the USA more out of courtesy than as a serious proponent of steam. We should not forget that the transition from steam to diesel in America was already in full swing and despite several vain attempts to stall this advance, including the mighty *John Henry* steam turbine of 1954, none would do anything to prevent the inevitable dominance of the internal combustion engine in North America. (In passing we might mention that in America when a steam engine was no longer of use it was said to have been 'retired', in many ways a far better sounding term than the one used here, the somewhat harsh term 'scrapped'.)

Consequently we can say without contradiction that in America at least Bulleid's was already a voice in the wilderness. Back in the UK Riddles too would have preferred to have finished with steam and replaced it with electrification but financially this was just not possible at the time. On the basis steam would have to continue for some years to come, we have the reason and justification for the building of the various Standard types; the side advantage of this being that some early form of uniformity might thus begin to be achieved with motive power on all regions. (As indicated previously by Cocks, former LNER man but now completely under the Bulleid spell, he would have liked to have seen a spread of Bulleid Pacifics throughout the country but which also immediately begs the question why this capable and professional engineer could be blind to their failings? No doubt, Doncaster, Swindon and Derby would have felt their own designs would be similarly suitable for a wider audience as well.)

However, as if to emphasise his own personal belief in a future for steam, there was also a veiled clue from Bulleid as to what was still to come. In this it may be inferred that he already knew that under a nationalised regime and without his own guiding hand British Railways would never allow Leader to work in traffic, although it can also be seen that in his own mind, he still intended to pursue his ideals of utopia still further for his article continued:

'While in the Leader class of engine the development of the steam locomotive has been carried a stage further, there is still much work to be done. The use of blast to create draft should give way to fans so that we can control the production of steam accurately. The exhaust steam

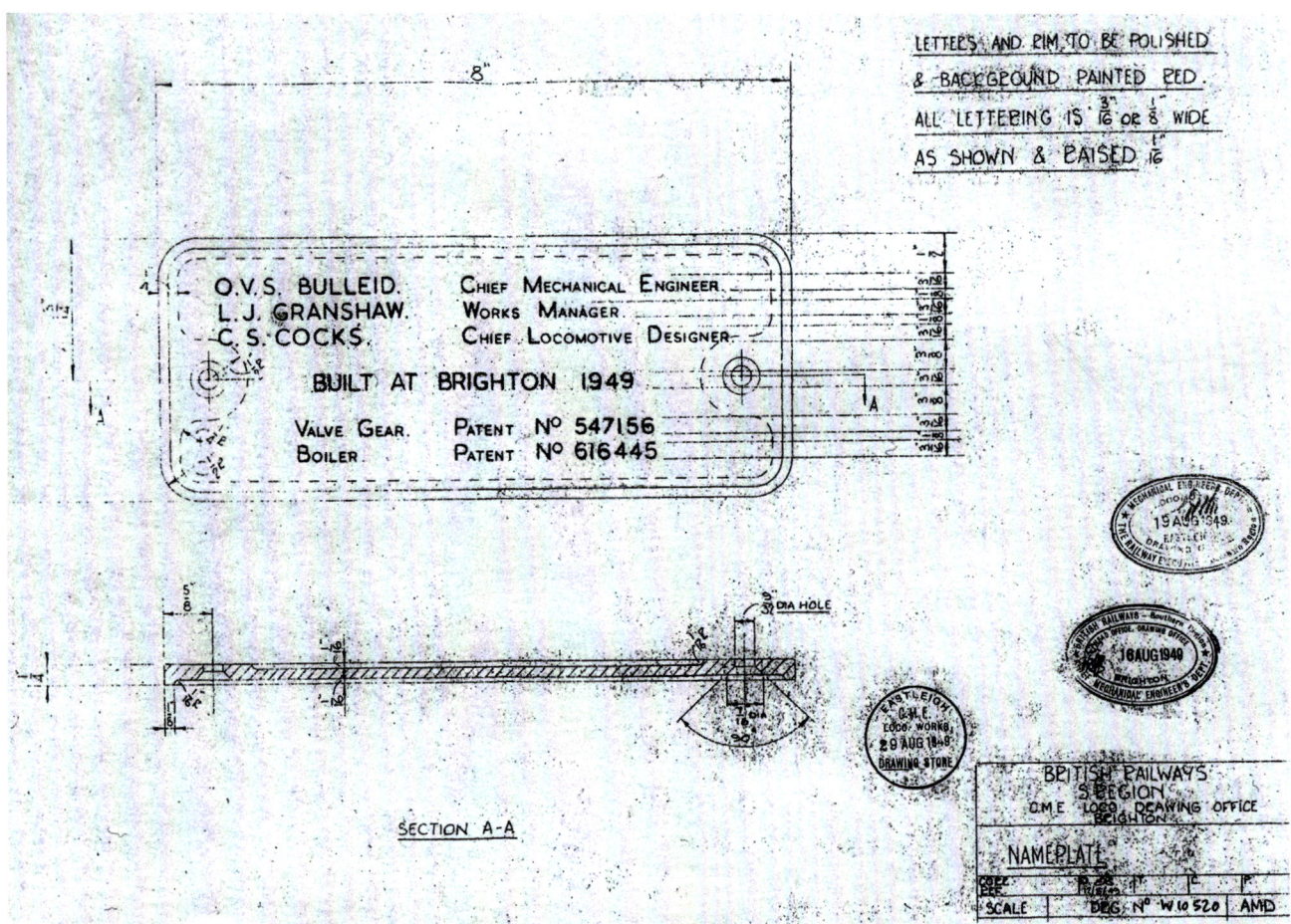

The works plate designed for but apparently never fitted to No. 36001. An unpainted original was found in a drawer at Brighton and was subsequently believed to have been in John Click's collection. He comments the inclusion of Granshaw's name was a bit 'naughty'. Possibly the only copy was put up for auction several years ago. The present writer was the underbidder at just above £1,000. Details of the vendor and successful purchaser are unknown.

should not be allowed to escape to the atmosphere but should be returned to the boiler. Experimental work already done encourages the thought that these two problems can be solved, and I commend them to the young engineers as worthy of investigation. I shall feel more than recompensed if I have shown that while the Stephenson locomotive may in some circumstances be dead or dying, this cannot be said of steam traction itself. If new designs be developed in the light of our present greater knowledge and the servicing of the locomotive be brought up to date – in short, if only we can demolish the conservatism which is destroying the steam locomotive rather than give up any of its customary ways – then we can look forward to a revival of steam traction.' (Elsewhere the article contained references to development on the Southern Railway in particular, but whilst Bulleid's ideas and influence come to the fore once again, there was nothing else necessarily radical.)

So, Bulleid clearly felt steam could be developed and what was to become 'The Turf Burner' would in fact be destined to be just another step forward along the way. Interestingly he refers to 'experimental work already done encourages thought that these two problems can be solved' – meaning the control of the blast by fans and exhaust steam being returned to the boiler. But exactly where had this been done? Certainly not in Bulleid's time on the Southern. The experiments with SR No. A816 (1930–35) may have been along similar lines but recall they were *before* Bulleid's time at Waterloo. To tie up a loose end on this particular topic, we should just mention that a few years earlier and prior to his retirement, Holcroft had been tasked by Bulleid with designing a heat exchange fitment similar to that on A816 but for the Merchant Navy class. A basic weight diagram was produced showing the equipment added to what was now a bogie tender attached to the class but nothing else is heard of the matter and certainly no practical experiment was ever carried out.

Elsewhere engineers were themselves generally facing up to the fact that it was potentially easier to pursue a course of dieselisation and eventual electrification. There was no doubt also political pressure in this area and whilst a number of skilled steam engineers were still to come, in reality the days of the steam designer being considered pre-eminent were rapidly drawing to a close. That is with one exception, and not this time Mr Bulleid.

To accompany the earlier similar views we also have this surreptitiously taken view of the broken crank axle on No. 36001. Without wishing to deliberately add fuel to the flame, recall too that another Bulleid designed engine, No. 35020 broke a crank axle at speed at Crewkerne in 1953. This resulted in ultra-sonic testing of the crank axles of all the members of the Merchant Navy class with a number being considered as likely to fail at some stage. Replacements (or was it a new design?) were fitted and no further trouble was experienced. But were the 1950 and 1953 failures due to design, manufacturer or materials? Those questions had not been answered, indeed folklore has it that the act of pressing the wheels of Leader on to the ends of the axles without having the crank webs suitable packed in the process may have been another contributory factor. *John Bell*

At the risk then of ignoring others there was really only one man contemporary with Bulleid who was also pursuing steam and that was the legendary André Chapelon in France. (Others of like mind namely Livio Dante Porta, David Wardale, Dr Adolph Giesl-Gieslingen would continue to develop steam and whilst achieving much success in their own right none was able to stem the demise of steam although they may very well have delayed it slightly.)

Chapelon meanwhile, and in very cruel summary terms, was using compounding and extremely free steam and exhaust passages to transform an already good steam engine into one which can only be described as phenomenal. What Chapelon had done in effect was to raise the power output of steam to figures almost unheard of on the French loading gauge. His 4-8-4 No. 242A1 on test produced 5,000 horsepower at the cylinders, the equivalent of 4,000 drawbar horse-power at 50mph; the figures speak for themselves. What was even more remarkable were the coal consumption figures, never more than 2.64lb per hp/hr. The grate too showed itself able to develop 1000hp per square metre of area. Truly this was a remarkable machine and, according to the Chapelon team, far from the limit that could in fact have been achieved. On the drawing board already were plans for a 6,000hp steam engine. Another stunning fact is that all this was achieved back in 1946 with France still suffering the ramifications of WWII and occupation. The impression given in the preceding narrative then was that Bulleid was a man ahead of his time – but Bulleid was very much behind the times when compared with Chapelon.

Unfortunately for Chapelon, in France politics would play its part. War had created the opportunity to rebuilt and re-equip the French railway system after the years of conflict. In many ways this was the equivalent of a blank canvas and this fact was not lost on the politicians of the day. Steam development was thus curtailed. Chapelon had shown it could be done, but it was not politically prudent, particularly in light of the fact that his No. 242A1 steam engine and other projected designs would then outperform any potential new electric locomotive then planned to be built. No, steam had to be seen as outmoded. Chapelon's other projected designs never got further than the drawing board.

Where we should hang our heads in shame is not to have noticed this ourselves, Bulleid and Riddles in particular lost what could well have been the chance to achieve true glory.

To return though to the subject of power output, and it should be remembered that in the UK, arguably the very best steam engines were in the league of the Stanier Duchess, the 'new' *Princess Anne*, the later rebuilt Merchant Navy and perhaps even a modern A2. Could we even include *Duke of Gloucester* with its steaming issues resolved as was achieved in preservation? Any of these types could with an engine in good condition, the best coal and a willing fireman ('men' might be needed) produce in the order of 3,000 indicated horsepower but still far short of what was happening across the channel. What was also a missed opportunity was to not take advantage of things such as the Giesel ejector and which when fitted by BR to a solitary original Bulleid 'Lght Pacific' No. 34064, it turned the engine overnight to the equivalent of a Merchant Navy. Now just imagine what the same fitment might have been done for the other classes mentioned.

Bulleid himself had long admired both the French nation and the abilities of their engineers, he was also fluent in the language. He had maintained what was probably more than just a professional relationship with André Chapelon, the two men had a great admiration for and friendship towards each other – Chapelon had of course travelled on Leader whilst the engine had been on test from Brighton, and whilst the Frenchman was reported as showing particular interest in the sleeve valves and firebox, paradoxically it may be considered a little strange that Bulleid had not perhaps incorporated any of the French principles in the Leader design.

Leaving aside the further development of steam in both Ireland and France, it would be fair to say that with the project now cancelled and the engines physically no more, it could be reasonably expected that the Leader project would be forgotten. But no, and it was not long before murmurings over the whole project were being aired in certain of the more technical and professional railway periodicals.

Accordingly it could only be a matter of time before the obvious blunt questions were being asked, and this came in the *Railway Gazette* of 25 May 1951, when an anonymous correspondent (but reported as writing from Woking) asked what was a perfectly fair question, 'I wonder if an appeal could be made through your columns for more information about this design? (*meaning Leader*). I know of no official information or photographs (*fifty years later we know both existed in quantity*) published about this interesting class, although it is now two years since the first one appeared from Brighton works. As far as my information goes only one "Leader" class locomotive has ever been steamed and that has been lying out of use in the open at Eastleigh since early

LEFT A positive of Leader was the excellent driving position. We hesitate to say 'unique to a UK steam locomotive design' as someone will no doubt come back with an example of a tank engine or similar. Against this was there was absolutely no protection for the driver at either end in the event of a front-end impact. In No. 1 end, the known controls, but basically duplicated at both ends. are identified as follows:

① Driver's seat. Non-adjustable. One fixed seat only provided in each cab.

② Regulator handle. The regulator rod to which it was attached ran overhead.

③ Cut-off warning plate. When coasting the maximum cut-off was cautioned to not exceed 4?%, that '?' is believed to have been 45%. At some point in Leader's history it is believed the maximum cut-off when starting was also reduced from 75% to 65% in an attempt to reduce the initial strain on the valves.

④ Driver's brake valve. The automatic charging system for the brakes meant there was no need for a separate ejector control.

⑤ Duplex vacuum gauge. (The image was taken when the engine was not in steam.)

⑥ Two steam chest pressure gauges No. 1 and No. 2 bogies, not identified as to which is which. Note the numbering goes to 320psi.

⑦ Steam heat pressure gauge, the valve/control for train heating is not identified.

⑧ Electric switches for indicator lights (6) and also coupling, reverser and steam chest gauges (4) – note the differing style of lampshades. It is assumed the group of six switches on the right are for the front exterior marker lamps. No electric red tail lamp was provided.

⑨ Reversing lever/reverser control lever. If the lever was right forward the loco was in full gear going that way. To notch up, the lever was pulled to the required position and the power reverser crept up to that point and stopped. Mechanical linking of the steam and hydraulic valves was needed to do this; a movement of the cab lever opening <u>both</u> together. Both closed again as the desired point of adjustment was reached.

⑩ Cylinders cocks (drain) – one lever for both bogies.

⑪ Whistle pull – reminiscent of the chain and handle of a WC cistern!

Not identified/shown: The wheel valve on the floor on the right. The whistle isolating valve, this was located out of camera at the top right of the cab above the right-hand window. (There were whistles at both ends with a separate isolating valve which isolated both whistles simultaneously mounted on the boiler.) The separate cab isolating valve was to prevent both whistles blowing at once. The small electrical switch below the mirror on the left-hand side of the cab is not identified. Might this have been for the cab light (not visible in the photograph) as it was above the centre window, or perhaps even the control for an electric windscreen wiper? Finally note the use of rivets along the horizontal axis of the doors. What appear to rivets also show up in places in other areas of the casing: clearly Mr B was not averse to these type of fastenings where it was considered necessary! *British Railways*

November. If this locomotive design is unfortunately unsuccessful there may be an attempt in official quarters to forget that it ever existed as has happened in the past with some experimental designs. *(On this the writer does not elaborate as to which ones.)* It seems odd that the extensive trials with this locomotive should appear to have been abandoned just when they appeared to be meeting with a fair measure of success. The locomotive apparently made several quite successful runs to Woking about October last year.'

So who was this anonymous correspondent? Perhaps someone from the 'inside'? Even having asked the question, the present writer feels it is necessary to comment we should not expect to find a serpent under every stone that is turned over – it could indeed have simply been a genuinely interested outside party.

British Railways did reply, but in so doing their response was curt. 'for varying technical reasons the experiments with the prototype "Leader" class locomotive were not as satisfactory as had been hoped and to obviate the expense which would be involved in continuing them for a problematical return, it has been decided not to proceed further with this novel design.'

It was a fair and an honest response, even if BR were now clearly on the defensive and, in reality, whatever they

In store at Eastleigh, 21 October 1950. The engine would make one more run less than two weeks later, after which she would stand unloved for a further six months before being taken away for scrap. Was this subsequent period of outside store from November 1950 to May 1951 in any way related to a possible sale to CIE? No papers appertaining to any such discussion has been located at the National Archives or the National Railway Museum. Riddles too fails to mention a possible interest/sale in his final report. Did BR reject an offer because they were cautious that if Bulleid were able to make it work in Ireland, there would inevitably be bad Press at home? Did the later *Sunday Despatch* article have its origins with a tip off from a disgruntled loco man at Eastleigh? *H.C. Casserley*

said had to be chosen very carefully. Unfortunately too this official response was not annotated to a particular individual, probably 'a spokesman' was all it was said. Might we doubt it was Rudguard!

British Railways had left themselves wide open but in the circumstances, this would probably have been the case no matter what had been said. Add to this the subsequent secrecy over the design itself, the costs, the trials and then the reasons for curtailment, plus the fact that the formal report from the dynamometer car tests and accompanying Riddles' reports would not be made public for a further thirty years, it is not really surprising that an increasing amount of conjecture would arise. Some of this would appear from various authors and in various publications that really should have known better but in Britain we seem to take delight in turning myth and conjecture into fact and as a result any number of incorrect and totally spurious allegations were made and similarly allowed to fester.

With hindsight the best option would probably have been to go on the offensive from the start. There were far fewer 'radical' journalists at the time compared with nowadays whilst additional 'trial by media' was also (fortunately) some way in the future.

Indeed Leader did show that certain of its ideas could well be utilised in the future. The body to bogie mounting without a central pivot (similar to that in a wartime tank) which instead had the 'body (superstructure)' of the steam engine resting on 'Mintex' pads was successfully copied for the SR-built diesel-electric designs 10201–3. It was likewise copied for the first generation main line diesel engines some years later – Classes 40, 44, 45 and 46. Similarly the axlebox 'dashpot' springing was adapted on what was to become the BR Mk 6 bogie used under a number of electric multiple-unit vehicles including the 4REP sets.

It had been thought that the 60 roller bearings salvaged from the Leader bogies (6 axles per locomotive and 1 at each end of an axle equals 12 per engine, multiplied by the 5 engines gives 60 bearings) might be used on the crank-axles of the Bulleid Q1 design and which had a propensity to run hot, but in the end, this was not pursued, due, it was stated, to the amount of modification that would have been required. This is perhaps slightly strange as in the period in question, 1951, the life of steam was still seen as projecting well into the future, future modernisation plans were still some years ahead and indeed even after the latter had been formulated there would still be major expense on a considerable number of steam engines, notably the number of Bulleid Pacifics that were rebuilt after this time. It also proves the point that these parts at least were on hand for all the class, perhaps all (or at least most) parts were in fact available for the five machines and it was a simple matter of assembly that never took place.

So it was that the Leader project refused to lie down, even if according to official sources the subject was now closed. Neither Waterloo nor Marylebone were prepared it seemed to comment further. Perhaps even others at Eastleigh and Brighton had similarly been told to decline comment. The enthusiast magazines in the meanwhile were similarly tight lipped – perhaps through choice.

The year 1952 witnessed nothing remarkable but then on Sunday 18 January 1953, the story again burst into the open and this time in the form of a front page 'Leader' (deliberate pun here!) of the *Sunday Despatch*. At this point the comments by Bulleid's 1964 biographer, Sean Day-Lewis may be the best to quote, and where the newspaper episode is treated with both an honest and unbiased approach.

'The supreme irony came two years later … when the *Sunday Dispatch*, a failing conservative newspaper, was suddenly tipped off about the story of the Leader class and decided that this was a magnificent stick with which to beat the concept of nationalisation – not because British Railways shelved the project, but because they did not do so earlier. It was the custom of such papers to find a story of this kind each week and blow it up to dominate the front page – no matter how old and stale the information. The "Leader" was certainly given the full treatment with a banner headline in thick letters, an inch deep;

RAILWAYS' BIGGEST FIASCO
£500,000 WASTED ON THREE USELESS ENGINES
THEY TRIED TO HUSH IT UP!
Three huge railway engines, which cost altogether about £500,000 to build, now lie rusting and useless in sheds and sidings – silent and hidden evidence of the biggest fiasco produced by Britain's nationalised railways.

This situation comes to light as the result of Sunday Dispatch inquiries, prompted by the threatened increase in fares and allegations of mismanagement on the railways.

The engines, 67ft. long monsters of the Leader Class, with driving cabins at each end, were built in 1948 and 1949 to "revolutionise" rail travel.

They were part of a £750,000 experiment undertaken by Mr O.V. Bulleid, Chief Mechanical Engineer of British Railways, Southern Region.

I can reveal that the region's officials regard the experiment as one of their biggest failures.

It was a failure that had been hushed up. From the start the plan to build Mr Bulleid's dream loco was kept secret, but late in 1948, the designer gave the British Association some details of "a revolutionary steam locomotive".

Extract from the *Sunday Dispatch* newspaper.

The first of the Leaders, known to railwaymen as No. 36001, was then being built at the Southern Region works in Brighton. It started its trials in 1949, and work began immediately on the other two.

From start to finish the "revolutionary" gave trouble. Workers at the Eastleigh (Hampshire) sheds frequently saw No. 36001 being towed back for repair by an "old fashioned" engine.

Firemen who worked aboard her during the set period reported the Leader was the most uncomfortable loco on the track.

Ventilation in the centre portion, where they stoked in a corridor running between the two driving cabs, was very poor.

One worker told me: "We all knew the three Leaders as 'The White Elephants'." Some who had ridden in them used less polite descriptions.

Frequently the "Flying Tramcar", as others called her, broke down.

She was chain-driven – immense chains more than two feet wide were completely enclosed in an oil bath. They caused endless trouble.

She was a streamlined job with no smoke stacks visible. Nearly everything about her was new in design. Leader was one of the most expensive locos ever built.

She carried four tons of coal and 4,000 gallons of water. The familiar trailing tender was done away with.

She was, in effect, two locos back to back, encased in steel, with one central firing point.

Railway maintenance workers, annoyed at attacks being made on them, say the money lost on this experiment could have been better spent improving their working conditions.

Mr Bulleid, the designer of the Leaders, is now working in Eire.

FOOTNOTE. – Nobody seems to have told British Railways' own magazine the story of locos 36001, 36002, and 36003. This month's issue gives pride of place to a review of the five years since nationalisation. Proudly, the writer praises the unified building of locomotives, carriages and wagons. Large scale production has, he says, considerably lowered the cost by millions of pounds.

The term 'Flying Tramcar' was certainly not one that had even been used before or indeed was used subsequently and may thus be said to be some form of unfortunate 'journalistic licence'. Having also reported the facts earlier in this work, the information within the newspaper was easily more inaccurate than factual.

Next day the *Daily Telegraph* followed up the story but managed to get the amount of money spent on the project into rather better perspective :

NOVEL ENGINE SCRAPPED
BRITISH RAILWAYS £150,000 TEST
A £150,000 experiment by British Railways to produce a revolutionary type of steam engine has been abandoned. The prototype, and two other partly finished engines of a new class of thirty to be called the Leader, have been broken up at the Southern Region works, Brighton.

The engine was designed by Mr O.V. Bulleid, when he was Chief Mechanical Engineer of the Southern Railway. Later he became consultant chief mechanical engineer to the Irish Railways.

A British Railways spokesman said yesterday: "The engine went on trial runs but did not come up to expectation. Meanwhile a second was nearly completed and the framework of a third was built. All three have been scrapped."

Firemen complained during the tests that they had to work under stifling conditions. But Mr Bulleid, now living in Eire, denied last night that the design was radically wrong.

"The locomotive was intended to meet the competition of electric engines, but built to use coal, the nation's fuel," he said.

"It was almost an enclosed box, with a driving cabin at each end, going right across the engine. In the middle was space for the fireman with a corridor at the side joining the two ends. The boiler was completely welded and was the first of its kind produced in an English railway shop.

"It did not require turntables or go into the sheds before starting on a return journey. During the trial run out of Brighton station, the acceleration was superb."

Mr Bulleid said he left the railways after nationalisation "because I did not approve of it and when I was offered a post in Ireland I was pleased to accept.

"In my opinion, there was little wrong with the Leader. The tragedy was that it was built two years too late."

Presumably Bulleid had been contacted by the *Daily Telegraph* and asked to respond but it was a very quick response as it was in print within 24-hours. Even so, his responses, if quoted correctly and not out of context, are perhaps slightly sad. If quoted correctly they can only give the impression of a man divorced from the reality.

So who had tipped off the Press? Something we will again probably never know. Most likely a disgruntled railwayman and, although cruel to say, perhaps tempted by the offer of sleaze money from the newspaper. What can be said with certainty is it would not have been an official British Railways source. Again according to Day-Lewis '"Why should we wash our dirty linen in public?" is the official British Railways attitude, 'the whole thing is still dynamite.'

As will have been gathered though, whilst the *Daily Telegraph* may have been basically correct in their response, no doubt directed to salient facts by a defensive British Railways, the *Sunday Dispatch* reports displayed an example of investigative journalism at the opposite end of the spectrum. But the damage was done, it could not be un-said and whilst factually the matter may have been put straight, the readership of the *Sunday Dispatch* was hardly the same as for the *Daily Telegraph*. As such, out of this was born rumour, misconception, inaccurate reporting and outright criticism of not just Leader but it seemed (at times) almost everything Bulleid ever had a hand in designing. (The image used in the newspaper came from an unknown Press photographer and eventually ended up in the photographic archive of *The Times*, but it must be said this archive has also absorbed several others photo libraries over the years.)

A veiled hint as to previous published inaccuracies has already been given in the introduction relative to two current-day writers, and whilst details of these indiscretions will not be given here, as an alternative the following three examples may well serve to indicate the almost open hostility that has been displayed in the past.

In this context the 1960 book by Ernest F. Carter, *Unusual Locomotives*, did its best to condemn the designer as a whole, '…in 1946/7, about 40 years after Sir Cecil Paget's grim experience with his unique locomotive, Bulleid's ill-fated six-cylindered "Leader" burst like a bombshell on the locomotive engineering world. He had defied traditional design and produced an engine which was as ugly as it was unconventional and as difficult to manipulate as it was inefficient. It was the first and last of its class and was broken up, its designer becoming Chief Mechanical Engineer of the Irish railways on the nationalisation of the British Lines.'

Aside from a brief couple of sentences which followed on the rebuilding of the Pacifics – that was it. The work and ideals of Bulleid condensed to less than a single page in a book running to in excess of 200 pages.

Some years later in 1987, G. Freeman Allen in his book *The Southern Since 1948*, the author commences what is, to be fair, a reasonable account of the project with the phrase: 'The genesis of this final definitely iconoclastic concept was the railway's immediate post-war requirement of more large-sized tank engines....'

Unfortunately from thereon the facts are supplemented by the by now well-known criticisms of the design although Freeman Allen does make one very interesting point at the end when referring to the controversy surrounding the Press article of 1953:

'And so it went on, not forgetting, naturally, to give management/labour relations any disruptive stir the opportunity offered.' The quote was then again made from the *Sunday Dispatch*, 'Railway maintenance workers, annoyed at attacks being made on them, say the money lost on this experiment could have been better spent improving their working conditions.' To this Freeman Allen added, 'A likely story, when one reflects on the railway unions' anxiety two and three decades later to see the money invested in APT's painful development not cut off, far from it, but greatly increased.' In this last statement Freeman Allen may well have been correct, but he was again applying 1980s perspective to a project of thirty years earlier.

Finally in most recent times Michael Rutherford. A man of considerable expertise and knowledge, writing in the November 2005 issue of *Backtrack*, in an article on F.W. Hawksworth at Swindon, he is of the opinion that, '... *(referring to an engineer who has)* spent all his working life in a drawing office environment or only one step removed from it ... Such a man is likely, when given the power, to either release all the pent up frustrations of his early career by becoming wildly radical (as with the case with Oliver Bulleid) or to heed his works and operating subordinates who are inevitably conservative, wishing to keep things as they are and know and to change things either very slowly or imperceptibly.' – the bracketed quote in italics is from the present author, that within the second set of brackets is as per Michael Rutherford. Mr Rutherford though was not totally correct in one aspect, Bulleid had not spent all his life in a drawing office environment. His time on the LNER also involved much footplate and other work.

So was Bulleid indeed radical in his designs or is this perhaps a slightly excessive description? The answer must surely depend upon the individual's definition of the word itself. Was Stanier radical in exploring turbine propulsion, Thompson on his rebuilds of Gresley locos, or Hawksworth with the use of 280psi boiler pressure on the 4-6-0 County class? Indeed according to discussion between the present author and the late A.C, (Tony) Sterndale who was in the drawing office at Swindon at the time, Hawksworth is purported to have included the high boiler pressure simply because 'if it was good enough for Bulleid then it is good

Fireman Sam Talbot seen in later days as a driver in the cab of a Class 33. Sam was justifiable commended for his efforts during the trials from Eastleigh. *Courtesy Mrs Talbot*

enough for us'. Perhaps radicalism is simply all a matter of degree and individual interpretation.

Whilst the three authors above have appeared to have been singled out, none of what they have written is factually incorrect. Any author recording fact is perfectly entitled to his opinion and it is indeed by assessing such opinion that a new perspective can sometimes be obtained. What is so wrong is when incorrect assessment, and therefore opinion, has been made and which, as referred to in the introduction, has been perpetuated again in more recent times. (Not by any of the three gentlemen mentioned above.)

Interestingly it does not appear any of the other Sunday or daily newspapers subsequently picked up on the story back in 1953, whilst contemporary news reports let alone movie footage of the engine whilst on trial are conspicuous by their absence.

Any news story will have a finite amount of interest, 'today's newspaper headline is tomorrows chip wrapper'. In the days that followed 18 January 1953 the same newspapers were dominated by the inauguration as Dwight D. Eisenhower as US President whilst at home the debate raged over the soon to be executed Police killer Derek Bentley. In the UK the story of Leader quickly went cold and perhaps this was just as well, for in Ireland, and

It is difficult to illustrate the actual 'figure of eight' movement described by the oscillating gear at the front of sleeves as originally fitted just in still images. However these two views may assist when comparing the position of the die blocks. One of the issues with the design of the valve gear, sleeves and oscillating gear was that of necessity there had to be a limited amount of play in each joint/bearing simply so that the respective components might move. However, wear, plus lubrication issues, may have increased that wear somewhat - which when compounded throughout a number of parts may have contributed towards failure. Issues with specific lubrication to the sleeves are well documented so far as No. 2039 was concerned and are said to have contributed to sleeve valve failure. Conversely, similar comment is not made to the same degree with No. 36001.

where the British newspaper headlines seemed to have only limited effect, Bulleid might well have caused further uproar when he unequivocally pronounced (referring again to Leader), 'we will probably do something of the sort over here.' Again a distinct reference to the future 'Turf Burner' (Leader Mk 2.)

But to return again to the *Daily Telegraph* report and in particular the alleged quote by Bulleid, 'The locomotive was intended to meet the competition of electric engines, but built to use coal, the nation's fuel.' Herein of course lies one of the continuing debates over Leader – that it was intended to burn oil and not coal.

Many individuals have in discussion over the years made reference to the fact that Leader was intended to burn oil. The simple question that comes with that is – where is the evidence? Nowhere is it mentioned in official SR records, nor in Riddles' report that this had been the intention. Indeed the only reference still located to suggest oil-firing is in some hand-written notes within the papers of the late John Click and now deposited at York. Here there is indeed a distinct reference that oil was the fuel Bulleid had indeed intended although unfortunately the note is undated. Even so the note continues that the traffic department themselves were opposed to the suggestion. Taking this one stage further, the record of drawings held at the NRM similarly has no confirmed reference to a drawing ever having been produced.

However we should not discount the topic just because there is no confirmation and instead, we should turn to more circumstantial evidence. At this stage we must also discuss briefly the contents of that NRM Southern Railway drawings register *https://www.railwaymuseum.org.uk/sites/default/files/2020–03/Southern%20Railway%20Locomotive%20Drawings%20and%20Microfilm%20Lists.pdf* – all 874 pages! This register lists locomotive-related drawings from the three works that amalgamated into the Southern Railway, namely Ashford, Brighton and Eastleigh. Despite the vast number of drawings listed – in excess of 17,000 – it is still likely this is nowhere near all that were produced on steam locomotive design over the three works in the 20th century and into the early years of BR. What we do have, for example, are (some) drawings on the various conversions to burn oil by most of the relevant SR loco classes prepared in the period 1946–48 but with one exception, which we will turn to in a moment.

But there is one teaser, which appears in the register under reference '30 130 SR W10634 Oil Burning Conversions 19-10-48'. Here we have 'Arrangement of fixing lugs for firebricks on firebox backplate 3" = 1" class 'Leader; Drawer 12, Drawing type PT, Condition 2'. So is this the proverbial missing link? It should be said that other classes that were converted to burn oil at the same time, King Arthur, T9 etc., have any number of entries covering, burners, pipes, flanges and so on and which of course leads to the conclusion that there may perhaps have been others, OR that this was indeed the only one as any further work on oil burning was curtailed. Recall too the oil burning 'debacle' had already come to an end when that one drawing was prepared, with the one exception all the oil burning engines on the Southern Region having ceased to work in early October. One other thing we might mention is that should anyone ever have the notion for a new build of Leader in its original form, that same register indicates the presence of a considerable number of component and parts drawings for the engine but nothing whatsoever on the sleeve valves (perhaps fortunately)!

So we return to the exception mentioned at the end of the previous but one paragraph. This exception in the little-known Terrier No. 515S which was converted at Brighton to burn oil in the summer of 1946 and reconverted to coal again in October 1947. At the time the official line was the conversion was, 'to give officials experience of oil-fired locomotives'. But who were these 'officials', surely a strange term which is not elaborated upon and similarly what could be gained from the conversion of a Terrier when no other tank engine conversions were planned? Hence might this have been a very early attempt in oil burning around the time the initial drawings of what would become Leader were being prepared? Further comment as to the rationale of No. 515S would now be pure speculation.

We should not though forget that the sheer obvious awkwardness of firing Leader allied to its offset fire-door all indeed do point to the fact that the coal firing aspect was very much of an afterthought.

So would oil-firing have made a difference? Certainly the disadvantages of oil were the smell, excess smoke if the burner and air flow were not correctly adjusted, potential leakage, and the fluctuations in temperature that were created within the firebox when the oil was reignited after having let the firebox cool down. Whilst this latter aspect could never be totally avoided even in Leader, Bulleid had gone some way towards dealing with the problem in consequence of the dry-sides. Leader would in many ways have been an ideal testbed for oil firing, she was of course already running on trial in November 1949 when West Country 34036 was converted back from oil to coal firing. It is perhaps a pity that oil was not pursued for 36001, it could not have changed history, but it might have made that history just a bit more palatable. (Another thought is did the prolonged running of No. 34036 on oil suggest the burner on this was being tried for No. 36001?)

From the preceding text it would be perfectly reasonable to conclude that with a fair proportion of the test runs reported as failures there was little choice for Riddles and the Railway Executive in condemning the Leader project. In so far as is known only two writers have either had access to or cared to study the BR reports on the engine and trials – J.G. Chacksfield and the present writer. To be fair, prior to 1985 the official reports were not publicly accessible, so there is excuse for inaccuracies in the past. It might then also be assumed that with access to the aforementioned reports little else can be added. But something else has now appeared, and what that is, albeit incomplete, does cast some doubt on the information contained in the official report.

It would appear that Brighton kept another record of the trials run, and what has survived are details of the

Engine record card for No. 36001. No other member of the Leader class was ever issued with such a record. Even so it does not provide full details of the numerous works visits etc., referred to in the text. Officially Leader can be seen to have run a total of 8,309 miles; we have no information as to how many miles were run by No. 2039 in her modified form.

SOUTHERN RAILWAY.

Scheduled Mileage _____ Depot _Brighton_ Class _Leader_ Engine No. _36001_

Reports received and sent to shops.	Engine arrived.	Work commenced.	Mileage since last Gen. Rep.	Class of Repr.	Boiler No.	Tender No.	Extension of Mileage.	Date to Work.	Repd. at.
20-12-49	16-12-49	16-12-49	None recorded	Weighing 1421			5,001	16-12-49	
7-2-50	2-2-50	2-2-50	—do—	" "			6,457	2-2-50	
25-4-50	17-4-50	17-4-50	—do—	L/Cas "			6,957	5-6-50	
27-6-50	20-6-50	20-6-50	—do—	L/Cas "			7,423	29-6-50	
4-7-50	30-6-50	30-6-50	—do—	Non/Class "			8,091	15-8-50	
4-9-50	28-8-50	28-8-50	—do—	Non/Class .			8,309	21-9-50	

Broken up. DE. 12/5/51.
of No. 3582.

tests, timings-delays etc., which took place on 5th, 8th, 16th, 19th, and 20th September 1949. The first two are of interest as these were the intended trials to Victoria, so we now have details of the actual running, the problems encountered en route, and the reason both runs were terminated early. Likewise the Crowborough run of the 20th September. All of these three trials officially being regarded as failures for various reasons. That of 5th September also involved the completion of the useful and comprehensive report by 'H.O. Inspector' E. Walton, which includes the damning sentence, 'Engine berthed in workshops at Brighton and so far as I am concerned have no desire to see it again.' The full text of the report together with the timings for the runs on the three days mentioned are appended on p.287-9.

But it is what is written by Brighton concerning the runs of 16th and 19th September that really cause questions. In the official report later presented to Riddles, all of the five runs mentioned by date were regarded as failures. As such here was the evidence piling up against Leader and would be part of that which was later used to condemn it, yet, and according to the Brighton report for 16th September – 'Running was satisfactory', and even more so on 19th September with 'The running of the trips from Brighton to Crowborough and back were very satisfactory.' In view of the importance of these comments, both day's records are reproduced as per the original documents.

If the runs then of 16th and 19th September were after all successful and not failures, how many more might have been likewise? How many more trips were similarly condemned and used as justification for the project to be cancelled? This is a bold accusation to make, and I do not accuse any person of deliberately manipulating the records. Riddles could only form his conclusions on the evidence presented to him and if that evidence was flawed then perhaps an incorrect decision might have been arrived at.

Without access to detailed records of more or all the runs, it is both unsafe and unwise to make further sweeping allegations. But here is the proof that two of the runs at least were not as previously viewed. Even so, two runs would not, on their own, have made a difference and we cannot discount the spectacular failures that later occurred. Neither can we pretend that the difficulties with the sleeve valves, crank-axle, overall and offset weight, or firebox lining did not occur. But how many other runs were regarded by one quarter as at least satisfactory and judged from another quarter as a failure? Perhaps indeed herein lies the answer, it depended on which side of the fence the judgement was taken from and so also from which side of the fence the report submitted to Riddles was compiled from. The traffic and chief mechanical engineering departments seem to have a different judgemental criteria. It might also go some way also to explain why the telegrams sent by Granshaw to Bulleid whilst the latter was away also appeared to add confusion compared with the official reports.

What is likewise puzzling is the fact that whilst these contradictions were occurring – in the autumn of 1949, Bulleid was still notionally involved although perhaps he was either not informed or even being deliberately kept away from reality.

11

Conclusions

It remains an everlasting pity John Clicks's own work was never published but, as mentioned before, that which remains is in part little more than a series of notes and consequently unsuitable for stand-alone publishing in its present form. Had it been developed, no doubt he would have revisited the text several times, adding extra detail as well cohesion between the various topics.

But as has also been stated, what he did record can now never be revisited and we must be grateful for the sources he did cover including when he spoke to Sir John Elliot. Click asked Sir John if he thought the railways had had their money's worth from Bulleid. Elliot replied at once, 'Yes. Oh God yes: no doubt about it'. Click adds, 'But was he bound to say that and equally importantly, what would the customers (traffic and motive power departments) say?' (I think we know the answer to that particular point courtesy of Messrs Nicholson and Townroe.)

It has been said that a CME can be a railway's most expensive chief officer; even that Bulleid was the most extravagant CME of recent times. If one allows that a man who makes no mistakes produces very little, then Bulleid's three as Sir John has called them, were the Leader, the Tavern Cars and the Double Decker. Even so and assuming Sir John's comment about 'money's worth' to be correct, they were but a small debit on a balance sheet hugely in the black. We might also question his criticism of the Double-Decker for this lasted in service for two decades and in the course of its work carried tens if not hundreds of thousands of passengers. True it had its weaknesses (the present author will admit he never travelled in it) but a product that served the railway for so long could hardly be described as a failure.

Click again, 'After 1937 Bulleid took longer than he should to get into his stride and then the war came: two years of warming up really. From that moment on he had a designer's market, demand knew no limit, ingenuity was offered full fling, increased productivity didn't need to be sold, the sky was the limit, people developed skills they had no idea they could master, there was a wonderful feeling of all being in it together, union problems receded, winning the war was a crusade in which all had a common purpose, methods had to be the best for the job, new materials the same, the learning rate shot up, women did men's jobs, new plant and machinery came in to match the need: yes, war did have its advantages. All those same assets were there to be re-exploited in peacetime.

'In 1945 the Southern was well placed to change over to production of rolling stock and locomotives to make up for the backlog over the war years. Bulleid was very lucky really, for there was so much to be done, and it was the policy of the Labour Government (whatever he thought of that) to maintain full employment, so that the only problems were, "..what do we do first and how do we re-organise"? Big enough problems, to be sure, but the sky was still the limit.

'Changes to design were resisted no matter where they came from: with the possible exception of the suggestions scheme. It was not unknown for one of us to "plant" a necessary change through this method as the only means of getting anything actually done. A change, even a minor one, immediately interfered with "standardisation", a shrine which OVB knew all about, and yet did not feel unduly constricted him.

'Almost all locomotive engineers have wanted to standardise but, on their terms, hence most who introduced new standards only really tacked them on to all their predecessor's creations whilst making a good argument for the elimination of much of what had gone before. Thompson's case being the worst on record.' (Click does not give further examples.)

'Bulleid was most modest in this respect. By 1947 he had come the conclusion that the Southern's needs could be met by only four steam designs: his two "Pacifics" and two classes of tank engine of which the embryonic "Leader" was the first and larger of the two. The "Q1" was regarded by then as a wartime necessity not to be perpetuated, and the second tank engine never got looked at very seriously.'

Click then talks about correspondence he had from Riddles (it is implied these were letters that passed between Riddles and Bulleid). He does not elaborate much and we have not located these letters either but Click does add one comment, "They could dispel the idea held by many for so long that something very underhand went on over the Leader's scrapping. I truly think it didn't."'

For a man who at times seemed to worship the ground Bulleid walked upon this is an honest statement to make and with all due respect to the memory of Click in the opinion of the present writer an accurate assessment as well. When I personally started my journey into Leader thirty-five plus years ago I came to a similar conclusion fairly early on. I like to think that John Click from an engineering perspective, and myself from a historical perspective, may have taken different routes in our studies but we converged with the same result and summarising my own words from that time, 'Leader did not fail us – but instead we failed it'. Why? Well simply put, it showed that steam development was not just still possible but worthwhile as well. True, aspects of Leader, the use of sleeve vales and the offset boiler were wrong, but the ability of the engine to produce steam, the total adhesion, the final chain drive giving smooth torque (subject to investigation into the unequal stresses placed upon the crank-axle by the design) and the clear view available to the driver were all worthy of further study. Leader should have been seen as means to an end, not the end of the means.

The trouble too for Bulleid was the lack of time history allowed him. Global conflict allied to impending nationalisation meant he was a man on a mission with limited time to achieve. And to achieve meant also to learn from the past, such as during his time with Gresley when we may presume he quickly realised that building single prototypes was not the best way of proceeding. With ten ('Hush-Hush') 10,000s and ten 'Cocks of the North' the investment incurred would have given the impetus to make them the success he felt both could have been. He would remember that lesson and perhaps that was another reason why the plan had been for five Leader engines.

Had nationalisation not occurred in 1948 (it likely would have been inevitable at some stage), then it is probably fair to say No. 36001 and her sisters would have achieved traffic status – or they would have dragged their designer down with them. Click seems to agree in the comment he makes apropos the naming of No. 34090, *Sir Eustace Missenden*, the man who had once so wholeheartedly backed Bulleid on the Southern and who had come over from Marylebone for the occasion. Missenden by then was wavering in his support for his former CME, and Leader in particular. Tantalisingly the next two sentences of Click's are completely unintelligible although the last few words are clear enough, 'Sir Eustace had had enough'. Pure conjecture then, and with Bulleid the age he was perhaps he was encouraged to retire gracefully. Unfortunately (or fortunately dependent upon one's perspective), the fact he went ahead with 'Leader Mk 2' meant the whole Leader saga was never really far from the mind.

Click again, 'When he looked back at "experiments" that had failed, Bulleid could often attribute the failure to some problem which improved technology either had or would make worth looking at again. For example, welded instead of rolled tube joints in a water-tube boiler, and the use of truly effective water treatment would make such a boiler on a loco feasible for the first time. He was right; it is always worth looking again at a failure and updating it. He was to do this on "Leader" but as history recounts, with too much optimism into the re-run.

'It had always puzzled me that Bulleid who was so plainly loyal in every way to his General Manager, Sir Eustace Missenden, and through him to the Southern Railway Board, turned what had started as a Traffic requirement for a replacement for Drummond's "M7" 0-4-4 tanks into a huge, all purpose, go almost anywhere challenge to electric traction.

'Very loyal, yes of course; but Bulleid took advantage to the full of any opportunities that came his way and could be used to further his professional aim. That, without much doubt would ensure he would go down in history as THE CME, who had taken radical steps to "return steam power to favour" by looking completely afresh at every aspect of design and maintenance.'

In *Bulleid of the Southern* – written we now know with much input from John Click (this is confirmed in letters between the two at the NRM) – OVB's eldest son Anthony set out the progress that would eventually culminate in No. 36001. Years later, the two would collaborate again when Click was undertaking his own research. The point to be made here being that there was no new eureka moment which Click was about to divulge for the first time. No evidence of anything sinister or underhand by anyone at British Railways. These were professional men, they may have disliked some of their peers, disagreed with the actions of their colleagues, but it would be rare to find underhand behaviour. And we say again, we have no evidence to support anything of that type having occurred.

Bulleid was born at a time of great expansion – Britain had given steam traction to the world – and arguably in the best years of his life, under Gresley, he had helped to develop steam power right up to the A4s which many regarded at the time, and have ever since, as the very pinnacle of the steam locomotive designer's art in Britain. Even so that was clearly not a view shared by Bulleid who as we have seen was determined to prove it could go further.

'Gresley's Pacifics, just like his own, were nothing but more or less successful stages in a progression towards an ideal steam locomotive that would successfully compete with *AND* see off, both present or up and coming competition by beating them all at their own game.' *(The words and emphasis here are exactly those of JGC as he has written them. A more egotistical perspective it would be difficult to find. Does Click really believe that Bulleid considered development of other traction would stand still whilst he caught up? Are we to be convinced that he*

It is always a risk to say 'the only' but certainly one of the very few steam designs to successfully operate with an offset boiler was the Shay type from North America, used mainly on logging railroads. Here the boiler was offset but the weight differential was countered with the steam chests and pistons on one side driving a gear train which in turn transmitted the drive to the respective axles. There were several differing designs and wheel arrangements but all following the same basic principle. The design type was also deliberately low geared. Such a concept would not have been suitable for main line use on the SR and certainly not as a replacement for the M7. *Wikipedia, creative common licence*

seriously considered technology – even if the use of that particular word might appear slightly out of context for the 1940s period – would have only limited advancement? Whatever one's views of Mr Bulleid and his work he was certainly no fool and to suggest otherwise is hardly appropriate.)

JGC continues, '(*Was Bulleid*) Biased? Yes, and why ever not. He had enormous confidence in Gresley and it was based, after the lessons of 1925 had been learnt (if not before), on solid results. Gresley was not blind to developments in other fields but took on the opposition. He investigated everything, every new thing, tried out what looked promising and adopted what was good, but it was Bulleid who did most of the reading for him, the fact finding, the visiting and the interviewing. But it was Gresley, after all had been said and done, who made the decisions, though.

'Bulleid regarded Germany's flying diesel set as humbug; and, on "Papyrus", showed that steam could improve on the best schedule between Kings Cross and Newcastle that the Germans could offer, and that steam power would allow greater passenger comfort, cost far less – and avoid that obnoxious diesel smell with which he never did come to terms.' Electrification was out of the question due to the costs involved.

Click's notes, as we have seen, afford a valuable and nowadays probably unique perspective into the mindset and visions of the last CME of the Southern. With only limited exceptions we have nothing comparable to any other CME whilst in later years Click was also in a position to be accepted by and so able to interview others in similar senior positions at the same time.

Click continues, 'The Southern under Sir Herbert Walker had built up the largest and most densely trafficked electric suburban services in the world; and steam, though still working important routes, had become the poor relation. Any ideas of seriously developing it (steam) in 1937 seemed highly unlikely. Sir John Elliot has called Walker's plans "electrification on the cheap"… a fair description when one compares it with the West Coast costs, for example; but, cheap or not, there was no money for much else.

'Walker had learnt to have complete confidence in Alfred Raworth, who was the Electrical Engineer at the time Bulleid arrived on the scene. He seems to have been a tough, even ruthless professional whose work must have been his life. I never knew him nor much about him, save that he was the only fellow Officer on the Southern with whom Bulleid didn't get on, and for whom he seemed to have less than his usual warm regard.

'Raworth represented the expensive, successful opposition, the sitting tenant holding the winning hand if you like, and with whom Maunsell had rather given up the unequal struggle. Leaving all that aside though, his methods did not appeal to Bulleid who was a persuader, winning (as he usually did) with sweet reasonableness, and certainly not given to charging his fences. A strong patriot to the core, Bulleid saw clearly the rise of the Nazis for what it was; but Raworth looking at the political system in Germany may have seen only what he wanted to see; a climate in which technical progress was undoubtedly flourished to the undoubted advantage of the Reichsbahn. Sir John Elliot said simply and bluntly "'Alfred' (Raworth) thought Hitler was right!". This worried Elliot; for he went on "I asked Eustace (Missenden) if we ought to have a word with him about it; but he said leave him alone, he's all right."'

Digressing slightly but again from Click, 'Before Bulleid arrived a new and important draughtsman had been taken on, not in the Electrical Engineer's Office but in Maunsell's Waterloo Office. Outside railway circles he was never well known, but his appointment was an important move to bring in new blood from industry to meet future needs. I refer to Percy Bollen, a quiet bachelor whose work was to be seen in all the electric and diesel electric locomotives built or authorised by the Southern. Every bit of these locomotives mechanical design was Bulleid's responsibility however much Raworth might disagree. Arguments did later ensue when Missenden tended to back Bulleid whereas Walker gave Raworth the benefit of any doubt. Bollen loyally helped, but he had to tread a careful path, and did so successfully.'

Click also confirms the present writer's assertions in his previous book, 'For the past forty years (Click was writing this circa 1990) it seems to have been thought that murder was done over the Leader programme. I know that was not the case for, bold though the Leader concept was, it was doomed not to succeed before its design was finished or building commenced, whichever came first. It was due, above all, to far too many ideas being incorporated in the one new design. That is something that Bulleid acknowledged himself in later years, and to say so now is in no way to do him an injustice to or spoil his enormous reputation. Rather the reverse.

'He WAS "ahead of his time" in lots of ways, he WAS undefeatedly an optimist, he COULD persuade people as no other man, he WAS getting older (though not in heart) and KNEW that time was not in his favour, but is it EVER in favour of ANY designer. *(The emphasis is again as per JGC's original writing.)*

'He found it difficult – even to the point of impossibility – to make his mind up. He was never quite content, feeling that there was always a better solution to a problem just around the corner. There always is something better, but time and the need, in his case to RUN a railway, call for a decision being made at some point. A "that's-as-good-as-we-can-make-it-now" stage. Let's get on and build!

'Bulleid always said the Leader was "two years too late", inferring that Nationalisation was the problem; and so it was because he was of course, no longer in sole charge after 1948. Subsequently far too long had been taken in Ireland too, chasing countless elusive ideas. I had said to OVB, "Look we cannot do everything on this one either", or his "Turf Burner" would never have turned a wheel.

'Production people's worst enemy is change for its own sake; or change for ANY reason, parochially speaking.

11 CONCLUSIONS

Almost the only view which we can confirm depicts one of the other members of the class, in this case No. 36002 under construction at Brighton. The date is 17 August 1949. By this time No. 36001 had been running for approaching two months and had begun to show up the deficiencies with the design. Many of the major issues were far too involved to have been rectified in No. 36002 but we still ask the question, were minor changes incorporated into the second engine in light of experience? In reality the answer is probably not. We also need to ask if the same urgency prevailed over No. 36002 or was the principal lesson learnt simply not to hurry so much in the build. If this were the case then it would backfire later for No. 36002 was so close to being complete when the order came to cease work. Had in fact she been ready, would she also have been trialled? *Don Broughton Collection*

213

It states volumes for Bulleid's Works Managers and their staff that no two of anything they built were truly alike, be it locomotives, carriages or wagons! Cocks and Lynn at the design stage, and the Managers during production, did their utmost to resist constant alterations. Bulleid's personality exerted constant and heavy pressure on those charged with interpreting his never ending flow of new ideas, and some older ones which he would trot out and which had to be challenged and shown to be impracticable for the umpteenth time. Stimulating? Of course; but it could be very wearing at the same time. It was to help make Cocks for one ill eventually I suspect.'

It might be said that Bulleid's intention with Leader was not specifically to produce the perfect locomotive but merely to prove a point, similar to the concept of the Decapod.

Ron Jarvis also briefly discussed the Leader trials with John Click soon after Riddles' report had been issued – Click had found a copy in one of the offices at Brighton. In discussion the point was raised about the extraordinary performance put up on the two occasions when 430 and then 480 tons were taken. Jarvis commented that he had tried to get Riddles to try a Leader boiler in one of the Garratts but without any success. Click's words again now, 'He said that Hargreaves (the Regional Metallurgist) was told by OVB to keep away from these boilers during their later construction (I have also had a similar tale from Byrne – [no details as to who this individual was]) and as a result he (is the 'he' Jarvis?) was aggrieved. When his opportunity came he told Riddles in a report that the first boiler at that time in steam had a welding defect and that he considered it unsafe to work. I have never known the exact location of this crack (?) but it was in a place very difficult to inspect so I presume it to have been on the right-hand side possibly where the siphon necks joined the underside of the barrel.'

Perhaps, in his later days on the Southern, Bulleid's view was that he had established himself with 'conventional' steam designs – although one could hardly consider the Merchant Navy and Light Pacifics as conventional, the Q was perhaps the closest. Despite too any relationship issues with Raworth, his contributions to the electric locomotives and also his rolling stock designs had proven his worth. Perhaps now was the time to question established practice and its right to exist. It appears to be that safe precedents were only subjects for distrust, to be substituted at all costs by something novel developed in a manner which might be described as instant engineering. Recall his words (to the Society of American Engineers), 'If only we can demolish the conservatism which is destroying the steam locomotive rather than give up any of its customary ways, then we can look forward to the revival of steam traction.'

His nibbana is that he would have liked to go even further in the direction of draughting by fan, and of finding means to return to the boiler the heat escaping in the exhaust steam. Perhaps the very shortcomings of the steam locomotive were indeed those which Bulleid attempted to remedy but recall too engineers of just as high integrity as Bulleid himself removed the chain-driven miniature valve gears from the Pacifics and scrapped the Leaders, not in any high-handed doctrinaire fashion, but reluctantly and after much travail in spirit, when economical and reliable service was still not forthcoming after repeated trials. Emotion will always raise a cheer for the lonely pioneer, but it is hard facts which will make the final judgement. When all has been said, however, one has to pay tribute to a very original and ingenious mind, to a man whose strong and controversial opinions resided in a most urbane and even endearing personality.

Bulleid vindicated?

Previously the impression may have been given that the intention may have been to criticise the designer as much as the design. If that appears to have been the case then I apologise at once. There has never been any intention or desire to criticise Bulleid the man, or his memory.

Instead the intention has always been to present the facts, or as many as it has been humanly possible to advise upon, and to use what is available to draw realistic conclusions.

So is it perhaps just possible that Bulleid was right? It is possible that circumstances – and circumstances over which he had no control – conspired to effectively kill Leader even before an objective assessment had been made? As mentioned initially in 2007, that conclusion has to remain a possibility.

Factually we know the timescale during which Leader was conceived and built was far from ideal. Over that Bulleid could have had no control. But ever since the word 'Leader' was first mentioned, there has almost been a concerted effort to discredit the design and with it the designer, concentrating on criticising the faults rather than promoting any potential benefits.

Here and now is not the place to enter a general discussion over Bulleid's other steam, diesel or electric designs. Much has been written on that score, some good, some bad, some well-reasoned, and some nothing short of scandalous. Referring though to the Pacific type, one area where the critics do seem to agree relative to the original design is that of the chain-driven valve gear, the weakness of which was stated to have been a major aspect of inferior design, principally due to the links stretching after only a short period in use and with consequential effect upon the valve timing. Indeed this was one of the reasons given to prove the need for rebuilding.

This statement appears to have been rarely if at all challenged in print in the past. And yet almost fifty plus years since the end of steam in daily service, now might be the time to put the record straight primarily as a result of a comment in the book, *Engine Sheds in Camera* released in 2005. This particular work centred around the photographs and recollections of former Salisbury Shed-Master, George Harrison, who recalls a conversation with Bulleid over the allegation of chain stretch. The response in a letter from Bulleid to Harrison was: 'Mr Smith, in his letter, spoke of chain-stretch and I think this must be a confusion with what I believe to be correct, namely that the links bed down onto the pins and it is this that results in the sag of the chain. It would require very high forces indeed to stretch the links themselves. I feel sure I told you that when the Eastleigh Works Manager reported to me this sagging, the makers asked me to tell him to hang up, side-by-side, from an overhead crane, the chain complained about and a new one and then let me know the difference. He did, and found none.' Indeed from an engineering perspective the links may very well wear but the likelihood of the chains stretching must be remote.

Vindication then for the original Pacific design at last. Bearing in mind that the valve gear on Leader was also similarly driven, it is well to trounce such an allegation before it is raised relative to the various sleeve valve failures.

Dealing also with the sleeve valves on Leader, a conversation between the author and a third party threw up what can only be described as an alarming accusation relative to the engine; it being suggested that whilst on trial at Brighton, there were occasions when *deliberate sabotage* took place to prevent test runs being successful.

Such is both a dangerous and insidious accusation to make and it must at once then be quantified. It appears one of the crews – so perhaps there was more than one – (the name Ted Forder was not mentioned) working on Leader from Brighton would deliberately introduce sand into the sleeve valves to promote failure. Analysis quickly revealed this was for personal gain only. The reason being that the crew were paid a daily rate for a complete test, if the run could be terminated early then they would thus finish their shift early yet still receive the same pay. At this stage I must state I do not believe it to have involved the regular test crew who are mentioned in the earlier text. So was this possible, and could it have happened, even more so was it a spontaneous act or was it even done with the connived blessing of a senior source?

Question, would it have been possible to introduce a foreign substance into the valve areas? In truth, unlikely, for with the presence of various engineers and technical men in the vicinity both during the preparations for and on the engine for many of the trials, opportunities may have been limited. Of course the crew would invariably have overheard talk amongst the technical fraternity whilst the determined individual will also invariably find a way. It is hard to believe for one moment that the senior individuals of the time who travelled as observers would have been party to such an act. Accusations perhaps, but not based upon fact.

No confirmed evidence then but circumstantial speculation remains. Why does Leader fail sometimes and not others? Why on one test in the autumn of 1949 between Buxted and Crowborough and with Bulleid on the engine, does it perform faultlessly in the morning, and then on a repeat run in the afternoon without Bulleid present, the engine fails? Coincidence – perhaps that is all it is. But again just as the individual may be thinking such suggestions are nothing more than hot-air, consider also the seeming reduction in sleeve valve failures after the engine was transferred to Eastleigh. We might conclude by adding that had a foreign substance been introduced into whatever mechanism then evidence of this would surely have been found when said defects caused were being repaired.

We now turn to the way the design and its faults were portrayed to Marylebone as a failure. The positive aspects of the engine, the total adhesion, the boiler's ability at raising

With the order to cease work given about 19 November 1949, No. 36002 was moved from the works to free up space and found a home in the Pullman shed. The unlikely combination of No. 36002 and a Pullman car are seen here just one week later on 26 November 1949, a combination that would never be seen outside.

Shortly after, No. 36002 was joined by the less complete No. 36003. The two engines at the back of the shed with the Pullman car – assuming it to be the same one – now nearest No. 36003. 20 December 1949. *Bluebell Railway Museum*

steam, and the superb braking system, are conspicuous by their absence as praise in the official reports. It was almost as if there was a fear of admitting aspects did in fact show potential. No, has been stated before, it could never have survived as per the original design, but surely it did not deserve to be condemned out of hand either. Those at Brighton in positions of power were the ones who had the future of the steam engine in their grasp. Conservatism (with a small 'c') would eventually hold sway, to speculate on the alternatives would be to go beyond both the remit and intention of the present work, although the whole subject of the potential for steam on Britain's Railways is one which would make for a lively debate. Perhaps we might have seen an engine numbered 37001 emerge – a Mk 2 Leader with the errors put right, and incorporating the lessons of the past century both from at home and overseas.

One final point worth mentioning is simply that Bulleid may have been portrayed as *The Last Giant of Steam* – the title of Sean Day-Lewis's biography on Oliver Bulleid – but he was certainly not the 'Last Man of Steam'. If we talk of the greatest, head and shoulders must be André Chapelon, he truly is the giant. But in many ways, Bulleid was probably not far behind even if not with No. 36001. Bulleid had the vision, he probably would have gone a lot further – and succeeded as well, if time had allowed. Where the likes then of Chapelon and Bulleid paved the way, others have since followed, even if their names may not perhaps be so well known. Engineers such as L.D. Porta, David Wardale, Phil Girdlestone, Shaun McMahon, Nigel Day, and Roger Waller come to mind. None has attempted to redesign Leader – so far at least, but each has indeed achieved with steam, and shown that Bulleid was indeed right to innovate. It was not really Bulleid who failed in 1950, but fate which contrived to fail him.

Was Bulleid right or was he wrong?

No matter what follows in this the final main chapter of this work there will still be dispute at the end. In terms of history six decades – more than half a century – have passed since the physical conclusion of the Leader project, the choice or terminology is to the individual's taste. Six decades also since the end the Southern Railway and likewise more than half a century since the end of Southern steam. The problem thus arises at how to deal with conclusions and controversy surrounding a design which today would easily be seen as obsolete from the outset. A design which, with our present-day knowledge, would never have got beyond the drawing board – probably not even progressed as far as a set of working drawings.

So to deal with the question 'Was Bulleid right, or was he wrong?' we have to view the situation piece by piece, as it existed all those decades ago. Attempting comparisons with a present-day railway system, or available technology and modern materials, will only cloud judgement.

To start with let us look at Bulleid himself. A skilled and competent engineer without doubt, but was he one of the greatest? Subjective opinion will take over here. If the reader believes the development of steam as per Bulleid

A relatively pristine No. 36002 outside the works and in the shadow of the signal box. Timeline: either when being moved out of the works to the Pullman shed, or in the process of transfer from Brighton to Bognor Regis. There she would be visible to all from passing trains and yet appears to have provoked little if any comment in the railway Press at this time. The exterior casing is in clean condition and has clearly been painted since the build view of the engine on page 213. As mentioned within the text, little needed to be done to complete No. 36002, she even has the shade over the coupling light added. This is No. 2 end.

In similar position to where No. 36001 had been stored prior to the latter engine's move to Eastleigh, No. 36002 awaits an initial move to store – whether Pullman shed or Bognor we cannot be certain. Covers are missing from the axle box leaf springs and it is not certain if the front windows are glazed. Sean Day-Lewis comments, 'just two days more and she would have been complete.' Alongside is the boiler and frames of what would have been No. 36004. *W.N.J. Jackson*

with the Pacifics and Q1 designs was appropriate, then clearly the answer was in the affirmative. If however he is judged just on Leader then it could be said the reverse might be the case.

Recall too Bulleid was not the only Chief Mechanical Engineer to have experimented. Throughout railway history there have been numerous examples of conventional or experimental designs which either failed, or came close, and in the end were not duplicated. Under that heading comes almost every British designer of the 20th century. We may give a few examples, not for the sake of condemning the individual or the machine but just to show people are sometimes remembered for what they failed to achieve as much as what they did. Churchward (County 4-4-0 and *The Great Bear*), Drummond (various 4-6-0 and 'double single' types), Fowler (*Fury* and the abortive Pacific design) – the list could be continued. Recall too that in previous years it was left to a successor to make a good engine even better, sometimes as a result of improvements in technology. Again some examples: S.O. Ell at Swindon with higher degree superheat, Ivatt with roller bearings on the last two Duchess class Pacifics, slightly controversial perhaps, but BR's own improvements to the middle big-end of the A4 class to prevent overheating, and then we have the rebuilding of the Bulleid breed. Might we realistically have expected a successor to Bulleid to sort out Leader?

At this stage then we once more have to consider the political and economic climate that existed at the time. Personally, for some years I was of the opinion that had the Southern Railway continued as a private company and nationalisation not occurred, then Leader would either have been made to succeed or, as actually did happen to the actual engine, it would have dragged its designer to similar oblivion. But other designers had also got it wrong

The next move by May 1950 – on an unreported date (or dates) – was when No. 36002 and her less complete sister No. 36003 were moved, singly or together is not known, from Brighton to Bognor for storage. 'Out of sight, out of mind' might well have been the phrase, but to be fair we have no idea whether this was because of pressure and continuing interest or it was just a simple matter of space constraints. The pair are seen here 'mostly' in the shed on 1 July 1950. Recall that at this time, No. 36001 was running trials from Eastleigh just 40 miles distant. In addition, the official line was that work had been 'suspended', although for the present the alternative term 'stopped' was really more accurate. *R.C. Riley/The Transport Treasury*

11 CONCLUSIONS

Once positioned, the two engines do not seem to have been moved but clearly the bush telegraph was still working as this is one of several similar views of the engines at this location. *Les Darbyshire*

in the past and without incurring such drastic retribution – although if we were still referring to a private company, then shareholders' money would be at stake, whilst the order for an additional thirty-one engines from November 1947 would no doubt also not have been confirmed. Thirty-six failures then? And Richards at the traffic department making ever more noises about the failure of the CME to deliver the tank engine power he so desperately needed, perhaps then indeed Bulleid would indeed have disappeared with his creation.

So the next question must then be, could Bulleid (or for that matter Riddles at BR) have made it work? Could it even have worked in the form it existed? The second question is easier to answer – an unfortunate no. In answer to the first question though it must be yes, but at what cost in redesign?

As regards costs, well that for the actual design, etc., is formally recorded. The project consumed a total of £178,865.[1] Exactly how this was distributed was as follows £40,783 8s 9d attributable to 36001, £6427 18s 1d on repairs and maintenance to the same engine and with the balance, £131,653 18s 2d, against the incomplete Nos 36002–5. 'A.F.C.' again is of the opinion that if the whole figure had been available for developing just the one prototype then the story might have been different. Probably that was never likely in the first place, as the Southern would have been unlikely to sanction such a considerable sum on one engine alone. Compared also with contemporary costs for alternative rail traction the price for Leader was not excessive. The pair of LMS Diesel Locomotives introduced in 1947/8 were stated to have accounted for £156,000, although it is not known if this included development or just production costs. (A similar breakdown on costs incurred before and after nationalisation is not known.)

Bulleid had intended his engine to be a go-anywhere, do-anything steam engine. Freed from the constraints of a steam engine designed specifically for passenger, goods, or shunting roles, Leader could in theory accomplish all of these and with equal aplomb. In some respects could be said for any large(ish) design, although the practicalities of a Castle, Merchant Navy, Duchess or A4 performing such roles might be questioned. (Yes, it did happen towards the end of steam when scheduling meant there was just not enough work for former express designs. This of course explains why so many specifically designed express classes were retired earlier than 'lesser' engines.)

So Leader was intended to be all things to all people. But Bulleid wanted to improve upon the design at the same time and by combining both schools of thought it was in reality a step too far. Having said that in some respects Riddles and his team did unintentionally succeed in the 9F later producing a machine capable of several roles, even if that was more by accident than design! In the 9F there existed a powerful machine equally at home on passenger or goods with small wheels and yet recorded at speeds of at least 90mph on more than one occasion. But in other respects it was a conventional steam engine – and not one that endeared itself to many firemen either, as all that power required a fair amount of human muscle to generate it. Had Bulleid worked on the principle of just smaller wheels and total adhesion it might have worked, but as we know that was not enough for the designer.

Dealing then with the mechanics first, the obvious place to start is with the sleeve valves. These did not work. They had not worked on the Paget engine, they did not work on *Hartland Point*, and they did not work on Leader either. (Day-Lewis comments that the 'features in common' between Paget's engine and Leader were 'largely coincidental'. In the opinion of the present author the tremendous similarity between the two and which was so radical compared with every other steam design is surely too much to be mere coincidence. In one area though Day-Lewis was absolutely right. Commenting on the features in common and the reasons for failure he continues, 'the same abortive result brought about by prejudice and lack of funds.')

Bulleid appeared determined to incorporate sleeve valves for the mistaken but commendable belief in increased efficiency and savings in space and weight. All these were indeed the advantages of the type but subject to the variations in speed, power requirements and vibration associated with a railway operation it was another story. All credit must be given to Bulleid for attempting to design out the likely pitfalls. The inclusion of axial rotation to the sleeve, the copious oil supply, these should have reduced the likelihood of failure, but it was still not enough. (A note in the files also refers to the sleeve valves originally to have been chrome plated. But this was countermanded as marked as, 'Cancelled by CME 10/12/48' – which 'CME' was this, Bulleid or Riddles?)

Certainly in later years Bulleid appeared to have accepted that the axial rotation connected to the sleeves was in effect a bad idea. This comes from correspondence between Bulleid and Reg Curl in 1965 in which he stated, 'The oscillating of the sleeves was abandoned because of a lack of

A final view at Bognor with just No. 36003 present. Whether this dates from the start or end of storage is uncertain. Whether sister engine No. 36002 was present but yet to shunted into position is also unclear. Be assured of one fact, No. 36002 was towed and certainly not steamed to reach here, whilst at the very least it is likely the connecting rods within the bogies had been removed and placed in the cabs – but seemingly not the drive chains on No. 36002 as the exterior casings remained in pace. *P.M. Alexander/Lens of Sutton Association*

Meanwhile what would have been No. 36004 was moved on accommodation (coach) bogies out of the works and stored nearby. This combination was not considered suitable for travel outside the immediate area and would remain in this or similar position until later scrapped. *S.C. Nash/Stephenson Locomotive Society*

time to do the experimental work needed; another side-effect of nationalisation!' Three years later writing to Curl again but this time from Malta, he continued on exactly the same theme, 'No one but those closely concerned could know it was the oscillating of the sleeves which caused so much anxiety and meant so many trials. *I often wish I had not listened to the suggestion of ……. that this oscillation would ensure proper lubrication of the sleeves as it had in the 'Tempest' aeroplanes' sleeve valve engines.*' (The italics are those of the present author, whilst the missing name is probably intended to be that of Sir Harry Ricardo.)

The number of times failures occurred due to wear, and seizures were a warning of what was to come. Possibly as with the Pacifics in an ideal situation he would perhaps have wished to incorporate poppet or Caprotti valve gear, but in the period in question and even though such gears existed, such opportunities were not available to him.

By using three cylinders per bogie, six on the completed engine, a wonderful even torque (allied to the provision of chain drive) would exist. Power transfer would be superb – indeed when it worked it was, whilst the acceleration could also be 'electric'. Recall the comment 'effortless' when witnessing the start from Eastleigh on 17 October 1950.

But to achieve such a smooth power take-off a multi-cylindered steam engine was essential and it was the desire to incorporate this that in turn had led to the use of sleeve valves in the first place. There was simply not enough room to use three full sets of Walschaerts or other valve gear between the frames. The maximum then would have had to have been two inside cylinders per bogie. Using more conventional valve gear but still retaining at least three cylinders per bogie conjures up a vision of a mixture of outside and inside cylinders – again this must be conjecture but in this latter scenario the smooth torque associated with the use of chains would have been lost.

In order for Riddles then to cure the cylinder problem, radical re-design to the cylinders and valve gear would have been necessary.

So far though everything has been negative, so now let us turn to one of the positive aspects Bulleid did achieve in the new design. The advantage of having a multi-cylindered steam engine has already been discussed, likewise the versatility of small driving wheels. But to apply steam to a design carried as it was on power bogies required flexible steam pipes. These had rarely been successfully developed before – recall the Gresley 'booster' and which it was stated occasionally resulted in 'fog working'. Here then Bulleid did achieve, such successes often conveniently ignored, and as is human nature, overshadowed by the failures.

Let us turn now to the final drive through the chain, the axle boxes, pedestal guides and crank-axles. All these are associated in the next group to be considered and which led up to both the actual failure and potential failure of the drive axle. Opinions here are again mixed. The final drive through chains meant that in order to incorporate chains with sufficient strength, it was not possible to afford two separate chains – one driving 'fore' and one 'aft' on each side of each bogie. Consequently the drive was split – centre axle to front axle only on one side, and centre axle to rear axle only on the other side. Again this was replicated on each bogie. The result was an obvious counter-pull across the centre axle. Without the machine subject to the pounding associated with steel-on-steel contact between wheel and track allied to the inevitable track irregularities that occur at points, crossings and the like, the result has to be undue stress upon the three throw crank-axle. Townroe was of the opinion that the problem was compounded by insufficient vertical movement in the horn guides of the centre axle and indeed that may well be the case. There is no formal evidence to support such a view.

A further opinion is given by J.M. Dunn (see Acknowledgments), who described himself as a 'running shed man', was that 'a standard gauge axle with three cranks of 7½in. throw looked strangely weak'. A little later the same author referring to the unsymmetrical final drive continued, 'This seemed to me to be a curiously un-mechanical arrangement which apart from causing uneven wear in the opposite axle boxes (which were all provided with roller bearings) of all three pairs of wheels, must have put a terrific strain on the, what appeared to me to be, already weak crank-axle.'

Again from those who wish to criticise Bulleid for the sake of it, folklore also has it that when pressing the wheels onto the end of the crank-axles, the space between the webs was either not packed at all, or insufficiently packed with hard timber as was the normal practice. Supposition has likewise been raised that there were pre-existing faults within the steel used for the axle. Another suggestion blames torsional vibration as the cause of axle failure, although as the rotating speed was just 272rpm at 60mph this is perhaps unlikely. Whatever may have been the reason, the undisputable fact was crank-axle failure after less than 6,000 miles running. As we cannot be totally certain as to the cause, we similarly cannot be totally certain of the necessary cure, likely one, all, or more of the statements above.

We now turn to the boiler, firebox, engine steaming ability and crew conditions. Make no mistake about it, Bulleid was a master at boiler design allied to water circulation. His boiler on the Merchant Navy class was arguably the most efficient at producing steam on any railway locomotive ever built in Britain – with the exception of Leader which was even better! Rugby testing plant were never able to reach the limit of evaporation of a Merchant Navy boiler – the un-rebuilt engine being tested, 35022, deposited so much oil on the rollers of the test house that it was considered unwise to proceed further! As such we can be certain that in the boiler for Leader, Bulleid would have designed a pressure vessel to the highest efficiency. Yet, and as reported, on any number of occasions Leader ran short of steam or was unable to maintain the required steaming rate.

For the moment let us return to the boiler and the firebox, which incorporated the thermic siphons. The conventional firebox is the area where the greatest heat is generated and consequently the greatest evaporation of water into steam will occur. But due to its complicated make up – two sheets held separated by countless stays – it was both expensive to construct and also to maintain. This was not assisted by the variations in temperature any such firebox was subjected to – one minute the demand for steam meaning an almost incandescent fire would be burning and the next a lesser demand. (Anyone who has ever travelled on a big steam engine working with a late cut-off and the regulator close to fully open will confirm the fire is almost white hot from the blast upon it and impossible to look at with the naked eye for any length of time.) Such variations (worse of course in an oil-burning furnace where the rise and fall in temperatures is both far faster and more dramatic) inevitably led to weeping from the firebox stays. In a number of designs the problem was accentuated by the use of copper for the inner firebox compared with steel for the outer firebox. The choice of metal determined by its efficiency at conducting heat, although again both will expand and contract at differing rates according to heat – hence the weep.

In Leader he went one stage further. Instead of a water-filled jacket surrounding the firebox, four siphons were provided and as such there was less difference in heating area compared with a jacketed design. The 'crown' of the firebox of course still existed – basically a water-filled canopy at the top of the firebox and it was to this that the four siphons were secured and as such their location (a triangular shape) from the crown to the base of the firebox afforded an additional advantage of supporting the crown itself.

In place of water filled firebox sides, Bulleid instead had plain welded sheets around both sides and the rear. A series of interlinked firebricks secured by small protruding hooks were intended to both retain the bricks and consequently the firebox heat and so afford some thermal protection to the crew.

Again in practice, this was a sound theoretical idea that did not work under operating conditions, for the reasons described above relative to a stationary engine compared with a moving locomotive. But what remains so amazing is the ability of the firebox and boiler to produce such a vast amount of steam, even when ultimately restricted by layers of firebrick reducing its volume. The transfer of heat to the syphons more than made up what would otherwise have been a shortfall. (Unfortunately we do have any figures available for the area of the syphons.)

Unfortunately too what none of the official records refer to is the evaporation rate of the boiler. This appears not to have been one of the items being tested – or if it was, it was not recorded. (Why we may ask? Was someone concerned this would show Leader's boiler was potentially more efficient, based on square feet of area, at producing steam than possibly any other railway engine ever built?)

Prove it – easy. It is known that the eventual grate area of Leader was reduced through the addition of either more

We move now to New Cross where Nos. 36002/3 spend some time, again in store, although by this stage it must have been obvious there would be no reprieve. Why New Cross? Well, perhaps Bognor had become 'too hot' and New Cross was certainly a less easily accessible location for the inquisitive. Unfortunately the depot also had a reputation as one where regular pilfering took place, with associated vandalism. That is not to suggest railway staff were involved, as culprits were rarely caught. New Cross was also a favoured location for storing locos temporarily out of service. Chalked on the side are the words, 'Property of the British Taxpayer' showing that feelings ran high even two years before the *Sunday Despatch* article. Again no definite dates for the moves to New Cross are available. *A.C. Sterndale*

than one row of, or an additional row of, firebricks. It matters not which. What is important is that we know without doubt the final grate area of Leader was just 25.5^{2}ft compared with the 43^{2}ft with which it had been designed.

A grate area as such was indeed compatible with an 'N' class 2-6-0, but it was smaller than that of a 'Schools'. Smaller than a Stanier 'Class 5'. And yet on its very last outing on 2 November 1950 and despite this reduced grate area the boiler was able to generate enough steam to lift 480t to 50mph on a rising gradient averaging 1 in 250 from a standing start. A poor steamer – rubbish! All this also from a total heating surface including the firebox of 2,387^{2}ft. (The comparative figures for a Merchant Navy were 2,451^{2}ft, and for a 'West Country/Battle of Britain' 2,122^{2}ft.) The basic problem was that most of the time the cylinders were wasting more steam than Leader's boiler could produce.

Still on the theme of what was a dry-back firebox, it appears that at some very late stage the thought occurred to either Bulleid or somebody in the drawing office that it would be a good idea to wrap a water jacket of sorts around the firebox, not to increase steam evaporation but instead to further supplement the insulation for the crew. Perhaps this may even have been around the time the external shape of the casing was decided upon. Whichever it was, the effect was counter-productive. The heat insulating abilities of the extra water were minimal, it added little to the available water capacity, and instead had a negative effect on the operation of the injectors, the latter situation in close proximity below the firing compartment and so close to the firebox. The physical location of the injectors as such was not an operational problem, their position was unaffected by heat. What did occur though was that aided by the heat of the water from the mantle tank, the feedwater was heated to the extent that the injectors were, to say the least, less efficient than they might have been. Of course had the concept of feed-water heating been incorporated in place of water treatment, then this would not have been an

No. 36002 is seen here on 23 May 1951, destined also to be her final day in London before she was towed south again back to Brighton and scrap. Compare the external condition with that when she had been put into store 18 months earlier, with some of the external marker lights broken. The issue with putting incomplete engines into store was that there does not appear to have been an inventory of what was present in the first place and consequently brass or copper fittings may have been unofficially removed without proof they were ever there in the first place. If it had only been known at the time probably the most valuable removable piece was the numberplate(s)! The 'old iron' soliloquy would certainly not have pleased Bulleid. *Brian Morrison*

Two almost nightmarish views of Nos. 36002 and 36003 in store; No. 36003 being the one with the holes cut in the cab ends for the marker lights that were never fitted. The Leader design was surely most unconventional steam design to run on Britain's railways in recent years but we might mention that according to E.S. Cox, in 1923 the LMS considered a 'Mallett' type engine for use on the Toton to Brent coal trains which at the time requiring double heading – a throwback to the Midland Railway 'small-engine' policy. This came to nothing but the concept of a large engine for the purpose was subsequently revived with the Garratt design of 1927. *Peter Dunk*

issue. Proof, if it were needed, of how the design evolved piecemeal rather than as a cohesive thought process.

Next we come to the conditions for the crew. It would be unfair to dismiss this as an irrelevance as so much has been made of the topic of heat, particularly for the fireman, in the past. But, and as again recounted before, misinformation has had its say. The actual temperature of 122° was discussed previously. Yes, Leader was hot and the working conditions were decidedly unpleasant. Bulleid in attempting to produce his ultimate steam engine with a reasonable degree of crew comfort had achieved the opposite and designed the heat in. Redesign would have been necessary. The union comment that the fireman could have been trapped in the event of a roll-over was a valid comment. Bulleid's desire to give the driver an unrestricted view ahead akin to that enjoyed from the front of an electric unit was just not feasible. It had also added complexity in duplicating the regulator, reversing gear and other controls through mechanical linkage and connecting the driving compartments at both ends. Possibly some of the problems with items such as the operation of the reversing gear were compounded by the very method of operation. The solution to all of this was a central cab where both men would work, thus separating the boiler and bunker portions. In other words a major re-design.

Finally on the subject of the boiler and firebox, we come to the note in Riddles' report over the X-ray examination of the boilers. This he had deemed necessary as the boiler barrel on Leader was not additionally riveted as was normal but was welded throughout. Here was another departure from tradition and one which was again viewed with suspicion. In Riddles' report, was this actual suspicion, or just over-caution? His comment upon not letting the remaining engines into service until their boilers had also been tested in a similar way is perhaps slightly strange. All the boilers for the Leader class engines would surely have been subjected to hydraulic and steam tests when built. The comments of Hargreaves earlier (*see* p.215) should be revisited at this stage.

(*But* – and again from Townroe, the first boiler for Leader was slow to make as Hargreaves, the Chief Metallurgist at Eastleigh, wanted every inch of welding X-rayed. According to Townroe, Bulleid sent for the negatives, saw no faults and told Hargreaves to desist. The story got around the staff and added to their anxiety about the way a boiler of that shape might behave under the normal stresses of expansion and contraction.)

It has been suggested to the author in the past that there was a suggestion of a problem with the boiler on

36001 and in the area of the welded seam but this could well have been rumour perpetuated in consequence of the incident referred to above. To suggest otherwise would be to imply that Riddles was sanctioning additional trials involving a steam engine having a 280psi boiler and which was then suggested to be likely to fail. Many things Riddles may have been, a fool he certainly was not.

We now come to the weight of Leader, which was far in excess of that originally projected. Indeed far from being able to work on the majority of company lines, the final design could only work on the minimum of company lines. The basic problem in this area was simply the offset boiler and weights that were subsequently added for some form of balance. Again as recounted in the text, even this was not enough, and a restriction had then to be as set on the one thing that could be easily varied – consumables. Hence the restricted amount of coal and water carried on the tests from Eastleigh.

The whole aspect of the offset boiler is perhaps one on the most puzzling aspects of the design. By placing the boiler in such fashion the results would have been obvious. Did Bulleid seriously believe that there would be no adverse effect? Did no one amongst his staff not advise him – or perhaps Bulleid's character was such it was not feasible to do so? During his time on the LNER he would surely have been aware of the *original* difficulties with the Gresley corridor tender, overheated bearings and the need for some balancing weights. Bulleid was in many respects a gifted and far-sighted engineer. (Another item of folklore is that he behaved the way he did as he was influenced by contemporary Sentinel designs particularly in relation to the 'engine' part of the design. And of course, the LNER did have Sentinel steam railcars.)

In many ways Bulleid could see beyond the straight-jacket approach to conventional steam engine thinking. But in the area of the offset boiler, and which was only provided so as to afford some means of communication between the crew, he was wrong. A 'dead-man's handle', duplicated brake controls, would have been sufficient. Centralising the boiler would have been a relatively easy step, it could have been achieved at the same time as a central cab where both men would work together.

The other aspects of Leader which have come in for criticism centre around auxiliary items, and primarily the reversing gear, smokebox duct and grate. The reversing gear problems may have been exaggerated by the complicated linkage involved, whilst the smokebox duct was in effect an early attempt at smokebox cleaning. A mesh screen as was developed and fitted to numerous steam designs in BR days would no doubt have worked. The grate too was perhaps unduly complicated, but the idea was sound, a little further in the development and it too would have worked perfectly well.

Having then criticised what must seem most of the design we have to ask what was left, and the answer is surprisingly quite a lot. But before leaving the negative aspects a few other issues need to be raised at this stage.

Many of the failings referred to were basic weaknesses in the design. Complications added without necessary thought as to how each might inter-react with the next. In effect, too many untried features in one design led to inevitable failure. But were any of these failures due to design, manufacture, assembly, or operational failure? Was the crank-axle failure due to poor-quality steel, were the sleeve failures due to haste in considering adequate lubrication in all areas? The questions are almost without end.

Returning to the positives, did the design of the engine, indicate or point towards the future? The answer to this is an undeniable yes. Leader showed that the development of steam was not finished, Bulleid was right in wanting to take the basic Stephenson locomotive further. The failure was not of the Leader design but the fact that at the time it appeared there were more obstacles against than there were benefits to be gained.

Certainly by the late 1940s the future for steam traction, not just in Britain but worldwide, was limited. The diesel engine was rapidly being developed, in America wholesale dieselisation was under way, and in France there were plans in place for major electrification. Britain could not stand in isolation. Riddles' remit under BR was to ensure the survival of steam until the public finances provided for replacement traction. He did this by attempting to provide a standard range of locomotives, without frills, until the alternative was available. How the individual may view the standard designs of Riddles is irrelevant in this context.

Bulleid's designs – the original Pacifics, and certainly Leader – just did not fit in. In effect it mattered not how Leader had performed, it was never going to be multiplied. The only time such a chance could have existed was if it had not only been 100% perfect off the drawing board, but possibly even 110% perfect. In the history of technological development has there ever been any machine that performed as such?

But that does not mean Leader was a waste of time either. The efficiency of the boiler, the locomotive on two power bogies (a form of sophisticated Kitson-Meyer perhaps), and other aspects of the auxiliary equipment showed there was still a potential for development. It was the fault of Riddles and his contemporaries that they did not take those ideas and use them as they stood or develop them further. Leader bequeathed only two real items, the body to bogie mounting, which has already been referred to, and the dashpot axlebox damping. This latter feature was indeed developed and incorporated into a very successful axlebox design on EMU stock. It was a pity what was not used concerned the Leader's braking system; 100% satisfactory and which operated akin to the air compressor and reservoirs on a diesel locomotive or large commercial vehicle. Obviously with Leader a vacuum was involved but the principle was the same – when the vacuum drops to a pre-set level, it was automatically replenished from a 'holding tank'. When both reservoir and holding tank had equalised, the ejector was brought into use automatically. It worked beautifully with one slight hic-cup in that the release valves were slightly slow

A remarkable and rare view showing the movement of No. 36002 from New Cross to Brighton on 24 June 1951 and seen passing Anerley. So perhaps a Leader did in the end venture down the Brighton main line, albeit on its way to scrap. (The single disc headcode is for the Quarry Line.) In charge is No. 31400, including a brake van, as No. 36002 was otherwise unbraked. This image must have been taken in consequence of inside information and indeed remains the only view located showing the actual movement of either No. 36002 or No. 36003 away from Brighton. In the background a new multiple aspect colour light signal has recently replaced the semaphore. *K.G.Carr, courtesy Peter Fidczuk*

No. 36003 'undressed in public'. Look carefully and the Ajax firedoors are visible and open. No. 2 end is nearest the camera with its water tank/coal bunker whilst the position of the offset boiler and mantle/shelf water tanks are also easily seen. These additional mantle tanks may well have increased the water capacity but at what cost? Did they in fact heat the water in the tanks too much so the injectors became unreliable?

Shunting around the Brighton complex, 23 March 1951, and proving No. 36003 came back to Brighton and was the first of three 'complete'(ish) engines to be cut up. The presence of roller bearings on all wheels made movement a relatively simple task – on most occasions. Although recall it had still not been enough to allow the works' Terrier to pull No. 36001 out of the shops two years previously in June 1949. The photograph allows a glimpse at yet another of the shelf water tanks running alongside the almost the whole length of the firebox/boiler on the 'blind' side, but in the process adding still more to the offset weight of the engine. No. 36003 clearly did not want to be dismantled as one bogie from the engine managed to derail whilst it was being moved into the works; fortunately coming to rest just short of fouling the main line. It would only be a temporary delay.

in operation. Again, not the fault of Bulleid or the design, this was down to the manufacturer of the valves. It can only be regretted that a similar system was not used on any other UK steam engine.

In the same way then that Bulleid's engine failed to affect the subsequent thinking of future UK steam design, so the same fate had befallen Paget years earlier. Indeed it is likely the same arguments and results affected this engine. It must forever be an anomaly in present-day knowledge that Bulleid as a mechanical engineer felt he could improve on a very similar design of 30–40 years earlier and yet went on to make not just the same but even more mistakes.

It might seem to the reader as if the purpose of this chapter has been to vilify Bulleid, but that is not the case. Indeed we now come to an even more contentious area, and where it appears there may even have been a deliberate policy against the engine. I both cannot and will not put into print any formal accusations, indeed I make none. What I do instead is, as before, is to point out fact; the reader alone may decide.

To start with then when the first engine was under construction, a power bogie was deliberately lifted off the ground and supplied with steam at just 8psi from an external source to both test and observe the operation. Everything ran perfectly 'like a sewing machine' – probably also the time the accompanying 'stills' were recorded. This test was a perfectly feasible and logical operation – and yet whilst the test was actually under way, the fitters in charge were instructed by, it was said, the Brighton Works Manager, to then reverse the engine without stopping it first. This has already been referred to in Chapter 1. Bulleid was advised of the incident by Doug Smith and Joe Hutchinson, and although both men entered the office of the CME with some trepidation, there was no fall-out.

But it must be questionable that with the majority of failures affecting No. 1 bogie why the opportunity was not taken to exchange the complete bogie with that from 36002 or 36003? It might have made all the difference. (It has been suggested that No. 1 bogie of 36001 may have been changed before the engine went to Eastleigh for its final trials and likewise the boiler may even have been changed.

Correspondence in 1989 between the author and B. Musgrave, who in 1949 was a draughtsman at Brighton, revealed that the latter was of the opinion that No. 1 bogie was in fact changed together with the boiler from 36001, this allegedly having taken place just prior to the engine's final transfer to Eastleigh in early 1950, the last item being swapped due to damage to the firebox sides. Such comment would surely have been mentioned in the official reports, but it is not, nor is it confirmed within any other source.)

Another question concerns the alleged water consumption for the light engine runs of 14th and 15th August and then the load trial on 21st August, with no mechanical work affecting the sleeves having been undertaken between those dates. Leader is supposed have run out of water running light and yet could then take a load over a greater distance without running out! Somewhere there is a grave inconsistency.

Finally consider the ability of the engine to haul its train on the very last run made. This showed the potential of the engine and even more particularly the design. But it was ignored by Marylebone.

What is also known is that very shortly after nationalisation, Riddles decided that there would be a change around amongst the senior mechanical engineering staff of the regions and for valid reasons. In this way he could gain first-hand and impartial knowledge from a fresh pair of eyes in relation to former company practice and designs – those for the LMS he probably knew himself. Such knowledge, plus the practical experience gained from the interchange trials of 1948 (although were the latter as much for show as for sound technical reasons?) was valuable in assisting with both the design and later construction sites used for the later build of Standard locomotives. But such interchange also meant there was now a direct line to Riddles which had not existed before. Previously Bulleid and his staff might well have tried to keep matters quiet until difficulties had been resolved but that no longer applied; everything was in the open.

The question has also been asked if despite the failure of Leader there was even a place for Bulleid working with Riddles, possibly as an ideas man as had been the case before, perhaps held 'in-check'? Here a quote from Riddles himself, when asked the very question by STEAM WORLD, may be appropriate:

'As a man I liked him and we got on well, but he was an individualist who wanted to do it his own way, and some of what he did was questionable. I couldn't fathom some of his thinking.' When asked about the decision to scrap 'Leader' he continued, 'It was the only sensible decision to make. The thing was 30 tons overweight, and the boiler so badly balanced it needed 2½ tons of pig-iron on one side to balance it up. Apart from that, the fireman was forced to stand so close to the firebox he was burning himself. The fireman had to lag himself with sandbags to deflect the heat. Was there a job for Bulleid after Nationalisation? – No, how could there be. Having been king of his own dung heap, how could he suddenly come and serve in mine? The surprise to me was that having failed on the Southern, he went to Ireland and failed there too.'

As we have said before, Riddles last sentence was wrong. Bulleid did not fail in Ireland; 'Turf Burner' worked. Yes, a few modifications were still needed but the lessons from Leader had been learnt. It was the wrong place, and the wrong time. A decade earlier and it could have been a different story.

Another oft-quoted mistaken view is once more from Day-Lewis. Generally this author's account of Bulleid, apart from also being the first book on the man and his work, is arguably one of the best overall, but in one area he has missed the point completely. The quote is referring to the time when the order came through from headquarters that work was to cease on Nos 36002–5. Day-Lewis; 'On that date No. 36002 was only two days from completion: after a few minor jobs like coupling up pipes and putting in cab windows the locomotive would have been ready for steaming. With the lessons learnt from No. 36001 she would surely have been a better engine than her older sister.' The same author might also be said to almost have romanticised relative to the trials of *Hartland Point*, as following that particular machines last outing and during which she fractured a sleeve at St Leonards – see p.75, he comments, 'And that was the sad end of No. 32039 … though the lessons she taught were invaluable.'

Both statements are simply not true. 36002 was built to the same design as 36001, she would have displayed exactly the same tendencies. The only possible variation was haste in the construction of 36001 had led to a slight warping of the cylinder blocks on the original engine. This had not applied to 36002 so sleeve valve failures may have been fewer but it is unlikely they would have been totally non-existent. Likewise time did not allow any of the lessons learnt from *Hartland Point* to be incorporated into the design. If they had the sleeve-valves might have been substituted. The guinea pig engine *Hartland Point* failed to serve the purpose it had been intended to do. If it had, work on the design of Leader would surely not have even commenced until trials with 2039 were complete.

So were 36001 and her sisters destined to be stillborn from the start, was the Leader project a triumph or a fiasco?

According to J.E. Chacksfield in his biography of Jarvis – the latter having been transferred from Derby to Brighton by Riddles – morale at Brighton around 1948–50 was slipping and whilst the drawing office at Brighton was heavily engaged in work on various modifications to the Pacifics (not the full rebuild as occurred later) a small section there was occupied full time also on similar modifications to Leader. Jarvis was also tasked by Riddles with reporting on the ongoing trials of 36001 and indeed some of the actual words and phrases incorporated by Riddles in the latter's own later reports to the Executive originated from the pen of Jarvis. He was similarly charged with overseeing the tests from Eastleigh later.

To all these men Bulleid was perhaps an irritation in his persistence in pursuing the untried concept of the improvement to the steam engine. But in reality Bulleid cannot have been said to have been wrong. Time-wise and location-wise perhaps he was misguided, but who

Conclusions

One of the very last views of No. 36002 in the course of being dismantled inside Brighton works on 30 June 1951. By this stage No. 36003 had succumbed to the same fate as indeed had No. 36001 at Eastleigh. The boiler and firebox have gone although the bunker, frames and bogies remain. Ironically alongside is a brand new BR Standard class 4 2-6-4T, and as mentioned before, precisely what the Southern had really needed in the first place.

can blame the man for trying? If Leader had been running perhaps two years earlier, then the outcome might well have been different.

To expand on this theme I can do no better than quote a slightly long passage from E. S. Cox's 1966 biography, *Locomotive Panorama Vol 2*, and in which the clash of personalities between Bulleid and the new British Railways regime is well described:

> With Bulleid on the other hand, there was rather a different situation which merits some description because of its unusual nature. To an extent unknown on other railways, he had been supreme autocrat within his own department, and had been able to impose his will upon a management otherwise pre-occupied with electrification.
>
> In locomotive matters on the former S.R. it could be said of him, as of Joseph in the Egyptian prison, that 'Whatsoever was done therein, he was the doer thereof.' An individualist of the deepest dye, he had no sympathy at all with the painstaking improvement of the breed which I have outlined, but wished with brilliant and dramatic improvisations to solve all the remaining problems of steam by quite other means. To him novelty was everything. If it would not work then this could not be the fault of the idea itself, but only of the incapacity of those who tried to carry it out or use it.
>
> The cross which he had to bear was that his developments with conventional practice were successful, sometimes brilliant, whereas his exercises in the bizarre, which he loved dearly as his brain children, often failed. A recent book (by Day-Lewis) has described in great detail the fascinating personality and the ideas, achievements and failures of this enigmatical man. He knew in advance that we were bound to introduce practice which was alien to his own thought processes, and to divert the activities of his assistants from frantically trying to solve the impossible into more normal channels. I recollect my first official contact with him after my new appointment when he assembled all his principal technical staff for lunch at the Old Ship Hotel at Brighton to meet me. His charm and tact eased a confrontation which could have been difficult, and he offered then, and loyally upheld later, every assistance from his people in what we wanted to do. He did not disguise his attitude however, and expressed in an extremely gentlemanly way, that he had cast his pearls before swine, and that if we found nothing to learn from his Merchant Navy and Leader, so much the worse for us. It intrigues the imagination to consider what policy would have been followed and what locomotive designs would have been produced had any of the above-mentioned men either taken Riddles' place or held the post of C.M.E. if the four individual railways had carried on exactly as before.
>
> In this context I must refer to a matter which caused the acutest embarrassment to Riddles and his officers at the time, and which it is difficult to write about objectively even after this lapse of years. I refer again to Bulleid's Leader class locomotive and the following are the facts of the case. Towards the end of the war the Southern Railway was considering a new design of tank engine, to handle cross-London freight traffic according to Bulleid's son in his book Master Builders of Steam, but, in our own records, for the purpose of replacing the Class 0-4-4 Tanks which would cover a slightly different kind of duty. Whatever may have been the true original need, the sight of Rayworth's C-C electric locomotive fired Bulleid with the idea that its outstanding advantage of being a 'total adhesion' machine ought to be equally applicable to steam traction. This was no new thought as witness Holden's 'Decapod' and various 'Fairlie' designs through history, but these all operated at low speed. With characteristic enthusiasm, Bulleid now enlarged the proposal and persuaded his management that what they really needed was an all-purpose, go-anywhere locomotive capable of hauling 480 tons passenger or 1,200 tons freight, and of attaining 90m.p.h. Accordingly, five of these unknowns were authorised by the S.R. on its 1947 programme, and anticipating success, 31 more were proposed for 1948. The newly formed Railway Executive approved the former and included them in its own 1948 programme, but having regard to their untried nature, cancelled the 31. Bulleid disclosed some particulars about the project in his Presidential Address to the Institution of Mechanical Engineers in October 1946. He listed therein ten objectives all of which were above reproach in the advancement of steam traction, and nearly all of which were capable of attack by more than one method. When we became responsible for technical matters throughout British Railways in 1948 we found this design almost completed at Brighton, and at once encountered an approach and a process of thought so alien to that of our own, with our different background, that our standards of judgment tended to flounder. The solution of the problem of designing a high speed double bogie steam engine seemed a task of some magnitude in itself, and we could not but be somewhat dazed to see that other novel and untried features were also crowded into the same framework to wit sleeve valve cylinders, driving wheels coupled by chains and an offset boiler having for firebox a row of thermic syphons encased in a firebrick lining without external water legs. We accepted untouched however, what this original mind was producing and on June 21st, 1949, No. 36001 was competed, with two others coming up strongly behind in the erecting shop at Brighton. Then followed trial running through to October 1950, on 90 days of which tests were carried out including two series of dynamometer car tests, but as is well known, there were continual failures and the engine was never able to enter revenue service.
>
> Some day and in another place, it may be possible for somebody else to give a full engineering account of all

A few weeks earlier than the Brighton view of No. 36002, the original engine No. 36001 sits awaiting its last journey to the works on 14 April 1951. Chains and padlocks have been tied around the access doors whilst it even looks as if the fireman's cab windows have been boarded up. *A.E. West, courtesy Mike King*

that happened in this period, but the engine encountered trouble after trouble in all of its unusual features. Successive modifications were made and to give these the best chance of success, Bulleid was specially retained for six months after his retirement in September 1949 in order to give advice and supervise the alterations. But all to no avail. Reliable running proved unattainable, and even in the final best condition to which the locomotive could be brought, its coal and water consumptions were respectively 68 and 47 more per d.b.h.p.hour than that of a Southern U class 2-6-0 tested under identical circumstances, this excess being due amongst other things to steam leakage past the numerous rings associated with the sleeve valves.

Further, the temperature conditions in the boiler compartment amidships were insupportable, and there was only one hero amongst the firemen on the Southern who was prepared to tolerate them even for test running only. I think that Bulleid believed to the end that with more drastic modifications success was just round the corner, but for Riddles and the R.E. enough was enough. Although regretting the outcome they could have no remorse that they had not given this novel attempt every reasonable chance to prove itself. At the end of 1950 it was decided to scrap the engine and the uncompleted chassis and finished components for the other four. As the engine remained unnamed, we shall probably never know who the Leader was to be who would provide the type name for this breakaway from convention had it fulfilled the hopes of its protagonist.'

Cox continued later with a brief description on Turf-Burner, and which for completeness is also included. Almost fittingly the brief comment made by him on the Irish connection was also right at the very end of his book;

'…we visited Eire, where Bulleid, then Chief Mechanical Engineer of the railways there, showed us much hospitality and laid on a display of motive power for us at Inchicore. There we saw the last fitful gleam of steam development in the British Isles. Nothing daunted by the fate of the "Leader" class on the Southern Region, this indefatigable enthusiast presented to us a reconstituted "Leader" having many of the same features, but with the added complexity of seeking to burn peat. For a long time previously one had seen occasional photographs of Irish locomotives of conventional design, looped with writhing external pipes curling in all directions, a veritable *Laocoon* of motive power. These were the guinea pigs upon which the attempt was made to solve the immense problem of reducing the high natural moisture content of this fuel. Bulleid took Bob Arbuthnot, President Elect, and

Inside Eastleigh works, work is progressing on dismantling No. 36001. None of the parts alongside appear to have any relevance to No. 36001 whilst the engine itself now sits on those huge wooden trestles. Notice where the numberplate has been removed, the clean original paintwork underneath is an indication of the amount of grime that had built up in the ensuing almost two years. The 'Not to be Moved' board would seem to be a bit optimistic. Interesting that the marker lights and whistle have been removed, might they have been considered for use on something else later?
Lens of Sutton Association

11 CONCLUSIONS

Still retaining its solitary headcode disc from the earlier running trials but clearly not going anywhere ever again. One of the last views of No. 36001 in a semi-complete state, above the frames at least. The marker lights and whistle have been mentioned with the previous image whilst the only other known parts that were salvaged were the roller bearings from, we think, all the bogies, considered for possible use on the Q1s but in the event not used. It is probably fair to say that 99% of the engines went to scrap. To quote John Click, 'Thus ended this last courageous attempt in Britain to produce a totally new concept of the steam locomotive.'

me, a half-dozen miles up the main line and back on this Irish "Leader" in its final shape. The locomotive certainly went and was clearly without some of the worst disabilities of its predecessor, but to the best of my knowledge, it never entered revenue service…'

The reference to the limited time available for steam after nationalisation now also needs to be taken further. With the development of other forms of motive power, diesel (and with varying forms of transmission and control gear, electric, mechanical, hydraulic etc.), electric, gas-turbine, all indicated that the way forward was the abolition of steam, progress for steam could only be made in the remaining years by simplifying maintenance and minor improvements to deal with ever-changing socio-economic conditions.

Returning to the standard of engineering on BR in the 1950s and it might thus be said that innovation was limited and with the result that design had stagnated – much the same way perhaps as Swindon had after 1930 – again I await the brick-bats. Indeed it took too long for items such as high-degree superheat, roller-bearings, differing exhaust systems (Kylchap/Lemaître) etc., to be accepted as able to improve reliability and performance without major engineering change. Possibly even alterations to valve gear operation, Caprotti in particular, may have improved steam performance and enabled standards of output to be maintained whilst all the while coal quality decreased. (*See also* comment by Barry Curl in Appendix X.)

Digressing slightly but it should not be forgotten that BR *did* in fact carry out one major steam experiment in the 1950s and which related to the fitting of a batch of the new Riddles' '9F' type with the Italian design of Crosti boiler. This was in effect a long pre-heating tube placed under the main boiler barrel and into which was directed what would otherwise be waste heat from the exhaust and so thus improve thermal efficiency.

The manufacturers had promised something like a 20% increase in efficiency and commensurate reduction in coal consumption. Unfortunately such results were not achieved and there followed a long and at times acrimonious discourse between BR and the Italian owners of the patent over payment of royalties.

The failure of the Crosti boiler to perform as per expectations was in reality only one of a long line of attempts over the years at improving steam engine efficiency and which never quite reached the goal intended. There is even indeed similarity with Leader, not because it is ever believed there was a serious attempt to fit a Crosti type of pre-heater, but in so far as their existed a genuine belief that improvement could be made.

Leader firebox and boiler lifted out of No. 36001 at Eastleigh minus the Ajax firedoor, which is perhaps another item retained, as this type, steam-operated on Leader and on the original Pacifics, were almost certainly interchangeable. 23 May 1951.

Before discussing this theme further with regard to 36001, let us conclude the Crosti ideal albeit in simplistic terms. The truth was there had indeed been the improvements promulgated by the makers on the Italian railways – but as far as is known only on certain classes of steam engine. In the main these were also old, and compared with more modern types, relatively inefficient designs. The Crosti variant was thus able to improve thermal efficiency to a far greater percentage on a steam engine of greater age than on a modern 1954-designed '9F'.

In many respects also here lies the fate of Leader. Bulleid had designed and built a machine which in theory at least should have showed considerable advantage in a number of areas. Unfortunately any advantage gained was more than overshadowed by the deficiencies that were only too apparent in others.

What is perhaps the most surprising is how a man with the obvious design capabilities of Bulleid persisted in the pursuit of ideas which had either never worked in a railway or other environment or had been clearly proven not to. By all means experiment, for it is not by this way that development occurs. But learn also from others. Failure to do so can only be described in clichéd terms, it being necessary to reinvent/rediscover the wheel.

From this it might then be perceived that now has come the time to criticise both Bulleid and Leader – wrong. Bulleid was right to try, but he was perhaps wrong in his final approach. British Railways were likewise right to scrap 36001, but equally wrong not to use the ideas it suggested.

Notes

(1) Allowing for inflation the original figure of £178,865 5s equates to £3,990,834.41 in 2004 figures. A single 1950 '£1' having increased in proportionate terms to £22.31 over the period.

12
'Leader Mk2'

The story of the Turf Burner is one that might equally be called 'Leader Mk 2'. How it evolved and why has been well covered by Ernie Shepherd in his 2004 book and so not need be repeated here. Suffice to say that after the failed attempt at purchasing Nos 36001 onwards from BR, Bulleid had this one remaining opportunity to prove a modern steam engine could be a viable proposition. Hence 'Leader Mk 2' is most certainly the appropriate label to use as the two shared so much in common. That similarity extended to the double-bogie, all adhesion locomotive, again chain driven but also with one important difference to 'Leader Mk1'. In 'Leader Mk 2', the actual 'engine' unit within the bogie was easily interchangeable. Here indeed was one of the changes Bulleid himself stated he should have incorporated into the Leader design, and no doubt he would have had time allowed for the original engine to have been developed further. Visually too the two were 'similar' but take care we use the word 'similar' with caution as even a quick glance will show that the Turf Burner had a more centrally placed cab – central that is along the length of the engine, the boiler/firebox was also not offset to one side – hence both crew were together. The fact the engine was also intended to burn peat meant that with a low calorific

'Leader Mk2' at Kildare. Similarity with her older sister? Certainly, although the lookout for the crew was not quite as good but at last both men were together. Again the boiler would come under suspicion (it was not off-centre) but it worked and when it ran, the engine worked well. The trouble was it just came too late. *R.A. Pocklington*

237

This was the experiment with the two boilers set up on the ground at Inchicore. An electric fan was used to force draught to a spare boiler from a 101 class locomotive, which was mechanically stoked from an oversize bunker at the rear. To replicate what would later be the Crosti feedwater effect applied to No. 356, a second smaller boiler was attached to the front with both sharing a common smokebox. The combined chimney emerged from the firebox of the smaller boiler, as seen here. The boiler was manually fed with sods of peat. JGC: 'by about six firemen … and the safety valve kept lifting. It was difficult: no; let's face it, impossible not to laugh, but there it was! Think, though. This rig was a "lash- up" but designed by a bold man, unafraid of ridicule and ready to do new research work into a problem. Meanwhile the wisemen had wagged their heads saying it was impossible, "aaaaltogether"!' OVB would prove them wrong. *R.A. Pocklington*

content, vast quantities of this fuel had to be carried and so at each end there were large hoppers for fuel.

It also cannot be denied that the Turf Burner worked and worked well. A few changes might have been desirable even necessary but it remained a *working* engine. Unlike Leader it was also just a single prototype although Bulleid must have realised that by the time the engine was built and running, steam, fuelled by whatever means, was in terminal decline in Ireland.

As how this extraordinary machine was conceived in the first place necessitates a brief revisiting of Irish railway history from 1939 onwards.

Prior to that time Ireland had imported good quality steam coal from Britain. Other sources had been necessary for short periods, years earlier, notably during the General Strike of 1926, but otherwise there was a regular traffic of coal across the Irish sea. This would all change after the start of WWII and despite a declaration of neutrality by the Irish government – sinking of coal transport from England seen as just one of many ways of affecting the UK economy.

Contrary also to popular belief, there is/was coal in Ireland, albeit low-grade. Mines existed and coal was mined in small amounts from near Carlow, west of Kilkenny, north west of Cork, east and south east of Limerick, and south east of Sligo.

Some imported coal did of course get through but the amount was restricted both for reasons of enemy attention mentioned earlier, and restricted supplies – less coal being mined in Wales and elsewhere as well and in consequence being retained for home (UK) use. (Although similar difficulties were experienced in Northern Ireland, there the situation was not so severe.)

By 1941 coal available to railway locomotives in the Republic had deteriorated to such an extent that 'duff' was being used, with the main depots in Dublin and elsewhere were down to literally 5–6 hours supply.[1] Previously too coal had been 'graded' upon arrival but now this was not possible. A service of sorts was just about maintained although by March, regarded as the peak of the fuel crisis, the fuel available was so poor that a five-hour journey by timetable might take three days to complete. Locos were simply running out of steam or fuel and stranded locos littered the system.

In an attempt to improve matters turf began to be used but in a conventional unmodified loco, only limited success

Side view of the modified former GSWR K3 2-6-0 No. 356, which like No. 2039, paved the way for what was to come. Bulleid had come to Inchicore in 1950 and so it was commendable that he had No. 356 modified and working as early as sometime in 1952. The engine is seen here in its original form with Crosti type pre-heaters either side of the boiler. Notice too the chimney which was used solely for lighting up. An amusing story from John Click on this very topic, 'After attending seven o'clock Mass, OVB would want to be off to his office and was generally there well before 9.30am, the official starting time. A CIE chauffeur always brought him in but that came with a problem. If he got OVB to Inchicore too soon the CME would want to go up to the latest carriage mock-up, or make an unexpected foray into some part of the works - when and where anything could happen! To kill time the driver thus went slowly and OVB found he could sketch, write, or set down his ideas for the day to come. Chauffeur and Bulleid had an arrangement; the latter asking the boss what speed he would like. The agreement was 20mph so he might draw or write, 30mph to read, and 40mph simply to arrive. One day I was going well and found, to my horror, that I had overtaken the Chief's car on my bicycle, fortunately I saw him drawing on squared paper and quite oblivious of everything else around. This turned out to be the lighting up chimney for No. 356 which was conceived in the car threading through Dublin's southern outskirts: it looks just the thing for sending smoke signals by deftly pulling and pushing the operating lever! The sketch would have been handed down to be developed into a working drawing.' *R.A. Pocklington*

was achieved. In terms of efficiency, the same weight of imported coal (although still not necessarily of best quality) produced 13,000 BTUs which compared with just 9,500 for turf. Turf was also volatile whilst containing 75% carbon, 25% ash and including a moisture content of 28–40%. Turf which had been dried and shaped into briquettes performed better but was not widely available. Indeed later trails in 1944 showed 100–105lb of turf briquette was burnt per mile and which was typically 25lb more than coal, even if the latter was of imported and of poor quality.

Experimentation and modifications to the blast pipe helped with one trial having achieved a consumption rate for turf down to 73lb/mile. Even so, it will be appreciated that far more volume of turf needed to be carried so some tender sides were built up with wooden planking to assist in taking on more fuel.

By the end of 1942 the fuel situation had been stabilised a combination of means. One of these was in the use of briquettes and Phurnacite, in total amounting to 30% of fuel used. Services were also being maintained by reducing loads and with the timetables altered. Fire cleaning points were also established to allow crews to clean fires after necessary effort by the engine – such as after surmounting a gradient. (The resultant debris, ash and clinker left by the lineside was considerable and when eventually all collected in later years was sufficient to fill a small quarry.)

A return to peace did not see a return to good quality coal and, as in the UK, oil firing was tried but, again as per the UK, took some time to get going – infrastructure, etc. By this time coal was again available but did not return to pre-1940 quality standards. It was thus against this backdrop that CIE were keen to develop a steam engine design largely immune to future fuel crisis hence the perfectly logical mandate given to Bulleid to develop a Turf Burner which could, if necessary, also be converted to oil.

Turf Burner worked – on turf that is, it never was modified/converted to burn oil. But just like Leader, history would repeat itself. It was the wrong place, and the wrong time period. A decade earlier and it could have been a different story. Click, who was with Bulleid in Ireland for some time, confirms this thought, 'Far too long had been taken in Ireland too, chasing countless illusive ideas. In all honesty, and modesty too, I had said to OVB, "Look we cannot do everything on this one either", or his "Turf Burner" would never have turned a wheel.'

We know Bulleid was a committed steam man and one who still clung on to his belief that a steam engine

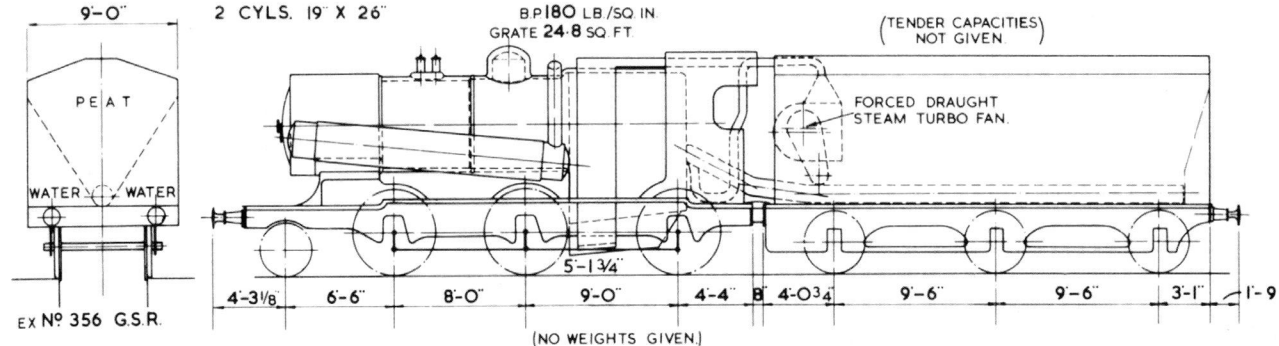
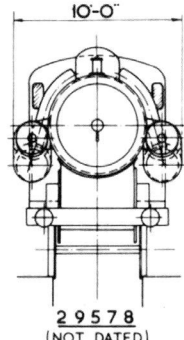

Not dated but believed to be the first Inchicore drawing for the rebuilt No. 356. This was before the decision was made to replace the turbo fan shown within the tender with induced draught from the separate bus engine.

could be developed that would be cheaper to build than the diesel competition and equally be more efficient than previous designs. He used as his rationale the 1948 report on Irish motive power by Sir James Milne, the last General Manager of the Great Western Railway (England).

Bulleid had been a contributor to Milne's report and now used some statistics from it to prove his case. For example on 1 January 1948 there were 461 broad gauge locomotives (referring to the standard Irish track-gauge of 5ft 3in) on its books made up of 65 classes – even if 23 of these classes consisted of just a single machine. As an example, the '101' class had 96 nominally identical locomotives but even these had several sub-classes. In addition there were 27 narrow gauge engines, two Sentinel steam railcars and the first of what would later total five 487hp diesel-electric shunters. Surprisingly fuel types are not mentioned by Bulleid.

More to the point was that availability for service was very low, with utilisation even worse. The maximum number of locomotives gainfully employed on any one day in 1947 was 348, whilst the average number working over the year was only 257; and that out of very nearly 500. The way was thus clear for Bulleid to propose improvement and although not confirmed anywhere so far located, it would seem logical to suggest that it was based on these figures that he made his case to be allowed to develop a 'modern' and efficient steam engine – *to burn turf*.

Bulleid's philosophy as to motive power was also summed up well in Paragraph 416 of the report, 'All new engines should be of the "mixed traffic" type and full use should be made of this dual capacity in the engine working arrangements. The engines should be designed as standard types to be perpetuated, subject to improvement in detail and reconsideration in the event of new developments; standardisation without stultification.' It went on '…it appears probable that all traffic requirements could be met by three of four types of engine exclusive of locomotives specially adapted for shunting duties', the last a reference to the first series of 487hp diesel-electric shunters by then in service, or very nearly so. Much of his philosophy again not that far removed from his Southern Railway days.

Click writes, 'Bulleid didn't always realise how much more limited in scale were the facilities at his disposal in Eire, and expected near miracles over his favourite projects; but also often got them. Quite what, or who, started him off on the idea of burning turf in a steam locomotive isn't clear, but the fact that it had never been done really satisfactorily would have been enough, for it offered him a challenge of the kind he most liked. It was also very politically acceptable in some quarters: especially as peat burning power stations had been commissioned some time earlier.'

Click comments reveal that he was perhaps not totally versed in what had occurred just a few years earlier. He similarly fails to mention any notion or indeed experience with oil as a possible fuel whilst from the forgoing it is perfectly reasonable to believe Bulleid's appointment in Ireland was based on a requirement to develop an efficient turf-burning locomotive. Even so we may ask the question did Bulleid agree to such a proposal or was it instead more of a transparent promise with Bulleid instead really wishing to continue his development of his 'ultimate' steam design? Even if the latter, it is interesting to note that he still did not copy the ideals of M. Chapelon.

Once settled at Inchicore, Owen Wynne, a senior member

By 1956 No. 356 had the Crosti type equipment replaced with banks of finned aluminium heaters. These were a development of a design again by Ricardo of Shoreham. Whether the change was made purely on the belief of increased efficiency, or concern over a possible patent issue, is not clear. It certainly cannot be said No. 356 in her revised form was in any way attractive, but that was not the point, for as with the earlier Inchicore tests, they were there to prove a point. Of necessity the original tender of No. 356 was enlarged by cutting and extending an old frame. Impatient to show what had been achieved, Bulleid invited the Minister of Trade and Commerce up to see No. 356 before there had been a chance to test her. The result was the engine fighting the tender on the first curve she encountered and 48hrs non-stop working necessary afterwards to put right the damage. The very long tender was necessary so sufficient turf could be carried to give the engine a useful range. On occasions turf had been used as a fuel on the Irish railways as far back as 1848. Dependent upon the type of coal, in proportion, turf could be slightly less than half the calorific value of the same weight in fuel. The external chute for any smokebox cleaning is interesting. The engine can be seen to be in light steam possibly recently having been lit up. *R.A. Pocklington*

From the rear, No. 356 looks even more menacing. At some point a form of vandalism took place with the word 'Turf' and the letters 'Experi' were painted out on the tender. Bulleid was not amused. Just creeping into view on the extreme right is the 4-wheel truck with the bus engine. *R.A. Pocklington*

The bus engine and truck: *note* the modern logo. At the time of John Click's journey on the engine from Inchicore south towards Cork, he noted the leaves of one spring on this 4-wheel truck were all broken but the trip went ahead anyway and they returned without derailment. *R.A. Pocklington*

of staff at the time Bulleid was in Ireland, recalled how he had requested they set up an experiment to burn turf in the Babcock & Wilcox stationary boilers in the powerhouse. 'I arranged to have a very large quantity of turf stacked in front of the firebox and six labourers were engaged to continuously throw peat into the firebox to maintain pressure. In due course OVS (*sic*) was telephoned to the effect that the boiler … was maintaining the required pressure'. On arrival 'when the safety valve blew' OVS was overheard by the labourers to say 'Well, it burns' a story that 'was to go the rounds for a long time afterwards' said Owen. Why was he so surprised, everyone in Ireland knew that turf 'was the primary fuel source in Ireland down the centuries'.

How John Click came to Inchicore to work with Bulleid appears to stem from August 1954 when he travelled to Ireland on holiday, but perhaps with the double intention of what we might nowadays refer to as a 'fact finding mission' allied to rumours that no doubt would have been circulating in engineering circles at both Rugby – where Click was now working – as well as elsewhere.

Again John Click's notes are not in any order and with several drafts of the same piece and once more with chunks missing. Even so it is possible to glean that he based himself at Dublin and consequently was close to the main works at Inchicore. As he also admits, 'what Mr Bulleid was up to was one magnet'.

This was clearly not a spontaneous visit either, as prior to travel Click had also written to Mr Meredith, the CME of the GNR. (Richard W. Meredith came to the GNR(I) from the GSWR having been working with Maunsell at Inchicore. He was appointed GNR(I) Works Manager at the start of 1926. He was especially interested in diesel engines, developing railbuses and railcars, patenting the Howden-Meredith steel and pneumatic railbus tyre. He became CME of the GNR(I) on 1 January 1951 and retired in Spring of 1957.) Meredith generously responded with footplate passes for the GNR. Click also wrote in advance to CIE who were similarly generous with the opportunity for a works visit and a similar footplate trip. In consequence of what happened later it is very possible Bulleid may even have been the one to 'pull the necessary strings' probably remembering the name of his former pupil.

Click again takes up the story, 'At midday (during his August 1954 sojourn) I was back in the Inchicore Offices and, nothing ventured nothing gained, asked if it was possible to see the CME. "Ah no, he's abroad; but would you like to see the Chief Draughtsman for a minute?"'

A few years earlier Bulleid had been commuting between Brighton and Inchicore both to oversee Leader at the former location and to commence his work with CIE. By 1954 of course visits away from Ireland would not have been connected with British Railways. Interesting too is Bulleid's comment when he finally left BR, as he thanked the Railway Executive for letting him get so much useful data 'for future work' – and now of course we know what that was intended to be!

Back at Inchicore and JGC, 'Paddy Mulvany was genial, but couldn't tell me, "…anyt'ing about the Turf Burner, f'r its a national secret, y'understand". I did; but then played my trump card. I had taken with me a copy of a 7mm drawing of the Leader and produced it now. "T'at's a fine drawing" said he, "did you do it … you did, can I have it?" After studying it, he beckoned outside, "Woodjou bring me t'at diagram of the turf borner for a minute!" He kept it upside down tantalisingly, but that was no real problem for we at Rugby had got used to reading that way up. It was one of the only two methods there of finding anything out! I thanked Mr. Mulvany, went into town and spent the next two hours sketching all that I'd seen - both ways up.'

A few days later Click wrote a 'thank you' letter – to Mulvany perhaps? – but concluding with '… "if there is ever an opportunity of doing original work under you, I would seriously consider dragging my English anchors." I hadn't the slightest idea that might either be possible, or practicable.

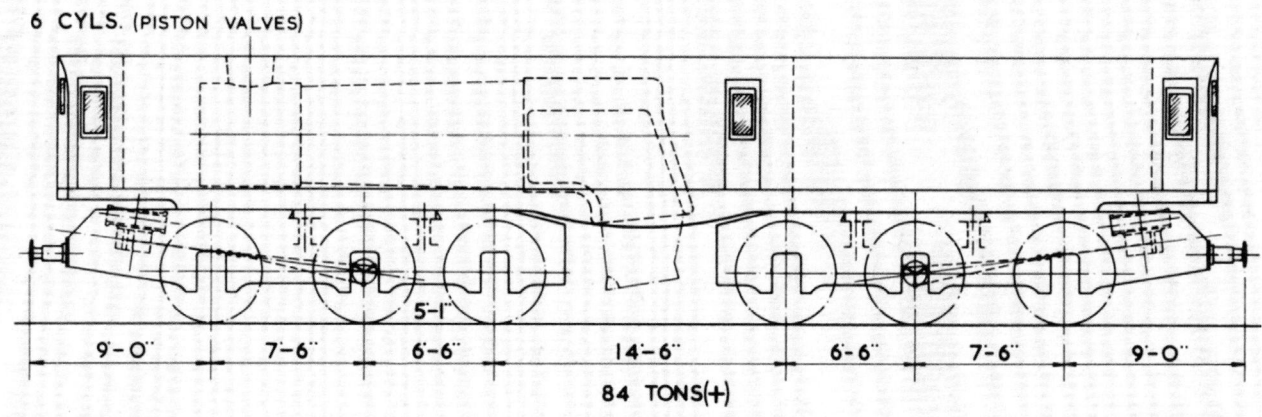

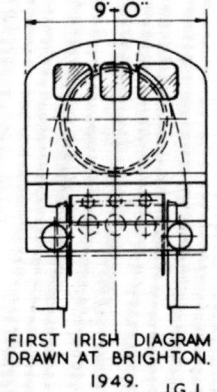

FIRST IRISH DIAGRAM DRAWN AT BRIGHTON. 1949. J.G.J.

First thoughts on a turf-burning locomotive prepared at Brighton (by whom?) in 1949. The visual similarity with Leader is immediately apparent although it will the noted the boiler is placed centrally. A multi-cylinder engine but now with piston valves and larger wheels but still with three cabs – was the fireman's cab now accessible from both sides? The weight shown with the ' + ' sign is interesting, the two ends being unequal; that at the front fixed with the boiler etc, whilst at the rear, fuel and water would change the numbers.

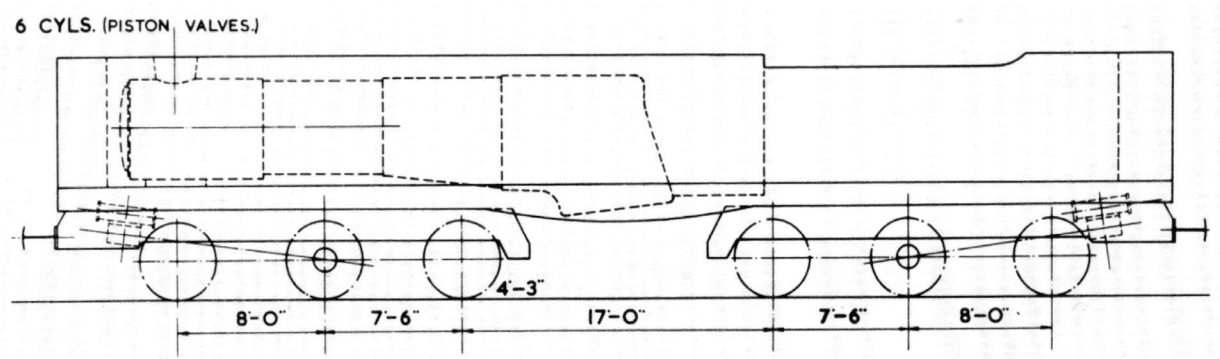

COMPARATIVE NOTES ON THIS DIAGRAM WERE:-

IRISH.		LEADER.
84	TOTAL WGT. TONS	114
14	AXLE-WEIGHT	19
6	COAL. TONS	4
5000	WATER. GALS.	4000

SECOND IRISH DIAGRAM DRAWN AT BRIGHTON. 1949. J.G.J.

A second Brighton drawing and this time with some useful comparative weights. The two end cabs are also of more uniform size. Smaller wheels are also shown. Again we are not told who the original draughtsman was.

The letter went off and I gave it no more thought but on the Friday, I was putting on my overalls before footplating home from Rugby to Euston on the 4.57pm up, ex Llandudno, when I was unexpectedly wanted on the phone. "Is thut you John?" came a familiar voice, "If you want thut job in Dublin yer to apply for it!" OVB must have rung C.S. Cocks in Derby at once. I had that rare feeling of being needed: walking on air, but what to do?'

In John Click's draft what follows next is a slightly strange recollection which is also certainly out of date. 'At Inchicore I was given a guide and I asked him to show me the Turf Burner. "Ah no", he said, "I mustn't show you t'at", but adding that he truly didn't know where it was. Eventually right at the far end of the works I thought I'd found it – there was an expanse of dirty grey dimly seen through two lines of carriage windows... Yes! "Now", I said hopefully, "If you stay here and I walk round the end of that coach you won't have shown me it will you?" "Oh, I will not," he agreed. As luck had it there was a coach alongside from which a good general view looked possible; so hoisting myself up over its buffers and in through the open corridor end I crept on all fours towards my chosen, and fortunately open, corridor window. As I slowly rose, I knew I was being watched, in that very compartment were four men frozen as if in a waxworks – playing cards! After a few seconds we all burst out laughing with relief: "deuce" certainly, or at least a draw.' We know Click was present at Inchicore during the tests with burning peat and then later on with Turf Burner engine. We believe he also returned to the UK in 1958 so this is likely to have been a subsequent visit, possibly even when the engine had been set aside.

However, and returning to 1954, Click did indeed take up the job in Ireland. 'Next summer (1955), I persuaded A. Ronald (Ron) Pocklington (who had come to us at Rugby direct from Vulcan Foundry) to come to Dublin with me. He was very interested in everything Bulleid was doing and had by then got to know No. 35022 at the Test Plant and had also ridden to Dover and back with me on No. 35028 working the 'Golden Arrow'. His was a more academic approach to a problem; whereas mine was more practical, so we tended to complement each other. On 'Clan Line' ARP took it all in good part until we crashed across the diamonds and plunged, rolling, through Sevenoaks, past the last electrified sidings and into the long tunnel. Diving in at 65 we accelerated steadily in total darkness until very near the end a spot of light. Initially, purple, then brown – getting larger – yellow and suddenly out into brilliant daylight – racing downhill at 85mph! It was a good baptism. Nothing subsequent did anything to diminish his admiration for the locomotive or its designer.' What Click and Pocklington's official job titles were is not reported, suffice to say they were both 'Assistants' to Bulleid (assuming this to be correct it is something of a coincidence that this was exactly the same term as had been applied relative to Bulleid and Gresley). The two were not as has been reported previously, 'seconded from BR' which in itself could have led to all sorts of suggestions relative to Bulleid's then current work.

Click himself speaks of his own first experiences in fond terms, 'Ireland as a whole was a wonderful retreat for the

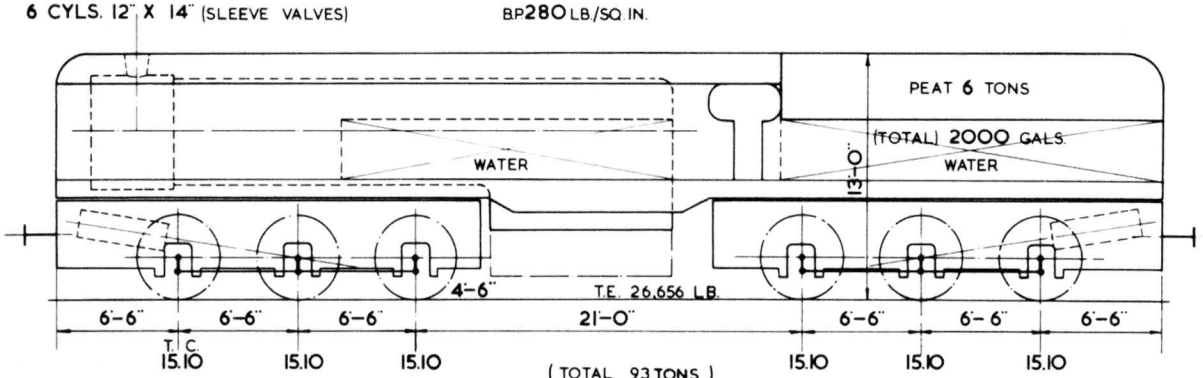

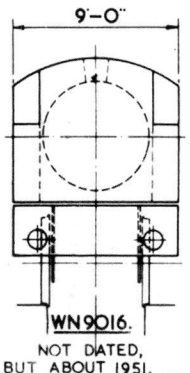

This time from 1951 and with a central cab. The very point made earlier about unbalanced weight between the two ends was of concern to the Inchicore drawing office who pushed for a symmetrical arrangement at both ends. Perhaps the lessons of 'Leader' were of concern?

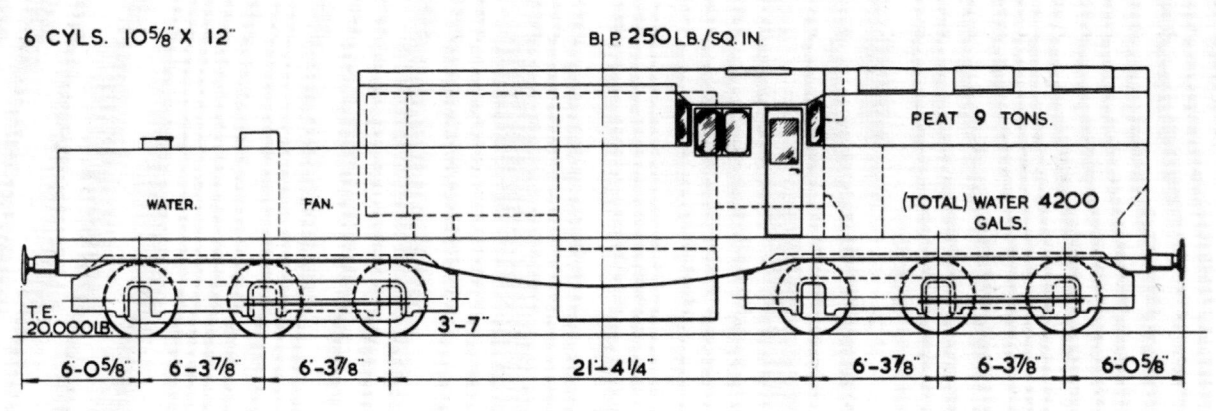

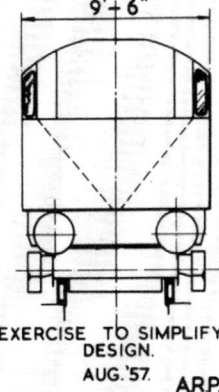

An idea that came too late was almost as per the Garratt arrangement, splitting the water tanks between the two ends and having the boiler amidships. This one was drawn by Ron Pocklington in 1957.

lover of the old and the quaint, but it was no way to run the various railways. Many locomotive engineers who later became more famous on this side of the water started in Ireland. Too many of their engines were still there in the fifties, though going fast. Bulleid's father-in-law's dinky little 2-4-2 tank actually hauled his Turf Burner out of the erecting shop. She regularly worked 'The Cab' (we later learn this to have been the nickname a 6-wheel coach) down to Kingsbridge station taking Inchicore staff to lunch there – that is until a shunter let two coaches down on to the six-wheeler, drove it up on to her buffer beam and wrote it off.' Without further reference (and in a caption for a photograph he clearly intended to send to us – the photograph has not been located) he speaks of other engines he observed from the period as well, 'This Aspinall 4-4-0 was standing in for No. 42 which must have been having a washout that day. The "Cab" is about to leave tender first and will return after lunch with the engine propelling the six-wheeler ahead of her. A number of these charming museum pieces were still doing quite important work when I left in 1958 and all had been superheated many years before, but I never saw Bulleid register the slightest interest in any of them … then there was this small Midland 2-4-0 designed by Attock which had worked the Boat Train from Westland Row in 1956. The volute springs on the leading axle are very unusual … more recently, and still very competent, were some of the Maunsell "moguls" adapted to the 5ft 3in gauge from sets of parts bought very cheaply from Woolwich after WWI … Watson, who produced some four-cylinder 4-6-0s based on Churchward's design seems to have made one or two

cardinal errors. He either believed all Swindon geese were swans or couldn't cope very well, or both come to that! All had been drastically rebuilt to two-cylinder engines, nearly all different; and two, though I missed seeing them at work, had Caprotti valve gear which Matt Devereux said had made them into very good engines indeed … I was up there looking for parts to cannibalise for the Turf Burner: such as ejectors and snifting valves – and I did find what I wanted!'

Some years before this and to test the idea of burning peat (dried peat had been used for centuries as a domestic fuel in Scandinavia, Scotland and Ireland) Bulleid had a stationary test rig erected within Inchicore works. This included an electric motor driving a large fan arranged to force draught to a spare boiler from a 101 class locomotive, which was mechanically stoked from an outsize bunker behind the rig. To simulate the subsequent Crosti-type feed heater a second, smaller boiler was installed facing the other way with both sharing a common smokebox. The combined chimney emerged from the firehole on this front boiler. The boiler was manually fed with sods of peat, 'by about six firemen … and the safety valve kept lifting.' (Perhaps even the same labourers from the earlier power station experiment!) Upon seeing it Click commented, 'It was difficult: no; let's face it, impossible not to laugh, but there it was! Think, though. This rig was a "lash-up", but designed by a bold man, unafraid of ridicule and ready to do new research work into a problem.'

Possibly even preceding this workshop test rig, the Chief Chemist had conducted his own experiments by stuffing smouldering turf up an old boiler tube and then blowing it with compressed air. He had got, transitorily,

The Leader Locomotive

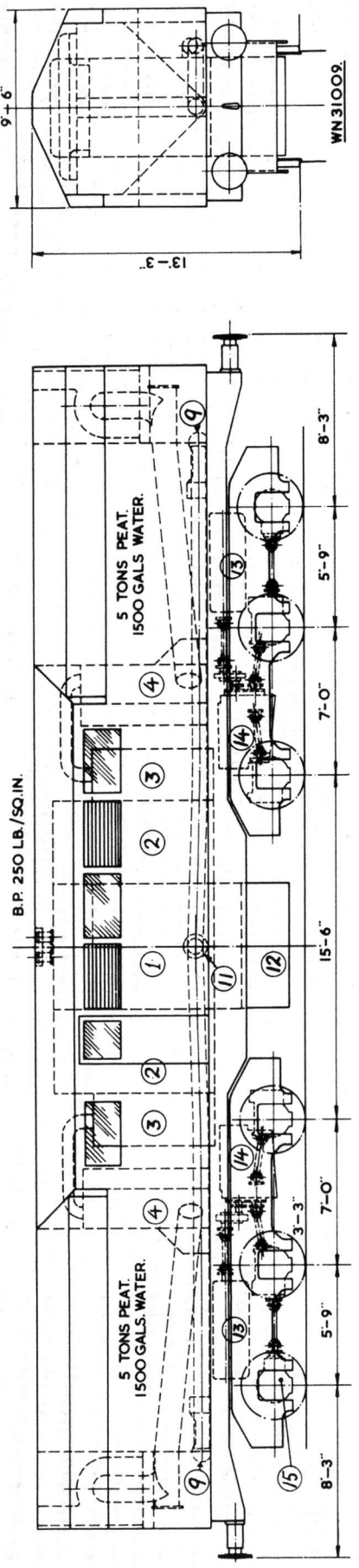
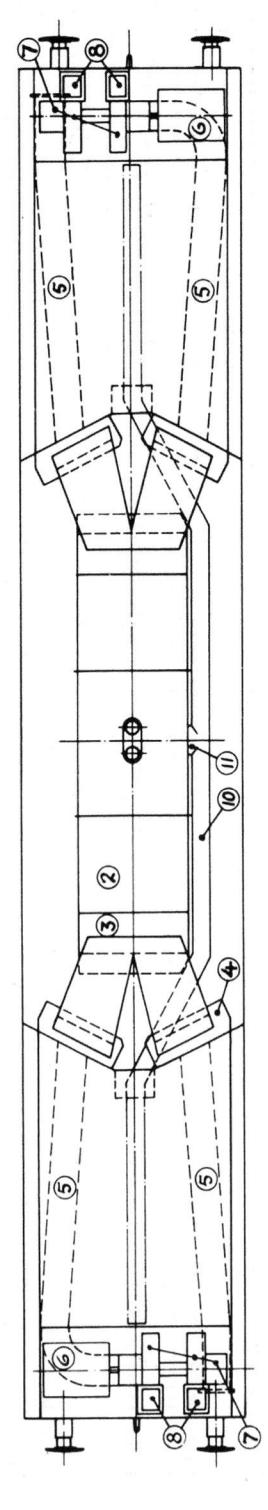

Almost there but with a Ricardo flat engine on the main frame and Mekydro drive to all axles. This design dates from 1954 at which time the Ricardo drive was abandoned, although we are not told why. Key:

1 Firebox section of boiler
2 Barrel sections
3 Smokeboxes
4 Feed water heater banks
5 Gas ducts to fans
6 Steam turbine driving fans
7 Inductions fans
8 Exhaust gas exits
9 Mechanical stokers
10 Turf conduits
11 Firing point (later changed to two points on the locomotive centreline, fore and aft of and just above the grate carrier)
12 Grate carrier and ashpan
13 6-cylinder flat Ricardo poppet valve engine mounted on main frame
14 Mekydro transmission gearbox, (as on Maybach diesel shunters)
15 Mekydro final drive units

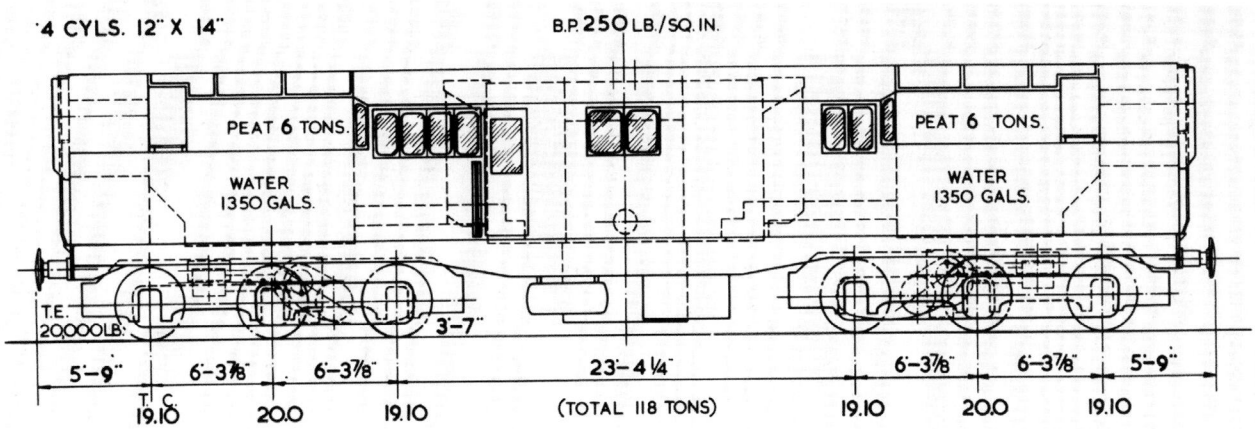
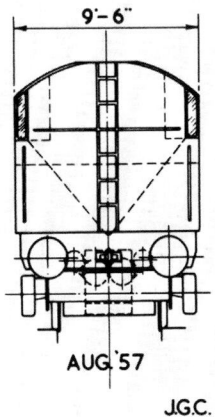

The final Turf Burner, the only obvious external change that came later was the addition of smoke deflectors. According to the 'HAV' book: 'When R.C. Bond saw the boiler design and was too surprised to say anything, Bulleid remarked, "I know what you are thinking, this could only be the work of the late Heath Robinson"'. Why did Bulleid go to Ireland? Many of the reasons are already explained but there is another explanation put forward by Click. 'as his "Leader" ran into more and more trouble OVB found himself fighting a losing battle from which he eventually had little option but to withdraw.' *(In this last sentence we have at last confirmation from a 'man in the know' of exactly the opinion several writers have come to in the past but without having the benefit of JGC's knowledge or experience. The present writer raised this very question with Click, 'Do you think "Leader" was dragging Bulleid down with it?', I was lambasted by Click for even asking it. At the time, and still now, I have not changed my intentions, wanting to try and 'explain' the man and why he behaved as he did; not to condemn him.)*

very high temperatures. Even so the risk was that at such high temperatures peat ash could form clinker and which explains the same question raised by Bulleid later. One thing Click does add is that even at the time of his visit(s) and subsequent employment, there was a distinct paucity of records as to what tests had been undertaken (presumably with peat?) and the results thereof.

Having satisfied himself the principles were sound, Bulleid as on the Southern, looked around for a guinea pig engine on which to try out his ideas. Chosen was a former Great Southern & Western Railway K3 class 2-6-0 No. 356 as a test bed. The modifications made included a new firebox fitted with tuyeres (these are orifices through which air is blown into the firebox to aid combustion), two Crosti pre-heaters either side of the boiler, which took heat from the exhaust to pre-heat the feed water, plus further pre-heating coils in the tender water tank. With the exhaust thus routed back along the engine and through the tender water it is not surprising to report the actual chimney was on the rear of the tender. Turf was fed into the firebox by means of an Archimedean screw although short of switching the screw off, the amount fed was difficult if not impossible to regulate. A Leyland internal combustion (from a bus) was also mounted on a small four-wheel wagon 'permanently' attached to the rear of the tender, this was used to drive the fan that created draft for the tuyeres as the firebox was otherwise sealed. (Recall also the comment from Paddy Mulvany at the time of his Brighton visit reference the chimney on the rear of the tender, 'By George, t'ats the very forst t'ing he wanted when he got here as well' – and which of course referred to No. 356.)

We have no definite date, but we do know No. 356 was working sometime in 1952. Click adds his own comments about his first experience of No. 356 probably during his 1954 visit and before he took up his formal appointment in Dublin, for he adds Bulleid 'cannily' said, "Well Click, if you can wait until tomorrow you can go out on the experimental locomotive." I instantly decided, "Yes, please". Finding a way of "explaining" why I'd not be back at Rugby next morning was a formality.

I was taken up to No. 356 which from the look of it hadn't turned a wheel for many months. The foreman had been told to prepare it for its run next day. 'Sh'yer can't go out on t'at t'ink; – it's a heap of scrap,' he said – altogether accurately! I had a good look round it, and had my doubts whether they'd ever get steam in it again. All the plates of the left-hand truck spring were broken (this was the truck carrying the bus engine) and I remember thinking if there's going to be a derailment it will only be at low speed in the yard. If we made it to the main line it would run.

Working pressure was reached before I joined the locomotive. No. 356 had been spruced up a bit, and sported what in the UK would be express headlamps and had a willing crew aboard expectantly wondering,

No. 1 engine being lowered into No. 2 bogie. This type of removable engine 'power-unit' was what Bulleid has wished for (too late as it turned out) for Leader. Had Bulleid (CIE) been able to purchase the Leader engines from the UK we can only speculate on what use they might have been and indeed in what form them they might have been used, experimentation leading to a new design perhaps? But sometimes modifying an existing build can even be more difficult than starting from scratch. The usual BFB wheels will be noted. *R.A. Pocklington*

As with Leader some time earlier, a completed bogie was placed on blocks and steam supplied from an external source for a test – it worked perfectly. The second bogie stands behind. *R.A. Pocklington*

Again akin to Leader, the bogies were pivotless, the body sitting on pads as seen here. As with Leader, the arrangement worked perfectly. *R.A. Pocklington*

as I was, what would happen next. I climbed up, got a welcome, had a look at the fire first, watched as the stoker was operated and got an impression of how turf behaved.

Draught, provided by the bus engine driven induction fan on the wagon behind the huge tender, was 'controlled' by a wire that disappeared over a pulley on the tender front and somehow reached its accelerator. This additional bus engine had become necessary as on the first trials, possibly when the engine had failed to achieve a successful round trip between Dublin and Cork (evidently the 'standard' test for a new engine), it was evident that forced draught was not on; and the original little steam turbines, notoriously uneconomical at part load, also gobbled up precious steam. The bus driven fan meant that forced (blown) draught gave way to induced, or sucking draught. Leaks henceforward would be into rather than out of the system. Space constraints though meant there was nothing for it but to mount the new arrangements on the separate wagon hitched behind the tender – even so, something else for the critics to jibe about.

The firing was very much an all or nothing affair. When the fireman wanted more steam he turned on the 'worum' (the stoker screw) and pulled the chain (which really was from some unfortunate loo) whereupon the bus engine went ' vrooOOM' taking a lot of the fire through the tubes, the smokebox, the bank of feed heaters, the labyrinth of ducks over the cab and through the tender, out of its back, into more flexible joints, through the fan and out of its 'chimney' in a gigantic plume of what would have called 'Golden rain'; but all before there was time to say 'turf smoke'.

It wanted gentle handling so I asked if I could have a go. Soon with the bus engine ticking over quite slowly and the stoker delivering a steady amount of turf she began to make steam quickly, and blew off keeping the safety valve up against the injector for a while. We were still by the Erecting Shop but it looked quite promising. We rumbled off with the exhaust beat getting lost somewhere in the tender but it didn't matter anyway – because steam production was by fan – totally divorced from the way the locomotive was worked. It was, not very surprisingly, possible to lose the fire in a trice or to smother it with too much new turf: after all we were dealing with a fuel with less than half the calorific value of an average coal and a quarter by weight of what went in was water, tending to put the fire out. Imagine it: for every ten pounds of 'air dried' turf that went on there were also two pints of water! Fly ash was a problem: it floated away prettily, and possibly harmlessly, still ignited. The danger was the larger, smouldering lumps, and what about clinker?

On the way up the bank to Clondalkin I began to get the hang of it – watching the fire and with the exhaust colour just the same as at Rugby – though everything happened faster. The quality of the fire bed changed very quickly, it was a full time and very demanding Job. The speed was only low but we held the water level quite easily. When we arrived everyone was pleased: 'Ah, you had hor steaming grand,' said one, 'we could've gone to Cork, sure we could'. It would certainly have been nice to have gone on a bit further; I was just getting the feel of it.

We dropped back down to Inchicore in the dark and what a sight it must have made from the lineside; fan wagon and tender first! Enough to make any Ballyfermot man who was 'after having taken a few' sign the pledge.

Just a touch of bus engine and a little turf every minute or so and we were enveloped in the beautiful scent of properly burned turf; delicate turf sparks floating by and me feeling here's a job I could tackle and get my teeth into. No. 356 never did venture out on to the main line again, it didn't need to, testing could and should be done standing still.

Back in OVB's office he wanted to know what I thought. I said that seeing the problem had made me far more certain that it could be solved, but that a much larger grate area would be needed.

But what 'problem' was this that Click was referring to as there is nothing in Click's notes. A reasonable assumption was that Bulleid had asked for Click's view as to whether peat was a suitable fuel, or something similar. To be fair Bulleid probably knew the answer himself but may well have been 'testing out the man'.

Whatever the case may have been, Clink continues: '"Was there any clinker problem?" he asked. My emphatic "No, none at all" was said in a way that must have made him consider as he added seemingly thinking out loud, "… so no sulphur either…". I made the point about there being no need to risk main line failure and he agreed, but said that "politically" it had to be seen to run. I remembered No. 32039's misfortune at Earlswood and fully understood.

'At that time No. 356 had Crosti type pre-heaters on both sides and draught was already supplied by the bus engine driven fan on a wagon behind. It had previously made one fateful trip to Cork but failed on the way back I

Possible a Saturday afternoon at Inchlicore as John Click comments this view was taken with the collusion of Ron Pocklington. 'One Saturday afternoon, when we had the shop to ourselves and it was really quiet, we put the loco onto her bogies. Billy Burnell had made an excellent job of a general arrangement drawing where, working strictly to figures, he had worked through this job on paper. She went down first time, and the close clearances underneath came out exactly as planned … Ronald Pocklington whose solutions to knotty problems such as the smokebox superheater, the main steampipes and the parking brake were valuable contributions to the overall success that was achieved.' *R.A. Pocklington*

The fuel used: peat; we are not told where supplies were obtained from or if it was in fact dried before being loaded into the bunkers. As to why peat was used may be traced back to WWII if not before. During WWII neutral Ireland had been starved of coal supplies, and what services did run, burned peat (turf to an Irishman) even though the locomotives themselves had been designed to burn good steam coal. Consequently the engines were immediately handicapped and didn't steam well or for long, as well as throwing out amounts of partly burnt turf. No special arrangements were possible other than to double and even triple head trains and to make frequent stops to regain steam or to take on yet more of this indigenous and plentiful yet wholly unsuitable fuel. It was railed to strategic points in modified, and otherwise scrap, six wheeled coaches known as creels. The emergency was hardly over before coal supplies were again interrupted by the 1947 crisis. Oil firing was then resorted to and was successful but it did add to the large backlog of boiler repairs deferred from the war because of material shortages then. A programme of buying in spare boilers, mainly for the more recent classes, was frowned on as being unlikely to be commercially effective. Instead, a five-year plan was proposed during which ten new steam engines would be built annually 'at Inchicore or elsewhere' supplemented by a further ten 'reconstructions', presumably from the better and younger classes. Eighty-nine of the 'odds and ends', so beloved of English photographers, were recommended for early scrapping. The 'museum' would soon not be quite no more but certainly a good deal less – or something like that.
R.A. Pocklington

Again, replicating Leader, the final drive was by chain and once more to alternating axles. The lower cover to the chain drive has yet to be added. *R.A. Pocklington*

Driving cab of the Turf Buner. Not quite the perfect view ahead for the driver; the need to have a more equal weight distribution had put paid to that, but no worse than many contemporary steam designs of later years anywhere in the world that were fitted with large boilers. *R.A. Pocklington*

was later told, and then seemed to have been dumped. OVB had copied the best (of what was new) it seemed but, in any case Crosti had not put in for an Irish Patent. He actually turned up at Inchicore on one occasion, Matt Devereux told me in 1986, and was seen by Johnny Johnston but got no joy. Quite what made Bulleid change the heaters is not clear, although possibly it was suggested by Ricardo at Shoreham (Bulleid had obviously maintained this relationship after he had left England.) By next summer (when I went over again) large panniers containing banks of finned aluminium heaters had been substituted. These were developed, it transpired later, from miniature cast aluminium alloy boilers designed by Riccardo for supplying small steam engines for use in what would now call "developing countries".'

Click continues on the subject of No. 356. 'A bus engine was all very well on the guinea-pig but the "prototype" had to have turbines and when I arrived at Dublin early in 1956, they had not only been ordered but soon arrived."

Referring now to both himself and Pocklington, 'nothing was more important than for us than to get some actual experience of "the turf" for ourselves; so accordingly No. 356 got altered yet again. For a week, and until the turf feed screw broke up, we did a series of useful tests which gave us the only data we had on what went on. The only thing we couldn't do was to use the superheater. What steam we did make and that wasn't used by the auxiliaries went out of the safety valves: it represented all that was left for traction and didn't look much. Even so, testing was very labour-intensive, but invaluable.'

Meanwhile what would later be designated 'CC1' was slowly taking shape in the workshops at Inchicore. Click had arrived after the principal design had been agreed and which, like Leader, consisted of a double bogie (six wheels/three axles per bogie) steam engine having a central boiler with a cab on either end of the boiler after which came a large turf hopper. The idea being that the crew would be able to have a reasonable view of the track ahead by looking either side of the turf bunker. The cabs were not connected but the driver and fireman would always be together. In order to maximise the heating surface the boiler and firebox was also almost rectangular even if this was a constant source of concern to some of VIP visitors who later saw and indeed travelled on the engine. (Appertaining to this topic, Click comments, 'The boiler for the Turf Burner, by its extraordinary design, frightened everybody; it was only a question of degree: everyone, that is, except OVB himself! When Cocks came over and rode with us, he told me, "They've all been invited, but they're afraid of the boiler so they've sent me!" When I first saw the boiler it had previously been fired, we were told, by, "sods of turf using pitchforks" with ring blowers in the chimneys at each end producing draught. The water level was said to have fluctuated wildly whenever its safety valve blew, a fact we verified two years later and cured by adding to the number of U-tubes connecting the central firebox to the two cuboid "barrels". Subsequent theoretical calculations by A. Ron Pocklington estimated a steaming rate of 20,000lb/hr.'

Click's own notes now add a totally new twist to the design and which shows that yet again Bulleid was not content with the design as it stood, for he comments, 'Shortly afterwards Paddy Mulvany disclosed that "Mr Bulleid is not after making up his mind about superheating"; and, later again, OVB himself told me he was looking for "plenty of wet steam so I can use the Anderson/Holcroft compression condensing system." Even if that system had ever worked as claimed (and remember it was tried on "N" class 2-6-0 No. A816, later 31816) there was a serious fallacy in his argument, simply because the amount of heat in the exhaust (with saturated steam) would be more in total due to the far higher steam consumption. In other words the classic reasons for superheating remained unchanged. By then, that meant radiant heating coils in the firebox which seemed "out" (because of the desire to put an oil fire in later on) or to do the best we could with a "superheater" (even if it might not be much better than a "steam dryer") in the smokebox. That we did, but not before being sent over to London to hear what Holcroft had to say. I'm afraid we found him very unconvincing.'

This is one of the few times oil is mentioned as fuel for CC1 but it is not clear if this meant heavy bunker type fuel or conventional diesel – but probably the former. Just to show CC1 was also only a stage along the road of development, the cylinder design that was actually installed was not, according to Click, what Bulleid had originally envisaged. Instead, 'he hankered for a three cylinder one (still) with sleeve valves and we would have "had a go" if time had been open-ended. It is also just possible that the loco might have had five cylinders!' Click does not elaborate further on this almost mind-numbing suggestion and we are left to speculate on what if anything Bulleid had in fact learnt from his experience with Nos 2039 and 36001. Without wishing to be personally rude, it appears to have been 'not a lot'. (The present writer when *attempting* to discuss both Leader and Turf Burner with John Click many years ago showed Mr Click a sketch – since lost – of a double-acting cylinder having a central con-rod driven by two horizontally opposed pistons, in appearance similar to that of a Westinghouse air pump. The question asked was, 'did this relate to the Turf Burner or Leader?' and by inference the answer was the Turf Burner, with the additional rider, 'we discounted that as unworkable very early on.' Sadly also one of the very few occasions John Click was willing to provide a practical comment.

Within the Inchicore workshops, history would again repeat itself as a finished bogie complete with its installed steam engine was run in in the Erecting Shop with steam supplied from an Aspinall 4-4-0 outside. It only needed about 5psi to be kept happily ticking over. Corrugated steam-pipes of the Alton type were fitted and which flexed to allow for bogie movement. This was a repeat of their successful use on No. 36001. The exhaust from both bogies was also combined. The actual engine complete with cylinders was removable, the idea being to substitute a fresh engine at an intermediate repair. The cost of a small number of spares would have been economically justified had a fleet of fifty been built, as was indeed the original intention. As to how and when this figure was arrived at, and equally when it was cancelled, is not reported.

Click again: 'Because the Turf Burner was fan-draughted, the exhaust steam did nothing – a fact that OVB continually

On test at Portarlington. Click is of the opinion that there were forces at work on CIE that must have viewed Bulleid's experimentation with not a little reserve. Was it coincidence that Click arrived just at the time No. 356 was due to make its second main line run? Probably yes, but from the theme of Click's comments it might almost appear Bulleid could have had some difficulty persuading CIE to build the bogie Turf Burner had this second trial also failed. He was probably under political pressure to prove his idea was feasible; he might even have been trying to convince himself at the same time. Even so the whole episode seems to have been almost a simple main line run with no apparent formal testing having taken place. *R.A. Pocklington*

More testing this time at the Dublin end of Portarlington, the painted end number CC1 shows up well. In the background are McMahon's Mills, which were rail connected. Click adds an amusing comment about the quiet running of the engine. 'Mick Keeley was asked to whistle at every telegraph pole so I could judge if the Britannia whistle could be heard clearly. As we rather thought it couldn't until the loco was very close, we substituted a CIE "screecher". At a time when linemen had got used to first hearing an A class diesel when still several miles off, the Turf Burner was very quiet and was a distinct hazard to the men on the line'.
R.A. Pocklington

complained about; he wanted its heat used, and he was quite right. His favourite ideas were using the Holcroft/Anderson (Click refers to it as Anderson/Holcroft) compression condensing system and/or drying the peat itself. Unfortunately all the available time (and space) were taken up making the loco go. Other worthy aims had to take second place, but we compromised by making it possible to turn some exhaust back into the tanks until the water got too hot for the Worthington feed pumps to deal with.'

All of the earlier trials were had been leading up to the building of the main locomotive, later numbered 'CC1' – once again Bulleid's numbering scheme was to the fore. No name was ever carried.).

When CC1 was finally completed in 1957 – the same year its predecessor No. 357 would be scrapped – Click had the rare privilege of being the first to move the engine in steam. Decades later we can only imagine the pride he must have felt, as in his own words, 'At last the day came to move the Turf Burner for the first time. To a bystander there I am sure my efforts would have looked very much as Granshaw's had to me on No. 36001 at Brighton. Bulleid had arrived much too early, waited a while and then told me to be sure and phone for him before I moved. I hadn't phoned but he drove up again later and then must have stayed. I cannot think now, as the only person there who had seen what had been done (and not done) at Brighton, why I didn't get a "buddy" loco over to act as a helper, or at least to be an

Modern engine, slightly less than modern rolling stock. *R.A. Pocklington*

anchor. She wouldn't go either way for some time. One wheel was in a very low rail joint but she wasn't in full gear either due to a part of the steam reverser having been removed and put back upside-down. Once this was put right, she did move … I had rehearsed this moment for months; in most of my dreams it had been easier!'

After this Click talks of a variety of experiences running with the engine on the main line, such as, 'To make sure what was going on underneath I had a seat welded on to the bogie and rode eleven miles on it. I told the driver it was deuced uncomfortable and I didn't want to be down there long. Michael Keely took me at my word and

Modern locomotive and this time modern rolling stock, the train is in the up side loops at Sallins. *R.A. Pocklington*

Dublin (we think, although Limerick has also been suggested) empty coaching stock and, as with the similar-looking trial with No. 36001 from Brighton, what might have been. *R.A. Pocklington*

reached a steady 60mph. It was enthralling to see the miniature valve gear (NOT this time in an oil bath) though the crankshaft was whizzing round at some nine rev a second and to feel the fan effect of the wheels. Back at Inchicore I had the seat burnt off, but OVB was very disappointed – he wanted a go too, and I believe he would have.

'Another occasion was when R.C. Bond and Bulleid's brother-in-law H.G. (George) Ivatt came over and rode on the Turf Burner; we got delayed at Clondalkin. Mr Bulleid travelled with us a number of times, once got up in a very French beret and wearing a white coat with gloves. (On another occasion M. Louis Armand, General Manager of the French railway system was also an interested observer. M. Armand had been inventor of the TIA '*Traitement Integral Armand*' water treatment system.) I tried several times to get him to drive but without success. But he chatted all the while; about the smooth ride, the hotness of the peat fire, and "Look at the interest those cattle are taking in us – they always recognised anything new!"'

Click also mentions another footplate observer, Cyril Fry, famed for his 'O' gauge Irish International Railway and Tramway System. Fry knew CIE's Chairman well and, through him, eventually got drawings out of OVB and had a model running – he even contrived to get an authentic turf smell from it. He added, 'Cyril and I both lived in Churchtown and I had the pleasure of seeing his railway several times; but, though I tried hard to get OVB to pay a visit he always said, "Oh no, if I went up I'd have the whole works making models, and that wouldn't do at all."'

By 1958 it must have been obvious there was to be no duplication of the design, but this did not stop interest from overseas, such as when in that year there was a visitation from the Birmingham Railway Carriage and Wagon Co. They had been invited over to look at the way the drive from the crank was coupled to the three axles by chains, superb even torque of course – but again this was as per its predecessor No. 36001. (No failed crank-axles on CC1 either.) In the same year CC1 was painted green and had a second set of smoke deflectors added '… eau-de-nil sash and a yellow warning pattern to OVB's own sketch,' according to Click.

Click had also now returned to full-time work with British Railways at Rugby by now, but was a visitor again later and shortly after the Institution of Locomotive Engineers' Summer Meeting in Dublin for which OVB had tried without success to get him back. Click adds – we may imagine perhaps wistfully – 'The "urgency of work" at the Testing Station had ruled that out.' It seems also that on the morning the Institution Members were to pay their visit, OVB had only managed to get No. CC1 into steam at the last minute – nobody had lit her up. So, late on he got her round to the head of the exhibits where, being last, she thus became first! This was an advantage because no shunting had to be done to get her out; hence after OVB had taken E.S. Cox to Clondalkin (10 miles from Dublin) and back everybody wanted to do the same, and many did: 'they are all steam men at heart,' OVB wrote. All marvelled, although whether that was wholly true or not, at Bulleid's persistence in getting authority for an

John Click at the controls of CC1. A final quote from him may also be appropriate here: 'CC1 the first steam locomotive in the world designed solely to burn peat – and also the last.'

View from the opposite side of the cab. *R.A. Pocklington*

even more innovative design than the 'Leader' to present to them for their delight. CC1 stole the show; but what followed? For John Click it was one last drive to Sallins, then *'finis'*: 'I had made the first move and also the last. She was quietly cut up in 1965.' Perhaps the VIP visitors were not really marvelling at the engineering prowess of the design but were instead seeing what was almost a fairground attraction.

That Summer 1958 ILE visit was also the swansong for CC1. All day long it had moved up and down up and down to Clondalkin giving footplate rides to VIPs. It had proved that peat could after all be used as a locomotive fuel. The order for fifty examples, for which a million punts had been kept in CIEs budget for some years, was gently forgotten.

What we should also remember is that CC1, just like No. 36001, never entered revenue-earning service. But unlike the Leader it never had to be hauled home, not even after a minor collision (Click does not afford any details of this) and this despite the jaunty angle of the buffers. It also never caused a minute's delay to other traffic and established a good reputation for speed out on the Dublin–Cork main line *and* it could even be said to have earned a small amount of revenue for the CIE; as on the occasion when it ventured to Kildare on a test run (36 miles) – one of the regular trial destinations. On this particular day the Station Master came and asked whether, 'as a great favour', the engine could move some wagons through the station for him; CC1 obliged. This was one of the few 'revenue-earning' tasks the locomotive ever did although folklore has it the engine was also used to make a few trips from Inchicore to North Wall on transfer freights. Smoke deflectors were added later, as was dazzle paint on both ends.

Notes

(1) *Locomotives of the Great Southern Railway*, p.320.

APPENDIX 1
G. Freeman Allen: *The Southern Since 1948*

Bulleid was the last British engineer to try and break the Stephenson mould of steam locomotive design. The genesis of his final, defiantly iconoclastic concept for the Southern was the railway's immediate post-war requirement of more large-sized tank engines to improve the working on its busiest branches.

In this context Bulleid's first proposal, submitted for the SR's 1946 building programme, was for twenty-five additional Class Q1 0-6-0s, for which previously-ordered material was still on hand; but that was resisted by the operators on grounds of inadequate lookout range for the crew when a Q1 was running tender-first. So Eastleigh busied itself drafting tank versions of the Q', ranging from an 0-6-4 through a 2-6-2 and 2-6-4 to a 4-6-4, all with 5ft 1in driving wheels: and all as deliberately innocent of the traditional grace notes of British locomotives outlines as the Q1. Bulleid himself, however, was set on a double power-unit locomotive, a concept which he had been nurturing since the end of the war.

The first drawing-board variation on that theme was a grotesque-looking 0-6-6-0T, in which a Bulleid Pacific-like shroud encased a Pacific boiler pressurised to 350lb/^{2}in that fed two three-cylinder 'engines'. Each axle was to be separately powered by its own 11in by 10in cylinder and valve gear; the cylinders of the leading 'engine' were mounted to the fore of the axles, those of the rear 'engine' in the reverse direction. The cab at least was in the conventional place, but by the end of 1945 Eastleigh had adopted a double-cabbed layout in one of the fresh 4-6-4T sketches which followed dismissal of the 0-6-6-0T proposal as impracticable.

Somehow Bulleid managed to parry reminders that the new design was supposed to be incorporated in the 1946 Building Programme and to pursue at his own pace his determined study of a double power-unit. By the spring of 1946 he had completed the outline of an 0-6-6-0 which, he submitted to the General Manager, would satisfy the Civil Engineer and, so far as the operators were concerned, would be the freight-hauling peer of a Q1 and a 'West Country' Pacific's equal in passenger trains, capable of up to 90mph despite wheels of only 4ft 3in diameter (later enlarged to 5ft 1in). Each six-coupled unit would be three-cylinder, with all cylinders driving with a very short stroke onto the middle axle, whence power would be transmitted to the other two by a chain system. The front engine would exhaust normally, but the rear engine's exhaust would be exploited as a feed-water heater. The boiler was again encased Bulleid Pacific-style, while the cab was well forward above the leading axle of the rear engine unit, leaving room at the rear for a massive combination of tank and bunker with a 2,500gal water and 4t coal capacity. In September 1946 this outline was accepted and an order to build was issued by the General Manager — but, only to the extent of five engines, at the agonised pleading of a motive power department which was aghast at the unproven character of so much of the design.

Bulleid put a June 1947 delivery date on the first locomotive of the quintet, which he was now minded to name after 'Leaders', starting with his own General Manager, Sir Eustace Missenden, and Winston Churchill (nameplates were never cast, though the projected class name stuck). Everyone knew that with detailed drawings not even begun or materials ordered, gestation of so revolutionary a machine within nine months would have been a miracle to match any in Holy Writ. But with nationalisation a certainty it was important to stamp the project with the appearance of work in a state of progress beyond recall. The Southern subsequently hung an even bolder 'hands-off' notice on the project by airily authorising a build of thirty-one more Leaders on the eve of nationalisation. Not so much as a bolt was ever ordered for them. And it was not until May 1948 that the main frames for the very first Leader were set up in Brighton works.

There is no room in this book to describe all the processes by which the Leader outline endorsed by the SR management in the autumn of 1946 mutated into the working model, No. 36001, which emerged from Brighton works almost three years later, in June 1949. One must, though, mourn one aesthetic sacrifice to the project: the gross deformation of the front end of Marsh Atlantic No. 2039 *Hartland Point* to turn this engine into a test-bed for the sleeve valves, exhaust arrangement and squat, rimless chimney now favoured for the Leader.

Above its frames No. 36001 had an orthodox smoke-tube boiler, pressurised to 280lb/^{2}in, but in the hope of a substantial maintenance cost reduction the firebox was of steel plate lined with refractory material in place of the customary stayed water-spaces. The firebox was to prove one of the machine's main frailties. The original lining was difficult to keep in place, but the remedy for that drastically diminished the grate area from 43 to 25.5^{2ft} and, with it, steaming capability. This was a critical factor, considering that six cylinders had to be fed.

Considerably reduced in floor area, the midships cab of No. 36001 was purely a firing position. To make the Leader appear even more competitive in operational flexibility at any speed with a diesel or electric, a driver's cab was added at each end of the locomotive, and a desperately narrow passageway led between them within the locomotive's casing, on one side of the boiler.

To make room even for this perilous passage the boiler had to be mounted slightly off the centre-line. This eventually threw up problems of uneven weight distribution; that had to be countered by inserting ballast weights in the passageway, a factor which naturally aggravated an already worrying excess of planned axle-loadings. Even the driving cabs were condemned as unhealthily hot, but working conditions in the firing cab were unbearably torrid. Temperatures here frequently climbed to 120°F and firemen were reduced to lagging their overall legs for protection. The trouble was that the cab had been designed with oil-firing in mind and this was the root of another evil for its occupants: the cab's area was too cramped for a free swing of the fireman's shovel.

Each three-axle, 5ft 1in-wheeled power unit was designed as a bogie for repair by replacement, like that of a diesel or electric locomotive. As in the original prospectus, each bogie had three cylinders, but of 12¼in by 15in, in a fabricated block, all driving to a three-throw crankshaft on the centre axle. The sleeve valves — another chronic source of weakness, because of their proneness to leakage and problems of lubrication — had Bulleid-Walschaerts gear, while the drive from centre to outer axles in each bogie was by chains immersed in oil baths. Total weight of the Leader in working order was no less than 130.5 tons, 20 tons in excess of preliminary design calculations, so that it would clearly be barred from many more SR secondary lines than the traffic department had been led to believe when it voted for the design to proceed to metal.

So far as No. 36001 was concerned the 18 months succeeding its completion were a chronicle of intermittent outings in steam, at first from Brighton over neighbouring lines in Sussex, and later from Eastleigh, most of them succeeded by retirements to works for adjustments of this or that component. No steam prototype in British history, surely, was so intensively nursed through its post-conception period. One test trip, it is said, had as many as eighteen anxious attendants crowded into its three cabs — how, heaven knows.

Nevertheless Bulleid himself was so confident of the Leader's eventual vindication that he proposed to retire from BR slightly ahead of time, at the end of September 1949, and move to the post of Consulting Mechanical Engineer which had been eagerly offered him by CIE in Ireland. His serene belief in his progeny's eventual triumph was epitomised in the title he selected for a paper he planned to read to the Institution of Mechanical Engineers in the autumn of 1950: 'Stages in the Development of the Steam Locomotive to restore it to its supremacy as the Ideal Railway Traction Unit'.

The Railway Executive eventually embargoed delivery of the paper, but initially its Mechanical Engineering Member, Robin Riddles, was surprisingly indulgent, even supportive of the Leader project. Convinced that it needed its progenitor's first-hand attention he persuaded Bulleid, without much difficulty, to retain command of the job until March 1950, in addition to his new responsibilities with CIE.

But by the spring of 1950 even Bulleid's ardent disciples on the SR's mechanical engineering staff, though their faith in the basic concept still flamed, were getting pessimistic about the amount of work and expense still needed to eliminate fallibilities in its detail. Total costs of the Leader project had already soared beyond £175,000, no fortune by today's money values, but frightening by comparison with the £16,000 it cost at the time to run another Stanier Class 5 4-6-0 off the production line. Any further work on Nos 36002–5 had been banned the previous November, though by then the second was nearing completion and the shell of the third had already acquired its bogies.

The veil was drawn over the whole project around November 1950. No. 36001 had moved base to Eastleigh early in the year. Then, in late September and early October, it was pitted against a Class U 2-6-0 in a series of tests with the Eastern dynamometer car with loads rising from 240 to 325 tons between Eastleigh and Woking. The results were damning. The Leader's coal consumption per ton-mile was 48% higher, and per drawbar horsepower/hour as much as 67.6% above the 2-6-0's. Its use of water was just as extravagant. Overall, the Leader's efficiency was rated 20.25% less than the 2-6-0's. After the dynamometer car had been returned home, a final trip was allowed No. 36001 on 2 November with 15 bogies of 480 tons, just to prove that it could meet its original load-hauling specification, and on this it put up the best, most trouble-free performance of its embarrassing life.

That, however, was a swan song. No. 36001 was dismissed to the Eastleigh works yard, there to rust until it was broken up, Nos 36002/3 were towed to New Cross Gate shed, where they sat out the following winter until they too were scrapped.

Both Railway Executive and SR kept discreet silence over the ignominious end of the Leaders until May 1951, when a Woking reader of the *Railway Gazette*, noting that the mutilated Atlantic No. 2039 had just been broken up, sought news of the cause for which it had suffered. Quizzed in turn by the *Gazette*, the Railway Executive now admitted that 'to obviate the expense which would be involved in continuing (the "Leaders") for a problematical return, it had been decided not to proceed further with this novel design'.

There was a ludicrous and much delayed postscript to the Leader episode, an egregious example of the desperate lengths to which some elements of the political spectrum's Far Right have gone — and will sadly still go — to belittle BR's management simply because it runs a nationalised industry. Early in 1953, with the Leaders long decently buried by the railway Press, the tale finally percolated to the *Sunday Dispatch*, a very Right-inclined paper fighting for a life it was soon to lose. On 18 January 1953 this disreputable sheet exploded with stark headlines proclaiming that it had unearthed the 'Railways' Biggest Fiasco! £500,000 wasted on three useless engines! They tried to hush it up!'

The story beneath was a pretty choice farrago even by gutter Press standards, as may be imagined from the think-of-a-number-and-treble-it' price-tag bannered in the headline. The whole sorry business, it was claimed,

The Leader Locomotive

had been brought to light ... as the result of *Sunday Dispatch* inquiries, prompted by the threatened increase of fares and allegations of mis-management on the railways.' The three engines,' the writer went on, his imagination taking livelier wing by the sentence, had been built 'to revolutionise rail travel. They were part of a £750,000 experiment undertaken by Mr O. V. S. Bulleid. I can reveal that the Region's officials regard the experiment as one of their biggest failures. It was a failure that had been hushed up. From the start the plan to build Mr Bulleid's dream loco was kept secret, but news leaked out late in 1948.'

And so it went on, not forgetting, naturally, to give management/labour relations any disruptive stir the opportunity offered. 'Railway maintenance workers, annoyed at attacks being made on them, say the money lost on the experiment could have been better spent improving their working conditions.' A likely story, when one reflects on the railway unions' anxiety two and three decades later to see the money invested in APT's painful development not cut off, far from it, but greatly increased.

To accompany the chapter in his book, G. Freeman Allen selected what the present writer has already described as possibly the most morose of all the photographs assembled on the engine – see page 143. It may not have been his choice, the publisher may well have had an input. Consequently rather than looking for negatives let us instead turn the clock back to June 1949 when there was still enthusiasm for the project. Grey clouds might well have been on the horizon but at the time they were certainly not black. No. 36001 is seen in Brighton works probably soon after her first steaming and whilst some teething troubles were perhaps to be expected there was every reason to believe the new design would be a success.

APPENDIX 2
Les Warnett: *Leader – The Mechanics*

Les Warnett was a fitter at Brighton during the time Leader was being constructed. Clearly also an enthusiast for the engine, his input into the technical side of the build is probably unique. Les had little to say on the trials, repairs or modifications to the engine, and which might even tend to imply to some of the staff it was just another job to be dealt with and it was not the practice to ask questions. After he retired Les lived quietly in a house at Wisborough Green and where in the hallway was a collection of Southern Region 'totems' plus one of the nameplates from Hartland Point. What follows has only been used once before and did not appear in the 2007 Ian Allan/OPC book.

The main body unit of Leader consisted of a full-length 'fish-belly' frame which supported the boiler and its ancillaries together with the fuel bunker and water tanks. All were enclosed within a framed sheet-steel casing forming a central fireman's cab with a driving cab at either end. All three cabs were interconnected by a narrow corridor on the left-hand side, assuming No. 1 end (smokebox) to be at the front.

To achieve this within the available loading gauge and having a boiler diameter of 6ft 4in, it was necessary to offset the boiler by 6in to the right-hand side, again viewed towards the front. The two power bogies were six-wheeled, chain-coupled units, each driven by a three-cylinder, simple expansion sleeve valve engine, and fitted with Bulleid's chain-driven variant of the Walschaerts valve gear. All moving parts were flood lubricated within sheet metal oil baths, including the spring rigging. The cylinders were pressure lubricated by a separate system.

A study of the photographs showing the locomotive in the course of construction reveals the extensive use of welded steel fabrication. Indeed, the whole theme of this was for saving weight allied to strength, the effect being to produce 'monocoque' assemblies where possible, leaving only those parts that might require inspection or periodic replacement easily serviceable. Indeed, with the exception of such components as the BFB wheel centres, tyres, buffer stocks, axlebox housings, superheater header and a number of relatively minor parts, the locomotive was largely fabricated or machined from plate, sheet, tube or bar. At this period electric welding was taking great strides forward and was a highly successful method of marrying steel together. It was a technique unparalleled in the history of steam locomotive construction, where hitherto heavy and expensive machined castings were assembled with either 'fitted' bolts or rivets. Of course, a bonus of this was that where prototype or one-off experimental work was involved, any minor changes in design during the course of construction could be adjusted by removal of the affected part by the welder. With Leader, various structures involved so many novel features that this facility was used to advantage. Components could also easily be modified where either fouls or errors occurred, as the side-effect of other modifications. Welding was restricted to specially selected men and their work was subjected to X-ray examinations

Main frame structure

The main frames were of welded steel fabrication and consisted of two inward-facing channel-section side members of varying depth braced by four major stretcher assemblies and two end channels. The overall length at the centre line was 64ft. 7in. with a nominal overall width of 9ft. For loading gauge clearance purposes however, both front and rear ends were set inwards to a minimum width of 8ft at the frame extremities. A distinct feature was the deep fish-belly of the actual side members. The maximum belly depth was 2ft 8in, the lower edge described by a 52ft radius located 1in forward of the longitudinal centre line. This blended into a 16½in channel depth on either side to extend over the lengths of the bogie support stretchers, after which the lower edge tapered upwards and the upper edge dropped downwards with a 9in radius to produce a 6in deep channel at each cab end. Each side member channel was braced by no fewer than twenty-seven vertical gussets. The front and rear beams were of 6in deep channel set forward at the centre portion to produce the familiar flattened bow front. The two bogie support stretchers were most complex and are perhaps best described as being made up of two transverse box-section longitudinal stretchers to form, in effect, a two-bar letter 'H', when viewed in plan profile. Each bogie was of course supported by two stretchers, the pair at each end being similar, though differing in certain details. Dealing with the common parts of both first, the front box section stretchers formed the supports for the four segment-shaped steel body-bearing plates. These were riveted to the underside of each stretcher section. Each bearing plate had a fenced segment-shaped enclosure, into which were flush riveted pads on which the superstructure was supported; four in each of the longitudinal stretcher sections and six in each of the transverse sections. Of the last mentioned, four out of the six were somewhat reduced in surface area, this being due to having shaped holes cut through the actual bearing plate and lower box section plates at the centre line to allow for the chimney duct on each bogie to exhaust into its respective box section.

The ends of each of the transverse box sections were profiled and welded into the channel-section side frame

Main frame assembly for No. 36001 at Brighton on 24 July 1948. Other components sit nearby, including on the left a bogie frame and in the foreground a cylinder block. *H.C. Casserley*

members. To allow the exhaust steam in the outer transverse box section of the rear stretcher to pass to the similar section on the front stretcher, a raised, flanged pipe was welded into the right-hand side of each top plate of the outer sections of both stretchers. A 7in internal bore, steel pipe connected both, being routed along the right-hand side of the locomotive to lie within the lower radius of the casing slope immediately above the right-hand slab water tank. To reduce condensation this pipe was wound with a thick asbestos lagging tape. The top plate of the outer transverse box section of the front stretcher only differed by having a suitably stiffened rectangular hole to which was stud-mounted the main exhaust pipe and through which the spent steam from both bogie units was exhausted. The front stretcher served an additional function by supporting the front boiler mounting. This involved additional extensions to the top plates of both longitudinal box sections to which were added 'Mintex' insulating plates. Both stretchers were welded into the main side frame members. There were two remaining major stretchers, again of welded steel construction. These were located between the two bogie support stretchers and served to support the boiler and firebox. Since the firebox mounting pad was 9½in lower than the main boiler mounting cradle pad, it was not practical to support the firebox on the top of a deep cradle structure. Instead a deep box-section cradle stretcher was located immediately to the rear of the firebox with the lower plate having two forward-facing extensions profiled to form support for the right-angle-shaped 'Mintex' pads. The lower plate was suitably gusseted to the underside to support the extensions. Finally, steel bracings were welded across the frames at both ends to provide support for the wood planking of the driver's cab floors.

Boiler, firebox and ancillaries

The all welded steel boiler of Leader was unique among steam engines although it had certain similarities to the earlier Paget design. The forward barrel section was of the two-ringed type with the front parallel section rolled to a diameter of 6ft with the seam butt-welded. The second tapered ring rear section was similarly rolled and welded but was coned to a maximum diameter of 6ft 4in at the rear. The taper occurred along the top only. Assembly of the rings differed from standard practice in being butt-welded together. The seams of both rings were positioned on the horizontal centre line but on alternate sides. The front tube plate was of ¾in thickness, flanged inwards and butt welded directly to the front ring. To the outside of the front ring was welded an octagonal flange for attachment of the similarly shaped rear flange of the smokebox. The firebox tube plate, at ⅝in thick, was similarly fitted and butt-welded, with the distance between tube plates as 12ft

ABOVE Early stages in the boiler/firebox construction: Eastleigh, 26 June 1948. The main barrel is seen to the right, complete with a chalked/painted line where the crown segment – visible immediately ahead – will eventually be added.

RIGHT Boiler and firebox crown added together with syphons, the latter have yet to be connected to the underside of the barrel.

BELOW Thermic syphon; one of four within the firebox. Their placing did mean accurate placing of coal to all parts of the grate was not easy and called for skill on the part of the fireman.

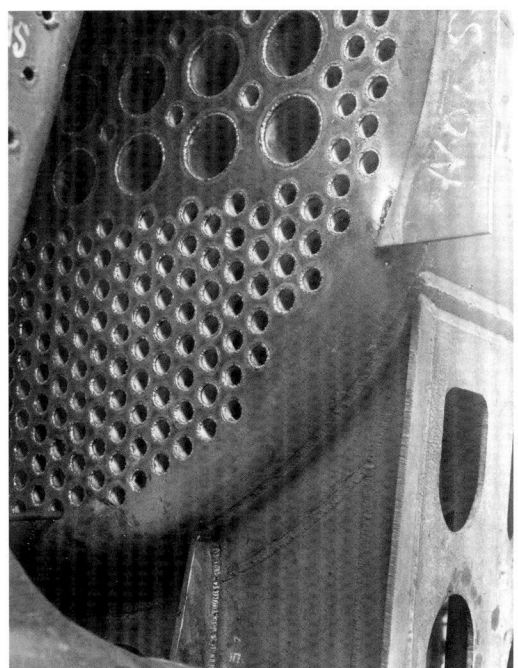

ABOVE Tubes welded into position: 36 large superheater flue tubes and 283 smoke tubes. This is the boiler on the right hand side with the firebox side sheets still to be added. *British Railways*

TOP RIGHT Progress at Eastleigh. Firebox side and back sheets still to be added. Recorded around 25 August 1948. *Reg Curl*

RIGHT Rear sheet being added, as yet the position of the butterfly-type Ajax fire door has still to be marked out.

6in. Within the boiler were thirty-six large superheater flue tubes and 283 smoke tubes, all welded directly into the tube plates following some expansion after insertion. This gave a total tube heating surface of 2,127^{2}ft. An external multi-valve poppet-type regulator valve was attached to a studded steel flange welded to the upper left-hand shoulder of the front ring.

Two standard 6in diameter Ross-pop safety valves were located on the top centre line at the rear end of the parallel centre ring. These were set to 280psi. It was with the rear section of the boiler that Bulleid departed from convention. He considered orthodox boiler stays a source of trouble and thus sought a cheaper method in both construction and maintenance. Accordingly, the customary water-jacketed firebox design was discarded and instead the top of the firebox was formed by an extension of the tapered barrel of the boiler in the shape of a slightly downward-sloping drum of segment section. The underside of this thus formed the firebox crown. This drum was butt-welded onto the rear ring as well as having a number of flexible rod stays. Conventional stays were provided between the top and bottom sections of the firebox top. To restore some of the heating surface lost by this exercise, four Nicholson-type thermic syphons each equally spaced 1ft 4in apart were provided. In addition to yielding an additional 260^{2}ft of heating surface they served to further anchor the firebox to the boiler. Each of the syphons drew water from just forward of the rear barrel ring, with a wash-out plug being directly on the elbow bend. Adjacent to the longest of the syphon necks was a downward pointing flange pipe to which was attached the manually operated blow-down valve associated with the TIA water treatment equipment. A total of thirty wash-out plugs were provided at strategic intervals on the firebox segment drum and front tube plate.

To contain the fire was a fabricated single-sheet box welded directly to the boiler. Supported on a rectangular base frame of angled steel, the front and side sheets were straightforward flat plates suitably stiffened by a lattice of steel strips welded to the outer faces. The rear was more complicated and was fabricated of six triangular steel plates to produce an angled back. In the left-hand rear face was a steam-operated firehole door similar to that fitted to the Pacifics. Butterfly-type twin doors were provided and operated by a pedal on the fireman's cab

From outside looking in. The positioning of the firebox door, to the left of the firebox is not fixed with the lower part of the two left-hand syphons also shown. Leader is believed to have unique in having four syphons – the Bulleid Pacific designs incorporated just two. The difficulty in firing is even more apparent now, placing coal to the front right-hand corner especially. (For an excellent drawing of the fireman's cab and layout therein, the reader is referred to the drawing by Philip Wilson on p146 of the HAV volume.)

A most unusual view from inside the firebox looking out! The image has been deliberately lightened as it also reveals a number of hooks on which the firebricks were hung.

floor. A manual back-up lever was also provided and attached to the doors themselves. Welded to the interior of the firebox was a defined pattern of steel lugs intended to support the refractory firebrick lining. As originally designed the firebox had a generous grate area of 43^{2}ft, the grate being of the rocking type and controlled by the fireman. The ashpan was also of steel sheet and of the double hopper type. Each hopper had two half-width 'flip-over' quadrant-shaped dump doors. Air flow to the grate was via dampers of the same size at front and rear under the control of the fireman. The existence of dampers to both front and rear was necessary due to the original intention of not turning the engine between duties. The uncluttered midships location, not unlike the well-known articulated Garratt designs, allowed full advantage to be taken of the space available for the ashpan. Provision was made for two boiler feed clacks, although in practice only one was used. This was mounted on the right-hand shoulder amidships of the front ring. A large eight-valve steam combine, with four wheel-operated and four lever-operated shut-off valves, was shoulder-mounted on the left-hand side at the front end of the tapered barrel

RIGHT The firebox as originally built with firebricks in position. The top drawing is a sectional elevation at the centre, lower left, cross section looking forward, and lower right cross section from inside looking out.

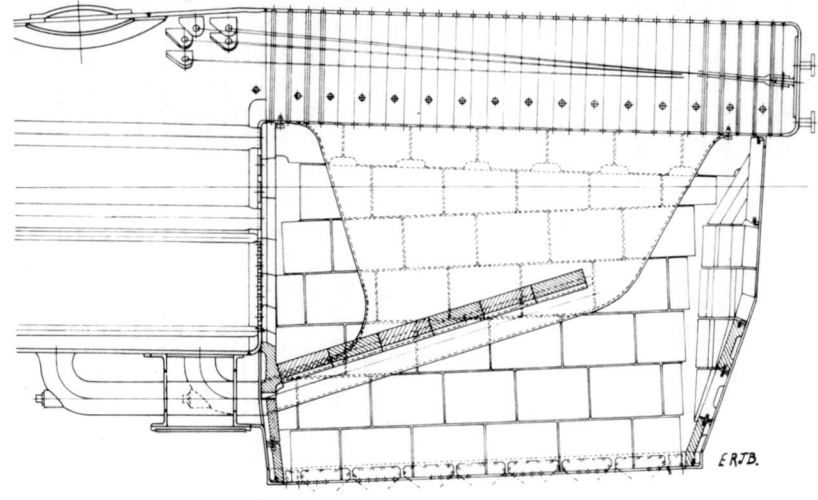

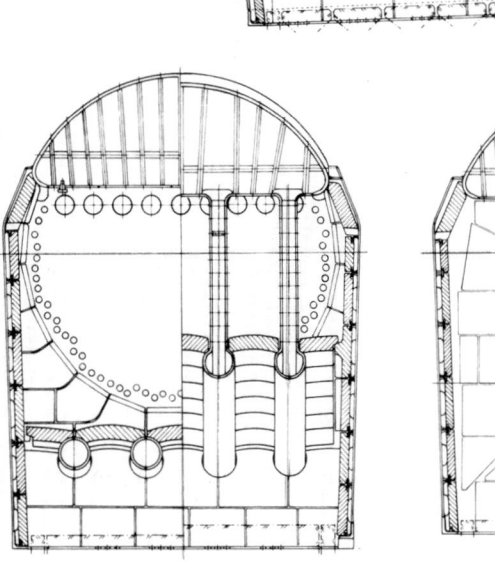

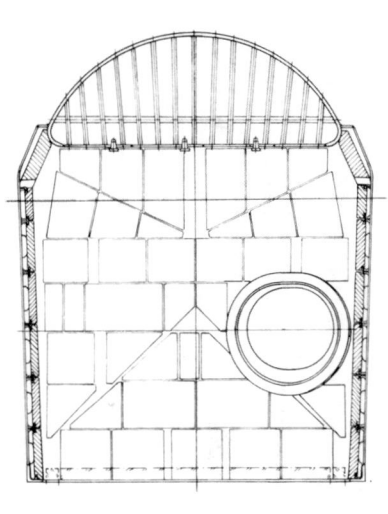

BELOW Comparisons with the previous drawings after thicker firebricks had been provided but which had the disadvantage of effective locking the grate – note the extension of the bricks at the lower corners. With the fire grate now locked because of the thicker lining, fire cleaning would have had to be done manually – difficult in the confined cab space and also with the four syphons – a further example of resolve one problem, and create another. Once more we may sympathise with the 'P & D' men.

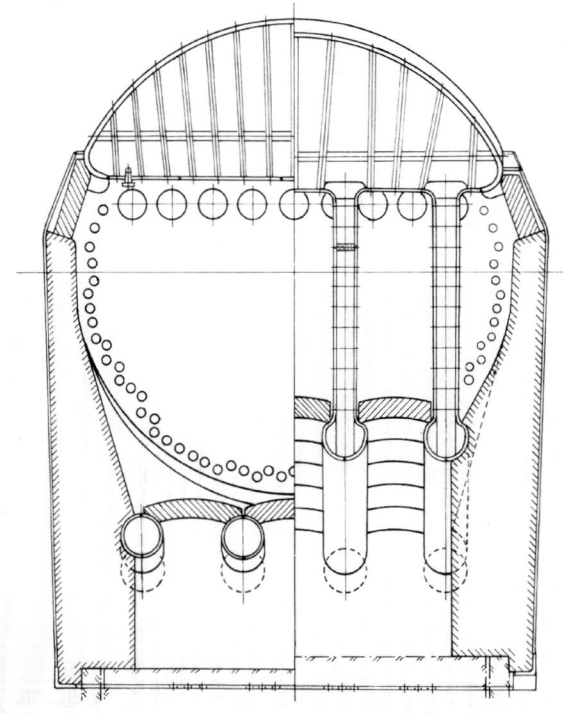

portion. Additionally, with the driver's controls segregated, the rear backhead was singularly devoid of fitments, the exception being a pair of water gauges which, when showing 1in of water, equated to a 3in covering of the firebox crown. Also within the fireman's compartment was the three-way TIA control and boiler pressure steam gauge. The principal boiler-mounting cradle was a very substantial fabricated steel support, located immediately ahead of the firebox and straddling the syphon necks. Similar but smaller mountings were welded to the underside close to the front of the first ring. The underside of each of the support mountings was flat and each bore down on to special 'Mintex' insulating pads located on each side of the frame stretchers. These were clamped in place but also slid to cater for boiler expansion. The boiler centre line was 9ft 4in from rail level. To reduce heat loss, the boiler and firebox were lagged with a fibreglass material which was held in place with thin iron wire. Additionally, the firebox was first sheeted with an aluminium foil paper before being covered with the insulating material. On completion, but before being lagged, a hydraulic test to 350psi was undertaken, followed by a 290psi steam test.

The original fire grate of the rocking type, controlled by the fireman. As originally built the grate area was 43^{2}ft, but successive additions of bricks eventually reduced this to 25.5^{2}ft. whilst a consequential disadvantage also meant the rocking grate was now locked in the one position – *see* previous illustration. *British Railways*

The hopper ashpan fitted with dump doors. *British Railways*

The TIA reservoir on the top of the bunker: also visible is the water filler accessed via the roof ventilator in No. 2 cab. There were no external steps on the engine leading to the water filler. From this angle, the tapering of the sides towards the ends is also visible. *John Click/National Railway Museum*

Feedwater

TIA-treated water was used to feed the boiler with the chemical carried in a tank atop the main water tank. This chemical reservoir was also fitted with a warming pipe. The manually-operated blow-down equipment was intended to be activated by the fireman for half a minute every thirty miles, earlier experience with the Pacifics having found that an automatic blow-down valve was insufficient to expel the mud and sludge which collected in the lower parts of the boiler. A recorder fitted in the fireman's compartment registered each time the blow-down valve was activated.

The treated water was fed into the boiler by two Davies and Metcalfe No. 11 Monitor-type injectors. These were mounted beneath the well of the fireman's compartment. Water and steam handles then protruded through the floor into the central compartment. Provision for viewing the operation of the injectors was by holes cut into the floor while an electric light beneath the floor allowed for the same to seen during darkness.

Smokebox

Since the smokebox was concealed beneath the outer body casing, it was designed to be solely functional. Fabricated from ¼in plate with a thicker plate used for the floor, it traced an irregular octagonal pattern and was mated with the similar fitment on the front of the boiler barrel. At the top the smokebox was flat in section, upon which two vacuum reserve reservoirs were mounted. The front the smokebox was flat, to which the smokebox door was attached. This took the form of an oval with a flattened top, the shape being dictated by the design of the smokebox. The whole was not dissimilar to the smokebox door shape on a Gresley A4, although in the latter case the unconventional shape was determined by the streamlined casing. Within the smokebox was mounted a Gresham & Craven single-cone vacuum ejector. The combined chimney and liner was of the convergent/divergent pattern and of large diameter to suit the design of the Bulleid modified Lemaître multiple-jet exhaust system. Top diameter of the chimney was 2ft 5in. When in position the chimney top was 12ft 8in from rail level. The body casing was attached to the chimney by an additional 1in wide flange. The

Inside the smokebox we see the base of the multiple jet blastpipe but no obvious sign of the ash duct. On the extreme left the timber board standing almost vertical is clearly a temporary feature! The shape of the smokebox door, flattened across the top is apparent. Only just visible at top right are the cylindrical shapes of two higher vacuum (25in) reservoirs placed longitudinally across the smokebox.

superheater header was mounted in the rear upper portion of the smokebox and accommodated four vertical rows of nine double-run elements. An additional 454^2ft of heating surface was provided. The smokebox plates were covered with thick 'Magnesia' lagging blocks while, to help reduce heat radiation into the front driver's cab, an insulated 'firedoor' was attached to the smokebox door. The locking handles protruded through this insulating material.

Fuel bunker and water tank

The designed capacity of 4,000 gallons of water and 4 tons of coal were carried in an integral tank/bunker assembly welded directly on to the main frame structure. The water tank arrangements were divided into three principal components: a main tank augmented by a secondary slab tank on the right-hand side and also what came to be dubbed a 'mantle shelf' tank near the central firing compartment. The main tank and coal bunker were centrally disposed and situated between the central fireman's cab and the driver's (No. 2 end) rear cab. In construction and layout the main tank and bunker was not unlike that of a conventional all-welded steel tender. The coal supply was in a bunker in the forward portion of the tank. This took the form of an asymmetrical hopper intended to self-trim the coal forward to the actual coal hole which, unlike normal practice, faced across the main structure. Ahead and immediately beneath this was the shovel plate. Aft of the shovel plate the bunker panel extended to the full height of the casing profile and was fitted with a single door slightly over 3ft 3in x 1ft 9in, through which access could be gained to the coal bunker. Within the fireman's compartment was a water gauge to indicate the remaining water reserve. Beneath the coal bunker the area was braced by a complex web of steel stretchers intended to act as baffles as well as absorb the loads created by water surge. An irregular-shaped sump plate was welded to the underside of the main water tank which combined a water feed well and strainer unit feeding the injector supply. The integral slab side tank was located on the offside of the main water tank and was slightly higher than the level of the main frames. Nominally 1ft 3in wide it was curved to that of the outer casing. The mantle shelf tank, dubbed so because of its shape, height and location, was built integral with the offside slab tank and of the same height. It enveloped the lower half of the rear firebox panelling to curve forward along the nearside firebox frame. It carried precious little water but was intended to afford an additional heat barrier between the hot sides of the firebox and corridor and the fireman's compartment. Each tank was connected with the next. The handbrake was bolted to the front face of the main end tank panel.

Reversing arrangement

The necessity to reverse both bogies simultaneously meant the reversing gear on Leader was a complex affair. Reversing was achieved by means of a steam cylinder rigidly attached to the main frames which then, by a series of gears, shafts, universal joints and splined shafts, transmitted the desired steam cut-off to each bogie. This steam cylinder was of the standard steam and oil hydraulic locking arrangement supported beneath a fabricated carrier frame welded to the underside of the main frame belly on the left-hand side of the engine. From this a reduced diameter piston rod extension operated the cut-off indicators in both driving cabs. All the working parts of the reversing arrangement were enclosed in individual oil baths and flood-lubricated. The weight-shaft sector arms, gears and bearings shared an extension of the main transmission oil bath on the 'front' bogie but, due to the staggered chain drive arrangement, the 'rear' bogie components were housed in a separate enclosure. Small rectangular oil bath boxes were fitted around the inner bearings of the power bogie drive shafts. The lower half of the main reversing oil bath was readily removable for routine maintenance and included a bolted circular inspection cover.

RIGHT AND BELOW The main steam reversing gear placed centrally below the engine. This had the task of adjusting the cut-off on both bogies simultaneously. At least with Leader there was never any report of one bogie attempting to pull in the opposite direction to its neighbour, although exact symmetry may sometimes have been in doubt. The greatest difficulty would have been attempting to move the reserving gear with the engine stationary on any form of curved track.

Brakes – control system

The brake control system together with the actual brake rigging was possibly the most sophisticated ever fitted to a steam locomotive. It consisted of an automatic vacuum brake system incorporating a new patented automatic ejector control. In place of the roar of a conventional ejector used to create and maintain vacuum, Leader was fitted with high and low pressure reservoirs and an automatic ejector system. When a drain was made on the low pressure 21in reservoirs these were automatically replenished from the two high pressure 25in reservoirs located atop the smokebox. This continued until both had reached the same level at which point the system would automatically charge in a series of small bursts, shutting itself off automatically when 25in had been restored. In practice the control system was both reliable and effective. Hence, when standing at the platform, the familiar roar from the continuous operation of the small ejector was replaced by intermittent short bursts from the single-core ejector — a new sound and totally unique to Leader. Allied to this the fully compensated clasp brakes on each of the twelve wheels gave the driver confidence in control and braking power.

Casing

The main frame structure supported a full-length sheet steel casing which enveloped the whole of the 'top works'. In plan it traced the same profile as that of the main frame structure and was not dissimilar to that of the Bulleid coach design. It was attached by two methods, either welding or bolts, dependent upon anticipated service requirements. For descriptive purposes the casing was subdivided into three parts, a centre parallel section through which the cross-section profile remained constant, and two tapered (in plan) end sections. In these the profile radii remained constant but the overall width reduced from 9ft to 8ft at the extremities. Modellers should note that the casing sides are not flat but describe a 50ft inward-curving radius. The front portion provided the enclosure for the larger of the two driving cabs, bow-fronted and with three flat facets, each furnished with a brass-framed window. Only the centre window could be opened although all three windows shared a common rain gutter strip across the top. Access to the cab was via a 1ft 10in opening on either side, each with a roller wheel-type sliding door which followed the same profile as the casing end. There were no windows in the doors, but above

Braking the rear nearside wheel of No. 1 bogie.

Casing attached to the main frames whereon is also the boiler. Firebox, bunker etc., being prepared to be slewed and perhaps then lowered on to the bogies. In the foreground set into the ground between the rails are the rollers used for valve setting. *British Railways*

each door was another rain gutter strip. Ventilation could be controlled by a 2ft wide, fore and aft, sliding roof panel which gave a maximum opening of 2ft 3 in. Within the cab was a wooden floor and a maximum cab height of 6ft 6in at the engine centre line. This decreased towards the sides, as seen in the photographs. From the cab front (No. 1 end) to the smokebox door the distance was 8ft 9 in, which allowed adequate room for opening the smokebox door. The problem of ash disposal from the smokebox was considered at an early stage in the design, it being recognised that a more efficient method than existing manual means was desirable. In the wake of the trial with No. 1896 it was first suggested that an ash duct of similar design should be provided on Leader. However, the space required for such a chute was needed for the steam turbine-driven oil pumps and the eventual ducted route was suspect due to its shallow angle of descent allied to bogie movement. As fitted the chute was of straightforward fabrication, bolted to the underside of the smokebox base to discharge the ash between the oil baths through a 6in square exit. It was under external mechanical control. The chute was later sealed and recourse made to manual smokebox cleaning. Had oil firing ever been installed then the need for smokebox cleaning would have been abolished.

The exterior casing was of thin steel sheet stiffened where necessary and supported in cross-section by formers. This was then welded to the main frame structure. At the rear the roof section was cut away to suit the profile of the coal bunker as well as the water tank filler and TIA container. The rear cab assembly was necessarily shortened to just 4ft due to the intrusion of the water tank and bunker assembly. Access to the bunker and top plate for water filling and TIA inspection was via the cab roof ventilation aperture at No. 2 end and accordingly three 15in wide steel rungs were welded to the tank end plate. Hand-holds were also provided at the tank end. A number of bolted panels were provided in the casing where this covered the smokebox, boiler, fireman's cab and water and bunker assemblies. These were to enable service access to various components. Apart from the chimney opening within the casing, further openings were provided for the safety valves, a single exposed whistle and thirteen washout plugs. All of these were on the boiler centre line which was necessarily offset 6in from the engine centre line. In the casing portion covering the firebox, two lines of 6½in x 6½in vents were cut along the 'flattened' shoulder portion on both sides. These had individual sliding shutters and were above the corridor space formed by the offset boiler and bunker. Within the fireman's cab and on the engine centre line was a rectangular sliding ventilator similar to those fitted to the driving cabs. Entry to the fireman's cab was by a single sliding door, similar to the driver's door but having a glass window. Alongside this was a triple sliding window not dissimilar to those fitted to the Pacifics in later years. Both the door and windows were protected by rain strips. Due to loading gauge restrictions it was not possible to fit a normal handrail and instead a vertical gulley was formed in the casing and fitted with a sunken handrail. Within the central fireman's compartment the floor level was lowered to form a well which created more room within the compartment. When entering from the outside the fireman stepped down into his cab which was provided with a wooden floor having cross-planks in similar fashion to the driving cabs.

As with the later bogies on the Turf Burner depicted earlier (*see* page 249), Leader had pioneered the centreless pivot arrangement for body-to-bogie positioning on a steam engine. But it was not the first such arrangement on the SR as Nos. CC1 and CC2, the two electric engines from 1941 and 1945 respectively, had a similar arrangement. No doubt having achieved success with this arrangement, it was copied on No. 36001. (As an aside, the electric loco numbered CC1 by the Southern also shared the same number with the Turf Burner some years later.) Four mounting/rubbing pads were provided on each bogie with a corresponding number on the underside of the main frames.

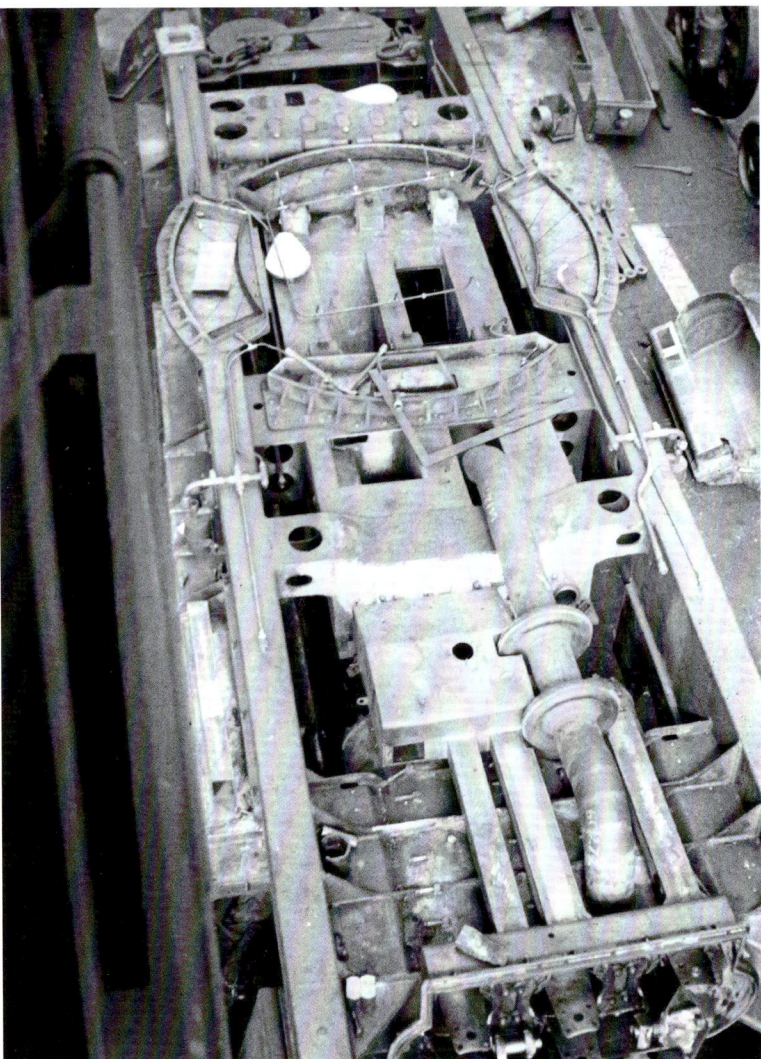

Electrics

Instrumentation lamps, inspection lamps, cab and other illumination, together with route indicator lamps, were all electrically lit. The 24V supply was provided by a single Stones-type TG1 steam turbine generator of 1kW maximum output. This was mounted in the corridor of the body structure alongside the boiler and beneath the regulator valve. A steam supply was obtained from the boiler manifold via a governor unit while the exhaust was taken directly into the smokebox. Six electric lamps were provided for headcode illumination at each end of the locomotive. Traditional steel brackets to support the more familiar headcode discs — or reversion to oil lamps in case of emergency — were also provided. The lamps were operated from banks of toggle switches in the driving compartments. The turbine generator also provided power for an electrically-driven windscreen wiper, clearing the driver's window only at each end cab.

Controls and instrumentation

The arrangement of controls and instrumentation was similar in both driving cabs. The exception to this was that the actual driving position was 'in line' with the corridor. Accordingly, when running with No. 1 end leading the driver was on the left-hand side and with No. 2 end leading he was seated at the right. In the latter case signal sighting was unaffected due to the uninterrupted forward vision. The controls in each cab were carefully laid out and could be reached by the driver from a single padded and swivelling seat.

Power bogies — pivots

One of the most interesting and unique features was the design of the two power bogies. Spaced at 34ft centres, they had no physical centre pivots, but relied on four very substantial segment-shaped bearing pads riveted to the top surfaces of the bogie assembly and located on the longitudinal and transverse centre lines of the bogie. These fabricated steel pads were lined with gunmetal bearing faces, machined with a matrix of oil grooves. A heavily reinforced outer 'fence' was welded to each of the segments to provide both radial pivot location and a means of power transference. It should be noted that the drawgear was attached to the power bogie buffer beams and not the main frames. Accordingly, power from the leading bogie had to pass through both front and rear pivots while each of these items had to be capable of withstanding either power or braking loads from both ends. Similar, but unfenced, pads were attached to the underside of the main frame structure. One of the advantages of the pivotless bogie was that it allowed the main steam pipe to pass through

Main steampipe.

each bogie adjacent to the vertical centre axis — the point of least movement — while sufficient flexibility in the design allowed the locomotive to negotiate curves down to a minimum radius of 5½ chains (121yd).

Bogie frame assembly

The bogie frame assemblies, like that of the main frame, were of welded steel fabrication. Both front and rear units were identical and each consisted of two box-section side frames braced by a complex of stretchers. These included the leading and trailing end beams, front and rear slide bar supports and inner and outer support stretchers. The last two named also supported the valve gear, motion and brake parts. Into the bogies were welded the cylinder fabrications, which formed the major structural component part. Other items such as oil baths were also added by weld as construction proceeded. Within the bogie side frames, which were hollow box-sections, an elongated triangular access hole was provided at each of the six spring 'stations'. These were necessarily stiffened and lipped, to which complementary-shaped steel cover plates were bolted. At the leading end the frames increased in depth on the underside to form a large area to which the cylinders were welded. The buffer beams were 7ft wide and of steel plate. Two additional pairs of 1in thick steel gussets were welded to the top plate extremities and were drilled with 2in diameter holes which acted as lifting lugs. The rear beam was of similar construction and in addition fronted three rear-facing triangular-shaped brackets to support the large brake cylinders.

Steam and exhaust pipes on the power bogies

To absorb bogie movement the steam-pipes were of convoluted steel, so giving an amount of movement without the fear of rupture. Both pipes passed down through the bogie in a 'swan-neck' turn, close to the hypothetical pivot point. They then plunged down through the oil bath to face the cylinders via an elbow turn. To reduce heat loss, the entire main steampipe run, with the exception of flange joints fitted where necessary, was lagged in metallic asbestos twine. The layout of the exhaust initially formed an integral part of the assembly since it was welded into the structure. A 7in internal diameter fabricated steel tube carried the exhaust from the cylinders until it was 'teed' into a short stub tube. The exhaust emerged from the bogies via a rectangular duct bolted to the top of the stretcher plate ahead of the front bogie bearing pad. The obvious difficulty of locating and maintaining the precise siting of the various sub-assemblies during welding was overcome with the use of a simple rotary welding cradle to which the frames were attached and then turned to the most convenient position ready for the next item to be added.

Horn guide pedestals

A pair of hollow flange-mounted cylindrical steel pedestal guides of 5½in diameter were attached to the underside of each bogie frame.

Axle boxes

All six axles were carried on Timken double-bow taper roller bearings. The utilisation of power transmission chains to connect the coupled wheels eliminated the need to maintain precise axle centres as would be the case with a conventional chassis fitted with coupling rods. Bulleid used this to advantage to 'resilient mount' the axle assemblies.

Wheels and axles

The six driving and coupled wheels of each power unit were of 5ft 1 n diameter and the same size as on the Q1 class. They bore the familiar Bulleid hallmark of BFB wheels which gave a more continuous support to the steel tyres compared with a spoke arrangement. Tyres were coned at a 1 in 20 inclination. By substituting chains for coupling rods the need for crankpins was dispensed with. Similarly, since the three-throw forged steel crankshaft of each unit was phased with 120° crank settings, no balance weights were required. The three-throw driving axle referred to was of hollow construction. The overall length was no less than 8ft 2⅝in which was necessary to accommodate the final drive sprockets. These were pressed on and secured with threaded flange caps screwed into the axle ends. Anti-rotation was afforded by a special hexagon/pentagon design, the brainchild of Reg Curl, at the time Chief Draughtsman at Eastleigh. The driving wheel centres were pressed and keyed using a pressure of 120 tons. Leading and trailing axle arrangements were similar except the axles were plain, although again hollow. It may be of interest to record that the cast wheel centres were pressed onto the axle ends without the tyres being added, and, although the axles were asymmetrical, by reversal they could be used for either leading or trailing application on each bogie.

Wheels and axles but note those seen here are for the front and rear of each bogie and due to the unsymmetrical drive are the sides without the sprockets attached. Folklore has it that some of the BR Standard Class 4 tank engines were originally envisaged to be built at Brighton incorporating BFB wheels. In the event 'standardisation' meant just that and there was no departure from the norm.

Seven blind axles for Leader. Two were required for each bogie consequently we are only one short for two complete engines. Unlike the crank axles, no issues were reported with these axles. *Reg Curl*

Visible under the casing is one of the centre axle final drive sprockets, which will be coupled by chain to an identical sprocket on the rear axle. By comparison the end of the front axle will be seen to be blind. On the opposite side the sprockets were fitted to the centre and front axles resulting in an unsymmetrical drive. Stephen Townroe was of the opinion that this unsymmetrical drive, the pull at the top in one direction and from the bottom on the opposite side, may have contributed to the failure of the crank axle on No. 36001, and yet the same unequal arrangement with final drive by chains was used on the turf burner seemingly without incident. We say 'seemingly' with caution, as whilst no similar axle failure was reported with TB, there is also no evidence to suggest the crank axles were ever subject to X-ray examination after the engine had completed any appreciable mileage. (We are not told now many miles TB actually did run.)

Chain transmission drive

A major deviation from normal locomotive practice was to couple the axles using chains and sprockets. This was an attempt to remove the inherent disadvantage of conventional cranks and coupling rods; namely, their inability to transmit constant torque throughout a revolution. Instead, 'Morse' multi-link inverted tooth transmission chains were used. However, because the chassis layout dictated that the sprockets should be on the outer extremities of the driving axles, the confines of the loading gauge would not permit sufficient space to drive both forwards and backwards on each side. The only solution, therefore, was to employ a staggered arrangement by driving forward to the leading axle on the right-hand side and rearwards to the trailing axle on the left-hand side.

Bogie spring rigging

For the spring rigging, laminated springs were chosen as being a particularly attractive application. They had the advantage of being both simply and neatly housed in the box section of the bogie frames. Here they performed under more or less ideal conditions, away from the enemies of grit, ash and dust and with the added bonus of being flood-lubricated.

Cylinders

The three cylinders in each of the two power bogies were each of 12½in bore and 15in stroke. They were also unique for modern-day steam traction in that the steam distribution was controlled by sleeve valves within the cylinder bores. Each three-cylinder assembly was in a steel fabricated structure welded directly into the bogie frame, thus eliminating the usual array of fitting bolts. The assembly

Cylinder boring. The cylinder assembly, later welded into the frame, was a fabricated steel structure with none of the usual nuts and bolts. It is believed the sleeves for No. 2039 (and later Leader) were machined at Eastleigh on a single lathe which had been brought down from Nine Elms decades before and apparently was the only one in any of the Southern workshops that could accommodate the task. Operated by just one man, it took up almost the length of the one wall within the Eastleigh machine shop.

consisted of three steel tubes welded between two substantial end plates. They had an overall length of 4ft 2in, a considerable distance when compared with the 15in stroke. To produce a central admission annulus and independent exhaust steam annuli at both ends of the cylinders, the three assemblies were rolled and welded from ½in steel plate in the form of open triple-bolted sections. Between each of the three annulus assemblies were welded separating plates and, as with No. 2039, the cylinders were enveloped in a full-length steam jacket. Prior to welding thirteen admission and thirteen exhaust ports were cut into the inside edge of each separating plate. The cylinder assembly was inclined downwards from the front towards the crank-axle at an angle of 1 in 8. Cast-iron liners were pressed into each cylinder, with holes provided to correspond to the admission and exhaust ports. The sleeve valves were merely tubes of cast Mechanite, a fine grain cast iron, machined to a sliding fit within the liners. They were then bored to house the pistons, with ports cut circumferentially around each end of the sleeve. The innermost rows were for steam admission and the outer ports for exhaust. Rings were provided at intervals between the sleeve valve and cylinder liner. Cast-iron piston heads were used, each having four sealing rings. Fabricated covers were provided at both ends, although these differed considerably in design.

Motion

The piston rods and crossheads were machined from a one-piece forging. Each rod was a nominal 2¾in diameter and secured to the piston head by a flange nut fitted with a split taper pin for final security. Connecting rods were of 'girder' section and 5ft 9in long. These were steel forgings of the simple strap type.

Sleeve valve motion

The sleeve valve motion was designed to give a variable figure-of-eight mode of operation. This was derived from two sources: a variable reciprocating motion controlled by an adaptation of Bulleid's patented valve gear, and a constant part-rotary or oscillating motion. This latter effect was imparted to the drive using the 'described use of a lever' principle and was intended to distribute the lubrication and reduce wear. The combination of these two modes thus produced the required movement. The Bulleid gear itself derived its motion from an independent three-throw crankshaft, chain-driven from the main crank-axle. Since the main crank-axle was a one-piece forging, the driven sprocket was a two-piece split gear secured by bolts. This gear was clamped between the centre and right-hand crank. An idler gear was provided which was supported by a bracket attached to the main bogie stretcher. The valve gear crankshaft was machined from a one-piece Mechanite casting and consisted of three unbalanced cranks again set at 120°. The shaft was carried on split bearings which were attached to fabricated steel supports extending rearwards from the main stretcher. The eccentric gear was a Bulleid speciality and he was able to reduce the frictional losses of conventional large eccentrics and sheaves, which he referred to as 'band-brakes'. Accordingly, a vertical drive was used to oscillate the expansion link, so enabling the cut-off to be varied. The eccentrics used were designed on the radial engine connecting rod principle, using one master rod. The expansion links were similarly miniaturised. Each sleeve was driven by an arm rigidly attached to the outer radius of the upper sleeve.

From the front, the centre and right-hand cylinders have their sleeves inserted as well as part of the oscillating mechanism.

The front view of a Leader bogie as originally built with oscillating gear intact. The reciprocating motion comes from the valve rod ① with ball-and-socket joint to allow the oscillating motion from the arc described by ball joints ② attached to lever ③ pivoted at ④. The whole was driven by rod ⑥ linked to the centre crosshead. An extension on the centre sleeve provides the same oscillation via ball joint ⑦ to the third sleeve. Extension lever ⑤ drives the mechanical lubricators. It is not clear what arrangement was made for the mechanical lubricators when the oscillating gear was later removed. All this was fine in theory but in reality, cumulative manufacturing tolerances and wear may well have been created greater movement than was designed for. In addition, folklore has it that Bulleid was told at an early stage that this mechanism was a potential source of trouble with the drive to the sleeves only provided at one central point – ⑥ on the drawing. One (un-named) draughtsman pleading (with who – probably not Bulleid) that the oscillating gear needed to be driven from two levers. He also gave the example of pulling out a drawer and then attempting to push it back on one corner – not unnaturally the drawer twisted slightly and jammed. No change to the design resulted.

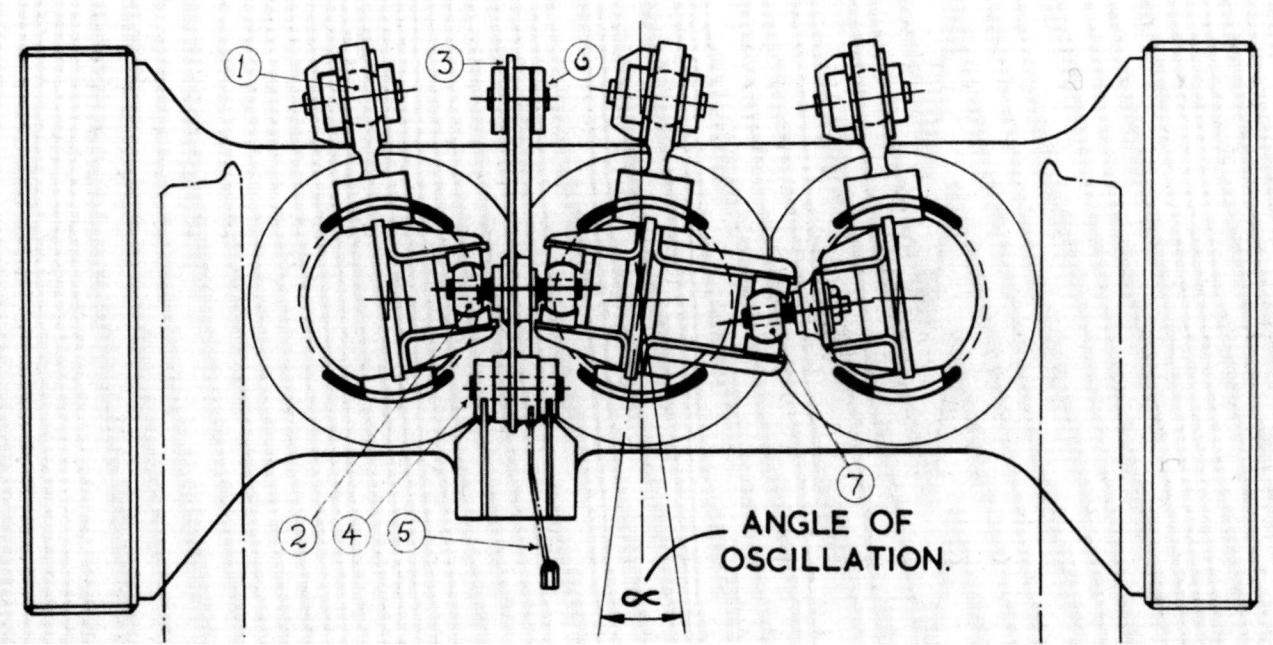

Oscillating gear

The initial drive for this was taken from the centre crosshead, not unlike the lap/lead arrangement of Walschaerts valve gear. A drop arm was attached to the right-hand side of the crosshead and used to drive a pendulum lever via a short link and so remove the angularity of the lever, each of the three sleeves being fitted with a driving beam. In operation the vertical movement described by the oscillating arm and derived from the pendulum lever, lifted two die-blocks. This raised the right-hand jaw beam assembly together with the right-hand side of the centre jaw beam assembly and caused the right-hand sleeve to partially rotate in an anti-clockwise direction, seen from the front. The centre sleeve adopted a clockwise rotation. Being diametrically opposite, the left-hand jaw beam assembly was thus moved downwards and took with it the die-block fitted to the trunnion of the left-hand jaw beam assembly. This caused the left-hand sleeve to rotate anti-clockwise. When Leader first ran, a cover was provided to the sleeve valve oscillating gear.

Seen from the underside we have the crank axle, connecting rods and sleeve valve drive via the chains seen, the whole will shortly be encased within the oil bath.

The valve gear on Leader was similar to that of the Pacific types except that the combination lever ①, supported from the swing link ②, was arranged for inside admission. Its motion is transmitted by valve rods ③ supported from the multiplying swing link ④ to plunger ⑤ at the exit from the oil bath and to the sleeve valve operating rod ⑥. The oscillating motion was added to the sleeves by pin ⑦ in lever ⑧ pivoted at ⑨ and driven from the centre crosshead link ⑩.

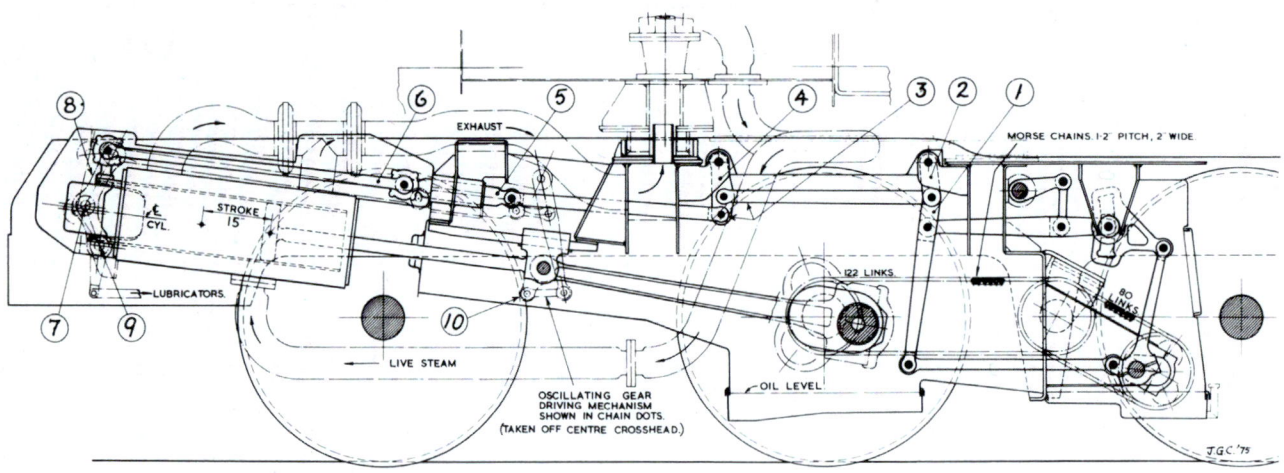

Cylinder cocks

The emission of exhaust steam condensate from the chimney together with condensate in the cylinders is both undesirable and hazardous. In the Leader design the problem was even more critical due to the long pipe runs involved in getting the live steam to, and the exhaust steam from, No. 2 bogie. Bulleid took steps to both prevent and reduce the problem. Prevention was by ensuring the fixed steam and exhaust pipes were lagged, while the design of the cylinders allowed for a steam flow around the admission and exhaust annuli. Two cylinder drain cocks were provided at the front and rear of each cylinder assembly. In addition, a third drain cock was attached to the main steam pipe elbows prior to entering the cylinders. Thus, by opening the cocks and cracking the regulator, steam could flow through the pipes, warming these and the cylinders and raising them to working temperature before being thrown out of the drain cocks. Control of the drain cocks was via a linkage controlled by a quadrant-mounted hand lever in each cab. As an additional safeguard, large blow-off valves were fitted to the front and rear covers of each cylinder. Under test at Brighton the crew maintained that the exhaust upon starting was more free of exhaust 'rain' than with a conventional steam locomotive.

Appendix 2 – Les Warnett: Leader – The Mechanics

Steam turbine, one of each bogie, for supplying oil to the oil bath enclosing the inside motion. *David Burnett*

Lubrication

Two independent lubrication systems were used on each bogie unit: a high pressure system for the cylinders, and a continuous-flow system for the remaining working components. Included in the high pressure system were the sleeve valves, cylinder liners and pistons, with the oil being delivered by three Wakefield No. 7 lubricators mounted on a welded carrier frame mounted on the right-hand side of each bogie. These were in turn driven by a link extending down from the sleeve valve oscillating gear. A series of copper pipes, valves and connectors then distributed the lubricant. The flow system was of the Bulleid oil bath type which fed the entire engine unit of each bogie. The oil supply for this was obtained from a sump and then delivered under pressure by oil pumps driven by a steam turbine, again mounted externally on each bogie. Photographs reveal the location of these exterior components, with the steam turbine easily identified by the tell-tale emission of steam. As well as lubricating the inside motion, separate oil baths were provided on the exterior of each bogie comprising two single and two double units. These enclosed the axle boxes, pedestal guides and roller bearings and, in the case of the double units, the final drive chain connecting the axles. The staggered arrangement of the chain drive, the reasons for which have been described earlier, accounted for the asymmetrical layout of the outside oil baths which are such a prominent feature of the Leader design.

Brake rigging

Mounted on the rear of each bogie were two 24in vacuum cylinders. These were connected via a 5in shaft to the brake operating levers, pull rods and compensating beams which formed an identical arrangement on each bogie. Power braking was afforded to all wheels.

Sundries and draw gear

With all six wheels available for adhesion and also driven, the risk of slipping was negligible. Hence, sanding gear was not provided and, indeed, never found necessary. The draw hook and coupling fitted to the two power bogies was of standard SR type cushioned by Spencer Moulton pads compressed at the rear of each beam by the securing nut. Electric lamps fitted to the underside of the front and rear edges of the body structure provided illumination when coupling at night. The 'voice' of Leader was achieved by a pair of brass whistles mounted one at each end of the locomotive adjacent to the topmost headcode indicator. These were independently operated from either end.

A fitter's nightmare, perhaps. The arrangement of pipes to the injectors under the fireman's cab. John Click recounts that poor joints in this area resulted in the central compartment being christened 'the Chinese laundry' due to steam leakage.

APPENDIX 3
The Views of the Professionals, Including Copies of Correspondence and Biographical Details

Charles Ware Attwell. 1906–1991. Harold Ware Attwell was born at North Tawton, Devon; his schooling included three years, 1919 to 1922 as a boarder at Queen Elizabeth's School, Crediton. Following this he served an Engineering Apprenticeship at Eastleigh Locomotive Works from 1923 to 1927.

At the completion of his training he did spells in the drawing offices at Eastleigh and Waterloo and then joined the Testing Section at Brighton in 1930 and eventually became Chief Locomotive Test Assistant for The Southern. In 1954 he was made Water Treatment Assistant and after a forty-nine-year career retired from British Railways January 1972.

Presentation of a set of cutlery to O.V.S. Bulleid, right, on 23 September 1949 a few days before his supposed official retirement at the end of the same month, aged 62. Also present are Sir Eustace Missenden, left, and Sir John Elliott. In the event Bulleid was persuaded to remain and to oversee the trials of Leader until the end of the same year. His role of consulting engineer to CIE (later CME) had begun in April of the same year and which partly explains how some early drawings for the Turf Burner had been prepared at Brighton. This was one of a series of images that appeared in the October 1949 issue of the *British Railways Southern Region Magazine* for October 1949 within an article 'Goodbye to the Southern's Famous C.M.E.' As might be expected on such an occasion, there were tributes rather than criticism. The Leader receives no more than a passing mention. In his own notes JGC adds a summary, 'Many people in the Drawing Office as well as in the Works got the impression that OVB only believed the last man he spoke to. He listened politely to views wherever they came from but was not usually influenced by others' ideas for very long at a time: for he was, above all else, constantly changing his mind. In my opinion this was a fault that often cost him dearly. He certainly kept everybody on their toes, but the frequent changes were very time-consuming. It has been described less kindly as 'keeping everyone dancing on hot bricks' by one anonymous critic. Some would have agreed, but it also meant that alternatives were given every consideration, and that's what good design is about. U-turns can be part of the process too, and our Chief made plenty of those as well. It could be very frustrating and very stimulating too but the most serious aspect of it all was the time factor. He was therefore less than keen in August 1946 when Missenden put him on to a committee charged with looking into future electrification. Worse, it was to be chaired by Raworth who had retired but was invited back to do the job. The Chief Accountant (believed to be Davidson), Robertson the Chief Civil Engineer, and Richards the Traffic Manager completed the team. They were to plan, cost out and stage the electrification of all lines east of Salisbury to Bournemouth inclusive. Warder was Secretary.' Later in 1948 Bulleid was away again, this time with Milne reporting on the motive power situation on the Irish railways. We know this was when he saw the opportunity for developing his ideas further in that country, We might also ask what exactly was going on with the progress on Leader doing his absences?

John Gaywood Click. 1926–1988. Premium apprentice under Bulleid from 1943 onwards. Much of Click's career has already been referred to previously within the text and so not need be repeated here. Suffice to say his entry in *Steam Index's Brief Biographies of Mechanical Engineers* (steamindex.com) probably sums up his character well. 'He was a perfectionist, had a delightful sense of humour, but was not an easy man to get to know well.'

Clifford S. Cocks. 1897–? Commenced his railway career with the GCR at Gorton and progressed with the LNER to a senior position in the drawing office at Doncaster works. Transferred to the Southern Railway in 1937 and quickly

RIGHT John Click in the cab of No. 36001, we think at Guildford. A complex individual, he remained a disciple of Bulleid throughout his life but would never achieve his youthful ambition to become Chief Mechanical Engineer. *J.G. Click/National Railway Museum*

BELOW Taken at Waterloo on the occasion of the naming of No. 34090 *Sir Eustace Missenden* on 15 February 1949. The assembled gathering is also a 'who's-who' of many of the principal players involved in the Leader story – job titles as per the rear of the print. Left to right: T.E. Chrimes (Superintendent of Motive Power); H.L. Smedley (Legal Advisor and Solicitor Railway Executive); W.J. England (ex-Superintendent of Operations); H.E.O. Wheeler (ex-Superintendent of Operations); R.G. Davidson (ex-Chief Accountant); O.W. Cromwell (Chief Officer for Labour and Establishment); R.M.T. Richards OBE (Deputy Chief Regional Officer); Sir Eustace Missenden OBE (Chairman of the Railway Executive); O.V.S. Bulleid (Chief Mechanical Engineer); John Elliott (Chief Regional Officer); S.W Smart OBS (Superintendent of Operations); R.P. Biddle CBE (Docks and Marine Manager Southampton); C. Grassmann (Public Relations and Advertising Officer). Note again Sir Eustace is unsmiling. To quote John Click again: 'Perhaps he was thinking of Leader and even regretting giving Bulleid so much freedom'. (Reference also *British Railways Southern Region Magazine* for March 1949 where this and other images together with an accompanying text record the occasion.)

Gordon Nicolson. Quote from A.B. MacLeod at the time when the latter was in charge of the railway system on the Isle of Wight, 'I noticed on Saturdays that frequently the operations [at Ryde Pier Head] were keenly watched by a schoolboy. I spoke to him one day and found he was very keen on railways. He lived in Ryde and his name was Gordon Nicholson. I employed him as a volunteer, unpaid, unofficial runner, who helped me a great deal in checking in the trains, finding out which engines wanted coal or had to go to depot at St John's Road owing to a minor defect, or even to be replaced by a standby engine. He much enjoyed doing this and felt he was "with it". His ambition was to become a railway man, but his father had other views; however, after Mr Nicholson had talked the matter over with me, he realised his son would not be happy in any other career. Mr Nicholson went to Waterloo to see the Chief Mechanical Engineer, and in due course Gordon became a pupil in Eastleigh Locomotive Works.' From *Rails in the Isle of Wight*, P.C. Allen & A.B. MacLeod. Allen & Unwin, 1967

became a disciple of Bulleid. He is reported as commenting that Bulleid's Pacific types could work all BR traffic and that the standard types simply increased the number of classes rather than reducing them. He does not mention his solution for freight. Click reports on Cocks as follows, 'CSC was short and stocky and when he had hoisted himself up he unerringly went straight to any weak point on the drawing he saw in front of him; he'd be ruthless, witty, devastating even. Sometimes a week's work would be covered in thick 2B pencil lines showing what he didn't like and then what was wanted; always explaining why, though. He was a great teacher, and though there are some now who would not own it, there can be nobody who worked under him who did not benefit from his example … Gradually Cocks's influence increased, there was some resentment but he was a dynamo, and he spoke the same ex-Doncaster language as the Chief. His feet were firmly on the ground and he realised he would have, and was already having to, restrain Bulleid's over-exuberance and higher flown fancies.'

Gordon Lloyd Nicholson. 1914–? A trained engineer, Nicholson was in charge of the Isle of Wight system during Bulleid's tenure but as we know also stood in for other more senior individuals at meetings. He later became District Motive Power Superintendent at Stewarts Lane. R.N.H. ('Dick') Hardy became shedmaster at Stewarts Lane in 1952 had Nicholson as his boss. Hardy recounts as follows, 'My greatest asset was G.L. Nicholson himself. He was a young man of 38 which was rare indeed for a Southern Region District Motive Power Superintendent. He was Southern through and through and yet quite different from any of his colleagues with whom I dealt, on that Region. To see him stalking down the signing-on corridor, through our outer office to his own sanctum — tall, military bowler, white stiff collar and furled umbrella — was a revelation even though his efforts to get me into a white stiff collar did not meet with the success they deserved. To know that he was steadfastly behind one was great, to experience the strength of his leadership and inspiration was even better for he was no extrovert leader who claimed the limelight but one who would delegate but expect his men to emulate his principles to the full. Furthermore, he had both a sense of humour and a sense of the ridiculous so necessary in running a motive power department in which the actors were so often hilariously funny, sometimes quite unconsciously.'

Nicholson was clearly not a fan of Bulleid so far as Leader was concerned. But that dislike would not have been personal and was instead based upon his loyalty and understand of what was needed in the form of motive power by the Southern Railway and its needs. What we have in his recollections, and we must add these were written by Nicholson approaching forty years after they occurred, is the opinion of man whose department was charged with providing motive power for the services scheduled by the traffic department. Motive power which, as recounted in the final paragraph of his recollections, was unreliable, expensive in lubricants and fuel and difficult to work on. The opinion of one man perhaps, but an opinion we should not set aside lightly.

In 1949 he penned a major article in the *British Railways Southern Region* magazine entitled 'The Locomotive Interchange Trials of 1948'. This ran over seven pages of the December issue. We do not know if he was subsequently active as a railway writer. (Leader was never considered for the interchange trails not least for the simple reason the engine was not even complete when the trials had taken place.)

Gordon Nicholson was later appointed Modernisation Assistant to the General Manager of the Scottish Region.

Stephen Collingwood Townroe. 1911–1991. Stephen Townroe recounted his own experiences of Leader to the author in correspondence dated July 1984 and in what can only be described as a masterly form of understatement. Describing the project in engineering terms first he then recounts some of the practical difficulties that were encountered and including, 'There were other little difficulties, such as breakage of the oil-pump drive, so that

Stephen Collingwood Townroe caught in the afternoon sunshine during his time as District Motive Power Superintendent at Eastleigh. The present writer owes much to him for help in unravelling the story of Leader. Notice the only locomotive portrait visible is a Maunsell design 'Lord Nelson'.

to get home without motion seizure the crew had to pour oil down through the cab floor. … Riding in 36001 might be imagined as sharing the inside of a small submarine with a hot boiler and smokebox, and sundry live steam pipes. The heat and humidity were almost unbearable.' He continued 'At the time of the dynamometer tests Bulleid was installed as CME in Ireland. I had hoped that he might pay us at least one visit to get first-hand information and to say a few words about his intentions, but he stayed away. He must have known by then that the Leader was a dead duck because he set about building a turf-burning version at Inchicore using piston, not sleeve valves and with an external driving cab. The late R.C. Bond, at the time Riddles' deputy, told me later of the interview at Marylebone at which Bulleid was told of the reasons why the Leader was not a practical proposition; care being taken to have every word taken down in shorthand!'

A later note to the present author from Townroe expounded on the autumn 1949 meeting between Riddles and Bulleid slightly further. Townroe recounted R.C. Bond as advising him of the 'rather difficult' discussion which had taken place between Riddles and Bulleid and 'about the impossibility of further progress and Riddles had to firmly insist that no more money could be spent.' This would then have been around the time the order was given for work to cease on 36002–5.

Townroe, again in correspondence to the author in 1984, wrote of Bulleid as follows. For obvious reasons this was not included in the original works:

'Bulleid soon left BR to become CME of CIE in Ireland. It was a revelation of Bulleid's ways of thinking that he proceeded to repeat his mistakes with a similar design to No. 36001, except that this time he put the enginemen in a separate cab. It was an experiment which the Irish railways could not afford and it, too, had to be scrapped without earning a penny or a punt. Such blindness to reality was/'is inexplicable.

'Those who worked on Bulleid's personal staff on the Southern found him an enigma. When approached for decisions on routine matters, they would receive the most illogical answers and after years of contact they had to admit, that they did not know what to make of him. He was a dreamer; certainly inventive and an originator (innovator) but lacking in hard common-sense. When he went into retirement, he was restless, and changed his residence at least five times.'

Townroe was similarly nothing short of abrupt in other ways when referring to the former CME, 'Bulleid was clever, self-centred, conceited, ingenious, charming with equals but inconsiderate and supercilious towards his underlings … he was a cold fish, he was erratic. Even his personal clerk often didn't know his whereabouts. He would

Reg Curl in his office at Eastleigh works during the late 1950s. Curl enjoyed a good relationship with Bulleid and was responsible for at least one detail on the Pacific types: the Hexagon/Pentagon means of securing the crank pins; the photograph of Leader on the wall will be noted. In his later career he took overall change of the apprentices and is recalled as a disciplinarian. As was fashion for the period, Reg was always most respectful when referring to the past. The John Click archive contains copies of letters sent by Reg Curl to Antony Bulleid (these later passed to Click) one of which starts, 'Dear Mr Antony, Please excuse my form of address to you, but there will only ever be *one* Mr Bulleid in my life. I still after a few years, miss very much, his constant companionship in correspondence … don't know why I got on so well with him – I wasn't afraid of him – perhaps that's the reason. I told him in later years that my work for him was the happiest years of my life, among 45 years D.O. I feel that many of the staff were not able to appreciate his calibre and in the main they feared him. Mr Munns the Works Supt – a good man – once said "Well, if he wants the chimney on the tender we'll 'b' well put it there! Ignorance!"' When steam records were being disposed of from Eastleigh in the mid 1960s, Reg was the one who saved much of the Nine Elms glass plate negatives – these now reside at the National Railway Museum. Reg had a son, Barry Curl, also an enthusiastic follower of steam who for years had a narrow gauge railway around the grounds of his home at Durley, Hampshire.

tell his car driver to be ready to leave for Eastleigh at 9am, leave him waiting until after his lunch and then tell him to drive to Ashford. His deputy, E.A.W. Turbett, was left to try and keep order in the CME Department affairs and kept clear of involvement in design… Bulleid was in workshops all his life. He had no first-hand outdoor experience as a District Traffic or Motive Power Officer. He did not discuss his design ideas with the users … hence nobody warned him that the inside of the Leader would be unbearable. Bulleid did not like people with practical experience and I am convinced that was why he did not talk about the MN design with my Chief in 1939, nor about the Bleeder in 1946. Now that he has passed away, I think that the truth about him can be written without any offence, and of course without malice.'

Townroe provided some personal notes as part of an article, possibly published later in the magazine of the Friends of the National Railway Museum. 'The story was one of repeated breakages of the valve gear components caused by valve seizures. The sleeves had then had their clearances increased to 36 thou.inch, after which steam tightness depended upon the rings, 32 per sleeve, which were a fitter's nightmare to fit properly. The refractory lining of the firebox had repeatedly came adrift – a problem already experiences the brick lining of fireboxes converted to oil-firing – but on the Leader the result was red-hot firebox sides. There were other little difficulties, such as breakage of the oil-pump drive, so that to get home without motion seizure the crew had to pour oil down through the cab floor. Riding in 36001 might be imagined as sharing the inside of a small submarine with a hot boiler and smokebox, and sundry live steam pipes. The heat and humidity were almost unbearable. The conditions for the engine crew in service were quite unacceptable and seemed to have escaped the designer. I witnessed the weigh table readings, and saw the needles hit the stops thus indicating axle-weights of over 25 tons. There was no conceivable way in which the excess weight could be shed to bring 36001 within the 18t 10cwt limit for secondary and 21t for main lines. At that moment the thing was obviously doomed. However Mr Riddles had evidently decided to let the Leader show its paces, if by any chance the design deserved to be developed. Somehow the Civil Engineer had been persuaded to allow 36001 to run between Eastleigh and Woking. Trial runs were made in the evenings when there was less chance of interfering with traffic. At the time of the dynamometer tests Bulleid was installed as CME in Ireland. I had hoped he might pay us at least one visit to get first-hand information and to say a few words about his intentions, but he stayed away. He must have known by then that the Leader was a dead duck… .'

APPENDIX 4
Details of Test Runs: 2039, 36001, etc.

CHRONOLOGY OF NO 2039	
12/05 – 2/06	Built by Kitson & Co. Given the number '39' by the LBSCR
12/08	Steam heating fitted
6/13	Named 'La France'
1/26	Renumbered and renamed by the SR. Now No 2039 'Hartland Point'
7/47	To Brighton Works for conversion
5/11/47	Ex Works from Brighton
3/12/47	Yard trial at Brighton in the presence of Bulleid and Ivatt
15/1247	Light engine together with 'E5' No 2404 to Lewes
1/1/48	Worked 3-coach set Brighton to Eastbourne
Jan 48	Daily test train Brighton to Groombridge via Lewes. Light engine runs Brighton to Three Bridges. 'K' class 2-6-0 propelled to Three Bridges and return
February 48	Works visits. Trip(s) to Eastleigh
Mar – mid-July 48	Test train on Coastway line Brighton to Lewes or Cowden? 3-coach set Brighton to Tunbridge Wells West and return. Similar load to Hastings and return
Mid July – August 48	Works visits?
September 48	Train of bogie utility vans. Works visit
December 48	Light engine trials to Hastings. Failed at St Leonards with broken valve rod on 19-12-48
Jan – Feb 49	Works. Trials?
14/3/49	Public passenger train Brighton to Redhill and return
16/3/49	Trial with 3 coaches Brighton to Redhill, failed at Earlswood
Apr – Jun 49	Special to Ashford with Bulleid on the footplate. Stock trains Lancing Carriage Works to Eastleigh. Works visits and storage
14/6/49 – 3/9/49	Brighton Works – overhaul
Sept 49	Stored at Brighton
17/2/51	Towed from Brighton to Eastleigh
24/2/51	Withdrawn from Eastleigh
28/2/51	Breaking up order No 958 issued
3/51	Scrapped Eastleigh Works

COMPLETE LIST OF ALL LEADER WORKINGS COMPILED FROM OFFICIAL SOURCES		
22/6/49	Initial trial trip	Failure
25/6/49	Light engine with E4 tank to Falmer and Groombridge	
26/6/49	Light engine with K to Eastleigh	
29/6/49	Light, Eastleigh to Brighton	Failure
7/7/49	Light to Falmer and Crowborough	
8/7/49	Light to Falmer and Crowborough	
12/7/49	Light to Falmer and Crowborough	
14/7/49	Light to Crowborough x 2	Failure
23/7/49	Light to Crowborough	
24/7/49	Light to Seaford	Failure
12/8/49	Light to Crowborough, Seaford and Lewes	Failure

	COMPLETE LIST OF ALL LEADER WORKINGS COMPILED FROM OFFICIAL SOURCES	
13/8/49	Light to Crowborough, Seaford and Lewes	
14/8/49	Light to Crowborough, Seaford and Lewes	Failure
15/8/49	Light to Crowborough, Seaford and Lewes	Failure
16/8/49	Light to Crowborough, Seaford and Lewes	Failure
17/8/49	Light to Crowborough, Seaford and Lewes	Failure
18/8/49	Trial to Eastleigh with 248 tons	Failure
20/8/49	Light, Eastleigh to Brighton	Failure
30/8/49	Light to Crowborough	
31/8/49	Light to Crowborough	
1/9/49	Light to Crowborough	
2/9/49	Light to Crowborough	
5/9/49	Intended trial to Victoria with 260 tons	Failure
8/9/49	Intended trial to Victoria with 260 tons	Failure
16/9/49	Trials to Crowborough with 180 and 271 tons	Failure
19/9/49	Trials to Crowborough with 180 and 271 tons	Failure
20/9/49	Trials to Crowborough with 180 and 271 tons	Failure
23/9/49	Light to Crowborough	
24/9/49	Light to Crowborough	
25/9/49	Light to Crowborough	Failure
27/9/49	Trials to Oxted, Crowborough and Lewes with 150 tons	Failure
28/9/49	Trials to Oxted, Crowborough and Lewes with 150 tons	Failure
29/9/49	Trials to Oxted, Crowborough and Lewes with 150 tons	Failure
30/9/49	Trials to Oxted, Crowborough and Lewes with 150 tons	Failure
3/10/49	Trial to Crowborough with 150 tons	Failure
4/10/49	Trial to Crowborough with 150 tons	Failure
9/10/49	Trial to Crowborough with 150 tons	Failure
22/10/49	Trial to Oxted and Crowborough with 150 tons	
23/10/49	Trial to Oxted and Crowborough with 150 tons	
24/10/49	Trial to Oxted and Crowborough with 150 tons	Failure
29/10/49	Light to Crowborough and Tunbridge Wells	Failure
30/10/49	Light to Crowborough and Tunbridge Wells	
31/10/49	Trial to Crowborough with 161 tons	
1/11/49	Trials to Oxted and Crowborough with 153 and 255 tons	Failure
2/11/49	Trials to Oxted and Crowborough with 153 and 255 tons	
3/11/49	Trials to Oxted and Crowborough with 153 and 255 tons	
4/11/49	Trials to Oxted and Crowborough with 153 and 255 tons	
7/11/49	Trials to Oxted, Polegate and Crowborough with 155 and 255 tons	
8/11/49	Trials to Oxted, Polegate and Crowborough with 155 and 255 tons	
9/11/49	Trials to Oxted, Polegate and Crowborough with 155 and 255 tons	
10/11/49	Trials to Oxted, Polegate and Crowborough with 155 and 255 tons	
11/11/49	Trials to Oxted, Polegate and Crowborough with 155 and 255 tons	
16/11/49	Trials to Oxted with 255 tons	Failure
21/11/49	Trails to Oxted and Polegate with 155 and 255 tons	
22/11/49	Trails to Oxted and Polegate with 155 and 255 tons	
23/11/49	Trails to Oxted and Polegate with 155 and 255 tons	
24/11/49	Trails to Oxted and Polegate with 155 and 255 tons	
25/11/49	Trails to Oxted and Polegate with 155 and 255 tons	Failure

COMPLETE LIST OF ALL LEADER WORKINGS COMPILED FROM OFFICIAL SOURCES		
29/11/49	Trial to Polegate with 153 tons	Failure
1/12/49	Trials to Oxted, Tunbridge Wells and Groombridge with 153 to 255 tons	
2/12/49	Trials to Oxted, Tunbridge Wells and Groombridge with 153 to 255 tons	
3/12/49	Trials to Oxted, Tunbridge Wells and Groombridge with 153 to 255 tons	
4/12/49	Trials to Oxted, Tunbridge Wells and Groombridge with 153 to 255 tons	
5/12/49	Trials to Oxted, Tunbridge Wells and Groombridge with 153 to 255 tons	
6/12/49	Trials to Oxted, Tunbridge Wells and Groombridge with 153 to 255 tons	Failure
12/12/49	Trials to Crowborough and Oxted with 153 to 255 tons	
13/12/49	Trials to Crowborough and Oxted with 153 to 255 tons	Failure
16/12/49	Light to Eastleigh and return	
27/1/50	Light to Tunbridge Wells	
2/2/50	Light to Eastleigh and return	
13/4/50	Light to Eastleigh	
6/6/50	Trial Eastleigh to Fratton with 332 tons	
7/6/50	Trial Eastleigh to Fratton with 332 tons	
8/6/50	Trial Eastleigh to Fratton with 332 tons	
12/6/50	Trial Eastleigh to Woking with 332 tons	
15/6/50	Trial Eastleigh to Woking with 320 tons	Failure
29/6/50	Intended Eastleigh to Woking trial with approx. 240 tons	Failure
15/8/50	Light Eastleigh to Botley	
16/8/50	Light Eastleigh to Botley	
18/8/50	Light Eastleigh to Fratton	
21/8/50	Trial, Eastleigh to Woking and Guildford with 231½ tons	
23/8/50	Trial, Eastleigh to Woking and Guildford with 264 tons	
24/8/50	Trial, Eastleigh to Woking and Guildford with 290½ tons	
21/9/50	Light Eastleigh to Fratton	
25/9/50	Trial, Eastleigh to Woking and Guildford with 241½ tons	
26/9/50	Trial, Eastleigh to Woking and Guildford with 275 tons	
27/9/50	Trial, Eastleigh to Woking and Guildford with 294½ tons	
28/9/50	Trial, Eastleigh to Woking and Guildford with 325 tons	
14/10/50	Light Eastleigh to Cosham	
17/10/50	Trial, Eastleigh to Woking and Guildford with 420 tons	
2/11/50	Trial, Eastleigh to Woking and Guildford with 480 tons*	Failure
Terminated at Basingstoke on outward journey		

In total, Leader made 91 reported outings, 71 starting from Brighton (including the final trip to Eastleigh on 13 April 1950), and a further 20 outings from Eastleigh. Of the 71 Brighton starts 45% were classified as failures. The figures from Eastleigh were better with just three reported failures – equivalent to just 15%, but as we know that does not mean the performance was faultless on the other occasions. The most runs in any month was in November 1949 when 16 days running was achieved. The second most runs being two months earlier in September 1949 with 14 days steaming. The least were in January, February, April, and November 1950 each recording just one day in steam March, April, and July 1950 had Leader not working at all.

The number of early trails from Brighton is explained as it was expected that apart from perhaps initial teething troubles, any issues might be quickly resolved and the class enter revenue earning service. However, as time passed and the difficulties with the design became more pronounced, so the tests reduced in number with all hope resting on more technical testing involving dynamometer car trials.

LEADER: Known works visits including for repair/investigation		
		Location
21-6-49	Engine emerges from Works - new	Brighton
22 to 24-6-49	To works	Brighton
25-6-49	Following successful trial run. Preparation for visit to Eastleigh	Brighton
30 June to 6-7-49	Repairs following return from Eastleigh	Brighton
15 to 22-7-49	Repairs, No 1 bogie	Brighton
24 July to 11-8-49	Repairs, No 1 bogie etc.	Brighton
18 or 19-8-49	Weighing, repairs to firebox lining, ash chute etc.	Eastleigh
21 to 29-8-49	Sleeve repairs etc.	Brighton
16 to 18-9-49	Blast pipe attention	Brighton
21/22-9-49	Sleeve repairs	Brighton
c.4 to 9 Oct-49	Firebox lining	Brighton
10 to 2/10/49	Firebox lining	Brighton
23 to 28/10/49	Sleeve repairs No 2 bogie	Brighton
16-12-49	Weighing	Eastleigh
Dec/Jan 1949-50	Adjustments to axle-boxes/springing /weights etc.	Brighton
2-2-50	Weighing	Brighton
17-4-50	Light/casual	Eastleigh
8-6-50	Main steam pipe and grate	Eastleigh
13 and 14-6-50	Buckley flange plate – smokebox	Eastleigh
19 to approx. 30-6-50	'Light casual'. Valve events checked, blast pipe cap changed, fittings for forthcoming Dynamometer Car trials	Eastleigh
30 June to 13-8-50	Crank axles replaced	Eastleigh
17 and 18-8-50	Oil bath repairs No. 2 bogie	Eastleigh
22-8-50	Attention to sleeves and some new rings fitted	Eastleigh
25 August to 19-9-50	Full set of rings fitted	Eastleigh

On trial from Brighton and passing Hurst Green Halt on 22 October 1949. This was a days of trials with 150t at the drawbar to Crowborough and then to Oxted. *K.G. Carr, courtesy Peter Fidczuk*

Comparative Performance Based on Average Results Obtained	'U' Class No 31630	'Leader' Class No 36001	% Difference 'U' class = 100%
Boiler Pressure lb/in	187	240	28.3 greater
Steam chest Pressure lb/in	167	135	19.2 less
Exhaust Pressure lb/in	1.81	7.3 6.0	
Smokebox vacuum in of water	2.34	4.00	71 greater
Inlet steam Temp ° F	478	546 564	
Exhaust steam Temp ° F	220	285	29.5 greater
Smokebox A temp ° F	570	574	0.7 greater
Smokebox B temp ° F	578	620	7.26 greater
Trip coal – pounds	1455	2457	68.8 greater
- lb mile	29.75	50.17	68.7 greater
- lb ton/mile	0.0818	0.121	48.0 greater
- lb/hour (running time)	1125	1830	62.7 greater
- lb/sq ft grate/hour	45	71.8	59.6 greater
- lb/DBHP hour	4.01	6.727	67.6 greater
Water – gallons	1245	1850	48.6 greater
gals/mile	25.44	37.78	48.5 greater
- lb/hour (running time)	9621	13790	43.3 greater
lb/ DBHP hour	34.34	50.66	47.5 greater
lb/sq ft evap heating	6.334	5.777	8.8 less
lb/ ton mile (incl engine)	0.702	0.912	30.0 greater
Evaporation – lb water /lb coal	8.554	7.532	12.0 less
Boiler efficiency %	78.29	71.22	9.0 less
BThUs/DBHP hour	53893	90262	67.5 greater
Overall efficiency %	4.72	2.82	40.25 less

COMPARATIVE PERFORMANCE OF 'LEADER' NO 36001, OCTOBER/NOVEMBER 1950		
	17 October	2 November
Load (tons)	430	480
Coal (total cwt)	52½	22 (Eastleigh-Basingstoke only)
lb/mile	59.6	-
lb/dbhp-hr	6.5	6.4
lb/sq ft grate/hr	125	130 (Eastleigh- Basingstoke only)
Water (total) gall	3,570	1,834
gall/mile	37.4	-
gall/mile (Eastleigh -Basingstoke only)	55.0	70.5
lb/dbhp-hr	41.0	51.0
lb/hr (Eastleigh- Basingstoke only)	19,000	24,500

TEST OF 17 OCTOBER 1950										
Place	Booked Time p.m.	Actual Time p.m.	Boiler Pressure	Steam-chest Pressure	% Cut-off	Water in Glass (F = 6½")	Smokebox Vacuum (in of water)	Temp F° Large Tubes	Temp F° Small Tubes	Remarks
Eastleigh	6.45	6.45	260	145 140	67 15	Full				
Allbrook Junc.		6.51¼	250 260 245	200 230 230	30 30 15	Full	4½ 8 6½	620 700 700	600 630 630	Engine worked very lightly to Allbrook Junc. and mainly due to this 5 min subsequently lost to Winchester Junction
Shawford		6.57	240	230	18	5 in	8	700	640	
Shawford Junc.			225	220	18		8	710	635	
St Cross Tunnel			225	220			8½	710	635	
Winchester		7.01¼	230	225	20	4 in	9	740	680	Shower of sparks from chimney about 20% being alight on reaching ground
Winchester Junc.			235	225			9	760	730	15 mph pws
Wallers Ash Box			250	240	20	2½ in	4	660	620	
Weston Box			240	235		2 in	7	720	680	
Micheldever		7.14½	220	205		2 in	8	720	685	BP and water in glass not maintained
Litchfield Tunnel			185	160		2 in	6	715	675	
Worting Junc.	7.19	7.23	200	60		2½ in				
Basingstoke	7.24 7.32	7.32	260 255	130 160	67 15	2 in	4	630	580	6 minutes taken to get engine set for water
Hook		7.46½	240	135	15	1½ in	5	670	630	
Winchfield		7.49	230	120	15	1¼ in	4	665	625	
Fleet		7.55¼	230	120	15	1¼ in	5	650	610	
Farnborough		7.55¼	230	120	15	1¾ in	5	645	600	
Brookwood		8.01	210	200	15					
Woking	8.05	8.03¼								To loal line. Sig checks.

Light engine working at Lewes. Notice the additional link that was in place on the couplings at both ends. Bulleid is reported to have said that had the engine worked on other railways (UK), then water pick-up gear and more coal would have been carried. We cannot begin to imagine why such a comment might have been made. To achieve the former would have been almost impossible with the existing design, the only space for water pick-up gear being amidships which was already cluttered with the ash pan. As Leader was also double ended presumably a scoop capable of working in either direction would have been required. As regards more coal, more coal equals more weight and Leader was already far heavier than intended. On other lines? Certainly not, no other region would have taken it. In many respects Bulleid was indeed a genius but in his comments here he has gone beyond that definition referring to the existing design. J.M. Dunn, himself a lifetime railway engineer, was also critical of aspects of the design when it came to maintenance. He adds, 'like other locomotives I have met, he presumably never expected his engines to require repairs between its visits to Works, but as one who has lived railway engines for nearly 40 years, I have very grave doubts as to how this would work out in practice.' *S.C. Nash/Stephenson Locomotive Society*

Appendix 4 – Details of Test Runs: 2039, 36001, etc.

TEST OF 2 NOVEMBER 1950										
Place	Booked Time p.m.	Actual Time p.m.	Boiler Pressure	Steam-chest Pressure	% Cut-off	Water in Glass (F = 6½")	Smokebox Vacuum (in of water)	Temp F° Large Tubes	Temp F° Small Tubes	Remarks
Eastleigh	6.40	6.40	260 / 270	240 / 130	67 / 25	Full	1 / 1¾	500	500	Started without difficulty
Allbrook Junc	6.45	6.45½	245 / 260	240 / 255	10 / 38	Full	2½ / 4	650 / 680	620 / 630	Pricker and dart used
Shawford		6.53½	230	225	18	Full	6½	730	680	
Shawford Junc.			220	210	18	Full	7	730	660	Pricker used
St Cross Tunnel			220	210	18	Full	7	730	660	
Winchester		6.58¼	245	240	18	Full	9	750	700	Pricker used
Winchester Junc.	6.59	7.01¾	255	225	18	Full	10½	760	710	
Wallers Ash Box		7.05	245	220	18	Full	10½	750	700	Pricker and dart used
Weston Box		7.07	240	225	18	Full	10	750	720	
Micheldever		7.09½	250 / 260	235 / 250	18 / 20	5½ in / 5 in	10 / 13½	785 / 800	750 / 780	
Litchfield Tunnel		7.12½	255	240	20	4 in	13½	820	800	
Worting Junc.	7.19	7.18½								Pricker used
Basingstoke	7.24	7.26								Sig. Stop 1½ minutes

293

APPENDIX 5
The Colour and Appearance of Leader

Just in case readers may think No. 36001 was a dull shade of grey throughout its life that is not so. There were several variations in appearance and colour, those known being listed below.

1. Black. Inside Brighton works around 20 June 1949 No. 36001 was painted gloss black all over. No front/rear number plates, side number decals or ownership details were shown.

2. Again on 20 June and probably continuing on the 21 June and the engine's first public appearance outside, the all-over black was replaced by all-over grey. (Similar to the term/tone 'photographic grey'.) Other details as above. Number plates front and rear fitted some time between 22 une and 28 June.

3. The next stage occurred at Eastleigh around 29 June 1949 and certainly in time for the VIP inspection. Livery all over grey. At Eastleigh the BR 'cycling lion' crest was applied centrally with words 'British Railways' passing through this. The number 36001 appeared in large decals underneath the emblem. Tyre walls painted white. Note the background to the numberplates was grey and not the more usual black and would remain as such throughout the life of the engine.

4. Upon returning to Brighton to commence trials, the 'British Railways' emblem and number were removed from the sides. In its place decals with the number 36001 now appeared on both sides but with these placed close to the access doors at either end of the engine. No ownership detail was shown. Five 'panels', bordered with standard black/red/white lines (although the white probably did not show much) were painted both sides of the engine. In this condition some images appear to show alternate light/dark paint but this is a trick of the light. Three panels with similar lining were applied at both ends. Note; the term 'panels' is used with caution as the paint applied was just to the borders and not within the 'panels' themselves. It should also be noted that where the centrally placed BR logo and number had previously been applied, the paint used to cover these did not entirely match the rest of the side and for the rest of No. 36001's life, certain images (in certain lights) show a slightly lighter patch in this area. (See p.149 and 151 as examples.)

5. As 4 above but around 20 September 1949 the oscillating gear at the front of the sleeves was removed from No. 1 end bogie. The oscillating gear at the front of both bogies was designed to have been protected by a curved dust cover. Whether this had been previously removed to facilitate observation of the oscillating gear during the running trials is not known.

6. On or about 22 October, oscillating gear also removed from No.2 end bogie as well. Comments above regarding the cover for this gear prior to its removal also applies.

7. Towards the end of June 1949, a circular hole was cut into the offside front of No. 1 end. This was to facilitate connections between the engine and the dynamometer car. Note also that when working from Eastleigh during the dynamometer trails (and possibly during some other pre-dynamometer trails), a canvas cover was stretched over part of the coal bunker.

John Click adds one final point to the livery story. 'At an early stage an unknown artist had produced a painting of Leader in overall black livery but lined out as per the first BR paint style for mixed-traffic locos. A print of this was doctored by Marylebone for internal consumption showing not only the "castrated cat" standing astride the BR "Catherine wheel" but in fact five versions; one for each panel. In the first the cat was preparing to spring at the wheel, the second showed him in full upward flight and so on... to the last panel where he was comfortably seated again, twitching his whiskers!'

Nos. 36002–3. These part completed engines appear never to have been painted. In its short life No. 36002 appears to have been all-over steel in colour although cast number plates were fitted at both ends.

It is important to note that despite the best endeavours of various skilled artists, Leader never appeared in any form of green livery.

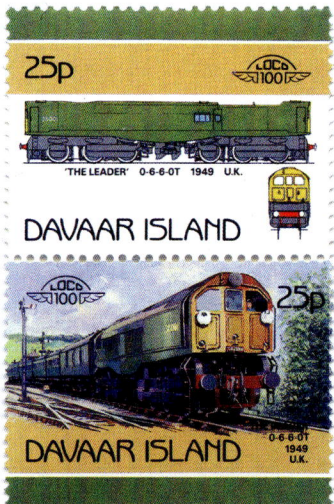

Davaar Island is at the mouth of Campbeltown Lock in Kintyre Peninsular, Argyll. Doubt exists as to whether these were or indeed could be used as genuine stamps. Three sets of six pairs each (12 stamps) featuring locomotives of the world were produced in 1983 (two sets of 12) and a third set in 1987. Leader was part of the 1987 issue. The yellow ends are probably best not commented upon.

Cold and lifeless at Eastleigh. Despite its massive appearance, we should not forget that the cab of Leader rode high in the loading gauge. J.M. Dunn in an article in *SLS* Journal No. 483 entitled 'I saw a Leader' commented that at 5ft 8in his hair brushed the cab roof at its tallest point. Recall the fireman's cab was in a well so there the headroom was greater. Leader's reputation and history is a mixture of truth, speculation and at times downright inaccuracy. Rumours for example that she spread the track and the asbestos clad fireman are just that – nothing more than rumour. Leader's reputation, the bad rather than the good, has always preceded it. The design of the braking system, the universal torque, the ability of the boiler to raise steam, the body-to-bogie mounting; all of these showed steam engine development was still possible but are conveniently ignored. Remember too Bulleid's earlier comment from years previous when he said just four steam types could work all the SR's loco-hauled steam traffic; Merchant Navy, Light Pacific and two types of Leader. (36001 was evidently the larger of the two). The Q1 was not included as this was considered a wartime and so temporary addition. Genius – or otherwise? *A.E. West/Mike King*

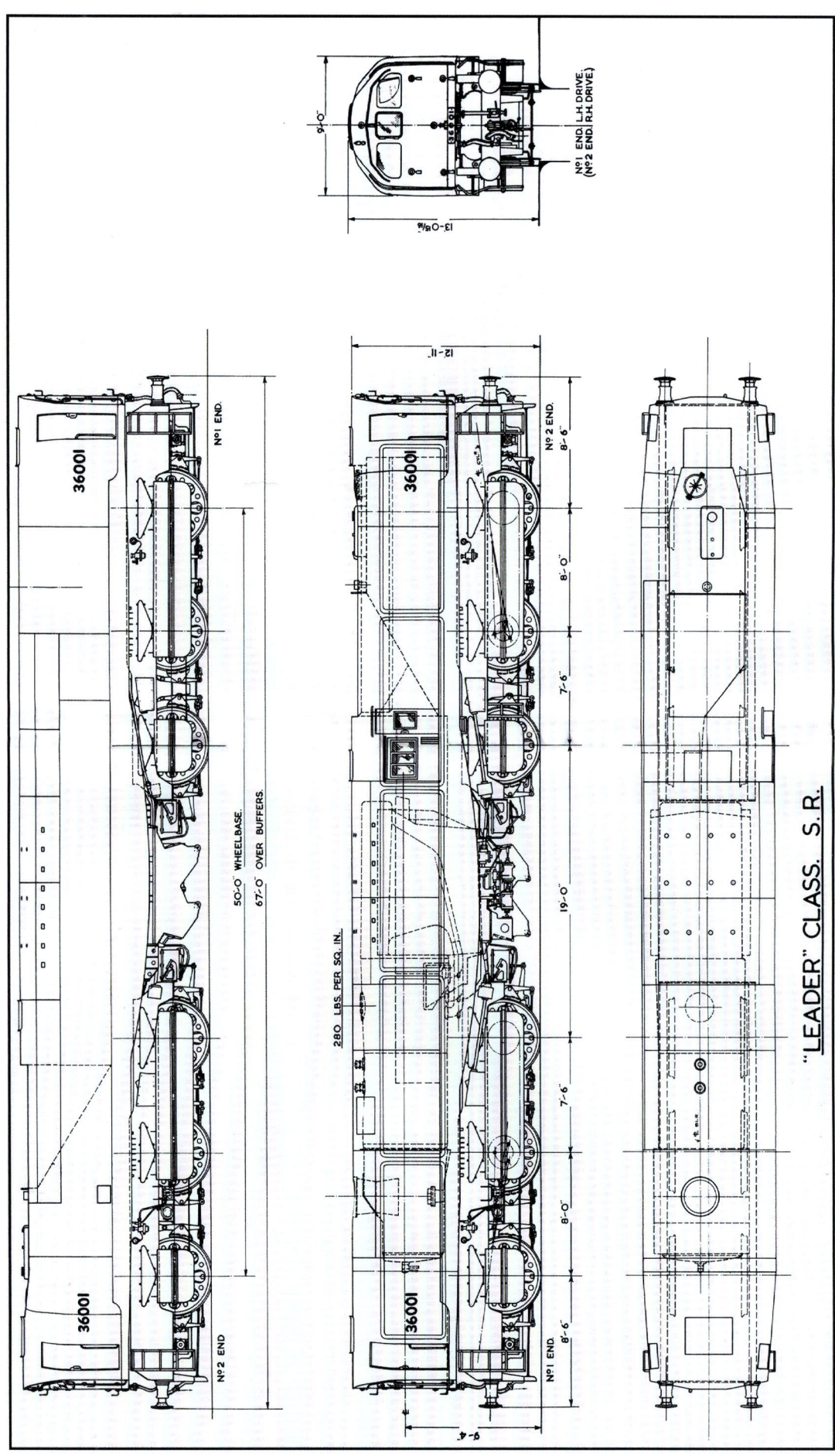

Leader reborn? Not quite. A spoof for the railway Press from the Swanage railway. Might Leader re-emerge as a 'new build'? The present writer sincerely hopes not, but as mentioned in the text a full size wooden mock-up of perhaps half the engine would certainly deserve a place in a museum to tell the story of one man's brave attempt to break the mould. One final comment: it is known Bulleid visited the renowned model loco builder James Stanley Beeson in Ringwood, we think just before Bulleid left for Ireland. The point of the visit was to discuss the building of a possible model of the Leader. For reasons that are unknown it did not progress further. From this we get the impression that Bulleid had a particular soft spot for the Leader design, whilst it was also rumoured he had at one time considered writing his autobiography – presumably covering all his work. It is not believed any work was ever undertaken and it would be left to his son Anthony Bulleid (HAV) to record his father's work. In Eastleigh though, Leader would not be forgotten even 40 years after its demise, as C.A.M.R.A (The Campaign for Real Ale) held a meeting at Eastleigh in 1991, the half-pint glass tankards for which featured an excellent representation of the engine.

INDEX

General

Atwell, Harold C, in charge of testing at Brighton 7
Bulleid, H A V, son of O V S, author of *Bulleid of the Southern* 6
Bulleid, O V S, his work on the Southern..........14, 16, 21
His work on the LNER, and visit to Vitré test centre with *Cock o' the North* 32
Source of inspiration for 'Leader' 90
Relations with Drawing Office staff 91-92
Chairs IMechE meeting, gives overview of future of railway motive power 97, 99
Presence at 1949 trials 152
Evasiveness on being pressed by Riddles for report on 'Leader' 152
Leaves for new post in Ireland..................................152
Writes to Missenden & Riddles 154
Leaves for new post in Ireland..................................152
Final ride on 'Leader'..188
Lecture to American Society of Mechanical Engineers, October 1949 197
Vindication of his work on the Southern 214-16
Was Bulleid right or wrong................................216-236
Bulleid's locomotive policy on CIE..............................240
Sets up experiment on turf burning at Inchicore........242
Uses ex-GSWR 2-6-0 No. 356 as turf-burning test-bed 247
Chapelon, André, French locomotive engineer 17, 83
Books on his work .... 35, (*Note 1*)
His proposals for further steam development 199
Click, John C, Bulleid apprentice 6
Comments on design process of *Leader* 38, 39, 41, 44
Comments on success of Fairburn 2-6-4T on Southern 95
Taking photographs of 'Leader's' construction..............96
His notes on Bulleid's time on the Southern...........209-13
First comments on Bulleid at Inchicore, and lack of realisation of Restrictions on facilities in Ireland 240
Sees drawing of 'Turf-burner.......................................242
Becomes Assistant to Bulleid in Dublin 244
Experience with turf-burning on No. 356 249

Is first person to move CC1 under steam....................255
Cocks, C S .... 13 (*Note 1*)
Cox, E S, locomotive designer, comments on Bulleid's points made at IMechE meeting................................99
Elliot, Sir John, Acting General Manager, southern Railway 44
Ellson, George, Chief Civil Engineer, SR, rejects Garratt proposal 21
Retirement, 1944...30
Granshaw, Works Manager, Brighton..........................11
Gresley, (Sir) Nigel, CME, LNER, work on LNER in '20s and '30s 22
Jarvis, R G, Chief Draughtsman, Brighton, report to Riddles 155/6
Letter in *Railway Observer*, 25 May 1951, 'What has become of 'Leader'?..............................200

Leader class locomotive

Construction & erection of locos; responsibilities of different Works...64
Genesis in Bulleid's mind 30
Idea for side passage (from Gresley corridor tender) 30
Similarity to Paget locomotive in principles 32
Principles of design 36-8
Suggestion that it should run on two power bogies 44
First outline of layout of power bogies 46
Use of sleeve valves...53, 54
Ricardo Engineering 53, 54
Traffic Requirements for 'Leader' (tonnages & routes)...56
Formal order to proceed to build.................................58
Ash chute trials on No. 1896.......................................60
Major problems associated with design of 'Leader' 101
Use of meehanite for sleeve valves 102
Boiler/firebox syphons 102
Brighton works woodwork shop – wooden mock-up of 'Leader' body 103
Leaders offset boiler: comparison with Shay locomotive in USA...104
Patent to cover new boiler design, no. 616.445 105
Feed-water heater compared to use of TIA treatment...106

298

Photography – ban during building	106
Bogie interchangeability	108
Further build authorisation, and cancellation	109, 112
Rising costs	113
First public appearance	116
First movement under steam, 22 June 1949	116
First mainline trial, 25 June	118
To Eastleigh, 26 June	119
Inspection by VIPs, 28 June	120
Return to Brighton, 29 June	124
Damage on return run	126
Trials. Mid-July	130
Further trials, mid-August, Crowborough, Seaford, Lewes	130
Weighing at Eastleigh (grossly overweight)	132
Return to Brighton, and repairs	132
Preparation for run to Victoria, 4 Sept.	133
Report of abortive run, 5 Sept.	134/5
Second abortive run, 8 Sept.	138-141
Further trials, late September – erratic steaming	145
Trials to end September, firebrick problems	146, 149
Successful period of trials, October/November 1949	150
Further trials, early December	152
Weight a major issue	153
Modifications to springs; extra ballast weights; firebox lining	154
Limitations as to coal and water carried	154
ASLEF unwilling to work locomotive; safety issues	158
Fitting of brick arch in firebox	162
Use of dynamometer car	162
First pre-dynamometer test, failed at Micheldever	167
Steam pressure troubles	170
Driving axle failures	171/2
Comparison trials made with 'U' class no. 31618	172
Further comparison trials with 'U' class no. 31630	173
Excess water consumption	173
Planning for dynamometer car trials, August 1950	174
First dynamometer test run, 12 August 1950	175/6
Further test run, 23 August	177/8
Water consumption problems	177/8
Another run (aborted), 24 August	180
Repairs at Eastleigh	181
More trials, 25-28 Sept	181-4
Final trial, 2 Nov.	188
Final report from Riddles, recommending scrapping	188-192
Nos. 36002 and 36003, incomplete, stored at Bognor	193
Nos 36002, 36003, moved to New Cross Gate, 11 Sept. 1950	193
No. 36002, dismantled at Brighton, 30 June 1951	194
No. 36001, dismantling began at Eastleigh, 25 Apr. 1951	194
Rumour that all five might be sold to Ireland	194
Some of the lessons learned from the project	202
Press story about 'Leander' 'fiasco', 18 Jan. 1953, *Sunday Dispatch*	203
Commentary on comments by other authors, E F Carter, G. Freeman Allen, Michael Rutherford	204/5
Drawings at national Railway Museum regarding oil-burning	205
Was 'Leader' intended to burn coal, or oil?	206
Conversion of 'Terrier' No. 515S as tests bed for oil firing	207
Trials reports from Brighton, Sept. 1949	208
Rumours of sabotage during trials	215
Description of 'Leader', by G. Freeman Allen, *The Southern since 1948*	258 (*Appendix 1*)
'Leader', The Mechanics, by Les Warnett, Brighton fitter	262 (*Appendix 2*)
Main frame structure	262
Boiler, firebox & ancillaries	263
Feedwater	269
Smokebox	269
Fuel bunker and water tank	270
Reversing arrangement	271
Brakes- control system	272
Casing	272
Electrics	274
Controls and instrumentation	274
Power bogies – pivots	274
Bogie frame assembly	275
Steam and exhaust pipes on the power bogies	275
Horn guide pedestals	275
Axle boxes	276
Wheels and axles	276
Chain transmission drive	277
Bogie spring rigging	277
Cylinders	277
Motion	278
Sleeve Valve motion	278
Oscillating Gear	280
Cylinder cocks	280

Lubrication	281
Brake rigging	281
Sundries and draw gear	281
The Views of the Professionals	282 (*Appendix 3*)
Atwell, C A	282
Click, J G	282
Cocks, C S	282
Nicholson, G L	284
Townroe, S C	284
Details of test runs on 2039 and 36001, etc	286 (*Appendix 4*)
Colour and Appearance of 'Leader'	294 (*Appendix 5*)

Images, General

The dynamometer car, on its way home, at Banbury after the trial	192
Southern Railway, Train Wreck, Shoreham Road bridge, 1927	28
Southern Railway, Brighton Works, interior	85

Images, 'Leader'

Southern Railway, Brighton Works, *Leader* Mainframe	86
Southern Railway, Eastleigh Works, Model *Leader Boiler*	87
British Railways, Eastleigh/Brighton Works, a 'Leader boiler	88, 89, 91
British Railways, Brighton Works, a 'Leader' boiler	90
British Railways, Eastleigh Works, a 'Leader' boiler	92
Bogie frames, Brighton Works	93
Bogie frames, with wheels	94
Bogie, almost complete, front end	95
Bogie, almost complete, rear end	96
Bogie, almost complete, rear end, No. 36001	97
Wheels, complete set for one bogie	98
Model of Motion	101
Tank & bunker under construction	102
Fireman's cab – interior	103, 104
Front of boiler and smokebox	105
Smokebox & Ash cute	106
Engine assembly – erecting shop	107
Boiler and smokebox on frame	108
Driver's cab, front end (no.1 end)	109
Side corridor, looking back from no. 1 end	109
Engine and cab, no. 1 end, mounted on frame	110, 111
Complete sleeve valve, with 'ears'	196
Sleeve inserted into 'Leader' bogie	196
A scored and broken sleeve	196
No. 36001, broken crank axle	199
No. 36001, interior driver's cab	200
No. 36001, in store at Eastleigh, 21 Oct. 1950	202
Valve gear, oscillating motion, two images	206
No. 36001, Engine record card	207
No. 36001 being wheeled, erecting shop	112
No. 36001 being painted, erecting shop	113
No. 36001 painted in glossy black, erecting shop	114, 115
No. 36001 complete, in works grey, Brighton, late June 1949	116
BR (ex- Southern Railway) no. 36001 after move to Eastleigh	118
BR (ex- Southern Railway) no. 36001 in front of Eastleigh Office Block	119
BR (ex- Southern Railway) no. 36001 in front of Eastleigh Office Block with drawing office staff (2 views)	120
BR (ex- Southern Railway) no. 36001 in front of Eastleigh Office Block (Head-on)	121
BR (ex- Southern Railway) no. 36001 (Official BR views, two broadside, one head-on)	122, 123
BR (ex- Southern Railway) no. 36001, at Eastleigh with class 0395 0-6-0 no. 30571.	124
BR (ex- Southern Railway) No. 36001, at Eastleigh (in colour)	125
BR No. 36001, leaving for Brighton, 29 June 1949	126
BR No. 36001, at Brighton, 29 June 1949	126
BR No. 36001, at Lewes, 17 August, 1949	128
BR No. 36001, at Brighton, 17 August, 1949	129
BR No. 36001, at Barnham, 20 August 1949	131
BR No. 36001, at Lewes, undated	133
BR No. 36001, at Brighton, (2 images)	134
BR No. 36001 at Oxted, taking water	135
BR No. 36001 at Dormans (colour)	136
BR No. 36001 at Dormans (b/w)	137
BR No. 36001 at Uckfield (in disgrace!), 20 Sept. 1949	139
BR No. 36001 at Crowborough (in disgrace!), 9 Oct.1949	140
BR No. 36001, en route, Lewes-Brighton (colour)	141
BR No. 36001 at Oxted, with train	142
BR No. 36001 at Oxted, with train	143
BR No. 36001, at Lewes, light engine	144
BR No. 36001, no. 2 end	144

Index

BR No. 36001 after running-round,
 at Oxted (colour)..147
BR No. 36001, at Oxted (colour) 148
BR No. 36001, being shunted at Brighton 149
BR No. 36001, in temporary store at Brighton............151
BR No. 36001, in the weigh house at Brighton..........153
BR No. 36001, unloved, last resting place at Brighton 155
BR No. 36001, final view at Brighton 157
BR No. 36001, at Eastleigh, ...159
BR No. 36001, inside Eastleigh Works 159
BR No. 36001, with train at Fratton June 1950 161
BR No. 36001, with train at Otterbourne,
 12/15 June 1950 163
BR No. 36001, at Eastleigh, being prepared for
 dynamometer car trials 166
BR No. 36001, taking water at Eastleigh 167
BR No. 36001, building the fire before the
 dynamometer car runs..169
BR No. 36001, two images of failed crank axle,
 no. 1 bogie, 7 July 1950 171
BR No. 36001, view from no. 1 cab of M7,
 No. 30027 shunting her around at Eastleigh 172
BR No. 36001, inside Eastleigh works, with visitors
 swarming over her 173
BR No. 36001, outside Eastleigh Running Shed,
 26 August 1950 174
BR No. 36001, inside Eastleigh works, 2 Sept. 1950...175
BR No. 36001, leaving Eastleigh shed.........................176
BR No. 36001, coaling, manually 177
BR No. 36001, dynamometer car attached.................178
BR No. 36001, dynamometer car attached, running
 through Eastleigh...179
'Lord Nelson' No. 30853, *Sir Richard Grenville*, seen
 from 'Leader' 181
BR No. 36001, waiting for the 'off' with test train......182
BR No. 36001, with test train (colour) 183
BR No. 36001, near Shawford, heading north............185
BR No. 36001, same place, same train, three-quarter
 rear view..185
BR No. 36001, test train, heading north near
 Otterbourne 186
BR No. 36001, test train, heading north near
 Otterbourne, from ground level 187
BR No. 36001, repairs at Guildford, 22 Aug 191
BR No. 36001, lifeless at Eastleigh.............................193
BR No. 36001, at Brighton, alongside No. 32039 195

BR No. 36002, under construction 213
BR No. 36002, construction ceased, in Pullman Car
 shed, Preston Park 215
BR No. 36003, stored, incomplete, with No. 36002,
 Preston Park...215
BR No. 36002, virtually complete, alongside 30935,
 Sevenoaks 216
BR No. 36002, alongside what would have been
 frames and boiler of 36004 217
BR Nos. 36002, and very partial 36003, in store
 at Bognor 218
Side view of No. 36003 at Bognor 219
No. 36003 alone at Bognor..220
Remnants of No. 36004 under tarpaulins, in the
 open at Eastleigh 221
Nos. 36002 and 36003 at New Cross..........................223
No. 36002 at New Cross, about to be towed
 to Brighton, and scrap 224
Two head-on views of Nos. 36002 and 36003
 at New Cross 225
No. 36002 under tow to Brighton by 'N' class
 No. 31400 227
No. 36003, 'undressed in public'................................228
No. 36003, and Brighton Works shunter,
 at Brighton 229
No. 36002, in course of being dismantled..................231
No. 36001, 14 April 1951, ...233
No. 36001, inside Eastleigh, in course
 of dismantling 234, 235
No. 36001, boiler, lifted from the frames 236
No. 36001, in pristine glory, illustrating G Freeman
 Allen's article 260
No. 36001, main frame assembly at Brighton.............263
No. 36001, three more images, August 1948,
 with four syphons in place 265
No. 36001, Firebox door, and from the interior
 of firebox, looking out 266
No. 36001, Original type of rocking grate 268
No. 36001, Ash chute in smokebox 268
No. 36001, locomotive top showing water filler
 and TIA reservoir...269
No. 36001, smokebox interior, showing base
 of multiple blast pipe 270
No. 36001, two images of steam reversing gear 271
No. 36001, brake gear, No. 1 bogie 272

No. 36001, casing attached to mainframe, complete with boiler, etc, and ready for lowering on to bogies 273
No. 36001, power bogie from on top, showing centreless pivot 274
No. 36001, main steampipe 275
No. 36001, wheels and axles 276
Blind axles for 'Leader' 276
'Leader', centre (crank) axle, final drive socket 277
'Leader', cylinder boring at Eastleigh 278
'Leader', power bogie from the front, two cylinders with sleeves inserted 279
Crank axle, connecting rods and sleeve valve chain drive 280
Steam turbine, supplying oil to oil bath 281
Pipes under the fireman's cab to the injectors 281
No. 36001, on trial from Brighton, passing Hurst Green Halt 290
No. 36001, light engine at Lewes 293
Image of 'Leader' on unofficial postage stamp (colour) 294
No. 36001, cold and lifeless at Eastleigh 295
'Leader'? – modern spoof for Swanage Railway 297

Images, Locomotives
No. 2039 *Hartland Point* 7
No. 36001 *Leader* 8, 11, 13, 15
No. 36002 10
BR Fairburn 2-6-4T, No. 42009 31
BR Standard 2-6-4T, No. 80010 33
BR (ex-LNER), Gresley 4-6-2, Class A4, No. 60033 *Seagull* 20
BR (ex-LNER), Class A4, 4-6-2, No 60017 *Silver Fox* 36
BR (ex-LNER), Class A4, 4-6-2, smokebox door 108
BR (ex-SR), Class Q1, 0-6-0, No 33036 39
BR (ex-SR), Class H, 0-4-4T, No 33036 43
LBSCR, Marsh Atlantic No. 39 61
LBSCR, Marsh Atlantic No. 39 (named *La France*) 62
LMSR, Beyer-Garratt 2-640+0-6-2, No. 4997 24
LMSR, Modified 'Royal Scot' 4-6-0, No. 6399 22
LMSR, Stanier 4-6-2, No. 6202 'Turbomotive' 23
LNER, Gresley 4-6-4, No. 10000 18
LNER, Gresley 4-6-4, No. 10000 (rebuilt) 18
LNER, Gresley/ Beyer-Garratt 2-8-0+0-8-2, No. 2395 25
LNER, Gresley 2-8-2, Class P2, No. 2001, *Cock o'the North* 27

MR, Paget sleeve-valve design of 1908 18
Southern Pacific Railroad (USA) 'Cab-in-front' 4-8-8-2, No.4232 37
Southern Railway, (ex- LBSCR), Marsh Atlantic No. 2038, *Portland Bill* 73
Southern Railway, (ex- LBSCR), Marsh Atlantic No. B39 (now named *Hartland Point*) 63
Southern Railway, (ex- LBSCR), Marsh Atlantic No. 2039, *Hartland Point* 64
Southern Railway, (ex- LBSCR), Marsh Atlantic No. 2039, *Hartland Point* (Front end, in course of modification) 66
Southern Railway, (ex- LBSCR), Marsh Atlantic No. 2039, ... 65, 67, 69 (c), 70
Hartland Point (Modified front end) 72, 74, 75, 76, 77
BR (ex-SR, ex-LBSCR), No.32039, *Hartland Point* 78, 79, 81, 82
(with BR ex-SR, ex-LBSCR, 0-6-2T, Class E4 No. 32577) 80
Southern Railway, Class I1X, No. 596 35
Southern Railway, Wainwright 0-6-4T, Class J, No. 1595 26
Southern Railway, Class LN, No.857, *Lord Howe* 21
Southern Railway, Class MN, No. 21C1, *Channel Packet* 38
Southern Railway, Class M7, 0-4-4T, No. 374 34
Southern Railway, Class N, 2-6-0, No. A816 .... 54, 55
Southern Railway, Class W, 2-6-4T (unidentified) 29
Southern Railway, Class WC, 4-6-2, No 21C133 (unnamed) 40
British Railways (Southern Region), Class BB, 4-6-2, No. 34090, *Sir Eustace Missenden* 100
Southern Railway, C-C Electric locomotive No. CC1/2 41
Southern Railway, N15, 'King Arthur' Class, No. 740, *Merlin* 50
Southern Railway, N15, 'King Arthur' Class, No. 783, *Sir Gillemere* 49
Southern Railway, 'River' Class 2-6-4T, No. 793, *River Ouse* 28
Southern Railway, Sentinel Steam Railcar. 56
Southern Railway, 'U1' class 2-6-0, No. 1896 59
BR 'U' class, No. 31618 164
BR 'U' class, No. 31830 165
Shay locomotives, offset boiler (two views) 211

INDEX

Images (the Turf Burner)

CC1 at Kildare	237
Inchicore, two boilers linked to experiment with turf burning	238
CIE 'K class No. 356 with experimental boiler	239
No. 356 with finned aluminium heaters	241
No. 356, from tender end	241
No. 356, truck with bus engine to provide draught for engine	242
CC1 Power unit being lowered into bogie	248
Completed bogie being steamed in works at Inchicore	248
Bearing pads for power bogie	249
CC1, nearly complete in Inchicore Works	250
Peat, as burnt in CC1	251
CC1, final drive (by chain, as in 'Leader')	251
CC1, driver's position	252
CC1, on test at Portarlington	253, 254
CC1, with test train	255
CC1, with test train, at Sallins, Co. Kildare	255
CC1, with empty coaching stock	256
CC1, view from fireman's side of the cab	257

Images (line drawing)

Southern Railway, drwg. No W6393 (double-ended Q1)	42
Southern Railway, drwg. No W5975 (0-6-4T)	44
Southern Railway, drwg. No. W6653 (4-6-4T)	45
Southern Railway, drwg. No. W6656 (0-4-4-4-0T)	47
Southern Railway, drwg. Un-numbered (4-6-4T)	48
Southern Railway, drwg. No. W6916 (0-4-4-4-0T)	51
Southern Railway, drwg. No. W7036 (0-4-4-4-0T)	51
Southern Railway, drwg. No. W7169 (0-6-6-0T)	53
Southern Railway, drwg. No. W7457 (0-6-6-0T)	105
BR (ex-Southern Railway) drawing, as complete, from *Railway Magazine*	117
BR (ex-Southern Railway) final drawing, un-numbered	117
CIE, first drawing of re-boilered No. 356	240
Brighton drawing of possible turf-burner	243
Second Brighton drawing of possible turf-burner, with weights	243
1951 drawing of turf-burner	244
1957 drawing of possible turf burner	245
1954 drawing of possible turf burner, but with single engine and Mekydro drive to all axles	246

A rebuilt Bulleid Merchant Navy pacific (this is BR No. 35010 *Blue Star* seen at Worting Junction west of Basingstoke with the down Bournemouth Belle). Rebuilding from 1956 transformed the design – as did a similar modification for the Light Pacifics. From an engine capable of prodigious but erratic performance, loved or loathed in equal measures (loathed more so by the maintenance staff), here was a modern machine that was reliable, predictable and far more economialc on fuel and water. All 30 of the Merchant Navy class were rebuilt plus 70 out the 100 Light Pacifics – the pending demise of steam put an end to the rebuilding programme. So the question is 'Could Leader have been rebuilt to become a useful part of the Southern steam fleet?' In its built form an emphatic 'No'. It could have been tinkered with certainly but that would not have addressed the fundamental issues that remained; weight, the firing position and the risks with the boiler/ firebox. Major re-design – basically a completely new engine would have been involved and with the Standard classes now prevalent any such option effectively disappeared on the stroke of midnight 1 January 1948 and Nationalisation. As has been said in the text, in effect Leader was condemned even before her built was complete.

Final turf-burner with each bogie having individual power unit	247
Four drawings of firebox, showing firebricks in position	267
Oscillating gear in front of sleeve valve cylinder	279
Side view of valve gear and oil bath	280

Images, People

Bulleid, O V S, designer of *Leader* 16
Bulleid, Missenden, Elliot: farewell presentation
  to Bulleid 282
Chrimes, T E, Southern Railway Running
  Superintendent 58
Click, John, at controls of CC1 257
Click, John, in cab of 36001 283
Curl, Reg. at Eastleigh..286
Forder, Fireman Ted, *Leader*'s fireman throughout
  trial, in the cab 127
Nicholson, G A..284
Riddles, Cox and Bond 194
Talbot, Sam, fireman during trials from Eastleigh 205
Townroe, S C 285
The 'Great and Good' of the Southern, many
  associated with design and building of 'Leader' 283

Locomotives, other

Q1, troubles with tender, when running
  tender-first...39, 40
W' class 2-6-4T, banned from use on passenger
  trains ....30, 35 (*Note 2*)
H1 4-4-2 No. 2039, use as a 'guinea-pig'
  for sleeve valves 63-68
Running trials with 2039 72-77
No.2039, dismantled at Eastleigh................................77
Irish 'turf-burner', first mention................................195
Reasons for use of peat ('turf') as locomotive fuel
  on CIE 237
Turf-burner (no. CC1) starts to take shape
  at Inchicore..252
Steam trials with completed bogie at Inchicore 253
CC1 completed in 1957 255
Visit by ILE, summer 1958 257

Morse chains, use on Bulleid pacifics.............................14
Mulvany, Paddy, Chief Draughtsman at Inchicore
  Visits Brighton 195
  Shows Click drawing of 'Turf-Burner' 242
  Anecdote about Bulleid and chimneys in tender......247
  Tells Click, Bulleid undecided about superheating
    on 'Turf-Burner' 252
Nicholson, G L persuades Missenden to reduce
  construction to five units.....................................85
Nicholson's views on Bulleid's character....................85-6
Paget Locomotive 18
Pocklington, Ron, photographer 7
Joins Click in Dublin as Assistant to Bulleid................244
Poppet valves, use on LNER...22
  Use elsewhere...35 (*Note 2*)
Railway Observer, timing of 'Leaders' construction....93-4
Richards, R M T, Traffic Manager, SR, scuppers idea
  of double-ended Q1 42
Presents requirement for M7 replacement....................87
Riddles, R A, CME of British Railways (in effect) orders
  all work on follow-on 'Leaders' to cease 150
Asks Elliot for costing details 151
Follows up with further request 152
Writes final report recommending scrapping 188-192
Rudguard, Lieut. Col. RE, Chief Motive Power
  Officer, bans 36001 138
Sevenoaks disaster, 1927 26
Steam locomotives, unconventional designs.................17
Southern Beyer-Garratt proposal 21
Southern Railway, needs for motive power
  in war years, 1939-45...26
Townroe, S C, Asst Dist Motive Power Superintendent,
  Eastleigh reaches compromise with ASLEF over
  'Leader' 158
Walton, E, Head Office Inspector, reports
  on abortive London run, 4 Sept. 134/5